I0884054

THEATER IN THE AMERICAS

A Series from Southern Illinois University Press

SCOTT MAGELSSEN *Series Editor*

Experiments in Democracy

Interracial and Cross-Cultural Exchange in American Theatre, 1912–1945

Edited by Cheryl Black and Jonathan Shandell

Southern Illinois University Press *Carbondale*

Southern Illinois University Press
www.siupress.com

Chapter 1 previously appeared as "Trying on *The Yellow Jacket*: Performing Chinese Exclusion and Assimilation," *Theatre Journal* 62.1 (2010): 75–92. © 2010 The Johns Hopkins University Press. Reprinted with permission of Johns Hopkins University Press.

Josefina Niggli materials used in chapter 6 courtesy of Western Carolina University Foundation, Cullowhee, North Carolina.

Chapter 9 copyright © 2016 by Elizabeth A. Osborne; chapter 10 copyright © 2016 by Garrett Eisler; chapter 11 copyright © 2016 by Lisa Jackson-Schebetta; chapter 12 © 2016 by Jonathan Shandell.

Chapter 12 previously appeared as "What Price Integration? *Anna Lucasta* and the American Negro Theatre," *Maroon: The Yale Journal of African-American Studies* 1 (2006): 107–32.

Printed in the United States of America

19 18 17 16 4 3 2 1

Cover illustration: Production of *Battle Hymn* by Michael Gold and Michael Blankfort, Experimental Theatre, New York, 1936, sponsored by the Works Progress Administration's Federal Theatre Project. *Courtesy of the Franklin D. Roosevelt Library and Museum, Hyde Park, New York.*

Library of Congress Cataloging-in-Publication Data

Names: Black, Cheryl, 1954– editor. | Shandell, Jonathan, editor.

Title: Experiments in democracy : interracial and cross-cultural exchange in American theatre, 1912–1945 / edited by Cheryl Black and Jonathan Shandell.

Description: Carbondale : Southern Illinois University Press, 2016. | Series: Theater in the Americas | Includes bibliographical references and index.

Identifiers: LCCN 2015041537| ISBN 9780809334681 (paperback) | ISBN 9780809334698 (e-book)

Subjects: LCSH: Theater—United States—History—20th century. | Theater and society—United States—History—20th century. | Race in the theater. | Ethnicity in the theater. | American drama—20th century—History and criticism. | Race relations in literature. | Minorities in literature. | BISAC: PERFORMING ARTS / Theater / History & Criticism. | PERFORMING ARTS / Theater / General. | PERFORMING ARTS / Theater / Direction & Production. | HISTORY / Modern / 20th Century.

Classification: LCC PN2266.3 .E94 2016 | DDC 792.0973/0904—dc23 LC record available at http://lccn.loc.gov/2015041537

Printed on recycled paper. ♻

This paper meets the requirements of ANSI/NISO Z39.48-1992 (Permanence of Paper) ♾

Contents

Illustrations

Experiments in Democracy

Introduction

Public Laboratories of Pluralism

Jonathan Shandell

The title and inspiration for this anthology come from reporter Dewey R. Jones's statement "Hedgerow theater is more than a theater—it is an experiment in democracy."[1] This sentence appeared in a 1932 profile of Pennsylvania's Hedgerow Theatre published in the *Chicago Defender*, a leading African American newspaper of the era. Jones visited the Hedgerow—a company founded and led by its white director, Jasper Deeter—and bestowed this striking bit of praise in recognition of the company's historic successes in fostering interracial collaboration and socialization on stage, behind the scenes, and among audiences. The Hedgerow offered a progressive model of democratic interaction and community building to the nation in an era marked by entrenched racial segregation and social inequity. Jones's provocative turn of phrase stuck with me and my coeditor, Cheryl Black, and called out for wider application within American theatre history before the civil rights movement. At a time when racial segregation was de jure in the American southeast and de facto everywhere else, when public transportation, schools, churches, and virtually all social organizations operated under strict policies of exclusion (based on gender, race, religion, or socioeconomic class), what role did theatrical performance play in testing and promoting more equitable models of democracy? How did artists and companies use the stage as a laboratory within which to bring heterogeneous communities together, to bridge divides of ethnic and cultural identity? What impacts did these experiments have in the nation's struggles toward greater inclusivity and social justice? The thirteen chapters in this anthology seek answers to these questions.

These chapters revisit interracial and cross-cultural "borrowings" among theatre artists, activists, and entrepreneurs staged across three decades of the first half of the twentieth century, attempting to assess these borrowings as experiments in racial and cultural inclusivity with the potential to move the nation toward a more just and democratic society. Many focus on theatre artists who used performance to seek paths across America's persistent black-white racial divide. Others consider how playwrights, actors, and theatre companies sought strategies for bringing Latino and Latina, Asian American, Native American, and Jewish American communities and cultural traditions into the nation's broader cultural conversation. The performance venues and activities examined include Broadway and the commercial theatre, left-wing and workers' theatres, folk plays, community-based performances, and certain works of the Federal Theatre Project. In total, this anthology highlights how a wide range of artists, working in an equivalently wide range of venues and artistic forms, aspired toward interracial and cross-cultural exchange both in the works they created and in the working processes they employed to create them.

This anthology—organized chronologically with respect to each chapter's subject matter—focuses on the decades prior to that post–World War II period in American history often labeled the civil rights era. The authors collected here investigate theatrical activities that preceded the more overt political activism against racial apartheid and discrimination seen primarily in the 1950s and 1960s. The decades of the 1910s through the 1940s were for the United States a period marked by a stark contradiction between mythologies and rhetoric about democracy on one hand and real social conditions on the other. The national public discourse brimmed with invocations of democracy, as political leaders sought to unify the nation against totalitarian forces abroad and fears of anarchism and revolution (whether real or imagined) at home. Yet progress toward realizing true democracy was slow or stagnant. Involvement in two world wars brought tensions between America's ideals and its social realities into stark relief. President Woodrow Wilson's famous call that "the world must be made safe for democracy" was complicated by the inequities and injustices suffered at home by African Americans, communities of newly arrived immigrants, and other marginalized minority groups.[2] The "Double V Campaign" launched by black newspapers during World War II—calling for victories over fascism abroad and over racist oppression on the home front—was one important reminder to Americans that antidemocratic actors and forces were located not only overseas. The internment of Japanese Americans, in flagrant violation of bedrock constitutional principles, was another. Amid these and many other disjunctions in the execution of America's ideals, certain artists used theatrical performance to test models of cross-cultural interaction and dialogue. Through their artistry, they sought strategies that might help the nation more closely resemble the just and inclusive democracy that it declared itself to be.

In her introduction to the anthology *Performing America: Cultural Nationalism in American Theatre*, J. Ellen Gainor identifies the early twentieth century as "one of the key moments in United States history when national consciousness came to the fore. . . . Essayists, artists, politicians, and others with opinions to voice shared freely their sense of the American national character."[3] The contributors to *Experiments in Democracy* follow the path set by *Performing America* in examining the contributions made by theatre artists to burgeoning national conversations of the era. Yet we offer our own distinctive focus through a particular emphasis on *interracial and cross-cultural exchange* within the theatre. Our concern is with America's sense of its *intra*national character, as we consider how various theatrical artists and companies worked to transform the ways that dissimilar groups within the nation oriented themselves toward one another. As political, social, and cultural forces conspired to reify and heighten feelings of cultural difference among groups of Americans, certain progressive-minded theatre artists worked to bring those disparate groups into closer proximity, partnership, and creative conversation. The *potential* for theatrical performance to connect dissimilar American communities in a spirit of shared enterprise and open dialogue, even when that potential is imperfectly realized, is the ideal that unites the various chapters in this volume.

In that light, this collection departs in its methodology from much of the existing scholarship investigating diversity and difference (with respect to race, ethnicity, religious affiliation, national origin, or sexuality) within American theatre history. An explosion of research in recent decades related to African American, Latino and Latina, Asian American, queer, Native American, Jewish American, and other minority-oriented traditions of theatre and performance has invigorated our understanding of the nation's stage history. A field that was once focused largely on a white Eurocentric and heteronormative canon now encompasses a rich kaleidoscope of dramatic traditions, identity groups, and performance practices. Many of the essays in this anthology draw upon and converse with recent work in these fields of research. But in the trend toward ethnocentric inquiries, theatre historians have tended to deemphasize how American theatre artists (both of the majority and from minority backgrounds) have used the stage as a vehicle to foster what Horace M. Kallen called "continuous, free and fruitful cross-fertilization" of cultures, traditions, aesthetics, and ideas.[4] This anthology seeks to fill that gap in the historiography of diversity on the American stage.[5]

Democracy versus the Melting Pot

At the onset of the twentieth century, the stage played an important role in circulating one of the most enduring images of American democracy. Israel Zangwill's 1908 drama *The Melting Pot* popularized a potent metaphor for civic engagement within the United States. The drama's hero—an idealistic young composer named David Quixano—is a voice of optimism for a new life inside the "golden door":

> America is God's Crucible, the great Melting-Pot where all the races of Europe are melting and re-forming! Here you stand, good folk, think I, when I see them at Ellis Island, here you stand . . . in your fifty groups, with your fifty languages and histories, and your fifty blood hatreds and rivalries. But you won't be long like that brothers, for these are the fires of God you've come to. . . . Into the Crucible with you all! God is making the American![6]

In Zangwill's drama, and in a wider national discourse, the melting pot metaphor portended the dissolution of ethnic differences into a new, homogenized Americanness in which all people held an equal stake and enjoyed equal protection. Citizenship in America's melting pot democracy presumed each individual's capacity for surrendering (or, at least, sublimating) traditional ethnic, racial, or religious allegiances and embracing a remade sense of self within a "great new continent that could melt up all race-differences and vendettas, that could purge and recreate."[7] For many, this possibility was an alluring antidote to the crushing prejudices and sufferings of an "old world" order. In the vision of the British-born Jew Zangwill, the real promise of American democracy was emancipation from the terror of the pogrom and the prospect of security and stability for suffering diasporic peoples.

The "melting pot" was one ideal that helped the nation come to grips with rapid changes in its demography at the turn of the twentieth century. Surging immigration had brought a huge influx of foreign-born citizens—mostly from Europe, but also in significant numbers from the Asian Pacific Rim—into the country. Nearly simultaneously, the tide of an African American "Great Migration" carried masses of black citizens away from southern rural communities and into northern and western regions in far greater concentrations than had previously been seen. Displacements and rapid population changes sparked serious national soul-searching, not only in terms of the meaning of "America" as a political or geopolitical entity but also around questions of internal civic positioning for the nation's collection of ethnic subgroups. How should vulnerable minority populations orient themselves within the social and cultural landscape of the United States? What strategies might serve to provide security and continuity for these communities on one hand and to solidify a sense of national belonging on the other? The "melting pot" was an ideal to which many Americans—both those within the majority and those seeking the benefits of greater inclusion and opportunity—could subscribe.

For others, however, the melting pot was a problematic model that foreclosed on claims toward individuality and cultural autonomy. Critics saw within the cauldron of assimilation not a future of liberty and equality for all but an insidious hegemony that served the interests of the powerful. In his 1916 essay "Trans-national America," Randolph Bourne proclaimed "the failure of the 'melting pot'" to supersede latent feelings of cultural difference among the country's ethnic and racial communities. Though Bourne was critical of a national fixation on assimilation, his advice to citizens of the United States was "not to fear the failure of democracy. It is rather to urge us to an investigation of what Americanism may rightly mean . . . [and] to assert a higher ideal than the 'melting-pot.'" His vision was of a democracy that celebrated and thrived on heterogeneity rather than of one that compelled absorption into what "a ruling class, descendant of those British stocks which were the first permanent immigrants, decide that America shall be made."[8]

This linking of the melting pot to the interests of "British stocks" reveals an oppressive racial politics at work behind assimilation and highlights the incompleteness of the social reforms of the Progressive Era (ca. 1890s–1910s). Perhaps the most significant expansion of democracy achieved by American Progressives was the ratification of the Nineteenth Amendment in 1920, which enshrined suffrage for women into the Constitution. But with respect to the barriers faced by racial and ethnic minorities, little in the way of tangible progress was achieved. Feelings of xenophobia and white chauvinism—heightened by global instabilities and the economic strains of the Depression—persisted in American society. Prevailing cultural narratives reinforced racial and ethnic hierarchies, as Gary Gerstle explains: "The allure of Nordic Americanization (or what some scholars have called 'Anglo-conformity') . . . was deeply ingrained in the movies and other aspects of mass culture." In subtle and not-so-subtle ways, Hollywood seduced American audiences with normative visions of a nation "in which Nordic types loomed large" while other groups remained hidden from view, banished to the cultural and political margins of the national experience.[9]

Inequality and invisibility was not what the melting pot was supposed to deliver to oppressed minorities. At one point in Zangwill's play, the starry-eyed David contends that "black and yellow" peoples could experience "the roaring and the bubbling" of "the great Melting Pot" just as readily as the "Celt and Latin, Slav and Teuton . . . Jew and Gentile." But this is hollow rhetoric, given America's ubiquitous privileging of whiteness and intractable pathology of racism. Freedom from oppression depends not only on a minority group's desire to assimilate but also on the majority's acceptance of that wish. For a nation whose standards of social privilege depended heavily (though not exclusively) on visible phenotypical traits like skin pigmentation, the hope that the white majority might "unite" seamlessly with non-white minorities "to build the Republic of Man and the Kingdom of God" was at best naive.[10] One snippet from Zangwill's dialogue reveals as much. A visiting Russian baron, challenged on his role in violently oppressing Jews in his home country, turns the table on his American accuser (the millionaire Quincy Davenport Jr.) by asking, "Don't you lynch and roast your niggers?" "Not officially," Davenport replies, in a potent reminder that some of the "fires" of the American experience burned outside of the great cauldron of democratic inclusion.[11]

Bourne's critique of the melting pot ideology extended the work of his contemporary Kallen, whose writings challenged utopic ideals of amalgamation and sounded an alarm about a rising tide of nativism and xenophobia in prewar America. Kallen envisioned the United States as "a democracy of nationalities . . . a single unit [that] serves as the foundation and background for the realization of the distinctive individuality of each *natio* that composes it and of the pooling of these in a harmony above them all."[12] He believed that true liberty and autonomy require a full, free, and public expression of that "distinctive individuality" for each of America's subgroups within the nation's public life. This is the philosophy of *cultural pluralism*. Pioneered by Bourne and Kallen, cultural pluralism inspired many other American social theorists of the early twentieth century, including George Santayana, Alain Locke, Louis Adamic, and Leonard Covello. Each of these theorists, in his own way, imagined a nation in which historically marginalized and disempowered groups could gain fuller hearings for themselves within the cultural landscape by affirming and proudly articulating their own histories and heritages rather than by seeking to dilute or homogenize them beyond recognition.

To crystallize the workings of cultural pluralism, Kallen countered the "melting pot" with his own evocative metaphor:

> As in an orchestra every type of instrument has its specific *timbre* and *tonality* . . . as every type has its appropriate theme and melody in the whole symphony, so in society, each ethnic group may be the natural instrument, its temper and culture may be its theme and melody and the harmony and dissonances and discords of them all may make the symphony of civilization.[13]

The richness of a symphony depends upon a conscious blending of dissimilar musical sounds. Members of an orchestra cannot play like soloists; they must listen attentively to their fellow musicians and work actively at attuning and synchronizing with them while artfully giving voice to the particular timbre of their own instruments. Cultural pluralism conceives of democracy neither as a single homogenized experience nor as a collection of isolated communities speaking only to and for themselves but as an active convergence and productive blending of variegated traditions. There are limits to this metaphor, as Kallen acknowledges: "A musical symphony is written before it is played; in the symphony of civilization the playing is the writing."[14] Thus true citizenship in a pluralistic democracy must move beyond a mere acknowledgment of difference. It must reject calls toward national homogeny and oppose instincts toward tribalism. Each participant in society, while maintaining a sense of self, must join the larger civic project of celebrating the voices of others and must also work consciously to bring his or her own voice into harmony with them.

The "symphony of civilization" never enshrined itself in the American cultural consciousness as readily as did the "melting pot." There was no popular drama to champion this vision of democracy to the public. But Kallen's vision of democracy has powerful implications for studying theatre history in its evocation of a creative process marked by live performance, group collaboration, and multivocal creative expression. Indeed, it is the vision that animates Dewey Jones's description of the Hedgerow as an "experiment in democracy" and is the concept that this anthology seeks to extend throughout the stage history of the United States in the early twentieth century. The chapters of this collection look to demonstrate how theatre artists across the era worked in concert with Bourne's and Kallen's hopes for democracy by promoting symphonic cultural variety over hegemonic, one-note Nordicization.

Though Kallen found his metaphor in the realm of classical music, the theatre may well be the creative art most closely aligned with his understanding of pluralistic democracy. As one introductory textbook puts it, "Theatre is unique because it is the only art for which the medium and subjects are exactly the same: the subjects of a play are human beings and human acts, and the mediums of a play are also human beings and human acts."[15] The democratic qualities of a symphony orchestra work only in the service of creating immaterial vibrations of sound. Other modes of artistic expression—literature, paintings, films, or architecture, for example—can also be created cooperatively; however, they too end in impersonal and disembodied media (paper and ink, paint and canvas, projected light, stone and brick). The theatre works uniquely with and through concrete actions performed by groups; interpersonal collaboration is its sine qua non.[16] The necessity of group interactions multiplies the opportunities for democratic social arrangements to arise, as artists and spectators interact with one another in a spirit of shared enterprise at every stage of the creative process. As those communities become inclusive, equitable, and participatory (rather than exclusionary, oppressive, or autocratic), the theatre recapitulates in miniature the very same dynamic that cultural pluralists envisioned for the nation as a whole.

The performances and artists discussed in this collection sought in some original and historically significant way to leverage the theatre's synergy with pluralistic democracy and, in doing so, to make their own original statement *about* democracy. Following recent trends in theatre scholarship, we take an expansive view of theatre as an artistic genre to include other modes of performance that incorporate dramatic storytelling, such as dance drama, radio drama, and scripted political rallies. These and other types of performances afforded to their creators a certain measure of insulation from real-world political pressures, providing opportunities for artists to test their democratic visions and allowing audiences to join and sample for themselves the new perspectives and possibilities contained therein. This anthology revisits many of those experiments, investigates how they worked, and considers what factors might have complicated or compromised their results.

Evaluating Experiments

With "experiments" as a central paradigm, the authors included here adopt the critical skepticism of a scientist who presumes that even the most carefully designed experiment can fail to produce its desired result or might have unintended consequences. Imperfect materials and flawed procedures can taint an outcome. A single experiment never fully solves the problem nor answers the question that inspired it. Successful results, when they do occur, raise more complex questions and demand further exploration. Most important, measurements taken and conclusions drawn from an experiment must account for the positionality and fallibility of its participants, observers, and interpreters. Thus the essays collected here seek to account for the blind spots, compromised methods, and unacknowledged biases at play in these theatrical practices. Even as American theatre artists sought to showcase progressive visions of a more inclusive democracy, intentionally or unknowingly their work sometimes perpetuated the antidemocratic values associated with inequalities of race, ethnicity, class, and gender. This book's contributors actively consider how the same gap between the ideal and the real that characterized the practice of democracy in the United States often complicated the work of theatre artists striving to perform more enlightened visions of that democracy.

Scientists invariably rely on the carefully controlled milieu of a laboratory to provide layers of protection essential for the success of their research. The unknown and potentially dangerous outcomes of experiments remain safely inside a laboratory's walls while harmful contagions stay out. The theatre can function in a similar fashion, facilitating the experiments that artists undertake in a process of creative discovery. The boundaries of a performance space can make for a psychic threshold of separation from entrenched patterns of discourse and social interaction, one that can allow for exploration of new possibilities. The human acts that are the medium and subject of theatrical performance are fictional and ephemeral in nature. Everyone knows that the "real world" will reassert itself when the performance concludes—an understanding that affords theatre artists some license to create onstage, provisionally, experiences that might not be viable elsewhere. American theatre artists in the first half of the twentieth century took advantage of that license, incubating staged visions of a different kind of American social landscape within hospitable environments that could foster their development.

In *The Souls of Black Folk*, W. E. B. Du Bois offered his now iconic observation that "the problem of the Twentieth Century is the problem of the color line."[17] As several chapters of this anthology reveal, here was a problem for which an array of theatrical American artists—from both sides of the trenchant black-white divide—explored remedies in the first half of the century. Visionary playwright Theodore Browne experimented with folklore, form, and narrative to meld an affirmation of "black masculinity" with a vision of "interracial communion" in his 1937 drama *Natural Man*, as Harry J. Elam Jr. argues (chapter 7). Choreographer Myra Kinch's efforts in this same period to use the idiom of modern dance to highlight and challenge America's undemocratic history of race are explored by Margaret F. Savilonis (chapter 8). Attempts at forging democratic interracial partnerships and projecting new visions of race liberalism are the focus of my study of the popular Harlem and Broadway juggernaut *Anna Lucasta* (chapter 12) and of Andrea Nouryeh's revisitation of the American Theatre Wing's much-heralded efforts to erase the color line within its Stage Door Canteens of the World War II years (chapter 13). Idealistically, and perhaps at times somewhat naively, the artists discussed in these chapters used performance spaces as sites where the alienation between black and white America, what Du Bois calls "the Veil,"[18] might be temporarily lifted or at least rendered more permeable.

Beyond Du Bois's perspective as an African American at the dawn of the twentieth century, we can now discern a multiplicity of "color lines"—each with its own "veil" of psychic dislocation—crisscrossing the sociopolitical landscape in this era. Our anthology revisits theatrical experiments along several of these other fronts as well. Ju Yon Kim's analysis of *The Yellow Jacket* (chapter 1) reveals the intersection of progressive ambitions and problematic acts of appropriation and stereotyping in one early attempt to integrate Chinese-inspired aesthetics with mainstream American cultural sensibilities. Experiments related to the experiences of Latino Americans are the focus of Eric Mayer-García's study of Ybor City's La Unión Martí-Maceo (chapter 3) and of Elizabeth Coonrod Martínez's reconsideration of the folk plays of Mexican American playwright Josefina Niggli (chapter 6). W. Douglas Powers, through his analysis of Lynn Riggs's drama (chapter 4), and Elizabeth A. Osborne, in her study of the Federal Theatre Project's radio series *First Americans* (chapter 9), focus on theatrical attempts to renegotiate questions of Native American identity and citizenship—indeed, the first "color line" to be drawn by Europeans on the continent.

In addition, authors collected in this volume attend to theatrical experiments that occurred at the intersections of traditional lines of American minority identity. Stuart J. Hecht's analysis of 1920s musicals explores fertile cultural exchanges unfolding on Broadway between African American jazz aesthetics and composers and lyricists of Jewish ancestry (chapter 2). In his study of the 1941 antifascist rally "Fun to Be Free" (chapter 10), Garrett Eisler reveals a collaboration of several artists working together to articulate an inclusive sense of "pan-ethnic Americanism" that they hoped would transcend divisions of race, religion, and national origin. The Theatre Union's efforts to undermine familiar American categories of race, ethnicity, and nationality and to unite disparate communities in a spirit of class solidarity is the focus of Cheryl Black and Anne Fletcher's discussion of the 1935 production of Albert Maltz's drama *Black Pit* (chapter 5). Lisa Jackson-Schebetta undertakes a new critical consideration of the multiracial character of the Theatre Guild's 1943 Broadway staging of Shakespeare's *Othello* (chapter 11). While other studies of this production have focused on Paul Robeson's historic appearance in the title role, Jackson-Schebetta brings the presence of the Puerto Rican actor José Ferrer into the foreground. Her study situates this historic production as a novel experiment with racialized bodies on the commercial American stage, one with important reverberations for both American democracy and wider hemispheric geopolitics.

What links the various experiments discussed across the chapters of this anthology—no matter how successful or problematic the endeavor turned out to be—is a bedrock sense of optimism that through performance the nation might improve its pursuit of a pluralistic democracy. Even more important questions follow: Did these "experiments in democracy" have any immediate effect? Did they, in the end, lead to some tangible measure of social progress? At minimum, the performance activities discussed here formed part of a vital cultural substrate: a public counternarrative against exclusion and oppression, one that helped condition the nation for the more overt activism on behalf of democracy to come later in the century. But one anecdote included in the *Defender* profile of the Hedgerow suggests a more direct social impact. Dewey Jones writes of a reunion between Wayland Rudd—a celebrated African American actor who performed at Hedgerow for several years—and one of his white collaborators, which took place months after both artists had departed the Hedgerow:

> I was with Rudd in the studios of the National Broadcasting Company in New York one night when a young white man came in with his mother and introduced her to us. "I heard you were to broadcast," [the young white man] said to Rudd, "and I wanted my mother to meet you." Later I learned that this young man's mother had objected strenuously to his going to Hedgerow because she had heard that he would come into contact with Negroes and she didn't feel that such contact would help a southern aristocrat in his fight to win success on the stage. But the boy defied his mother and spent three years with Jasper Deeter. Later he returned home and completely changed his mother's point of view, and she showed this change by coming to the studio to meet a Negro and congratulate him on his acting.[19]

This anecdote is strikingly similar to some of the testimonials from those who patronized the Stage Door Canteen in New York (see chapter 13). But how many more such stories could be told? In what other ways did the activism of American theatre artists directly inspire more democratic actions and thoughts by others? Individual experiences like this mother's conversion away from racist animosity too often go undocumented and thus remain outside of the reach of historians who seek to gauge the impact of the theatrical work they investigate. Even so, we offer this anthology as a testament to the potential for the theatre both to envision a more just society and to bring the nation closer to its realization.

Notes

1. Dewey R. Jones, "Hedgerow Theater Sets New Standard in Solution of American Race Problem," *Chicago Defender*, 17 December 1932, 10.

2. Woodrow Wilson, "Essential Terms for Peace in Europe," in *Woodrow Wilson: Essential Writings and Speeches of the Scholar-President*, ed. Mario R. DiNunzio (New York: New York University Press, 2006), 402.

3. J. Ellen Gainor, introduction to *Performing America: Cultural Nationalism and American Theatre*, ed. J. Ellen Gainor and Jeffrey D. Mason (Ann Arbor: University of Michigan Press, 1999), 8.

4. Horace M. Kallen, "Culture and the Klan," in *Culture and Democracy in the United States: Studies in the Group Psychology of the American People* (New York: Boni and Liveright, 1924), 42.

5. See, as one illustrative example, Marc Maufort, ed., *Staging Difference: Cultural Pluralism in American Theatre and Drama* (New York: Peter Lang, 1995). Though there are points of overlap between that anthology and this one, particularly in the use of the term "cultural pluralism," there are key differences between them. Maufort writes in his introduction:

> The terms "cultural pluralism" or "multiculturalism" are considered here in their broadest sense. They do not necessarily involve the social and anthropological underpinnings from which they emanate. . . . Consequently, cultural pluralism, as the word is used here . . . focuses on *the more general concept of the "other,"* i.e. any member of American society that does not belong to the hegemony. (1, emphasis added)

In contrast, this collection returns to Horace Kallen and Randolph Bourne's original conception of "cultural pluralism" as a process of dialogue and exchange among disparate American voices and traditions and strategically applies that paradigm to the study of American theatre history in the early twentieth century.

6. Israel Zangwill, *The Melting-Pot* (New York: Macmillan, 1917), 32.

7. Ibid., 179.

8. Randolph Bourne, "Trans-national America," *Atlantic Monthly*, July 1916, http://www.theatlantic.com/ideastour/idealism/bourne-full.html, accessed 6 July 2012.

9. Gary Gerstle, *American Crucible: Race and Nation in the Twentieth Century* (Princeton, N.J.: Princeton University Press, 2001), 170.

10. Zangwill, *Melting-Pot*, 183.

11. Ibid., 110.

12. Horace M. Kallen, "Democracy versus the Melting Pot," in *Culture and Democracy in the United States: Studies in the Group Psychology of the American People* (New York: Boni and Liveright, 1924), 124.

13. Ibid.

14. Ibid. There is a certain irony in Kallen's use of a symphony as an alternative metaphor to the "melting pot," given the project of David Quixano (the protagonist of Zangwill's play) to write a symphony in celebration of the "melting pot" and American assimilation.

15. William Missouri Downs et al., *The Art of Theatre: Then and Now*, 3rd ed. (Boston: Wadsworth, 2013), 10.

16. The more recent genre of solo performance falls outside of the historical parameters of this study. In this genre, a solo work written, staged, designed, and performed by a single artist still requires the interaction of one performer with a live audience to reach its finished form.

17. W. E. B. Du Bois, *The Souls of Black Folk* (Chicago: A. C. McClurg, 1903), xxxi.

18. Ibid.

19. Jones, "Hedgerow Theater Sets New Standard," 10.

1. Trying on *The Yellow Jacket*

Performing Chinese Exclusion and Assimilation (1912–28)

Ju Yon Kim

Advertised as a "Chinese Drama Played in [the] Chinese Manner," George C. Hazelton Jr. and J. Harry Benrimo's *The Yellow Jacket* opened on Broadway in 1912 to enthusiastic reviews.[1] In the play, the governor of a Chinese province decides to kill his first wife and their son, Wu Hoo Git, in order to be rid of the physically deformed child and to elevate his second wife. The farmer charged with carrying out the murders secretly spares and raises Wu Hoo Git, and the young hero later successfully pursues his birthright and the yellow jacket befitting his social position.[2] Depictions of Chinese characters on the American stage were not uncommon in the nineteenth and early twentieth centuries and ranged from spectacular portrayals of China in various productions of *Aladdin* and the Ravel family's *Kim-ka!* (1847) to plays featuring Chinese characters in the United States, which appeared after the midcentury rise in emigration from China.[3] Benrimo, one of the writers of *The Yellow Jacket*, performed as a Chinese immigrant in Francis Powers's *The First Born* (1897), a popular realist drama set in San Francisco's Chinatown. *The Yellow Jacket* was unusual, however, in adopting dramatic conventions associated with the Chinese opera as well as Chinese narratives, characters, and settings. Theatre critics who had grown tired of the naturalistic sets dominating American drama of this era applauded the play's more abstract and unfamiliar aesthetics.

The Chinese theatrical conventions that Hazelton and Benrimo supposedly borrowed included a stage decorated with "Chinese banners," "signs of good cheer," and "huge lanterns";[4] the use of chairs, tables, cushions, and other basic properties to represent various settings, actions, and objects; a visible orchestra playing cymbals and gongs; and a "Property Man" who would move about the stage during the performance to manage the set.

The script of *The Yellow Jacket* directs the Property Man to provide swords to fighting characters, toss shredded paper to represent snow, and hold a pole to represent a weeping willow. In addition, it instructs him to read a newspaper, smoke, and eat during specific moments of the performance when he is presumably not working. As discussed in more detail below, the playwrights' claims about the origins of the performance (as the translation of three Chinese dramas) and the authenticity of its representation of the Chinese theatre would become apocryphal—in part through Benrimo's own efforts to recast the work as an "American" creation. The play nonetheless offered Broadway audiences accustomed to dramatic realism a radically different theatrical experience.

Now largely forgotten, *The Yellow Jacket*'s remarkable success in the first half of the twentieth century presents the intriguing question of how a performance first advertised as a "Chinese drama" became heralded as "a classic of the American theater," particularly in an era when immigration exclusions enforced strict boundaries between "Chinese" and "American."[5] In chapter 2, Stuart J. Hecht revisits the tensions between nativism and immigrant cultural production of this era with respect to Jerome Kern and Oscar Hammerstein's musical *Show Boat*. Such tensions are also relevant here. *The Yellow Jacket* tested racial and cultural boundaries, bringing into focus how social and aesthetic distinctions between "Chinese" and "American" emerged and shifted in relation to each other during the same era. A central contention of this chapter is that *The Yellow Jacket*'s ultimately short-lived transformation from amusing Chinese spectacle to modern American masterpiece reflects its flexible participation in contemporary debates about theatrical realism and experimentation, popular culture and high art, and acceptable and unacceptable "foreignness." My study demonstrates that while *The Yellow Jacket* straddled apparently conflicting categories, the play did not subvert these binaries so much as initiate negotiations about which lines of cultural and racial demarcation could and could *not* be crossed.

Nevertheless, performances of *The Yellow Jacket* made the interface between "Chinese" and "American" available for theatrical and social experiment and play. On the one hand, the drama affirmed notions of racial peculiarity and white normativity through theatrical devices that foregrounded the estranged perspective of its European American viewers; on the other hand, it simultaneously encouraged those same spectators to see differently by seeing *as* the Chinese. Performances offered viewers an opportunity not simply to discern the presumed alienness of the Chinese but also to simulate the experience of Chinese spectatorship. In particular, the play's integration of nonrealistic "Chinese" staging with the Property Man's performance of his tasks and other quotidian behaviors made it possible for its audiences to engage—alongside the actors—in provisional racial crossings. Critically celebrated for its aesthetic innovations, *The Yellow Jacket* was also a laboratory of social experimentation in its performance of interracial and cross-cultural exchanges.

Property Man (*center*) with Wu Sin Yin and Tai Fah Min in a scene from *The Yellow Jacket* by George C. Hazelton Jr. and J. Harry Benrimo. *Photograph by Arnold Genthe. Courtesy of the Library of Congress, Prints and Photographs Division, Arnold Genthe Collection: Negatives and Transparencies.*

Seeing and Playing in Yellowface

On 12 November 1916, *New York Times* theatre critic Alexander Woollcott offered an effusive welcome back to *The Yellow Jacket*, which had first opened at the Fulton Theatre on Broadway four years before:

> The return of "The Yellow Jacket," if only for ten honorable matinees, is a cause for august rejoicing. The fascinating Chinese play, wrought somewhat in the Chinese way, was frozen out of New York at the end of its first brief visit four seasons ago. Since then it has been to the end of the world and come back again.[6]

Although favorably received in 1912, *The Yellow Jacket* was hardly a hit at the time. In the four years of its absence from New York, however, it had traveled to London, Spain, and Russia; the 1916 revival led to the domestic success that its supporters thought it had deserved its first time around. Attesting to its continued popularity, revivals followed in 1921, 1928, 1934, and 1941.[7]

Woollcott saw the play's belated success as an example of a regrettable popular tendency to overlook artistic genius: "It is sometimes the tragedy of a rare and beautiful play that it cannot find its public in time."[8] His assessment, however, obscures the complex intersection of social and aesthetic developments that shaped the play's reception. In the early twentieth century, the use of naturalistic stage sets had reached its height in the United States, particularly through the influence of director David Belasco. By the time of *The Yellow Jacket*'s first opening, a backlash against this theatrical "illusionism" had developed. In July 1912, theatre critic Clayton Hamilton of *The Bookman* attacked Belasco's sets as distracting, expensive, and unimaginative.[9] This complaint against Belasco was just one among many directed at the American theatre during this period by critics who also lamented the theatre's emphasis on entertainment and novelty over aesthetic development. Opening on 4 November 1912, *The Yellow Jacket* made its first appearance in the midst of these frustrations with illusionism, mass entertainment, and the apparent inadequacy of American drama.

Although press coverage noted the drama's lofty language and sentimental plot, its ostensibly "Chinese" metatheatrical conventions became the focus of public attention.[10] Interpretations of what these conventions meant—in terms of the play's aesthetic and commercial appeal and in its relationship to Chinese and American theatrical practices—were hardly uniform or static. Markedly divergent characterizations of the play emerged, reflecting a tension between the continuing appeal of the realistic stage and the growing influence of modern experimentation and between a desire to see this play as an authentic representation of the "Orient" and a need to claim it as an important product of American theatre.

The performance begins with the appearance of the "Property Man" who "enters indifferently from the opening at center of curtain, strikes thrice on a gong and exits" (233). A figure dressed as a "Chinese scholar," operating as the Chorus, then speaks to the audience directly, introducing the play and adding, "Let me impress upon you that my property man is to your eyes intensely invisible" (234). In asserting the invisibility of the Property Man, the Chorus only highlights his visibility and the peculiarity of the convention. Arranging props and sets throughout the performance, with apparently little concern over interrupting the performance, the Property Man became the most publicized aspect of the production. According to James Harbeck, "Reviews often spent half of their length on the staging and gave more column inches to the property man than to all other performers combined."[11]

Although Hazelton and Benrimo could claim that they included the Property Man in order to be faithful to Chinese theatrical practices, they were selective in the elements they chose to adopt for *The Yellow Jacket.* Krystyn Moon notes, for example, that the play significantly deviates from the Chinese opera by having the actors speak, instead of sing, almost all of their lines.[12] The Chorus is another key divergence from its "Chinese manner." In their foreword to the play, Hazelton and Benrimo explain that the Chorus replaces the signs normally used within Chinese theatre to establish scenes (232). Yet the role of the Chorus clearly exceeds that of a place marker: both character and guide, he explains aspects of the performance while providing abstruse commentary. For example, he advises the audience, "Observe well with your eyes and listen well with your ears. Be as one family, exceedingly happy and content. Heaven has no mouth. It makes men speak for it" (234). Such nonsensical "wisdom" and exaggerated erudition establishes the Chorus as a humorous caricature of a Chinese scholar, a racialized adaptation of an ancient Greek chorus. Thus, the claim that *The Yellow Jacket* was a "Chinese drama" warrants careful scrutiny.

Furthermore, although it is possible in broad strokes to evaluate the accuracy of *The Yellow Jacket*'s imitation, such a comparison risks eliding the vitality of Chinese theatrical practices and forms, which elude the fixity ascribed to them by the play. Opening during a time of significant political change in China and severe restrictions on Chinese immigration to the United States, *The Yellow Jacket* perpetuated a depoliticized and disembodied notion of "assimilable" foreignness. Fixing Chinese opera's diverse styles into a single, comprehensively scripted play set in an indeterminate time, *The Yellow Jacket* reiterated Orientalist images of an archaic and unchanging East. Just a year before its opening, however, a major revolution had begun in China. As a play supposedly based on traditional Chinese drama, *The Yellow Jacket* certainly had no obligation to engage with news of contemporary upheavals in China. Yet its ahistorical representation of "Chinese theatre" obscured the aesthetic dynamism and political import of the Chinese regional theatres. Colin Mackerras notes that Chinese theatre went through major transformations during the Qing dynasty (1644–1911), including the decline of the aristocratic *kunqua* drama, the rise of popular regional theatres, and the increasing politicization of the stage.[13] Actors were deeply engaged in the struggles of the 1911 revolution that led to a republican government.[14] Although the basic plot of *The Yellow Jacket* traces a regime change, the Chorus's humorous "philosophical" framing of the narrative and public discussions of the play's formal innovations (vis-à-vis American theatre) glossed over the political relevancy of a cultural form that was implicated at the time in a national revolution.

The significance of Chinese theatres moreover extended beyond China, through their presence in immigrant communities. Diasporic Chinese theatres were important centers of immigrant society and, according to Nancy Y. Rao, "took an active role in defining the historical, geographical, and social positions of Chinese Americans."[15] Emerging in the mid-1800s, these immigrant theatres had by the turn of the twentieth century become popular tourist attractions in San Francisco and New York. The first Chinese theatre in New York opened in 1893 but closed just a year before *The Yellow Jacket*'s first run, and more than a decade passed before another theatre devoted to Chinese opera opened in New York.[16]

The absence of both a large Chinese immigrant population and a Chinese theatre in New York at the time of *The Yellow Jacket*'s opening was likely crucial to the play's success. Pointing to a shift in American representations of the Chinese at the turn of the century from sly cheats to refined mandarins, Dave Williams observes that hostility toward the Chinese declined somewhat after the passage of the Chinese Exclusion Act of 1882.[17] Moon similarly tracks a shift from "unconditional hatred" to "fascination" prompted by immigration restrictions, the revolution in China, and the return of popular depictions of Chinese culture as (charmingly) backward.[18] If (as Robert G. Lee observed of the mid-1800s) the increasing presence of Chinese immigrants spurred representations of the Chinese as menacingly alien rather than safely foreign,[19] their shrinking numbers at the turn of the century seem to have motivated a reverse movement. Distanced both spatially (through restrictions on Chinese immigration) and temporally (through representations of an unchanging East), the Chinese could become quaint and interesting again.

The decline of Chinatown theatres also meant that when *The Yellow Jacket* opened on Broadway, it could claim to represent Chinese opera without the competing presence in New York of these immigrant theatres—where property men went about their tasks without a script stipulating indifferent behavior and no chorus was present to explain the performance. Instead, the use of white actors in yellowface—that is, in makeup and costumes that signaled "Asianness"—fully realized the physical absence of Chinese and Chinese American peoples in the play's reproduction of the Chinese theatre.[20] In studies of early yellowface performance, Lee and Sean Metzger link the practice to anxieties about contamination and assimilation.[21] Gaining popularity during the mid-1800s, yellowface performances persisted into the twentieth century. The practice became part of what Moon describes as "a more totalizing racialization on the stage"[22]—that is, the integration of more facets of a production (including makeup, costumes, sets, and music) into an all-encompassing theatrical representation of racial otherness.

Adopting "Chinese" stage conventions as well as fashions and melodies, *The Yellow Jacket* exemplifies this trend of creating an integrated theatrical experience. Yet as I show in this section, the play's "totalizing racialization" was especially expansive, extending past the stage to encompass the audience. With the "Chinese threat" legally curtailed, the complex racial identifications activated by Hazelton and Benrimo's drama recall the contradictory mix that Eric Lott finds in blackface minstrelsy, where "transgression and containment coexisted."[23] *The Yellow Jacket*, however, specifically cultivated this ambiguous relationship through dramatic conventions that prompted spectators to conceive of themselves as yellowface *viewers*. In particular, the Property Man's casual mannerisms and execution of daily tasks were critical to enabling the audience to assume dual—but not equal—roles as white and "Chinese" spectators. In one sense, *The Yellow Jacket* asked its audience to watch its presentation of the Chinese in order to enjoy a simulated experience of Chinese spectatorship. At the same time, the drama constantly and unmistakably reminded its white audience of the certainty of their *not* being Chinese.

In its presentation of the "Chinese theatre," the drama explicitly projects an audience that would find the play mystifying. In his opening monologue, the Chorus not only explains that the Property Man should be understood to be "invisible" but also warns viewers that "much of our acting will be strange" (233). In declaring that the performance will *be* strange, as opposed to suggesting that it may *seem* strange, the Chorus normalizes the perceptions of those who *do* find it strange. The Chorus then repeatedly reminds audience members of their estrangement from the culture presented on the stage by providing them with explanations of the performance. Similarly, Wu Sin Yin, the first character of the enacted narrative to speak, proclaims, "By your gracious leave, with many apologies, I will state in all modesty, for your edification only, for of course I know who I am and how great and august I am, while you are not so favored, that I am Wu Sin Yin, the Great" (235). Through this affected and convoluted language, Wu Sin Yin (like the Chorus) breaks the fourth wall and takes for granted the audience's lack of familiarity with the aesthetics of the performance. Thus, although the play does allow for two possible audience perspectives—that of Chinese spectators for whom its conventions would be the norm, and of Western spectators who would find those same gestures strange and incomprehensible—it privileges the latter as the primary mode of viewership.

While less overt than the Chorus or Wu Sin Yin's remarks to the audience, the Property Man's performance of the mundane reinforces *The Yellow Jacket*'s estrangement of the aesthetics of Chinese theatre. When informing viewers that the Property Man is invisible, the Chorus instructs them on how to see his behaviors "properly"—just as an audience accustomed to the Chinese opera might. Yet as Williams argues in his reading of *The Yellow Jacket*, "These conventions, wrenched from their theatrical and cultural context, do not fit organically into the performance as they would in a Chinese theatre. Instead, they become quaint distractions from the story, the exact opposite of their original function."[24] A "property man" in the kind of Chinatown theatre that Benrimo purportedly visited would have taken a purely practical role managing the stage and would not be considered part of the performance itself. But Hazelton and Benrimo scripted in great detail the behaviors and mannerisms of their Property Man. Their stage directions not only call for the Property Man to arrange the set but also direct him to smoke, read a newspaper, hurt himself accidentally, eat a bowl of rice with chopsticks, and misplace a cushion before correcting his mistake; the script even specifies his attitude as "indifferent" and "complacent." The play therefore does not simply *use* Chinese stage conventions; instead, it *mimics* the application of these conventions in its reenactment of a specific staging of a "Chinese drama," which was then reproduced every time *The Yellow Jacket* was performed.

The presence and actions of the Property Man, however, generate a sense of intimacy as well as difference between the performance and the audience. As a carefully scripted impersonation of those who manage sets in Chinese theatres, the Property Man is both the most stylized and the most ethnographic aspect of the play. The simulated mannerisms, habits, and even "mistakes" imbue the role with an air of authenticity. In other words, the apparent banality of his performance reinforces its realism. An article on Arthur Shaw, who originated the role, stressed the skill required to play the part faithfully: "For two hours and a half this property man moves among the actors as though invisible to them and to the spectators. The slightest bit of overplaying, the least stooping to buffoonery, the merest suggestion of theatricals on his part would ruin his impersonation and mar the whole play."[25] The desired effect was a kind of naturalism, as though the actor were an actual property man rather than a scripted character. Shaw reiterated this point to explain why his part was more difficult than it appeared:

> Suppose I took a notion to get interested in somebody out in the audience! Can't you see how quickly the whole illusion would blow up! Or even suppose that I became excited about the play or anything save my work as a property man, can't you imagine how soon I'd be fired? . . . I don't dare do anything except loll around and pretend to do nothing in a nonchalant, lackadaisical, celestial way. But in reality I am working all the time.[26]

Portraying his work as a carefully maintained "illusion," down to the "nonchalant, lackadaisical" attitude assumed to be the natural manner of the Chinese (or "Celestial"), Shaw explained that his performance had to seem unaffected in order to replicate an authentic experience of the Chinese theatre for his audience. The subtle enactment of mundane behaviors thus lent the play an impression of ethnographic credibility.

The Property Man's apparently indifferent execution of and occasional deviations from his duties therefore heighten the sense that the audience is witnessing a realistic representation of Chinese drama. In doing so, the performance generates two—ostensibly opposing—effects. On the one hand, it accentuates a divide between viewers who would through familiarity be indifferent to his behaviors and those who would be fascinated by the novelty of these same behaviors. In reviews of the play, writers stressed this difference in perception, noting that Chinese spectators familiar with the theatrical conventions replicated in *The Yellow Jacket* would not see them as strange or comic. The *New York Times* explained, "[The Property Man's] menial assistants are supposed to follow him in sublime invisibleness. And the effect, to our eyes, should be merely amusing, whereas to the Celestial it is all taken in deadly earnest."[27] Watching the Property Man doze off or apathetically kick away a prop, Broadway audiences could take pleasure in seeing what would remain "unseen" to a Chinese viewer accustomed to such conventions. In describing the contrasting perspectives of the Celestial and non-Celestial viewer, however, the article ignored the extent to which the play assimilates and returns the gaze of the latter. While the very banality of the Property Man's behaviors augments the drama's claim to ethnographic accuracy, their careful replication in every production and embodiment by a white actor in yellowface present these actions as notable rather than ordinary. The play's double movement of implying the "naturalness" of the Property Man's behavior to Chinese spectators while affirming its strangeness to European American audiences therefore materializes racial particularity as a way of *seeing*, as well as a way of being.

Moreover, because *The Yellow Jacket* was performed in major American and European theatres with white actors in yellowface, opportunities for Chinese and Chinese American actors or spectators to trouble its presentation of the Chinese theatre were limited. Despite the decline of Chinatown theatres before *The Yellow Jacket*'s first Broadway run, their popularity as tourist destinations and as the subject of books and articles at the end of the nineteenth century meant that Americans were not entirely unfamiliar with the kind of performance reflected in the play. Yet while Chinese performers were also guilty of replicating stereotypes for commercial gain, productions in China or by Chinese immigrants for their communities offered a much less mediated and less comfortable experience for Western spectators than did this performance on Broadway.[28] In a 1903 account of a visit to a Chinese theatre, E. M. Green described the confusion of American tourists trying to understand what they saw.

> A row of Americans extend on either side from the rear wall to the front of the stage. The faces of these onlookers bear that stupid expression always noticeable in people listening to a language they do not understand. The hideousness of the occidental costume is made glaringly apparent by the somber color, yet graceful lines, of the every-day dress of the old men and children who lounge about on the stage behind them and by the exceeding beauty of the costumes of the actors.[29]

Green's account highlights the awkwardness of these encounters in less controlled spaces—where Chinese spectators and actors seemed unconcerned with the tourists' discomfort and could potentially return their gaze to judge the expressions and clothing of these tourists as inappropriate or strange. Performances of *The Yellow Jacket*, on the other hand, offered a safe space in which Western audiences could observe the foreign without actually confronting foreign bodies that might disturb the integrity of their vision of self and other.

And yet, even as performances of *The Yellow Jacket* promoted a sense of racial and cultural difference, they also allowed viewers to dabble with the prospect of looking differently (without looking different). Its experiments in trespassing the lines between "Chinese" and "American" became most salient when its viewers experienced the play from *both* of these spectatorial positions. Articulating this experience, critics who attended the 1912 and 1916 productions on Broadway recounted how they vacillated between identifying with and distancing themselves from the performance. Clayton Hamilton, for example, asserted, "They [the play's producers] have invited their American audience to laugh at these [Chinese theatrical] conventions; and they have forced their audience, by this very act of laughing at them, to grow so familiar with the Chinese conventions as to accept them ultimately as media for the expression of delicate poetry and poignant pathos."[30] A *New York Times* article similarly observed that the play allowed for both amusement and empathy:

> The curious thing about this Celestial drama is that we are augustly asked not merely to accept the conventions but to be amused by them at the same time. And it is the amazing thing about "The Yellow Jacket" that entering into the spirit of the adventure, we do just this. We not only laugh delightedly at the detached boredom of the efficient property man and the comic insufficiency of his snowstorm, but we follow with bated breath the humiliation of the Daffodil and submit utterly to the unforgettable enchantment of the languorous flower boat.[31]

These accounts suggest that *The Yellow Jacket* simultaneously positioned these audience members as both American *and* Chinese spectators: the former laughing at the strange conventions, the latter engrossed by the dramatized narrative. Thus, while the play affirmed a view of Chinese culture as foreign, it also allowed spectators to "grow so familiar" with its conventions that they could appreciate the "poetry" and "pathos" conveyed, just as Chinese spectators habituated to such performances might do. The Property Man, moving fluidly between the "staged" world of Wu Hoo Git and the "real" world of his daily labor and providing the play with both slapstick comedy and ethnographic credibility, was the key device that allowed the audience to try on Chinese spectatorship. Productions of *The Yellow Jacket* therefore enabled their primarily white American audiences to see the Chinese and to see *as* the Chinese, simulating a racial crossing while making unnecessary the actual presence of the Chinese, who continued to be subject to immigration exclusions. The yellowface of the actors onstage found a reflection in the simulated yellowface of audience members, who could imaginatively inhabit the spectatorial position of the "Other" without sacrificing the distanced perspective to which they comfortably returned.

From Chinese Drama to American Classic

While *The Yellow Jacket* allowed Broadway audiences to delight in the possibility of trying on Chinese spectatorship, its successes abroad prompted its creators and supporters to obscure their own initial endorsement of the performance as an authentic portrayal of the Chinese theatre. Rather, they sought to diminish the play's loose borrowings of Chinese aesthetics and to establish it as an exclusively *American* contribution to modern theatre. The play's partial replication of the Chinese theatre, which initially lent it the impression of authenticity, later allowed Benrimo to claim that it actually evinced a calculated *inauthenticity*. Much like the Chorus insists on the "invisibility" of the Property Man (who remains clearly present to the audience), the playwright claimed in a 1928 *New York Times* article that "'The Yellow Jacket' is not a Chinese play."[32] Benrimo asked the public to blind itself to the production's imitation of the Chinese theatre and to see its experiment in cross-cultural exchange as an exclusively American invention.

Much of the initial publicity surrounding *The Yellow Jacket* described the drama as "new," "novel," "quaint," or "strange." Advertisements promoted it as "The Laughing Novelty"[33] and "The Sensational Novelty of the Year!!"[34] Articles about the play reiterated this point with headlines such as "Something New and Strange in Drama."[35] A review printed immediately after its opening proclaimed, "For besides reflecting a very great deal of charm and sentiment it contains no end of good fun. In fact, the first audience alternated between loud laughter at its grotesquerie and hushed awe at those portions of the play which developed the more serious motives."[36] Hamilton (who had criticized the public's preference for "novelty" in playwriting) nonetheless raved, "*The Yellow Jacket* . . . deserves to be recorded as the most remarkable artistic achievement of the present season."[37] Given Hamilton's attack on Belasco, his praise of *The Yellow Jacket* can be understood in part as a jab at excessive illusionism. *The Yellow Jacket* therefore provided critics an opportunity to vent their frustrations with existing theatrical practices while suggesting new paths for American drama. *The Yellow Jacket*'s "novelty" thus fused popular entertainment with artistic innovation: critics could praise its creative use of non-Western theatrical conventions, while the general public could enjoy its "strangeness" and "quaintness."

This drama could feasibly occupy both roles because, even as it seemed to reject verisimilitude in its staging, it asserted a different sort of overarching realism in how it represented Chinese culture. As Erika Fischer-Lichte points out, the play is invested in maintaining an "illusion of reality [that] is proclaimed to be the reality of *another* stage: the Chinese stage."[38] However unfamiliar and stylized the conventions deployed, this double framing of the play as an imaginative representation of the dramatic narrative and an accurate reproduction of Chinese theatre allowed *The Yellow Jacket* to lay simultaneous claim to both artistic innovation and ethnographic authenticity. While Hamilton might have appreciated *The Yellow Jacket*'s metatheatrical conventions, he saw the work as a faithful depiction of the Chinese theatre. He called *The Yellow Jacket* "a veritable Chinese play" and wrote, "It may probably be stated as a fact that Mr. Benrimo knows more about the Chinese stage than any other American today. It occurred to him that it would be interesting to devise a play out of the traditional materials of the Chinese theatre and to present it precisely in accordance with the conventions of the Chinese stage."[39] Hamilton thus embraced the "precise" reproduction of Chinese theatre, even if he did not appreciate the meticulous details of Belasco's sets. *Current Opinion* offered a similar claim: "Mr. Benrimo's observations of the Chinese theatre in San Francisco have enabled him to steep his pen in realism."[40] Highlighting that the play was a product of the playwright's firsthand observations and the actors' meticulous imitation, these writers emphasized that it exemplified an ethnographic, if not dramatic, realism.

Nevertheless, when *The Yellow Jacket*'s European tour and subsequent revivals in the United States established it as a pioneering work of modern American drama, this rise in status necessitated a complex maneuvering away from its associations with popular entertainment and ethnographic verisimilitude. The evocation of Chinese "Otherness," which allowed *The Yellow Jacket* to bridge the ethnographic and the aesthetic, presented a particular challenge to the play's assimilation into a nascent American dramatic canon. *The Yellow Jacket*'s international tour began when Benrimo took the drama to London after its critically lauded but financially unsuccessful Broadway run. Max Reinhardt's decision to produce the play in Berlin and Konstantin Stanislavski's sponsorship in Moscow secured *The Yellow Jacket*'s new reputation as an innovative American drama embraced by respected theatre artists abroad. Productions in Madrid, Vienna, and Budapest followed performances in major German and Russian cities. The enthusiasm with which European theatre practitioners received this work is not surprising, given the interest that Reinhardt, Edward Gordon Craig, Jacques Copeau, and others had previously espoused in Asian theatre.[41] These avant-garde European directors of the early twentieth century developed stylized theatrical productions and simplified stage designs that drew inspiration from a range of performance traditions, including Chinese opera and Japanese Noh and Kabuki. Arthur Feinsod recounts that these developments in European theatre gradually made their way across the Atlantic and began making an impact on American theatre artists and critics around the time of *The Yellow Jacket*'s opening in 1912.[42] The attention that the play received while abroad, understandable in this context, further validated the praise it received from domestic critics as a welcome departure from existing practices in American theatre. Heralded at the time as the first American play to receive such a widespread and favorable response in Europe,[43] it seemed to represent a possible turning point in American drama—an emergence from the shallowness of second-class entertainment to establish itself as a national art that deserved international recognition.

To assume this new role as a renowned American drama of aesthetic depth and complexity, however, *The Yellow Jacket* needed to shed its old clothes as an entertaining novelty and authentic imitation. Any praise of this work as a meticulous depiction of Chinese theatre could imply that it was an uncreative imitation rather than a work of formal experimentation. According to Jack K. W. Tchen, by the late nineteenth century, the "American imitation and emulation of Chinese luxuries" evident in colonial times had been replaced by an opposite impulse: "With the rise of a destined sense of American civilization, the Chinese were cast as the embodiment of slavish imitators—the opposite of the free and happy Americans."[44] Despite repeated descriptions of the drama as a replication of the Chinese theatre, which would seem to belie stereotypes of the derivative Chinese and the innovative American, a *New York Times* article on *The Yellow Jacket*'s return to Broadway reveals a striking resistance to seeing China as a source of inspiration:

> This tardy appreciation of a beautiful example of native dramatic literature will be seized as capital by those who love to proclaim that America is a nation of imitators, incapable of appreciating its own art until it bears the stamp of alien approval. In this case they will be wrong, for the circumstances are misleading. It is probably true that the mass of theatergoers is ignorant of the wide popularity of "The Yellow Jacket," and that the true explanation of the belated enthusiasm is that it arrived four years before its time—before the leaven of the new stage movement had begun its upheaval of the native stage.[45]

This critic's prediction that the play's success would support claims that the United States was "a nation of imitators" seems to allude to its "Chinese" story and staging. Yet the subsequent reference to the "stamp of alien approval" reveals that the alleged imitation is not of Chinese but of *European* theatre practitioners, those who enthusiastically endorsed the play after its modest first run. Emphatically claiming *The Yellow Jacket* as a "native" creation, the writer does not consider the possibility that the drama's simulation of Chinese theatrical practices would also confirm accusations of American mimicry.

This turning away from the play's debt to Chinese theatrical practice fits into the tradition of "American orientalisms," identified by Tchen, which "began with some admiration or fascination for an actual Chinese thing, idea, or person, then went through a phase of emulation and mimesis, and ended with European American mastery and dominance."[46] The temporary incorporation of *The Yellow Jacket* into the ranks of important American drama might suggest a broadening of cultural borders to encompass Chinese influences. Yet subsequent efforts to establish the drama as an expressly *American* contribution to modern theatre revealed instead that its "emulation and mimesis" of Chinese opera became problematic, necessitating a complicated set of circumventions and erasures.

The play's success in Europe led to a refigured understanding of its "Chinese" and "American" elements, with the former diminished as constituting the less significant, decorative aspects of the play. Celebrating *The Yellow Jacket*'s international success, one article described it as having "American parentage, Chinese trappings, and cosmopolitan appeal."[47] In other words, this play was an American creation *masquerading* as Chinese. Similarly, Woollcott welcomed the drama back to Broadway by characterizing it as "a Chinese play, wrought *somewhat* in the Chinese way" (emphasis added), simultaneously affirming and casting doubt on the authenticity of its representation. Woollcott elaborated, "But here is an additional aesthetic pleasure—the pleasure some of us always feel in the deliberate recapture for the moment of some ancient or alien accent, a pleasure we feel in our innocence whether the re-creation be authentic or not. It is authentic enough for our purposes."[48] With questions of authenticity thus dismissed, for Woollcott, aesthetic merit lay only in the authors' active reworking of the mere "accent" or inflection of a foreign culture.

The issue of the accuracy of the play's representation became entirely irrelevant, however, with Benrimo's declaration in the *New York Times* that "'The Yellow Jacket' is not a Chinese play." In an article titled "Legend and Truth: The Facts about 'The Yellow Jacket,' Again in Revival Here," which appeared on 4 November 1928, on the occasion of the play's second New York revival, Benrimo explained:

> We borrowed not so much from the Oriental theatre as from the Chinese philosophy of life. In looking for a plot that would lend itself to Chinese treatment, we hit upon the underlying theme of "Pilgrim's Progress," substituting Chinese morality for that of Puritan England. In other words, we carried a boy from the cradle to the grave in a fashion plausible to the Occidental mind, and yet developed the tale in an Oriental atmosphere. We made use of Chinese imagery, symbolism and morality, but the basic vitality of the play was American. It is not a translation nor an adaptation, only clothed in Chinese garments.[49]

The "truth" about *The Yellow Jacket*, according to Benrimo, was that it was an American and not a Chinese play. Despite repeated assertions to the contrary circulated sixteen years earlier, Benrimo insisted that the origin of its plot was Anglo-American and specifically aligned the play with the plot of John Bunyan's *The Pilgrim's Progress*. Meanwhile, he relegated its "Chinese" aspects to superficial "garments" surrounding a core of American "vitality."

Benrimo stressed, moreover, that he and Hazelton saw *The Yellow Jacket* as a corrective to dominant American theatrical practices: "Hazelton was an easterner and knew nothing about China or the Chinese theatre. But he agreed with me that it was something better than the realistic drama which demanded fresh butter on the stage if the plot called for fresh butter."[50] While press coverage of *The Yellow Jacket*, particularly during its first Broadway run, described it as both a departure from the prevalent realism of the American stage *and* a careful imitation of a Chinese performance, Benrimo explicitly associated his work upon its return to Broadway with artistic experimentation and "native" creativity—the traits most amenable to positioning the play as an important work of modern American drama. Insisting that the drama was American and not Chinese, however, also required that Benrimo admit to fraud. In the article, he acknowledged,

> I am not . . . a Chinese scholar. The legend that I am, like that which created the impression that "The Yellow Jacket" was a translation from the Chinese, was the invention of the press department sixteen years ago. My collaborator, George C. Hazelton, wasn't a very good showman and refused to pretend that he knew Chinese. So the responsibility fell on me.[51]

With this confession, Benrimo effectively invalidated much of the publicity surrounding the play's initial run and made endorsements of his expertise on Chinese theatre seem ridiculous in retrospect.

In characterizing the Chinese elements of the play as "trappings" and "garments," or in terms of an "ancient or alien accent" that is authentic "enough," Benrimo and admirers of his drama pushed to dissolve the performance's presumed referent. Whether or not this affected how most theatregoers regarded *The Yellow Jacket* is difficult to establish, although Benrimo's decision to publish his "confession" suggests that the prevailing view then was that the play simulated Chinese performances. Furthermore, even Benrimo's overt attempt to change public perception of the play may not have affected how audiences *experienced* the performance: as Woollcott's 1916 article on the Broadway revival makes clear, recognizing that *The Yellow Jacket* does not accurately represent Chinese theatre did not necessarily deprive the audience of a pleasure that came from the impression or "accent" of authenticity.

Few critics today would dispute the accuracy of Benrimo's claim that the play is more American invention than careful imitation. Yet I would also propose that to the extent that the Property Man joins two definitions of performance—as "doing" and "representing"—his onstage activities obstinately resist dismissal as the mere flavor or inflection of Chinese theatrical practices. However scripted and rehearsed his stage business, the Property Man must nevertheless manage the objects that prompt the audience and the actors to "see" a snowstorm or a weeping willow. This work is what enables the rest of the performance to exercise—or to be an exercise of—the American imagination. Whether or not the Property Man faithfully replicates those who manage stages in Chinese theatres, his "doing" of common tasks connects them not through mimesis but through practice. In this sense, Arthur Shaw was correct in remarking about his role as the Property Man, "I am working all the time."[52] In the slippage between representation and practice, between playing a role and working a job, the Property Man bears a material affinity—albeit one that is always transient and partial—with the property men whom he evokes. To the extent that shades of the Chinese body linger on the stage, however distorted to serve as an effect of American ingenuity, they emerge not in the play's exotic accoutrements or in the Property Man's humorous "Celestial" expressions but in those (never fully registered) moments of the performance when he is simply unrecognized labor.

The story of *The Yellow Jacket* is a chronicle of travels taken, imagined, and forbidden. In its treks from New York to Moscow and back, *The Yellow Jacket* moved (if always partially) from amusement to art, authentic to fake, Chinese to American, while serving as a medium through which actors and audiences could try on racial Otherness (and Benrimo could try on the hats of expert and fraud). The play's mobility stands in contrast to its static portrayal of China as a distant, unchanging world and to the nation's contemporaneous barring of Chinese immigration. In a final twist, however, *The Yellow Jacket* lost much of its popularity after the mid-twentieth century, slipping out of the ranks of prominent American plays. Meanwhile, post–World War II changes to U.S. immigration policy finally overturned restrictions on Asian immigration. Despite the play's many circulations, its depiction of Chinese theatre—which in hindsight invites critique as an Orientalist caricature—preserves it as a fascinating object for analysis but makes future travels as an enduring theatrical production unlikely.

Notes

1. *The Yellow Jacket*, advertisement, *New York Times*, 30 October 1912, 22, Proquest Historical Newspapers, http://proquest.umi.com, accessed 16 June 2005. All subsequent *New York Times* citations are from Proquest Historical Newspapers website.

2. The play refers to the yellow jackets that were bestowed as a sign of imperial favor during the Qing dynasty. While the authors make use of the idea that the jacket is a sign of high social status, the play does not suggest a familiarity with the actual practices surrounding its distribution and use.

3. Today, *Aladdin* is more commonly associated with the Middle East; these nineteenth-century theatrical productions, however, were set in China. For an extended discussion of *Aladdin* and *Kim-ka!*, see Krystyn Moon, *Yellowface: Creating the Chinese in American Popular Music and Performance, 1850s–1920s* (New Brunswick, N.J.: Rutgers University Press, 2005), 23–26.

4. George C. Hazelton Jr. and J. Harry Benrimo, *The Yellow Jacket*, in *The Chinese Other, 1850–1925: An Anthology of Plays*, ed. Dave Williams (Lanham, Md.: University Press of America, 1997), 235. Subsequent citations are in text.

5. "J. Harry Benrimo, Actor, Playwright," *New York Times*, 27 March 1942, 23, accessed 16 June 2005.

6. Alexander Woollcott, "Second Thoughts on First Nights," *New York Times*, 12 November 1916, X6, accessed 16 June 2005.

7. James Harbeck, "The Quaintness—and Usefulness—of the Old Chinese Traditions: *The Yellow Jacket* and *Lady Precious Stream*," *Asian Theatre Journal* 13.2 (1996): 241.

8. Woollcott, "Second Thoughts on First Nights."

9. See Arthur Feinsod, *The Simple Stage: Its Origins in the Modern American Theater* (New York: Greenwood Press, 1992), 28.

10. Harbeck, "Quaintness," 241.

11. Ibid.

12. Moon, *Yellowface*, 99.

13. Colin Mackerras, "The Drama of the Qing Dynasty," in *Chinese Theater: From Its Origins to the Present Day*, ed. Colin Mackerras (Honolulu: University of Hawaii Press, 1983), 92.

14. Ibid., 112.

15. Nancy Y. Rao, "Songs of the Exclusion Era: New York Chinatown's Opera Theaters in the 1920s," *American Music* 20.4 (2002): 426.

16. Su Zheng, *Claiming Diaspora: Music, Transnationalism, and Cultural Politics in Asian/Chinese America* (New York: Oxford University Press, 2010), 94.

17. Dave Williams, *Misreading the Chinese Character: Images of the Chinese in Euroamerican Drama to 1825* (New York: Peter Lang, 2000), 113.

18. Moon, *Yellowface*, 112.

19. Robert G. Lee, *Orientals: Asian Americans in Popular Culture* (Philadelphia: Temple University Press, 1999), 28.

20. *The Yellow Jacket*, however, may not have always been performed in yellowface when it was produced in smaller community stages. The Collection of Chinese Theater Images in California at the San Francisco Museum of Performance and Design includes a photograph captioned "Performance of the Yellow jacket [*sic*] by the Hawaii Chinese Civic Club dramatic chapter in 1950s," which shows an ostensibly Chinese Hawaiian cast. While outside the scope of this paper, a performance of the play by Chinese Americans in the 1950s would activate different meanings and effects than the Broadway productions analyzed here.

21. Lee, *Orientals*, 43; Sean Metzger, "Charles Parsloe's Chinese Fetish: An Example of Yellowface Performance in Nineteenth-Century American Melodrama," *Theatre Journal* 56.4 (2004): 651.

22. Moon, *Yellowface*, 118.

23. Eric Lott, *Love and Theft: Blackface Minstrelsy and the American Working Class* (New York: Oxford University Press, 1995), 234.

24. Williams, *Misreading the Chinese Character*, 172.

25. "Acting, Acting, All the Time, but Not a Word to Speak," *New York Times*, 1 December 1912, X8, accessed 16 June 2005.

26. Ibid.

27. "Something New and Strange in Drama," *New York Times*, 3 November 1912, X6, accessed 16 June 2005.

28. Jack K. W. Tchen, *New York before Chinatown: Orientalism and the Shaping of American Cultures* (Baltimore: Johns Hopkins University Press, 1999), 153.

29. E. M. Green, "The Chinese Theater," *Overland Monthly and Out West Magazine*, February 1903, 7–9, APS Online, Proquest, http://proquest.umi.com, accessed 24 June 2005. Subsequent APS Online citations are from this same website.

30. Clayton Hamilton, "Yellow Jacket," *The Bookman*, December 1912, 382, APS Online, Proquest, accessed 14 September 2005.

31. Woollcott, "Second Thoughts on First Nights," X6.

32. J. Harry Benrimo, "Legend and Truth: The Facts about 'The Yellow Jacket,' Again in Revival Here," *New York Times*, 2 November 1928, 118, accessed 16 June 2005.

33. *The Yellow Jacket*, advertisement, *New York Times*, 15 November 1912, 10, accessed 16 June 2005.

34. *The Yellow Jacket*, advertisement, *New York Times*, 1 December 1912, X8, accessed 16 June 2005.

35. "Something New and Strange in Drama," X6.

36. "'The Yellow Jacket' Is a Real Novelty," *New York Times*, 5 November 1912, 13, accessed 16 June 2005.

37. Hamilton, "Yellow Jacket," 382. In an article titled "What Is Wrong with the American Drama?," which appeared between *The Yellow Jacket*'s first two Broadway runs, Hamilton argued that theatregoers' preference for novelty prevented the cultivation of profound, imaginative American plays. Clayton Hamilton, "What Is Wrong with the American Drama?," *Bookman*, May 1914, 314, APS Online, Proquest, accessed 24 June 2005.

38. Erika Fischer-Lichte, *The Show and the Gaze: A European Perspective* (Iowa City: University of Iowa Press, 1997), 81.

39. Hamilton, "What Is Wrong," 314.

40. "Reading the Heart of the East through the Drama," *Current Opinion*, January 1913, 35, APS Online, Proquest, accessed 24 June 2005.

41. Arthur Feinsod, *The Simple Stage: Its Origins in the Modern American Theater* (New York: Greenwood Press, 1992), 55.

42. Ibid., 28.

43. "Play That Went Round the World," *New York Times*, 26 November 1916, X7, accessed 16 June 2005.

44. Tchen, *New York before Chinatown*, 292.

45. "Play that Went," X7.

46. Tchen, *New York before Chinatown*, xx.

47. "When Grandees Give 'The Yellow Jacket,'" *New York Times*, 11 March 1917, X5, accessed 16 June 2005.

48. Woollcott, "Second Thoughts on First Nights," X6.

49. Benrimo, "Legend and Truth."

50. Ibid.

51. Ibid.

52. "Acting, Acting," X8.

2. Jazz, Jews, and Modernism on Broadway

From *Lady, Be Good!* to *Show Boat* (1924–27)

Stuart J. Hecht

The year 1924 proved a watershed for American democracy on Broadway. That year, Congress passed the Immigration Act, effectively closing America's doors to the mass migration of immigrants—particularly Italians and eastern European Jews. Ironically, that very same year, Jewish artists began a long run as the dominant force in American musical theatre. At a point where nativism asserted a national homogeneity, Jewish artists responded with bold artistic visions of American cultural pluralism on the Broadway stage. George and Ira Gershwin unveiled their debut production, *Lady, Be Good!* Others, such as Richard Rodgers and Lorenz Hart, followed with their own jazz-based musicals that challenged nativist American values by celebrating urbanity and modernity. An early instance of American "culture wars," the tensions between nativist feelings and assimilating immigrant culture on Broadway culminated in Jerome Kern and Oscar Hammerstein's *Show Boat* (1927). Through this landmark musical, Jewish musical artists—asserting cultural ties with African American culture and music—promoted an inclusive vision of America, tacitly defying those parochial forces that sought to expel them. This chapter assesses the impact of an unspoken cultural alliance within Broadway musicals of the mid-1920s between artists of Jewish heritage and the jazz music derived from African American culture; such an alliance produced an influential expression of a decidedly modern, diverse, and forward-looking vision of America.

Prior to 1919, Broadway stood as the pinnacle of American popular culture. Though controlled largely by Jewish producers, Broadway's productions tended to reflect predominantly Protestant values. The half-dozen years following World War I were dominated by so-called Cinderella shows such as *Irene* and *Sally*: musicals (despite the presence of modern women characters) whose sensibilities and musical aesthetics remained starkly traditional. *Lady, Be Good!* changed the theatrical landscape by introducing to the Broadway stage urbane characters, clever and only slightly cynical, whose songs and dances were flavored with jazz. This urbanity reflected the Gershwins' secular Jewish American sensibilities. Broadway became the site whereby those sensibilities, at odds with traditionally established national norms, found opportunity and expression.

Lady, Be Good! came on the heels of a crescendo of American nativism that was grounded in rural and small-town experience and located primarily in the Deep South. The long-dormant Ku Klux Klan had revived itself in 1915 around the trial of Leo Frank. Frank was a Jew from New York, educated at Cornell, who had moved to Atlanta to manage a pencil factory. He was accused, on shaky grounds, of murdering young factory worker Mary Phagan. Local media coverage of the trial brought out vicious anti-Semitism. Frank came to represent in the Atlanta public's imagination not just a legal defendant but rather the Jew as outsider. Following Frank's conviction and death sentence, protests erupted in northern cities on his behalf. Georgia's governor commuted the death sentence to life imprisonment, on the grounds that he had received an unfair trial. However, in 1915 Frank was kidnapped from his work camp and lynched by a gang that included some of Georgia's most prominent citizens.[1] The Klan gained additional visibility in D. W. Griffith's 1915 classic film, *The Birth of a Nation*, a work that reinforced negative minority stereotypes and popularized nativist sentiment.

Reactions to the First World War also fed American nativism of the period. Anti-German sentiment ran high during the war years; individuals and businesses with German-sounding names in northern cities were attacked, causing many to change their names. After a decade of writing songs with decidedly ethnic titles, characters, and subject matter, Tin Pan Alley songwriters abandoned the practice. To us today, prewar hits such as Irving Berlin's "Cohen Owes Me Ninety-Seven Dollars," "He's a Ragpicker," "It Takes an Irishman to Make Love," or "I'll Take You Back to Italy" seem politically incorrect; but in their own era, given the commercial appeal of these songs, it seems that some ethnic populations enjoyed being celebrated in this manner. World War I pressured American popular culture into a new type of patriotic homogeneity. In the postwar years, the "First Red Scare" and the J. Edgar Hoover–orchestrated Palmer Raids targeted immigrants for their presumed anarchistic or Bolshevik sympathies. Emma Goldman was sent to Russia. Nicola Sacco and Bartolomeo Vanzetti were arrested and then executed on questionable grounds. Goldman was Jewish, and Sacco and Vanzetti were Italian; their public persecutions solidified apparent linkages among nationality, politics, enforcement, and prejudice.

During the presidential election of 1924, both political parties appealed mostly to the rural vote. At the Democratic convention, William Gibbs McAdoo (enjoying strong support from the Ku Klux Klan) almost defeated Al Smith, the Irish Catholic governor of New York. After one hundred ballots, John W. Davis was chosen as a compromise candidate who could still appeal to voters in largely WASP rural and small-town America.[2] Seeking the same rural vote, Republican president Calvin Coolidge's campaign featured an auto caravan across America. In its vanguard was a truck painted with portraits of Coolidge and running mate Charles Dawes with a placard that read "Common Sense" and "Brass Tacks." Most significantly, painted on either side of the truck was the image of a farmhouse—no person in sight—supposedly depicting Coolidge's birthplace. There was no hint of urbanity or ethnicity in the presidential campaigning of 1924.[3] These historical and political trends toward nativism culminated in the aforementioned Immigration Act of 1924, which effectively closed America's doors after almost a half century of welcoming "your tired, your poor, / Your huddled masses yearning to breathe free."

The songs of Berlin and his Tin Pan Alley and Broadway peers presented an influential response to nativist national values and tastes. Broadway shows played first to a commercial New York City audience and then (when successful) toured nationwide—spreading urban offerings to nonurban regions. By the 1920s, the makeup of Broadway audiences was becoming heavily Jewish. As such, musicals reflected—and supported—the tastes of that public, as well as those of Broadway composers, lyricists, and librettists (most of whom were also Jewish). However, it would be a mistake to assume that Broadway artists deliberately shaped their material in order to make political statements; their endeavor was a commercial one designed primarily to entertain. Nonetheless, the sensibilities and experiences of the increasingly Jewish Broadway community found shape and expression for a national audience through this creative work.[4]

For one example, consider the 1924 *Music Box Revue* by the Russian-born Jewish composer Irving Berlin. The show included what on the surface appears to be a comedic song, written for Fanny Brice, to be sung with a Yiddish accent, titled "Don't Send Me Back to Petrograd." In a telling final line, Brice's character begs to remain in America, singing, "I'll even wash the sheets of the Ku Klux Klan."[5] More vivid examples are found in the creative output of the Gershwins. George and Ira's parents came from Russia, making these brothers second-generation American Jews. Raised with exposure both to liturgical music and Yiddish theatrics, George and Ira assimilated themselves in many ways to American social and cultural norms. Though not college educated, the Gershwin brothers were the product of the New York City public school system and of a community that treasured education as a means to achieve the American dream. By 1924, both had artistic achievements of their own: George as a pop composer and Ira (working under an assumed name) as a lyricist. With *Lady, Be Good!*, they teamed up with one another and joined forces with another sibling duo—the vaudeville dance stars Adele and Fred Astaire—on a mainstream Broadway musical like none that had come before it. Their new musical collaboration would embrace the latest musical trends by featuring a score composed entirely of jazz.[6] *Lady, Be Good!* opened only months after America officially closed its doors with the Immigration Act.

George's early fascination with jazz drew him toward the influence of black stride piano players James P. Johnson and Willie "the Lion" Smith. His own musical compositions blended strains of this tradition with Jewish liturgical influences and the conventions of Tin Pan Alley. George's music was thus an amalgamation of the cultures of several poor New York City neighborhoods. Ira loved light verse, especially the writings of W. S. Gilbert, and also developed a love for slang—as evident in his compressed lyrics to the song "'S Wonderful" (which included made-up words like "fash" for "fashion" and "pash" for "passion").[7] Before World War I, jazz and slang belonged to disreputable urban street culture. Staid nineteenth-century Victorianism still ruled the Broadway stage, but inroads were made just beyond Broadway's geographical citadel. Eubie Blake and Noble Sissle's all-black *Shuffle Along* (1921) proved an unexpected hit with both white and black audiences.[8] The kings of the Broadway revue—Florenz Ziegfeld and George White—soon hired the show's dancers to teach their own dancers jazz moves. But the scripted musical genre did not succumb as quickly. George Gershwin teamed up in 1922 with lyricist Buddy DeSylva to write *Blue Monday*, a one-act jazz opera performed by white singers in blackface, set in Harlem. This opera proved commercially unsuccessful. When George introduced "Rhapsody in Blue" in early 1924, accompanied by Paul Whiteman and His Concert Orchestra in New York, the blending of jazz strains with classical orchestrations made jazz suddenly respectable—setting the stage for *Lady, Be Good!*

Though the plot of *Lady, Be Good!* is somewhat slight, its milieu and sensibilities proved powerful. The play opens with brother and sister Dick and Susie Trevor (played by Fred and Adele Astaire) flat broke, having been evicted from their home and finding themselves out on an urban street. They crash the party of a wealthy friend and, while there, endure a series of comic mix-ups. In the end, Susie marries Jack for love rather than for money—though it turns out, fortuitously, that her love *has* money. No sentimentality here: the pace is fast with little time to pause and indulge, let alone reflect. Nor are there any lessons to be learned as Susie hits the jackpot both romantically and (unexpectedly) financially. Along the way, the characters deliver a series of syncopated Gershwin numbers, including "Fascinating Rhythm," "So Am I," "The Half of It, Dearie, Blues," "Little Jazz Bird," "I'd Rather Charleston," and the title number, "Oh, Lady, Be Good!" These songs served to show off the modern dancing styles of the brother-and-sister leads, Adele and Fred Astaire.

Born in Omaha, the Astaires (much like the Gershwins) melded the old into the new with flash and pizzazz. By 1924, the Astaires had become bona fide vaudeville stars, having just returned from rubbing shoulders with England's aristocracy thanks to their "puttin' on the ritz" sense of polish and style.[9] They had become in real life what their image suggested: witty, toe-tapping American sophisticates. The characters played by the Astaires are young, energetic, optimistic, and, above all, entirely urbane—matching perfectly the mood and style of the Gershwins' music. They seemingly have no cares and do not take things too seriously, beyond the need to assist one another and the desire to improve their financial lot by romantic means. Their personal loyalties overshadow their superficiality, as they blithely bounce off others while attending to their own interests. It is all materialistic and lighthearted entertainment, a glittering fantasy of modern life—definitely not the kind of musical that cares about traditional small-town values, domesticity, or sentimentality. *Lady, Be Good!* ignored America's puritanical past to take pleasure in 1920s hedonism.[10]

Lady, Be Good! marks a significant shift in the American musical. In one sense, this shift was one of musical aesthetics; scholar Deena Rosenberg notes, "In *Lady, Be Good!* the Gershwins introduced a new kind of modern theatre song, as well as a higher level of musical-dramatic coherence than the 1924 Broadway norm. In fact, the score, on its own and in relation to the book, set high standards for musicals to come."[11] *Lady, Be Good!* was also noteworthy as a gesture of cross-cultural exchange, linking a certain set of Jewish American sensibilities with African American musical traditions on the Broadway stage. Though never "Jewish" in its characters or story line, *Lady, Be Good!* depicted an open, contemporary, urbane society of the sort embraced and embodied by the Gershwins and their Jewish musical theatre cohorts. Just as the Gershwins set aside any direct reference to their own ethnic heritage in favor of modern cosmopolitanism, so too did the stories they wove and the songs they wrote. The show promoted modernist notions of urban progress, sophistication, and elegance: a "Roaring Twenties" attitude that rejected Victorianism by celebrating flappers and cigarettes, fast cars and bathtub gin. The show's music and the lyrics ran counter to the WASP sentimentality that had dominated the previous generation of musicals. It was a brashly defiant rejection of old-fashioned Americana, one that trumpeted the arrival of Jewish artists as Broadway's dominant creative force. The Gershwins danced with the Astaires, with still-invisible black musicians providing the accompaniment.

Taken together, this represents a heady set of unspoken democratic cultural alliances—a direct challenge to nativist elements promoting a narrower vision of American authenticity. *Lady, Be Good!* asserted a vastly different perspective, aligning jazz with the search for acceptance and wealth in modern America. Leo Frank may have been brutalized by southern bigots, but there were many more like him out there, such as the Gershwins themselves: a generation of assimilated Jews who were rapidly gaining acceptance within the highest reaches of American life, even winning applause for doing so. A jazz-infused Broadway musical composed by Jews signified a rise of representational, democratic cultural expression in an age of some distinctly represented antidemocratic politics.

The success of *Lady, Be Good!* set the stage for a flurry of subsequent jazz musicals. It proved particularly inspirational for a wave of Jewish artists—notably Richard Rodgers and Lorenz Hart—who the very next year began their own startling string of hits. Rodgers's scores tended to blend Jerome Kern–inspired ballads with Gershwinesque jazz numbers, with Hart's lyrics providing intellectual allusions and clever wordplay. Rodgers and Hart's compositions, like those of the Gershwins, reflected a sensibility as sophisticated as New York City itself. However, the high point of the Broadway revolution started by the Gershwins in 1924 came three years later, not with Rodgers and Hart but through another Jewish writing duo—Jerome Kern and Oscar Hammerstein II—and their landmark 1927 musical, *Show Boat*.

Show Boat: Cementing Jazz and Jews

If *Lady, Be Good!* broke down Victorian walls, *Show Boat* cemented new structures into place by embedding a diverse and democratic modernity firmly within the American ethos. *Show Boat* traced the evolution of the new, suggesting modernism was organic and inevitable and, as such, just as inherent to American life as anything that preceded it.[12] Drawn from Edna Ferber's 1926 novel of the same name, *Show Boat* is generally acknowledged as the first fully integrated book musical. While this designation refers to its use of music and lyrics to develop a serious plot, this musical was "integrated" in another way: in its dramatization of a racially mixed community with a somewhat racially mixed cast and creative team.[13] While recognized for its excellence and its contribution to forwarding the musical form, *Show Boat* also asserted an inclusive vision of America. Its plot depicts a forty-year period, from 1887 to 1927 (which was the year of its Broadway opening). As such, *Show Boat* was rooted in the past but also decidedly up-to-date. Its characters collectively proclaimed the American identity of its era.

Show Boat follows a series of couples who form a kind of family unit, through two generations, from past to present. Cap'n Andy and his wife, Parthy, parents to Magnolia, operate the titular vessel, a Mississippi River steam paddleboat named the *Cotton Blossom*. Cap'n Andy is both the boat's skipper and the actor-manager of its onboard company of performers. Working for them are three other couples. Frank and Ellie are married, vaudeville-style performers who sing and dance. These two ultimately discover a downtrodden Magnolia and urge her to return to show business, thus salvaging her life. The *Cotton Blossom*'s stars are the unwed couple, Julie and Steve. Though seemingly devoted to Julie, Steve eventually disappears without explanation. The third couple is husband and wife Joe and Queenie, African American workers who run the kitchen and keep the ship stocked. Though Queenie scolds her husband for laziness, it is Joe whose reflections on the Mississippi echo through the drama with his recurring singing of the pseudogospel anthem "Ol' Man River." One more duo, Gaylord Ravenal and Magnolia, are the drama's romantic leads, a Mississippi gambler paired with an innocent ingénue. Gaylord and Magnolia wed, experience great joy and sorrow, and birth the next generation—their stage-star daughter, Kim.

The characters of *Show Boat* embody a rich cross-section of America. Cap'n Andy comes from the West. He is a doting father but a questionable husband, a man of loose morals who sneaks around trying to avoid the forbidding eye of his wife. Parthy, by contrast, comes from New England and represents the puritanical East. Though harsh, she is protective of those in her brood and urges them toward self-improvement and better lives. It is fitting that this western man and eastern woman meet at the place in the nation where East meets West: the ever-shifting Mississippi River. This sense of the mighty river as a living presence echoes through the lyrics of "Ol'

Man River," in which Hammerstein features Joe as philosopher, learning life's lessons from the river itself—especially on how to endure suffering. The Mississippi stands as a symbol of America's anguished soul. Its waters pulse through the nation as the prime means of transporting lives; it is also the body-politic's central artery, keeping this earthbound nation alive.

As the play progresses in time, the *Cotton Blossom* moves slowly but inevitably from south to north, traveling roughly two thousand miles and traversing forty years in time. The southern origins of this journey play out through the politics of miscegenation, the romantic comingling of black with white. Its opening song, "Cotton Blossom," establishes how, on this showboat, the black crew members work while the white passengers play, defining the boat as a microcosm of the entire American experience (most particularly that of the nineteenth-century South). But the story's path leads through geographical, chronological, and cultural change. By play's end, the *Cotton Blossom* docks in New York City, with the same Queenie who initially ran the downstairs kitchen now dolled up in flapper clothes, enjoying a new freedom to "play."

Early in the drama, Magnolia meets Gaylord, a prototypical Mississippi gambler complete with top hat, cane, and genteel southern manners. He is a dreamer who attracts Magnolia but, in the end, causes her much hardship and pain. In one sense, Gaylord personifies the South and Magnolia the North, but there are other dimensions to these multilayered characters. For instance, a southern sheriff pursues Gaylord before he shifts his attention to Julie. Gaylord gets along just fine with Queenie and Joe. Perhaps Gaylord can best be understood as a southern maverick, living just outside the region's societal rules and norms. In that sense, the *Cotton Blossom* becomes a type of Noah's ark: a safe haven for those who do not fit into prevailing political and social norms and are riding out the flood.

Almost from the start, evocations of American racial pathology find their way into the musical. With the young Magnolia hanging out in Queenie's kitchen, Julie begins to sing "Can't Help Lovin' Dat Man." Queenie asks Julie, "How come y'all know dat song? . . . Ah didn't ever hear anybody but colored folks sing dat song."[14] Julie shrugs it off, but Queenie is perceptive here: Julie has African American ancestry, though she passes for white in society. Shortly thereafter, the southern sheriff boards the *Cotton Blossom* to accuse Julie of having mixed blood, making her relationship with Steve a violation of miscegenation laws. This comes as a shock to all but Julie, who leaves with little fuss despite Steve's protestations. This is a decidedly southern incident; such an arrest would not have happened with the *Cotton Blossom* docked in the North. There is no mention in the script of whether Cap'n Andy or Parthy know of Julie's passing as white. If they do, they clearly do not care. Nor is racial prejudice an issue for Magnolia; it is her custom to hang out in Queenie's kitchen, talking with the cook and her husband. The *Cotton Blossom* can mostly float past the societal troubles and restrictions found on shore. When Julie is taken away, it is Magnolia who bursts into tears, having formed a special bond with Julie. Tellingly, Magnolia fails to understand why such distinctions matter.

Magnolia is also oblivious to Gaylord Ravenal's history as a Mississippi gambler. In her eyes, he represents a certain southern type: gracious, polished, and charming. He and Magnolia fall in love at first sight but must keep their romance secret from the suspicious and puritanical Parthy. Thanks to the loving but amoral Cap'n Andy, the two escape to wed when he diverts his wife long enough for the nuptials to occur. Assuming the *Cotton Blossom* began its trek in New Orleans,[15] it is particularly fitting that Gaylord and Magnolia end up at the northern end of mid-America, in Chicago of the "Gay Nineties," where they place their daughter in a Catholic girls' school while they live the high life. When Gaylord's luck runs out, he leaves his destitute wife and daughter behind. In time, Magnolia finds success on the stage. Their daughter, Kim, grows up and becomes a star in her own right in New York. Magnolia's *Cotton Blossom* past returns to her—literally—to support her as she launches a new life and guides her own daughter into the future.[16]

A parallel narrative in *Show Boat* unfolds through Kern's varied score. The show's musical styles shift as the boat travels through time and space. The early numbers in *Show Boat* echo nineteenth-century banjo songs, traditional African American folk tunes, and (with "Ol' Man River") Negro spirituals. When Magnolia and Ravenal first meet, they proclaim their love through the operetta-styled "Make Believe," which evokes the mid to late nineteenth century. Act 2 opens in Chicago at the 1893 World's Fair, where the newlyweds and their parents sing the spritely "Why Do I Love You?" By 1904, Magnolia (having been abandoned) auditions at the Trocadero nightclub in Chicago, where the alcoholic Julie sings of her latest beau, "Bill" (Steve apparently long gone). Spotting Magnolia, Julie secretly steps aside, never to be seen again. Her sacrifice enables Magnolia to audition successfully with Julie's old "coon song," thereby linking the two women again and making Magnolia the rightful inheritor of Julie's cultural and professional mantle, forever surrogate mother and child. Thus Magnolia stands as the child of east and west, of black and white, with a childhood rooted in America's South but with her adulthood fashioned in America's North. Her life and consequent views represent a synthesis of a diverse and multiracial American experience.

Culture and time advance next through a period song, when Magnolia must win over her first audience (significantly on New Year's Eve) by singing the "old favorite" "After the Ball." Cap'n Andy, unexpectedly present, cheers her on. This pivotal moment reunites father and daughter, old showbiz with new showbiz, and ties together through song the nineteenth and twentieth centuries. By 1927, Magnolia achieves Broadway stardom, dragging the legacy of the rest of the nation with her to the nation's commercial and entertainment center. Her daughter, Kim, now an adult, follows her example by becoming a star in her own right as a jazz dancer. To reinforce the evolution from past to present, Queenie reappears dressed as a flapper, telling Joe how modern girls nab men with the song, "Hey, Feller!"

The progression of song styles meticulously marks the passage of time, with two meaningful interruptions to the chronology. Charles K. Harris's 1891 hit song "After the Ball" originated in the hit musical *A Trip to Chinatown*. The song's inclusion near the end of *Show Boat* encouraged its 1927 audiences to hark back to the previous generation. Similarly, Joe Howard's 1904 song "Good-Bye My Lady Love," sung and danced by Frank and Ellie, was a familiar vaudeville hit of a previous era and served a similar function in the musical. As these nostalgic songs were familiar popular favorites from the past, their performance within the musical captured and brought into sharp definition evolving cultural values and beliefs embedded in the passage of time since their debut.

Much as *Show Boat* charts historical changes in styles of American popular music, it also documents an evolving history of American show business over those same years. That history starts with the showboats themselves, which date back to the 1820s. The musical then enacts a nineteenth-century melodrama along with elements of minstrelsy and vaudeville and (with the inclusion of "After the Ball") a reference to an early musical, *A Trip to Chinatown*. There are also references to Chicago's Columbian Exposition, with its midway entertainments, and to the developing nightclub scene via the Trocadero. The drama's conclusion, set in 1927, contains simultaneous metatheatrical references both to a Gershwin-style jazz musical and to *Show Boat* itself. In other words, Kern and Hammerstein used a history of American music to underscore the forward progress dramatized in their musical: from the prejudicial toward the enlightened, even as the recurring anthem "Ol' Man River" rolls along throughout.

In these ways, *Show Boat* becomes an argument against backward-looking American nativism. Rather than let the Klan define American identity, *Show Boat* offers a more progressive, democratic sensibility. It decries racism and laws against miscegenation, presenting a portrait of an America in which black and white citizens of different social classes can develop rich relationships. It describes the Mississippi as the lifeblood of all of America and projects this vision mostly through African American eyes, with an awareness of a history of suffering and injustice. It is the story of the evolution of black music, framed by the artistry of a Jewish composer and Jewish lyricist, with roots deep in geography and time—thereby trumping the Klan's exclusionary claims to a prejudicial "authenticity." *Show Boat* is also a celebration of urban modernity. The narrative starts in New Orleans, but its characters' lives come to fruition first in Chicago and later in New York City. The inclusion of the Columbian Exposition as a setting underscores the "miracle" of modern Chicago rising from the ashes of its great fire, driving forward with industrialization and technological advancement. At this exposition, historian Frederick Jackson Turner famously introduced his "frontier thesis," which proclaimed the death of America's uncivilized recent past and applauded its present and future. That the musical then moves quickly to 1927 New York, to the very same Broadway in the very same year as *Show Boat*'s debut, reinforces the drama's values as the most modern of modern, in the most urbane of urban centers.

Show Boat is thus a study in progress, a carefully crafted account of how America itself moved from parochialism to multiculturalism, from the rural to the urban, from the old-fashioned to the modern. It suggests that this evolution has been both organic and inevitable. *Show Boat* portrays its present modernity as the natural outcome of all those forces at work once-upon-a-time that allow the aging Magnolia and Gaylord to pass the torch to Kim. Kim inherits much from her parents and their traditions, even as she ends the play dancing to a new kind of music. In Ferber's novel, Magnolia and Gaylord name their daughter Kim because she was born on the *Cotton Blossom* as it reached a point on the Mississippi River near the convergence of three states, Kentucky, Illinois, and Missouri, her name coming from the first letter of each. Thus Kim is explicitly a product of the heart of the nation with the river as its core. Furthermore, those three states epitomize the historic conflict of the Civil War. Kentucky was a border state, Missouri experienced some of the worst internecine bloodshed, and Illinois was the home of Lincoln. Kim's birth launches a new chapter of healing for the nation's future, moving on from war-torn grievances and grief. Kim dances jazz, even as Queenie now dons flapper gear. This is the vision of contemporary America expressed by a trio of Jewish artists—Ferber, Kern, and Hammerstein—who situate these characters, and themselves, as rightfully living and working within an inclusive America, the Klan be damned.

Oddly, the first production of *Show Boat* featured the Italian American actress Tess Gardella playing Queenie in blackface and otherwise utilized African American actors alongside white performers.[17] This was perhaps the first instance of an integrated cast for a major Broadway musical; it certainly was (Gardella's burnt cork notwithstanding) the first successful Broadway musical to feature an African American actor in a serious leading role (Jules Bledsoe as Joe). The statement made by the musical *Show Boat* was thus mirrored by the onstage cast, much as the show's finale metatheatrically depicts an actual Broadway theatre in its present era. The performance had direct and immediate bearing on the world beyond the proscenium, with the fact and fiction validating one another.

In the novel, Julie auditions at a club called Joppers. In the musical, the site of that Chicago audition is changed to the Trocadero. The real-life Trocadero was opened by Florenz Ziegfeld's father in 1893 in anticipation of the Columbian Exposition of later that same year. The club was failing when young Ziegfeld returned from Europe with a new act, the strongman Eugene Sandow. Florenz Jr. promptly put Sandow on display at the Trocadero, thus saving it (and rescuing his father financially) while also launching his own producing career. So there is a clear parallel built into *Show Boat* between the Illinois-born impresario Ziegfeld Jr. and the birth of Magnolia's own career. But there is still more to this story. Ziegfeld agreed to produce *Show Boat* to coincide with the opening of his own new Broadway venue, the Ziegfeld Theatre. Work on *Show Boat* was delayed, however, forcing Ziegfeld to inaugurate that theatre with *Rio Rita* instead. But it was at the Ziegfeld Theatre that Florenz sought to start a new chapter in his producing career—with a new playhouse featuring a radically new sort of musical. The 1927 audience for *Show Boat* saw Kim's performance at the Ziegfeld Theatre both within the fiction that is *Show Boat* and within *their own lived experience.* Just as Ziegfeld's professional roots began at Chicago's Trocadero (making his father proud) and led to a new kind of show at the Ziegfeld Theatre, so too did Magnolia's professional career start at the same Trocadero (where Julie had already appeared) and led to her proudly watching her daughter play the Ziegfeld Theatre. We assume the producer named his new theatre after himself; perhaps it was also to honor his father of the same name. Given all this, is it also safe to presume that Ziegfeld had a hand in shaping some of *Show Boat,* though the exact nature of his contributions is not known. Thus Ziegfeld aligned himself with the events depicted in *Show Boat* and, by implication, its democratic message.

Show Boat thus affirmed that the roots of American pluralism ran deeper than those of the Klan. It asserted that the black-white experience was indigenous to America and that Broadway's new aesthetics were authentically American: the perfect expression of a nation that functioned thanks to its very diversity. The musical was, in 1927, the latest link in a long cultural current that spanned generations and, like the Mississippi River, flowed from the very base of the nation and served as its ongoing, life-giving heartbeat. As *Lady, Be Good!* had initiated a blend of Jewish black jazz into a modern synthesis, *Show Boat* cemented those creative exchanges as legitimate and authentically American. American Jews could thus join others to lay claim to the worlds depicted on the Broadway stage.

Postscript

Following *Lady, Be Good!* in 1924, the Gershwins rattled off another eleven shows for the Broadway stage. Some were in the same jazz/romantic comedy vein: witty, often even silly romances filled with plenty of jazz melody, rhythm, and tap dance. But strewn among them were three works that sought to expand their theatrical voices into the arena of political satire: *Strike Up the Band* (1927), *Of Thee I Sing* (1931), and *Let 'Em Eat Cake* (1933). These three musicals are also highly comedic. Yet where *Strike Up the Band* and its sequel, *Let 'Em Eat Cake*, vaguely address international affairs, *Of Thee I Sing* zeroes in on the United States and its domestic politics. The Gershwin brothers' English predecessors, W. S. Gilbert and Arthur Sullivan, had perfected the art of satirizing Britain's governmental institutions through their operettas. In *Of Thee I Sing*, the Gershwins showed some courage in doing something comparable for America—holding its politicians and political processes up to lighthearted but serious comic roasting.

With the acerbic George S. Kaufman and Morrie Ryskind as librettists, *Of Thee I Sing* won the 1932 Pulitzer Prize for Drama, the first musical to be so honored. But it is worth emphasizing Ira Gershwin's deliberate addition of one word—a decidedly modern "baby"—to the familiar phrase from our national anthem that gave the show its title. This addendum to the lyrics was not just irreverent slang; the word was a marker of domesticity and other traditional American values. This Gershwin vision of American democracy included both the old and the new, American-born and immigrant, seeing merit in all, in sharp contrast to the exclusionary tactics of backward-looking nativists. Hence *Of Thee I Sing* is in line with both *Lady, Be Good!* and *Show Boat*. A new, inclusive approach to the American musical theatre continued to flourish, seven years past the 1924 closing of America's doors—and well beyond that.

George Gershwin's fascination with creating a black jazz opera famously came to fruition in 1935 with his *Porgy and Bess*. Much as Edna Ferber had spent time in Virginia collecting firsthand research when writing the novel *Show Boat*, so too did Gershwin visit South Carolina. Whether these works hold up as "authentic" or not today, both artists strove to be as accurate as possible in their depictions of peoples and events. Such an approach reflects each artist's respect for others: democratic ideals put into artistic practice.

Notes

1. A sensationalist local press encouraged anti-Semitic takes on Leo Frank's trial, further inspiring northern protests that proclaimed Frank's innocence. The events surrounding Leo Frank's trial and subsequent lynching shocked Atlanta's Jewish population. Some fled Georgia, and those who remained began to retreat from secular public life. Northern Jews responded to Frank's lynching by founding the Anti-Defamation League. For more, see Steve Oney, *And the Dead Shall Rise: The Murder of Mary Phagan and the Lynching of Leo Frank* (New York: Vintage Books, 2004).

2. Irving Berlin attended the 1924 Democratic National Convention and was frightened by how close McAdoo and his Klan constituency came to winning the party's nomination. See, for example, Laurence Bergreen, *As Thousands Cheer: The Life of Irving Berlin* (New York: Viking, 1996).

3. Larry L. Krug, *Coolidge-Dawes Lincoln Tour 1924* (Atglen, Pa.: Schiffer, 2007).

4. See Stuart J. Hecht, *Transposing Broadway: Jews, Assimilation and the American Musical* (New York: Palgrave Macmillan, 2011); the source for the increased percentage of Jews in Broadway audiences and among professional musicians comes from *Encyclopedia Judaica*, ed. Fred Skolnik and Michael Berenbaum, vol. 15 (Farmington Hill, Mich.: Macmillan Reference USA, 2007), 219.

5. *The Complete Lyrics of Irving Berlin*, ed. Robert Kimball and Linda Emmet (New York: Alfred A. Knopf, 2001), 214.

6. Another jazz musical, the all–African American *Shuffle Along*, predates *Lady, Be Good!* But *Shuffle Along* was staged outside of the geographical area generally understood to be "Broadway" and for the most part did not draw a regular Broadway audience.

7. Deena Rosenberg, *Fascinating Rhythm: The Collaboration of George and Ira Gershwin* (Ann Arbor: University of Michigan Press, 1997).

8. For evidence that George Gershwin saw *Shuffle Along*, see Howard Pollack, *George Gershwin: His Life and Work* (Berkeley: University of California Press, 2006), 76. Pollack describes how Gershwin socialized with the leading

black musicians in Harlem at that time. For a discussion of *Shuffle Along* and its links to Jews and to modernism, see Ann Douglas, *Terrible Honesty: Mongrel Manhattan in the 1920s* (New York: Farrar, Straus and Giroux, 1995). Douglas also links urban jazz with modernism and the modernist values that dominated the Jazz Age.

9. Not only did the Astaires' London success lead them to socialize with English nobility, but these connections eventually caused the sibling act to break up. In 1932 Adele retired from the stage in order to marry the English lord Charles Cavendish.

10. Douglas also links the Astaires' dance to black jazz roots, despite their outwardly WASP personae; see *Terrible Honesty*, 359–31.

11. George and Ira Gershwin, *Lady, Be Good!*, Nonesuch Records, 1992, compact disc; liner notes by Deena Rosenberg, 27.

12. The best historical account of *Show Boat* can be found in Miles Kreuger, *Show Boat: The Story of a Classic American Musical* (New York: Oxford University Press, 1978). For an insightful racial analysis of the show, see Todd Decker, *Show Boat: Performing Race in an American Musical* (New York: Oxford University Press, 2012). See also Scott McMillan, "Paul Robeson, Will Vodery's 'Jubilee Singers,' and the Earliest Script of the Kern-Hammerstein *Show Boat*," *Theatre Survey* 41.2 (2000): 51–70.

13. The creative team for *Show Boat* included Will Vodery, an African American, as choir director and vocal arranger.

14. Oscar Hammerstein II and Jerome Kern, *Show Boat*, in *American Musicals: 1927–1949*, ed. Laurence Maslon (New York: Library of America/Penguin Random House, 2014), 23.

15. In Edna Ferber's novel, Julie is evicted from the boat by a sheriff in the state of Mississippi. Edna Ferber, *Show Boat* (1926; New York: G. K. Hall, 1981).

16. Perhaps the real showboat is Magnolia herself, as it is, in the end, her story. Kim also chooses a career on the stage, walking in her mother's footsteps; she is, perhaps, another showboat traveling down similar waters.

17. Gardella makes for a revealing study in the ambiguities of racial categories and public receptions of racial identity in this era. Italians were not wholly accepted as "white" in the early twentieth century, affording Gardella something of an ambiguous status with the public that may well have affected audience reception of her portrayal of a non-white role. Furthermore, Gardella was well known to audiences prior to *Show Boat* for her turns as the minstrelsy-derived character "Aunt Jemima" on the vaudeville stage; this history certainly added more complexity to the public's view of the actress behind the burnt cork.

3. Reconfiguring Race and Citizenship

The *Teatro Vernáculo* of La Unión Martí-Maceo (1930–40)

Eric Mayer-García

> If we rely on history to tell us what happened at a specific time and place, we can rely on the story to tell us not only what might have happened, but also what is happening at an unspecified time and place.
>
> —Trinh T. Minh-ha, *Woman, Native, Other: Writing Postcoloniality and Feminism*

In November 1932, a crowd of theatregoers gathered in the large hall of Sociedad La Unión Martí-Maceo (the Martí-Maceo Society), one of Ybor City's many mutual aid societies. Adjacent to Tampa, Ybor City was established in 1885 by tobacco factory owners to house workers. Tobacco workers, mostly emigrants from Italy, Spain, and Cuba, created mutual aid societies for their respective communities; La Unión Martí-Maceo provided benefits and social activities for Cubans of color in Ybor City.[1] A diverse audience of tobacco workers—women and men, Cuban and Spanish, black, white, and *mulato*—came to the Martí-Maceo theatre to see a group of well-known players who regularly appeared at the Centro Obrero (the Labor Hall). They performed one of the latest hits from Havana, *La loca de la casa* (The crazy woman of the house, 1929) by Agustín Rodríguez—an outrageous satire in the style of *teatro bufo*, with stock characters and popular music. The play depicts a mysterious countess confronting Monico, the *negrito*: a blackface stock character who personifies the Cuban national character as irreverent, mischievous, and macho. Challenging social norms within both the world of the play and the audience, the countess pounces upon Monico, professes her love, and calls him her count before vanishing behind the curtain with a promise to return soon with an opulent ring. Alone onstage, Monico shares with the audience his perceived stroke of fortune:

MONICO: (*Pinching himself*) Monico . . . Monico . . . are you awake? Yes! Really awake without a doubt! . . . She is into me in a really serious way and all because of this little body! It's not my fault, but the fault of the Catalonian that was my father and of Catalonia. I am the image, although a little darker, of the land where they produce the very scent of manliness! It's silliness gentlemen. And I do not know if a spirit told it to me, or if I dreamt it: that this little body was worth so much! It already begins to bear fruit, and how so, nothing less than getting to toy with a ring worth millions![2]

Monico's satisfaction with the appeal of his *cuerpectio* (little body) as the object of the countess's desire violates the *bufo's* customary gender roles, as he emulates the typical behavior of the licentious mixed-race *mulata* character. Monico also transgresses racial categories by moving between them. He attributes his sex appeal to his Catalonian father and, in doing so, performs his mixed-race heritage and presents himself as *mulato*. Monico also identifies with his peninsular ethnic heritage, becoming "the image, although a little darker," of Catalonia itself. In this moment, Monico troubles the lines between black, *mulato*, and white; Cuban and Catalonian; masculine and feminine; *negrito* and *mulata*.

Performed on the Martí-Maceo stage in 1932, Monico's utterance created multiple meanings for the diverse audience assembled in the haven for Cubans of color living in the racist crucible of the Jim Crow South. His humorous transgressions must have incited laughter. At the same time, Monico made critical gestures toward the structural tropes of Cuba's complex and often painful colonial history. As the offspring of a peninsular Spaniard and an Afro-Cuban woman, Monico embodied a common metanarrative of Cuba's origins as a *mestiza* nation. By playing the part of the *mulata* stock character, he both evoked and disordered the power relations of white Cuban and peninsular male objectification of mixed-race women of color. Monico's preoccupation with the newfound value of his "little body" recalled, with biting irony, the commodification of black bodies during the slave trade. While transgressing lines of race as the *negrito*, Monico ultimately alluded to the fissures in his own status as a blackface stage character that degraded Afro-Cubans and belonged to a national imaginary of racial privilege.

In the epigraph, Trinh T. Minh-ha reminds us of the interdependent relationship between historiography and storytelling.[3] This chapter seeks to fill the gaps in the story of the theatre of La Unión Martí-Maceo by approaching archival play manuscripts as remnants of the "unspecified time and place" of cultural memory. Through analysis of these manuscripts and other surviving records, I attempt to describe "what might have happened" as Ybor City's Afro-Cubans used theatrical performance to assert their citizenship as transnational Cubans and U.S. Americans. By bringing focused attention to specific productions of *teatro vernáculo*—a blanket term for the many porous and contiguous genres of Cuban popular theatre, including *teatro bufo*, *zarzuelas* (a dramatic-lyric genre), and variety theatre—I argue that members of the performance section of La Unión Martí-Maceo entered into a discourse on race and citizenship. Their contributions to that discourse arose from and amplified their community's experiences as Afro-Cubans within the United States. Through skillful manipulation of popular conventions and performance traditions, these 1930s productions of *teatro vernáculo* called into question representations of race, ethnicity, nation, and gender. Artists and audiences participated in a critique of segregation and racial exclusion and created performances that reconfigured the political, cultural, and social parameters of citizenship from a transnational Afro-Cuban perspective.

The most extensive archive documenting theatre performances of La Unión Martí-Maceo is housed at the University of South Florida Libraries Special Collections. The Sociedad La Unión Martí-Maceo Records contain three unpublished scripts: a typed manuscript of Rodríguez's aforementioned *La loca de la casa*, a *juguete cómico* or one-act farce with popular music; a handwritten manuscript of a social drama called *Hambre* (Hunger, n.d.); and a handwritten copy of the second half of a *juguete cómico* called *Los novios* (The betrothed, n.d.).[4] Within his broader history of Hispanic theatre in the United States, Nicolás Kanellos analyzes *Hambre* and *Los novios*, both of which he finds relevant to the social and economic realities of the Martí-Maceo Society.[5] However, no single study has yet been dedicated to the theatre of La Unión Martí-Maceo, and the archival script of *La loca de la casa* has received no scholarly attention to date.[6]

The reconfiguration of *teatro vernáculo* from a transnational Afro-Cuban perspective runs parallel to playwright Josefina Niggli's innovative use of the popular *género chico* to assert Mexican and Mexican American belonging in the U.S. American ethos through a process that Elizabeth Coonrod Martínez describes in chapter 6 as "(re)visioning." Martínez argues that Niggli brought "her own experience in Mexican culture, and her distinctive awareness of social inequality and the peasant class, into greater social currency for English-speaking American audiences." Similarly, those in the Martí-Maceo Society did not limit their audiences to Afro-Cuban members alone, involving white Cubans and other immigrants in their theatre and its critical "(re)visioning." While most social and cultural activities of Ybor City's mutual aid societies were exclusive to members and their families, theatre was an exception. The theatre of La Unión Martí-Maceo was a space where the entire Ybor City community could come together, regardless of racial division. For instance, on 11 November 1926 a group of local journalists organized a tribute in the Martí-Maceo theatre for New York–based Afro-Cuban lawyer Bernardo Ruiz Suárez, author of a treatise on race and democracy in Cuba and the United States: *The Color Question in the Two Americas*.[7] The celebration included the performance of an original *bufo* play called *El muerto vivo* (The living dead) and was open to everyone "sin distinción de razas" (regardless of racial difference).[8] Similarly, the 1932 production of *La loca de la casa* sheds light on La Unión Martí-Maceo's pursuit of the democratic and inclusive character of cultural pluralism and transnationality outlined in the introduction to this volume.

In the 1890s, members of the Cuban community of Ybor City played an important role in their home country's struggle for independence against Spain, contributing to forward-thinking visions of Cuba as an autonomous nation that transcended colonial hierarchies of race. On 26 November 1891, poet and revolutionary leader José Martí delivered a famous speech titled "Con todos y para el bien de todos" (With all and for the good of all) calling for white Cubans to unite with black Cubans in resistance to Spain. In some ways, the Cuban enclave in Ybor City exemplified Martí's ideals in its social relations. White and black Cuban men received comparable wages for the same work. Workrooms in factories were racially integrated, and black Cubans moved around more freely in Ybor City's public sphere than in other parts of Jim Crow Tampa.[9] Cigar workers of all races raised coffers for the independence movement, and through the collaboration of Cubans in exile and forces on the island led by Afro-Cuban general Antonio Maceo, the movement all but defeated Spain before that progress succumbed to U.S. intervention. After founding one of the only known racially integrated Cuban social clubs, El Club Nacional Cubano, Octubre 10 (The October 10th Club), the Cuban community of Ybor City was a bastion of the racial fraternity that Martí, Maceo, and others envisioned.

The end of Cuba's struggle for independence, ironically, coincided with an upsurge of Jim Crow segregation in the U.S. South. Cubans of Ybor City increasingly felt pressure to divide their community according to the color lines of the U.S. South. Thus a contradiction emerged between the Cuban community's legacy in dispelling racial hierarchies and the growing institutionalization of segregationist practices adapted by its mutual aid societies. In 1900, Cubans of African descent were forced out of the previously integrated October 10th Club.[10] The expelled members founded Ybor City's first Afro-Cuban club, then called the Sociedad de Libre Pensadores de Martí y Maceo (The Society of Freethinkers of Martí-Maceo), while those remaining in the October 10th Club—who self-identified as and passed for white by both Cuban and U.S. criteria—renamed their group El Círculo Cubano (The Cuban Club).[11] It is difficult to establish to what extent U.S. conceptions of race mediated this process of segregation, as social pressures exacerbated racial divisions already existent in the community.[12]

Historically, race in Cuba has functioned differently than in the United States. In chapter 11, Lisa Jackson-Schebetta explains how the Spanish colonial hegemony that once connected Latin American worlds introduced theopolitical and ethnic-racial identity categories, which imbued the idea of race within concepts of ethnicity, nation, and religion. Spanish colonial models differed from models of race brought to the Americas by British colonialists. By the turn of the twentieth century, Cubans defined racial categories in ways apart from the black-white binary that prevailed in the United States. Cuban racial typology included *blanco* (white), *trigueño* (wheat-colored), *mestizo* (mixed race), *mulato* (mulatto), *moreno* (dark-skinned), or *negro* (black)—categories that were more flexible and porous. The emphasis in these terms pertains to skin color and phenotype, and none of these categories laid a claim to racial purity. In fact, lack of racial purity was an important marker that set any Cuban apart from being a Spanish colonial subject. Traditional racial hierarchies have privileged *blancos* over *mulatos*, and *mulatos* over *negros*. Social class also worked as a racial determinant. A person of color in a high social position may have moved between being a *mestizo* or *moreno*, depending upon whether his or her higher status was recognized or not.[13] It remains unclear to what degree Cuban conceptions of race determined how the October 10th Club segregated itself. However, what is clear is that the contrasting color lines of both Cuba and the United States played a part in determining who became white and who became black in Ybor City.

Struggles over nation, race, and citizenry in Cuba incessantly shaped local understandings of related struggles in Ybor City. In Cuba during the 1920s through the 1940s, Afro-Cuban organizations fought against attempts to impose forms of public segregation and protected their right never to be excluded from public spaces—a right guaranteed by the first Cuban constitution of 1901.[14] However, groups that forged political agency for Afro-Cubans against racial oppression throughout Cuba's history—such as Afro-Cuban *sociedades*, *cabildos de nación* (fraternal societies for distinct African ethnicities), or the Partido Independiente de Color (Independent Party of Color)—were themselves racially and ethnically segregated institutions. Although segregationist practices forced Afro-Cubans out of the October 10th Club, Ybor City's Afro-Cubans did not define the break as an acceptance of racial subordination. By modeling their new organization after an Afro-Cuban *sociedad*, the founders of Sociedad La Unión Martí-Maceo positioned the organization within a tradition of political agency, social ascendancy, and self-determination.

Theatres became a vital outlet for this political and cultural impulse, articulating the transnational existence of their audiences by adapting local themes to traditional performance practices. The large theatre in La Unión Martí-Maceo's hall was quite active.[15] It became a focal point of club members' social life and an important venue for all-black performers in Tampa. This theatre was remarkable for its inclusivity in relation to other social distinctions, including age and gender. Women participated significantly. The *sección de damas* (ladies' committee) planned and raised funds for club social events, including theatrical performances by both youth and adult troupes. The women of the club also led youth programs, organized dances, taught music lessons, and directed youth theatre productions.[16] Club members took the stage in concerts, dances, serious drama, and most notably *teatro vernáculo*. Surviving scripts from the club reveal that these popular comic dramas carried potent sociological and political resonance with audiences.

Scholars have grappled with the complexities of *teatro vernáculo* and other forms of popular cultural expression, giving attention to their coexisting hegemonic and subversive potentials. For Cuban theatre historian Rine Leal, the most lasting contribution of the nineteenth-century *teatro bufo* was that its social, racial, and ethnic type characters spoke in "Cuban." This "Cuban" language derived from multiple "distortions" to Castilian Spanish.[17] Each "distortion" enunciated a distinct kind of *cubanía* (Cubanness) as a deliberate break with Spanish culture and colonial empire. Meanwhile, several of these sonic interventions articulated *cubanía* as necessarily African and Afro-Cuban through racial and ethnic impersonation. Recognizing this postcolonial double-consciousness manifested in *teatro bufo*, Inés María Martiatu argues that through the performance of blackface characters, the genre also became a mechanism for the exclusion and devaluation of a racially different (Afro-Cuban) Other.[18] Jill Lane, however, reads these performances as an epistemological threshold into racial inclusivity and Cuban nationhood, arguing that blackface performances in *teatro bufo* throughout the nineteenth century rehearsed a *mestizaje* (racial miscegenation) that made Martí's call for a Cuban nation transcending racial division imaginable.[19] Lane's analysis of *teatro bufo* and related *vernáculo* genres as components of an epistemic shift in nineteenth-century Cuban national consciousness also applies to twentieth-century Ybor City—given how the cultural memory of Martí's call for racial solidarity haunted later *vernáculo* performances, particularly within the hall that bore Maceo's name hyphenated with his own.

Afro-Cuban perspectives dominated representation and reception of *teatro vernáculo* performances at La Unión Martí-Maceo's theatre. Race becomes an important lens for understanding the relationship of Afro-Cuban spectators to the characters, particularly regarding both the *negrito* and the *mulata* characters. The *negrito* propagated stereotypes of black Cuban men as cunning, barbarous, violent, and immoral. The *mulata* depicted Cuban women of color as licentious, socially ambitious, and dishonest. Presenting an Afro-Cuban perspective on *teatro bufo*, Martiatu argues that confrontation with these characters and their stereotypes is often a painful experience for Afro-Cubans.[20] How then did perception of these characters change when performed by Afro-Cuban actors, or when performed in a space that belonged to and virtually defined Ybor City's Afro-Cuban community, or when characters evoked specific affiliations with immigrant workers across lines of racial and ethnic difference? The history of *teatro vernáculo* performances at La Unión Martí-Maceo suggests alternative meanings that the *negrito*, the *mulata*, and the theatrical traditions to which they belong might have conveyed. The transmigration between Cuba and Ybor City and the resulting fluidity of La Unión Martí-Maceo's ever-shifting membership placed the theatre simultaneously within two cultural frameworks. Tensions between two distinct racial orders—one extending from Cuba through its diaspora, the other found domestically in the United States—may have produced ruptures of racial scripts through which artists and audiences could question racisms on multiple levels.

The surviving scripts of *La loca de la casa* and *Los novios* provide some evidence of this subversive process. In these *juguetes cómicos*, humor arises through the distinctively Cuban sensibility called *choteo*, a satiric and "irreverent attitude toward imposed order."[21] In *teatro vernáculo*, *choteo* often depicts a challenger situated in a position of authentic "Cubanness" who launches a vulgarly comic attack on authority, prestige, or propriety.[22] As Kenya Dworkin y Méndez writes, "The more irreverent the farce, the more highly critical the tone."[23] In *La loca de la casa* and *Los novios*, *choteo* targets racial, social, and gendered hierarchies through the machinations of the infamous comic trio of the *negrito*, the *mulata*, and the *gallego* (a daft and unwashed Galician immigrant). As a microcosm of the wide spectrum of Cuban type characters belonging to *teatro vernáculo*, the *negrito*, the *mulata*, and the *gallego* have come to represent a snapshot of the Cuban nation in colloquial understandings.[24] Regarding race, the trio represented black, white, and *mulato* Cubans. In relation to gender, the *gallego* and the *negrito* exhibited the normative masculinity of *machismo*, a kind of chauvinism descended from the Mediterranean honor code. The *mulata*, on the other hand, was sexualized and commodified, especially in the performance of *guaracha*: a fast-tempo Cuban music genre with picaresque lyrics written for the character.[25] As the object of sexual desire, and as the offspring of a marginalized woman of color and a white Cuban or Spaniard in a position of power, the *mulata* embodied Cuba's history of colonialism, commodification, and transculturation. With respect to nationality, the *negrito* and the *mulata* represented native Cuban *criollos*, whereas the *gallego* represented Galician immigrants and their social status as a poor foreign minority within early twentieth-century Cuba.[26] However, the *gallego* performed a different kind of Cubanness. By transplanting his contemporary Galician culture into the Cuban *ajiaco* (stew), this character personified the transculturation that sustained Cuba as a heterogeneous and creolized society.[27]

Preserved in a typescript in a loose-leaf notebook, *La loca de la casa* contains information regarding production dates and cast. A label affixed to the cover states (in English), "The play was first produced at the Payret Theatre in Habana, Cuba 1929. Played here in 1931."[28] This note seems to be the work of an archivist; "here" presumably refers to the theatre of La Unión Martí-Maceo. However, in conflict with the date on the label, the note "Tampa Florida Noviembre 5 de 1932" appears on the final page of the script.[29] The script belonged to Manuel García, who played the character Mondoreño, the *gallego*. García, a *bufo* actor known locally for playing *negrito* roles, eventually became a member of the Federal Theatre Project's only Hispanic unit in Ybor City.[30] The names of other cast members are handwritten next to the list of characters in the typescript copy, and in some cases only a first name appears. For example, Chela (who is listed as playing Rosa, the *mulata*) may have been Chela Martínez, a well-known local actress who also joined the Federal Theatre Project and led a group that performed social dramas, *zarzuelas*, and *teatro vernáculo* at the Centro Obrero every Sunday beginning in 1931.[31] The names of two other regular Centro Obrero performers—García and "Funny lady" Jennie Rodríguez (Loca)—also appear in the cast list. Although the national and racial identities of Martínez, García, and Rodríguez cannot be determined with certainty, they likely were white Cubans or white Spanish immigrants and not associated with La Unión Martí-Maceo (as their names do not appear in the registry of members between 1915 and 1938).[32] Thus the script copy of *La loca de la casa* documents multiracial collaboration on the Martí-Maceo stage and illuminates important connections between the performances at the Centro Obrero and the theatre of La Unión Martí-Maceo.[33]

Agustín Rodríguez, the author of *La loca de casa*, was a Spanish playwright of Cuban *teatro vernáculo* whose popular works often appeared at the Alhambra Theatre, the most important theatre for *teatro vernáculo* during the 1920s and 1930s. The play debuted at Havana's Payret Theatre, a venue that catered to the Cuban capital's elite families.[34] The plot of *La loca de la casa* begins when Monico (the *negrito*) and Mondoreño (the *gallego*) arrive at a house answering the same ad for a job. Realizing they are in competition with one another, they begin to fight. Rosa, the *mulata* maid, breaks up their row by threatening to call the police. After things cool down, the elite *criollo* owner of the house, Don Álvaro, hires them both. Álvaro exits with Mondoreño to show him his new job in the garden, leaving Monico alone. Loca (a crazy woman) enters, confessing her undying love to Monico, whom she mistakes for Conde Carnido, a Spanish count within her delusional fantasy world. Loca later finds Mondoreño alone and takes him for Embajador Tilbor, the ambassador with whom she is having a secret affair. Loca draws both Monico and Mondoreño into believing they are Conde Carnido and Embajador Tilbor—Spanish nobles competing for her affections.

The confusion created by the "happy idea" of Loca's romantic fantasy allows for temporary transgression of gendered, racial, and social hierarchies, thus undermining (if only temporarily) the prevailing racial order. *Choteo* in *La loca de la casa* works through this "delusional" transcendence of gender, race, and class. Whenever Monico starts to invest in the prestigious title bestowed to him by Loca's fantasy, another character soon bursts his bubble, deflating his pretentions. After Monico first crosses paths with Loca, he considers bragging about his lucky fortune to the *negritos* working in the shoeshine parlor. He imagines them dealing him "the kind of *choteo* that has yet to be seen and that none of you has ever seen before." Thus Monico immediately relates the dubiousness of his new status as a noble with his susceptibility to being *choteo*-ed. Later, when Monico starts to believe that he actually *is* Conde Carnido, Rosa deals Monico a morsel of the *choteo* he imagines when she refers to him as "Conde Carnero" (Count Mutton). The same thing happens to Mondoreño. When Mondoreño is drawn into believing that he *is* Embajador Tilbor, he unwittingly pronounces the name of his new alter ego as "*empaquetador del Tibor*" (packer of the chamber pot). Here Mondoreño commits a clear act of auto-*choteo*. The *choteo* reaches its climax when Monico (as Conde Carnido) and Mondoreño (as Embajador Tilbor) confront each other. Seeing Mondoreño with a ring that Loca had promised to him, Monico tries to reclaim it by right of his presumed noble Spanish heritage.

> MONICO: Look, drop the familiarities and respect me as I am in my house and in use of a title that, by my ancestors, belongs to me . . .
>
> MONDOREÑO: Well, look at this *chico*, I've outdone you. *(Showing him the ring)*
>
> MONICO: But what do I see? My ring?
>
> MONDOREÑO: Your ring, get out of here you swine. Listen friend, since when have they named you a count? Tell me fool, have you ever once seen a black count? Look wretch, go and sell linens, or better yet clean my shoes, which is the best you can do . . .
>
> MONICO: I am going to tell you, *gallego*, proceed with caution because it won't be me who will fire you out of here like a salty zeppelin, because I am the count, and that heritage comes from my grandmother, which by natural law, I inherited from my mother.[35]

Monico and Mondoreño pull out their knives. Loca enters and breaks up the fight, proposing to solve the rivalry by allowing both suitors to marry her. Mondoreño and Monico, displaying mutually held sexist attitudes, reject Loca's proposal. Monico declares that "civilization and the law prohibit it" and that such a scheme "would only occur to a *loca*." Mondoreño fervently agrees, saying, "This thing about two husbands is no more than the thought of a *loca*." By calling her *loca*, the two set off her crazy trigger, sending her into a violent rampage as she shortly returns with a revolver and takes aim at Monico and Mondoreño. Ironically, the two rivals unite in reaffirming traditional gender norms but in doing so bring about the abrupt end to their short-lived status as Spanish nobles within Loca's fantasy world. Here *choteo* satirizes the characters' *machismo*, exposing that their sexism unifies them across racial and ethnic differences and simultaneously betrays them in their temporary transcendence of race and class hierarchies.

In the closing scene, the *juguete* plays out a common *bufo* motif, wherein the *mulata* (Rosa) responds to the advances of the *gallego* (Mondoreño) and rejects those of the *negrito* (Monico). Rosa admits that she may be of Monico's race, but she wants nothing to do with him.

MONICO: You see, this is how these salty Galicians are, so very haughty with you women of color. It's because of you with your tale of lightening the race [*aclarar la raza*]. You entice the bald *gallego* in such a slippery way. Keep on that way you wretch, and next he'll be running off to Spain, leaving you with such a parcel of little colored *mulatos* that no one can decipher, and then you'll be sorry. . . .

ROSA: Listen you *moreno* [dark] loser, you must know that although I am of the same race, it is not possible for me to be with a monkey, so forget about it and drop those kinds of pretensions with me. I am not the *loca* and I fire off the truth.[36]

Rosa rejects Monico, but her rebuttal indicates a more inclusive understanding of the "Cuban race," an ideological concept of a *mestiza* or *mulata* nation in which all share a connection to African ancestry.[37] In this sense, Rosa's rejection of Monico is not a rejection of his race as a Cuban of African descent (a status she shares with him) but rather of his darker skin color. Monico's accusation of Rosa's "slippery way" highlights the important slippage between these two very different constructions of race that Afro-Cubans move between—one based on phenotype and skin color and the other constituted by ethnically African aspects of Afro-Cuban identities. Monico echoes Rosa's intraracial prejudice when he calls her out for propagating, as a *mulata*, the "tale of lightening the race," referring to race here as color and phenotype. *La loca de la casa* satirizes the desires of the *negrito*, the *mulata*, and the *gallego* to identify as less black, more ethnically Spanish, and of a higher class. Yet through Loca's fantasies, the performed transgressions of gender, race, and class foreground their own construction, before their hegemonic weight returns in the final scene.

The play's conclusion may be considered a reification of racial hierarchies and a moral judgment against Loca's fantasy of a world where race goes unnoticed. From the perspective of the elite bourgeois audience that frequented the Payret Theatre, Rosa's "truth" justifies racial hierarchies as it critiques Loca's fantasy as an allegory for Cuban racial fraternity. However, for Afro-Cubans, dispelling the idea of racial fraternity did not simply support racist attitudes. Such a perspective also exposed racial fraternity as a hypocritical political platform that sought to obfuscate difference so as to squelch political agency for Cubans of color. The play's parody of the Cuban nation—as enacted through the *mulata*, the *negrito*, and the *gallego*—critiques "color-blind" politics by equating such an outlook with Loca's delusions. The more Monico and Mondoreño try to transcend their social position within that fantasy world, the faster they internalize the real-world colonial hierarchies they seek to defy. On the Martí-Maceo stage, *La loca de la casa* challenged the naive hopes that the racial order of a colonial past could be simply wished away and that the Cuban nation could move beyond racial division while ignoring racial inequality. The play's *choteo* critiqued race relations in Ybor City's Cuban community, where white Cubans separated themselves from Afro-Cubans on account of the desire for upward mobility and the fear of being persecuted as black in the U.S. South.

In the final moment before the curtain, Mondoreño asks Rosa to dance a *son* with him to celebrate their dalliance. *Son* became the most popular genre of Cuban music during the mid-1920s, combining Spanish *canción* (ballads) and guitar with Afro-Cuban rhythms and percussion instruments. Its presence at the end of *La loca de la casa* exemplifies the convention of *obras bufas*—in which all characters, despite their differences or unresolved tensions, dance to popular music genres with creolized Afro-Cuban elements. The 10 October 1925 edition of a local newspaper tells of the Arango-Moreno Bufos Cubanos (a group on tour from Cuba) inviting the public to their performance at El Círculo Cubano to get to know Cuban *sones* (plural of *son*).[38] The orchestra and cast performed Cuban *son*, *boleros* (slow tempo romantic ballads), and *danzón* (Cuba's first popular music featuring African rhythms) as *entremeses* between one-act *sainetes* and *juguetes cómicos*. This programming format was commonplace for *teatro vernáculo* performances at the Centro Obrero, where a local Afro-Cuban orchestra, El Sexteto Floridiano, played *son* and *rumba*, a genre defined by call and response singing, percussion, and dance.[39] The instances of *son* and *rumba* in *La loca de la casa* and *Los novios* enact an important linkage between *teatro vernáculo* and Afrocubanismo—a cultural movement that proliferated Afro-Cuban themes, art, literature, and music in order to articulate a new sense of Cubanness that was transcultural and compatible with being a nation of color.[40] The music of these two *juguetes cómicos* exposed local audiences to the force of Afrocubanismo in reimagining nation and demonstrated the power of performance in making interventions in public discourses on race and citizenship.

The second example of *teatro vernáculo* performed on the stage of La Unión Martí-Maceo is a *juguete cómico* called *Los novios*. The archival script is incomplete: a handwritten copy in a composition notebook. Through *choteo*, mistaken identity, and the romantic comedy plot structure, the play parodies the tragic interracial romances of popular Cuban *zarzuelas* of the same era. Popular *zarzuelas* like *El cafetal* (1929), *María la O* (1930), and *Cecilia Valdés* (1932) reimagine the colonial past of nineteenth-century Cuba on stage. Based on its parody of these *zarzuelas*, *Los novios* was likely staged during the early- to mid-1930s. The play takes place on a rural estate, as the suitor Don Rafael arrives to seek the affections of Lucía, the daughter of the elite white *criollos* Don Pepe and Doña Castula. No one has met Rafael before his arrival. Don Pepe mistakes Rafael's servant, a *gallego* named Santiago, for Don Rafael himself. Lucia, making the same mistake, embraces Santiago—inciting Rafael's anger. Further misidentifications ensue. Don Pepe, thinking his own servant Eliotropo (the *negrito*) was the one embraced by Lucía, attacks him, demanding, "Is it true that you were hugging *her*?" But Eliotropo thinks Don Pepe speaks of Sofía, the *mulata* whom Eliotropo loves. Meanwhile, Eliotropo spies Sofía in the embrace of Rafael, who in turn is mistaken by all for his own servant Santiago. Through this comic exchange, Eliotropo misconstrues Don Pepe as the father of Sofía; Don Pepe, in turn, mistakes Eliotropo as the boyfriend of his daughter, Lucía.

D. PEPE: Is it true that you were hugging her?

ELIO: Me. No Señor! It was the other guy.

D. PEPE: Who?

ELIO: (*fuming*) The servant of your daughter's boyfriend.

D. PEPE: What?

ELIO: *Sí* Señor! Hugging her in my presence.

D. PEPE: So, what do you have to do with it?

ELIO: How am I not going to have anything to do with it? . . . I am going out with her.

D. PEPE: With my daughter?

ELIO: Oh . . . She's your daughter? She hasn't told me anything about it.[41]

Mistaken identity in *Los novios* drives the humor and sets up the play's parody of the conventions of tragic interracial romance plots found in popular contemporary *zarzuelas*.[42] Such tragic love affairs present the traumatic emasculation of Afro-Cuban men and the vilification of Afro-Cuban women through colonial paradigms of race and gender. *Los novios* draws on the romantic comedy plot to undermine these tropes. In the end, the confusion that fuels the comedy is sorted out, and the lovers return to their rightful partners according to normative social roles. Eliotropo reunites with Sofía, and Rafael unites with Lucía. The conciliatory nature of the comic resolution restores the racial order in a much different manner than in the *zarzuelas*—which convey a troubling sense of morality through the deaths of lovers who transgress racial boundaries. *Los novios* refuses to reproduce the violence and hegemonic morality of the tragic romance, instead addressing colonial hierarchies through comic subterfuge.

In *Los novios*, *choteo* unsettles those colonial hierarchies, taking aim at Don Pepe's patriarchal rule. *Choteo* targets Don Pepe as the *machista* patriarch who cannot maintain order over his own estate. The confusion begins when Santiago, the *gallego*, misunderstands Don Pepe's use of the word *yegua* (mare), which in Cuban slang can refer to a man's "woman," a term analogous to "old lady." Santiago's dialogue implies the existence of an earlier scene missing from the manuscript, in which Don Pepe refers to Lucía with the term *yegua* (while mistaking Santiago for Lucía's suitor Don Rafael). Later, after having searched for and encountered an actual mare, Santiago returns and complains to Doña Castula that her husband has cheated him.

> CASTULA: Where were you?
>
> SANTIAGO: I was doing business with your husband, who is a greater liar than the devil.
>
> CASTULA: How so?
>
> SANTIAGO: He told me to go to see her [the *yegua*] and told me that she was well educated.
>
> CASTULA: And how did she seem to you?
>
> SANTIAGO: Well she doesn't write, doesn't wear shoes, is very dull, and when she saw me she gave me a couple of kicks and a bite.[43]

Santiago's confusion owing to his literal interpretation of *yegua* does *choteo* to the misogyny of Don Pepe's *machismo*. The play's *choteo* takes its irreverence to a level of grotesque disfigurement, equating Pepe's way of "doing business" (that is, the business of marriage) with bestiality. Indeed Don Pepe's authority is a function of the colonial racial and patriarchal order that consolidates social and political power with elite white *criollo* men. Fissures in that order grow as the *choteo* reveals Don Pepe to be a shameless philanderer, the father of illegitimate children, a perpetrator of bestiality, a liar, and a cheat. Through its unique blending of *choteo*, mistaken identity, and the romantic comedy plot structure, *Los novios* exemplifies a retooling of *teatro vernáculo* and its characters for the theatre audience of La Unión Martí-Maceo. The play's dramaturgical innovations recalibrate the racially exclusionary national imaginary staged by *teatro vernáculo* and tragic *zarzuelas* to create avenues of engagement, self-representation, and authorship for Ybor City's Afro-Cubans.

In creating its particular innovation of *teatro vernáculo*, *Los novios* reconfigured the nineteenth-century Cuban imaginary to reflect a critical perspective, performing a politics of racial inclusivity for the audience of La Unión Martí-Maceo's theatre. This audience, with its predominant transnational Afro-Cuban makeup and spectatorship, likely mined parallel meanings from *La loca de la casa*'s *choteo* of "color-blind" nationalism and its critical resonance with race relations among Cubans in Ybor City. Artists appearing at La Unión Martí-Maceo engaged in a vibrant critique of dominant ideologies on nation and race in Cuba and of race and citizenship in Ybor City. These performances advanced new ideals of a racially inclusive citizenry, ideals developed through the transnational movement of tobacco workers and touring performances between Havana and Ybor City, continuously revised through Afro-Cuban struggle and agency in Cuba and in the U.S. diaspora.

Notes

1. Gary R. Mormino and George E. Pozzetta, *The Immigrant World of Ybor City: Italians and Their Latin Neighbors in Tampa, 1885–1985* (Urbana: University of Illinois Press, 1987), 5–6, 64–67.

2. Agustín Rodríguez, *La loca de la casa*, Sociedad La Unión Martí-Maceo Records 1853–2000, series 6 Miscellaneous Files, box 19, folder 8, University of South Florida Special Collections, Tampa, 13. All translations from the originals are by the author of this chapter.

3. Trinh T. Minh-ha, *Woman, Native, Other: Writing Postcoloniality and Feminism* (Bloomington: Indiana University Press, 1989), 120.

4. A fourth script copy, contained in a loose-leaf notebook with "Sección de Declamación de La Unión Marti Maceo" [*sic*] (Performance Section of the Martí-Maceo Society) written on the cover, is archived in the Círculo Cubano Collection, box 10, folder 6, University of South Florida Special Collections, Tampa. The notebook contains sides for the character Doña Quiteria from the Spanish *juguete cómico* titled *El autor del crimen* (1875) by Vital Aza.

5. Nicolás Kanellos, *A History of Hispanic Theatre in the United States: Origins to 1940* (Austin: University of Texas Press, 1990), 168.

6. This chapter focuses on *La loca de la casa* and *Los novios* as examples of *teatro vernáculo* encapsulating a distinct theatrical discourse on race and nation. *Hambre* and *El autor del crimen* are outside of the scope of Cuban *teatro vernáculo* and thus less pertinent to my argument.

7. Bernardo Ruiz Suárez, *The Color Question in the Two Americas*, trans. John Crosby Gordon (New York: Hunt Publishing, 1922).

8. "Homenaje al Dr. Ruíz," *La Gaceta de Tampa*, 8 August 1924, 1; "Homenaje al Dr. Ruíz," *La Gaceta de Tampa*, 9 August 1924, 1.

9. Nancy Raquel Mirabal, "The Afro-Cuban Community in Ybor City and Tampa, 1886–1910," *OAH Magazine of History* 7 (1993): 20.

10. Nancy Raquel Mirabal, "'Más que negro': José Martí and the Politics of Unity," *José Martí in the United States: The Florida Experience*, ed. Louis A. Pérez Jr. (Tempe: ASU Center for Latin American Studies, 1995), 62.

11. Mormino and Pozzetta, *Immigrant World*, 186.

12. Susan D. Greenbaum, *More Than Black: Afro-Cubans in Tampa* (Gainesville: University Press of Florida, 2002), 119; Mirabal, "'Más que negro,'" 63–64.

13. Pedro Pérez Sarduy and Jean Stubbs, "The Rite of Social Communion," in *Afrocuba: An Anthology of Cuban Writing on Race, Politics, and Culture*, ed. Pedro Pérez Sarduy and Jean Stubbs (Victoria, Australia: Ocean Press, 1993), 8–9, 12; Antonio López, *Unbecoming Blackness: The Diaspora Cultures of Afro-Cuban America* (New York: New York University Press, 2012), 28–30; Ruiz Suárez, *Color Question*, 80–83.

14. Alejandro de la Fuente, *A Nation for All: Race, Inequality, and Politics in Twentieth-Century Cuba* (Chapel Hill: University of North Carolina Press, 2001), 57, 78–80.

15. Kenya Dworkin y Méndez, "From Factories to Footlights: The Original Spanish Language Cigar Workers' Theatre in Ybor City and West Tampa, Florida," in *Recovering the U.S. Hispanic Literary Heritage*, ed. María Herrera-Sobek and Virginia Sánchez Korrol, vol. 3 (Houston: Arte Público Press, 2006), 335.

16. Greenbaum, *More Than Black*, 172, 207.

17. Rine Leal, "Prologo: La chancleta y el coturno," in *Teatro bufo: Siglo XIX, antología, tomo 1*, ed. José Triana (La Habana: Editorial Arte y Cultura, 1975), 18.

18. Inés María Martiatu, "Sin similcutancia posible. Una mirada otra al teatro bufo cubano," in *Bufo y Nación: Interpelaciones Desde el Presente*, ed. Inés María Martiatu (La Habana: Editorial Letras Cubanas, 2008), 9.

19. Jill Lane, *Blackface Cuba, 1840–1895* (Philadelphia: University of Pennsylvania Press, 2005), 16.

20. Martiatu, "Sin similcutancia possible," 12–13.

21. Lane, *Blackface Cuba*, 120.

22. José Esteban Muñoz, *Disidentifications: Queers of Color and the Performance of Politics* (Minneapolis: University of Minnesota Press, 1999), 119–20, 135–41; Jorge Mañach, *Indagación del Choteo* (Barcelona: Linkgua ediciones, 2009), 21.

23. Dworkin y Méndez, "From Factories to Footlights," 336.

24. Laurie Frederik, *Trumpets in the Mountains* (Durham: Duke University Press, 2012), 281n1. Frederik, an anthropologist, notes that the comic trio is commonly explained by Cubans as having been "representative of the groups comprising the new Cuban nation [and] is often a blanket statement about the historical importance of Teatro Bufo in general."

25. Rosa Ileana Boudet, "Alhambra: Choteo y simulacro," in *Teatro cubano: Relectura cómplice* (Santa Mónica: Ediciones de la Flecha, 2011), 18; Karen Thomas, *Cuban Zarzuela: Performing Race and Gender on Havana's Lyric Stage* (Urbana: University of Illinois Press, 2009), 43; Alicia Arrizón, *Queering Mestizaje: Transculturation and Performance* (Ann Arbor: University of Michigan Press, 2006), 100.

26. Jorge Castellanos and Isabel Castellanos, "El negro en el teatro cubano," in *Cultura Afrocubana, tomo IV, Letras—Música—Arte* (Miami: Ediciones Universales, 1994), 239.

27. Increasingly throughout the early twentieth century, Cubans understood their national community and culture as heterogeneous and *criollo* (creole), qualities resulting from the transculturation of Amerindian, West African, Hispanic, and Chinese elements.

28. Rodríguez, *La loca de la casa*, cover.

29. Ibid., 31.

30. A. de la Peña, "Sociales," *La Gaceta de Tampa*, 23 August 1930, 1; Kanellos, *History of Hispanic Theatre*, 158.

31. Kanellos, *History of Hispanic Theatre*, 171.

32. "Registro de Socios de la Sección Familiar, de La Unión Martí Maceo," Sociedad La Unión Martí-Maceo Records 1853–2000, series 2 Membership Files, box 7, folder 3.

33. In fact, Jennie Rodríguez performed the leading roles in two unnamed plays in a benefit for Manuel García at the Centro Obrero on 25 December 1932. Given the proximity of the benefit to the date in the script, it is likely that *La loca de la casa* was performed in repertoire as one of these two unnamed plays. See "Beneficio," *La Gaceta de Tampa*, 23 December 1932, 1.

34. Eduardo Robreño, *Historia del teatro popular cubano* (La Habana: Oficina del Historiodor de la ciudad de la Habana, 1961), 68.

35. Rodríguez, *La loca de la casa*, 19.

36. Ibid., 30–31.

37. De la Fuente, *Nation for All*, 183, 185, 187.

38. "Círculo Cubano," *La Gaceta de Tampa*, 10 October 1925, 1.

39. "Función extraordinaria," *La Gaceta de Tampa*, 21 December 1932, 1.

40. De la Fuente, *Nation for All*, 180–83.

41. *Los novios*, Sociedad La Unión Martí-Maceo Records 1853–2000, series 6 Miscellaneous Files, box 19, folder 10.

42. Don Pepe's fear of Eliotropo's presumed affair with his daughter parallels the forbidden love scenario between Lázaro, a black slave, and Flor, the daughter of a planter, in *El cafetal*. Eliotropo's desire for revenge against Rafael for his presumed affair with Sofía echoes the rivalry between a free man of color and a son of a planter over the love of a *mulata* courtesan in *María la O* and *Cecilia Valdés*.

43. *Los novios*.

4. A Cosmogony for the Marginalized

Lynn Riggs, Mythmaking, and Multiracial-Homosexual Apologetics (1931–32)

W. Douglas Powers

More than seventy years after the musical *Oklahoma!* premiered in 1944, the following words still hold true: "There has been a surprising minimum of applause bestowed upon Lynn Riggs, who wrote 'Green Grow the Lilacs' and who seems to be the forgotten man of the musical show based upon it."[1] Despite having written the source material for *Oklahoma!*, playwright Rollie Lynn Riggs does seem to be forgotten. As a playwright he was prolific, yet his many experiments with theatrical style make his plays difficult to categorize, and his works are rarely staged or studied.

Likewise, as an individual, the man himself defies neat classification. One-sixteenth Cherokee through his mother, Riggs always self-identified as a Cherokee; he called himself an "absorbed Cherokee," to denote his status as an Oklahoma Cherokee who had lost what was perceived by white America as his "Indianness" because of dilution of Native blood.[2] For Riggs, being a Cherokee meant being of mixed blood; in 1910, only 21.9 percent of Cherokees in Oklahoma identified as full-blooded, while 77 percent identified as mixed-blooded (0.8 percent did not report).[3] Twenty years later, Oklahoma's full-blooded population had decreased to 17.3 percent.[4] So while "full-blooded" was (in a Eurocentric, traditional sense) the standard for racial purity and thus an authentic Indian identity, the reality was that more than three-quarters of the Cherokees in Oklahoma held (like Riggs) a mixed-blood identity.

As Riggs's life history reveals, blood quantum is, of course, no reliable measure of any individual's sense of cultural belonging. Born in 1899 in Indian Territory—the area that merged with the neighboring Oklahoma Territory in 1906 to form the state of Oklahoma[5]—Riggs was only an infant when his mother (one-eighth Cherokee) died. His father remarried a Cherokee woman prone to violent outbursts, prompting Riggs's father to shuttle his children between the family's home and those of his white relatives. Riggs nonetheless remained culturally connected to this Cherokee heritage, learning hundreds of old Cherokee chants as a boy and living among the dense Cherokee population in and around Claremore. Concrete particulars about Riggs's childhood are scarce, partly because the writer was vehemently reticent about revealing himself. In 1929, he wrote to friend Barrett Clark, "I don't like my life very well, after all, and there's no point in its being made public."[6] Riggs held a deep and conflicted attachment to his birthplace until his death from cancer in 1954.

Indeed, there are other, more significant complications with which to wrestle in affixing identity labels to Lynn Riggs. In the inspired queer reading of Riggs's play *The Cherokee Night* titled "Lynn Riggs as Code Talker," Creek-Cherokee author and literary theorist Craig S. Womack suggests that Riggs's closeted homosexuality not only affected his anguished relationship with his home state but also helped forge his self-perception as an Oklahoman and as an Indian. According to Womack's "Oklahomo Theory," as an "absorbed" (that is, mixed-blood) Cherokee, Riggs viewed Indianness through the lens of his queerness. The playwright's feelings of alienation and nonconformity due to his homosexuality mirrored his sense of his own mixed-blood Indian ancestry.[7] This chapter extends Womack's analysis to argue that *The Cherokee Night* as well as *Green Grow the Lilacs*—the source for Richard Rodgers and Oscar Hammerstein's seminal musical *Oklahoma!*—are more than coded literary subterfuges for their playwright's repressed sexual orientation. Rather, these plays may be interpreted as variations of a cosmogony, or creation story, through which Riggs could condemn or affirm his own disenfranchised identity in the universe. In the process, Riggs envelops within his theatrical cosmogonies a range of American fringe-dwelling groups—pre-statehood Oklahomans, mixed-blood Cherokees, and homosexuals—who exist both outside and within the confines of a racially pure, heteronormative white United States of America. Such resonances can emerge only through a reassessment of the aesthetics of Riggs's dramaturgy.

In her article "Mixedbloods and Bloodlust in *Cherokee Night*," Muscogee academic and theatre professional Julie Little Thunder condemns the inclusion of Lynn Riggs's 1932 play *The Cherokee Night* in the anthology of American Indian dramas *Stories of Our Way*. Little Thunder asserts that Riggs's play "distorts native cultures and perpetuates racist stereotypes, demonstrating how authors of minority ancestry, with no real connection to their culture, may inadvertently reinforce the view of the dominant society."[8] Little Thunder finds "two especially noxious stereotypes dominat[ing] *Cherokee Night*: [Riggs's] view of the mixedblood condition as degenerate, and his belief in an innate 'Cherokee bloodlust.'"[9] On the surface, her assessment seems justified. Mixed-bloods figure prominently in *The Cherokee Night*, an enigmatic and disquieting play consisting of seven interconnected (yet achronological) scenes detailing the troubled and violent lives of Cherokees of varying degrees of blood quantum in the early days of Oklahoma statehood. But Little Thunder misreads *The Cherokee Night* as realistic or naturalistic. Though the play employs Darwinian concepts of heredity and environment and is imbued with verisimilitude, Riggs departs from the representational style familiar to American theatregoers of the 1930s. The drama weaves together interconnected tragic stories of mixed-blood Cherokees in its seven out-of-sequence episodes; its style more closely resembles the German-inspired aesthetics of American expressionism than conventional fourth-wall dramaturgy. Expressionism "is characterized by intense subjectivism, a violent antipathy to society and to the family, a powerful lyricism that takes precedence over plot and character, and a lack of psychological delineation resulting in type characters and symbolic abstractions."[10] *The Cherokee Night* must be interpreted in this light, as a figurative and subjective narrative rather than as a "slice of life" that seeks to document mixed-blood experience in a realistic manner.

The Cherokee Night structures its social message—an indictment of white American patriarchy and its hegemonies concerning Native peoples—thematically, rather than through a linear cause-and-effect structure. The incidents of the play represent a search, a journey through "stations" on the road to martyrdom. The drama's protagonist—or, more precisely, its collection of mixed-blood characters that functions as a group protagonist—is sacrificed to the materialism, hypocrisy, or heartlessness of others. In keeping with the conventions of expressionism, Riggs reduces his plot to a demonstration of his thesis and his supporting characters to types (such as the noble savage, the whore, and the desperado). Linguistically, Riggs employs a distinctive Oklahoma dialect:

> A MAN: (*Leaping to his feet, excitedly.*) When I was a boy back in the Ozarks, I used to go a-barefoot. And I'd steal apples. And sass my Paw. I'd beat the ole cow. I'd be mean to my little sister and brothers. I wouldn't be thankful jist to be a-livin'. I was always wantin' sump'n. *And* a-gettin' nuthin'. *And* a-cussin'. *And* a-swearin'. And a-gettin' next to

> all the girls like a wild hoss. And I was a-gettin' wickeder and wickeder when Jonas come along, praise the Lord! And I follered him, praise the Lord! And I lissened and heared him, praise Jonas! And I'll die happy like I'm a-livin', praise the Lord on high![11]

All of the play's distortions and symbolic representations of the external world reflect its protagonist's internal terrain. Dominating the mise-en-scène of *The Cherokee Night*, looming to some degree over each vignette, is Claremore Mound: the site of a brutal 1817 massacre by Cherokee warriors of Osage women, children, and elderly while their men were away hunting. Riggs sets the stage for the first scene by writing: "*From a place of darkness a gigantic teepee thrusts itself up into the light—white and glistening . . . no smoke rises from this ghostly habitation. But somewhere inside is the muffled thud of a drum and the sound of deep voices.*"[12]

The events of *Cherokee Night* become strange and fantastic, so as to elucidate the emotional perspective of its mixed-blood characters. In scene 4, a group of mixed-blood Cherokee boys search the woods for the site of a brutal murder over a card game between African American men (who are referred to in the text with that most offensive of epithets). After discovering the artifacts of the crime and succumbing to a primal, ecstatic, and stereotypical war dance extolling bloodshed, the horrified boys discover actual blood on their hands. Riggs's stage directions read:

> *Then slowly, rising from the warmed and fertile earth, a giant Negro, naked to the waist, lifts himself into the sun from behind the thick underbrush. His black body glistens. He stares off toward the fleeing boys, stretches himself, comes forward a step from sun into shadow, in a movement real and ghostly, as if he were two presences: the murderer undismayed by his crime, and the very emanation of the dead man himself. He stands a moment in the gloom, his dark hulk tremendous against the sun, his eyes following the boys; one hand moves itself forward to a blackberry spray, in an uncalculated reflex, gathers two berries and lifts them idly to his mouth. The he yawns. Then the sun dies. All below becomes dark. . . . A drum is beating—harsh and troubled.*[13]

Thus the overall theatrical effect created again manifested an expressionist aesthetic "of allegory clothed in nightmare or vision."[14]

Indeed, Riggs's dramaturgy contains more epic, even cosmological, resonances in how the playwright positions his own Otherness. The playwright not only speaks in code about his own identity but also constructs new mythologies—conforming to identified patterns of the "sacred" and the "profane"—that allow for a ritualized destruction and recreation of a desired, ordered cosmos through performance. In Mircea Eliade's estimation, the "sacred" "manifests itself, shows itself, as something . . . of a wholly different order, a reality that does not belong to our world, in objects that are an integral part of our natural 'profane' world."[15] Daniel L. Pals clarifies this distinction between these modes of being by describing the "sacred" as the "sphere of the supernatural, of things extraordinary, memorable, and momentous,"[16] in contrast to the "profane," which encompasses the "realm of everyday business—of things ordinary, random, and largely unimportant."[17] Eliade writes:

> The man of archaic societies [*homo religiosus*] tends to live as much as possible *in* the sacred or in close proximity to consecrated objects. The tendency is perfectly understandable, because, for . . . the man of all pre-modern societies, the *sacred* is equivalent to a *power*, and in the last analysis, to *reality*. The sacred is saturated with *being*. Sacred power means reality and at the same time enduringness and efficacity. The polarity sacred-profane is often expressed as an opposition between *real* and *unreal* or pseudoreal. . . . Religious man deeply desires *to be*, to participate in *reality*, to be saturated with power.[18]

The profane world can also be construed as a world of chaos, while that of the sacred corresponds to order; the journey from the profane to the sacred is "fraught with perils . . . from the ephemeral and illusory to reality and eternity."[19] In its aesthetics, and ultimately in its social outlook, *The Cherokee Night* embraces and articulates this polarity of sacred and profane.

Reflecting on his technique in *The Cherokee Night*, Riggs explained in a program note for a 1932 production at the Hedgerow Theatre,

> The time sense, or rather the lack of chronological sequence, is not to be thought of as a stunt. The intent of the play, stated in Scene One in somewhat supernatural terms, is meant to carry the play forward in space exactly the same way as the mind—dealing with the subject—draws out of the past or future or present, impartially, the verbal or visual language which will serve best to illustrate and illuminate a meaning.[20]

The meaning Riggs speaks of is chaos and disorder: the catalytic void that follows the archetypal expulsion of mankind from a primordial paradise and the resulting separation from the sacred. The central allegory of the play equates a metaphorical night—that is, the chaos resulting from a break with the sacred past—with the historic alienation of the Cherokees from their tribal history. This metaphor is exemplified in the play's mixed-blood characters, who are emblems for Riggs himself. In *The Cherokee Night*, Riggs personifies post-statehood Cherokee identity as the mixed-blood. After some sort of historic fall from grace—which might be Oklahoma statehood, the Allotment Act of 1887, or (as discussed later in this chapter) Riggs's own birth—those with depleted Native blood attempt either to assume a white persona and its materialist and individualistic values or to cling in vain to a distorted image of their cultural Otherness based on racist white stereotypes of red devils or noble savages.[21] Exiled to a confused wasteland out of balance with the natural world, absorbed Cherokees become entangled in a range of sordid activities, including grave robbing, incest, prostitution, and murder. They find themselves doomed to extinction, either through total assimilation or death.[22] Riggs's persona of the absorbed Cherokee is most strikingly delineated in the final scene of *The Cherokee Night*, in which the provocatively named half-blood Edgar Breeden, also known as Edgar Spench, arrives seriously wounded on the doorstep of full-blood Gray-Wolf. Edgar's two last names indicate his unstable, dualistic identities. Pursued by white vigilantes, Edgar confesses to wife desertion, rape, and murder—acts he attributes to the presence of his Indian blood. Gray-Wolf, on the other hand, ascribes Edgar's ugly deeds to the *dilution* of his Indian blood.[23]

These two characters (Indian and not-enough Indian) personify sacred and profane identities. Gray-Wolf underscores his connection to the sacred by proclaiming, "I'm full-blood—Cherokee. I live peaceful. I ain't troubled. I remember the way my people lived in quiet times. Think of my ancestors. It keeps me safe."[24] Spench's inability to defend his criminal actions reinforces his profane identity: "I tried ever'thing. Tried to farm. Too restless. Cattle herdin', ridin' fence. Sump'n always drove me on. The bosses! Burned down their barns, rustled their cattle, slept with their wives. Shot the bastards down—! Sump'n inside—no rest, I don't know—Bad blood. Too much Indian, they tell me."[25] In the end, the white posse murders Breeden/Spench in cold blood; his wife, Marthy, and pregnant mistress, Florey, are left to make sense of his death.

> MARTHY: . . . You tried to do right. It was too much. You was hounded day and night, inside and outside. By day, men. At night, your thoughts. Now it's over. Sleep. Rest now. (*She shifts the child in her arms, looks down at it.*) But here's your son. In him your trouble. It goes on. In him. It ain't finished. (*She turns, calls to a young woman, who is weeping quietly.* FLOREY *comes over to her.*) Florey. Here's Florey Newcomb,

bearin' your child. You're at rest. Sleep. Your disgrace, your wickedness, your pain and trouble live on a while longer. In her child, in my child. In all people born now, about to be born. (*Her face becomes luminous, as her mind gropes toward an impersonal truth.*) Someday, the agony will end. Yours has. Ours will. Maybe not in the night of death, the cold dark night, without stars. Maybe in the sun. It's got to! It's what we live for.

FLOREY: (*Sobbing, crying out.*) He's dead! How can you stand there! Edgar's dead!

MARTHY: (*Compassionately, trying to comfort her.*) It's what he wanted. He'll rest now. Let him die.

FLOREY: But it goes on, it goes on!

MARTHY: In our children, yes. In our children's children, maybe no.[26]

Breeden/Spench's death can be seen as both the destruction of chaos and the reconstruction of order. The cosmos regains its stability when Gray-Wolf orders the white vigilantes to stay away from the outlaw's body: "Leave us. It's *our* dead."[27] Riggs's stage directions describe "a curious and solemn ritual," underscored by the beating of a low and throbbing drum, as the old full-blood and the dead man's wife and pregnant mistress cover his body with a blanket.

In an Eliadean sense, this collective act restores a paradise founded on community rather than on individual isolation. Tribal communion prevails over the selfishness embodied by Breeden/Spench (whom Gray-Wolf identifies as "a man that don't like no one's life but his own").[28] Such individualistic thinking was inspired within the Cherokee Nation by the U.S. government's passage of the Dawes Act of 1887, which sought to eradicate Indian nations by abolishing communal ownership of tribal lands. The Cherokees resisted the Dawes Act until the Curtis Act of 1898 eliminated tribal governments, allowing Cherokee tribal lands to be distributed in 160-acre allotments. White speculators further complicated matters:

> [They] immediately began defrauding [Indians] through complicated legal maneuvers. They even plundered the land holdings of orphans and other children, and this practice became particularly widespread and ugly after oil was discovered on Indian land. As they were defrauded of the lands, the poorer Indians retreated onto marginal land in the hills, living on the very edge of existence, many squatting on the land allotments of friends and relatives. . . . When the Great Depression came, they almost starved to death.[29]

Lineal descent from an ancestor on the Dawes Roll remains the only criteria for enrollment in the Cherokee Nation. As of 2002, membership exceeded two hundred thousand members, whose degree of blood ranges from full-blood to 1/2,048.[30] For many of mixed ancestry, the questions of tribal identity and blood quantum that Riggs wrestled with in his drama are still present. Such questions tend to be even more complicated among other Native American tribes, whose criteria for citizenship are much more selective than those of the Cherokee.[31]

Riggs spent his adulthood on the run like Spench: away from Oklahoma, in the liberal-minded artistic enclaves of Santa Fe, New York City, and Hollywood. He returned to his home state only for brief, sporadic visits; he did not go back for his father's funeral in 1951.[32] Phyllis Braunlich's biography of Riggs, *Haunted by Home*, suggests that his homosexuality, rather than a mixed-blood identity, drove him from his native soil. Riggs did not write overtly about his sexuality and remained closeted to all but his closest friends in his literary and artistic circles.[33] Rather than overtly acknowledge his sexual orientation and confront social prejudices of his era, as Womack posits, Riggs employed the metaphor of the culturally disenfranchised mixed-blood Indian as a symbolic expression of his own tortured insecurities and estrangement from respectable society as a closeted gay man.

Riggs not only developed the mixed-blood Indian of post-statehood Oklahoma as a metaphor for the closeted homosexual but also employed the post-statehood *white* Oklahoman, who lives silently on the outskirts of civilization, for the same symbolic purpose.[34] Indeed, the copresence of white and mixed-blood metaphors in his dramaturgy demonstrates the bifurcated nature of Riggs's own identity. Riggs once described the community of white Oklahomans—who, in all likelihood, also had some diluted degrees of Indian blood—as a group whose members were "much admired and much maligned, [but] have been not quite known—a shifting fringe of dark around the campfire, where wolves, perhaps, and unnamable things lurked."[35] Womack argues that the metaphor of the white post-statehood Oklahoman is better understood as "the inner terrain of the closeted gay man than as an actual literal rendering of Oklahoma and its people." He posits that Riggs's depiction of these Oklahomans presents a gay sexual frontier of the 1930s dominated by silence, fear of discovery and of self-recognition, secret meeting places, self-loathing, and "a sense of cannibalism even, of being devoured by a dark other, and being such a devourer oneself, secretly feeding on one's own."[36] Riggs himself acknowledged, in what is perhaps the closest he ever came to "outing" himself, that he too was born "just outside the rush of light" and understood the voiceless Oklahoman, considering it his duty to speak—"falteringly, imperfectly, incompletely"—for these quiet outsiders through his plays and poetry.[37] Thus *The Cherokee Night* enfolds an inclusive cross-section of Americans—white and Indian, gay and straight, and any others finding themselves on the "shifting fringe" of the national culture—within its metaphorical vision.

These doomed, silenced types living "outside the rush of light" are not at all representative of the characters Riggs etches in his better-known play *Green Grow the Lilacs* (who find their way into its musical adaptation, *Oklahoma!*). Produced by the Theatre Guild, *Green Grow the Lilacs* premiered on 26 January 1931 and enjoyed considerable success in New York, with Franchot Tone originating the role of Curly. *Green Grow the Lilacs* was purportedly in the running for the 1931 Pulitzer Prize for Drama.[38] But the drama's success pales in comparison to the acclaim achieved by composer Richard Rodgers and librettist Oscar Hammerstein II with *Oklahoma!* The 1943 musical continued the experiment of integrating drama, song, and dance notably attempted earlier by Hammerstein and composer Jerome Kern in their groundbreaking 1927 *Show Boat* (as discussed by Stuart J. Hecht in chapter 2).[39] The characters that populate both play and musical are vibrant and lusty, from an envisioned golden age that predated both statehood and Riggs's own childhood. Describing the quintessential Oklahoma of his play while writing it in France on a Guggenheim Fellowship, Riggs said:

> [*Green Grow the Lilacs*] is about a vanished era in the Middle West—an era a little more golden than the present one; a time when people were easier, warmer, happier in the environment they had created. Song flourished. There were the usual human anguishes, of course. But there was wholeness in the people, there was great endurance. And in spite of ignorances and darknesses, there was a cool wisdom our radios and autos have banished forever. Even the speech of the people, backwoods though it was, was rich, flavorous, lustrous, and wise. And the songs are now forgotten, except for a few which have gotten into anthologies.[40]

Womack argues that within Riggs's writing, the golden era that preceded statehood and the darker one that followed represent two contrasting sides of Riggs himself; he is at once the droll balladeer cowboy in *Green Grow the Lilacs* and the troubled mixed-blood of *The Cherokee Night*. He notes, however, that

Riggs never addresses what caused the expulsion from Okie Eden. Nor does he deal with the disastrous effects of this putative white paradise on tribal nations. . . . These two time periods, and the transition between them, occurs in Riggs, not in Oklahoma. Again, this is an Oklahomo's interior landscape rather than Oklahoma physical geography.[41]

In other words, Riggs's "Before Statehood," or "B.S.," is precisely that. The Indian Territory of *Green Grow the Lilacs* and later the Oklahoma of *Oklahoma!* exist only within Riggs's imagination. They are the myths within which a closeted gay Indian could escape the oppression of reality and even reinvent himself through ritual reenactment; they are a theatrical never-never land—within which Riggs does not have to grow up and wrestle with his sexual demons—where love is courtly, straight, and soaked with song. For Riggs, this Oklahoma existed before statehood and, most important, before *himself.* The "expulsion from Eden" coincides, in a sense, with the maturation of Riggs's own sexual identity, which was nearly contemporaneous in history with Oklahoma statehood. Homosexuality—chaotic in the sense that it does not fit into a natural scheme of things—needed to be evicted to retain order. In contrasting but symbolically parallel ways, both *Green Grow the Lilacs* and *The Cherokee Night* enact the expulsion of gay identity.

In the preface to *This Violent Empire: The Birth of an American National Identity,* Carroll Smith-Rosenberg notes that

> the need to violently exclude Others seen as dangerous or polluting has formed a critical component of the United States' national identity from the Alien and Sedition Acts of the 1790s through Joseph McCarthy's war on domestic Communists to the present. . . . Difference perceived as dangerous, disdained as polluting, demanding expulsion, [has therefore] formed a critical component of America's . . . national identity.

America's ostensible pluralism still requires the construction of a "normative national culture" based upon "a romanticized national past" that can stand in opposition to a threatening cast of "Others, domestic and foreign, [who] represent all that . . . true Americans do not wish to be. . . . To fear and dehumanize . . . Others, to ruthlessly hunt them down, is truly American."[42] In this sense, both *The Cherokee Night* and *Green Grow the Lilacs* are truly American plays.

Tellingly, the greatest threats to order in both scripts are *sexual* threats—no surprise considering Riggs's consuming fear of his own sexuality. *Green*

Grow the Lilacs' Middle Eastern peddler (a character type also found in Riggs's earlier play *Knives of Syria*), however, is basically a harmless, comic, exotic Other who in Riggs's version sells Jeeter (the character who becomes Jud in *Oklahoma!*) the "frog-sticker" that kills him, but in the musical he ultimately assimilates by marrying into the community. Jeeter poses the more sinister threat to the play's social order as a sexual predator who spends the majority of his time hidden away in a dark smokehouse, surrounded by pornography. In some sense, Jeeter personifies Riggs's homosexuality, hidden and unwholesome; the elimination of this unwanted, unhealthy sexuality is imperative to preserving the golden age.

Jeeter also demands comparison with the Booger figure of the Cherokee Booger Dance—a ritual performance (perhaps known to Riggs) in which Cherokees wear masks with sexual connotations. A Booger Dance mask might feature a large, pendulous gourd for a penis-like nose, surrounded by a base of opossum fur resembling or suggesting pubic hair. Booger Dancers impersonate non-Cherokees intruding upon an evening of Cherokee social dancing. Their vulgar obsessions with sex are at odds with decorous Cherokee society, posing a direct threat to traditional Cherokee culture. Beautifully dressed Cherokee women join the Boogers in the sacred Eagle Dance, in which the women symbolically invite these vulgar outsiders to join them in their dancing. As the women continue dancing serenely, the Boogers desecrate the purity of their movements—mocking the hospitality of the Indians and symbolically miming the cultural rape of the Cherokees. The Boogers exhibit their gourd phalluses and obscenely bump and grind, while the women (unperturbed) continue to dance with great dignity. At the close of the dance, the Boogers boisterously depart in search of other wholesome folk to corrupt. They run off into the night, as spectators erupt in sidesplitting laughter, only to return later as well-behaved Cherokee men as the social dancing and the party continue.[43] Jeeter's transgressive sexuality mirrors the profane defilement evident in this ritualized reenactment of encounters between Cherokees and white outsiders.

In response to *Oklahoma!*, Robert Benchley wrote in the *New Yorker*, "After rereading Mr. Riggs's drama (a very fine and original one, by the way), I can't see that the version at the St. James [*Oklahoma!*] has omitted anything of consequence."[44] In fact, profound differences exist between the final scenes of *Green Grow the Lilacs* and those of *Oklahoma!* At the conclusion of the musical, the community celebrates not only Curly and Laurey's union as man and wife but also the territory's imminent admission into *the* Union, the United States. Both events are sacred, and the promise of statehood warrants the rousing title song. Following this exercise in nationalism, Jud—the "bullet-colored hired man" (code for his mixed-blood identity)[45] who lusts after Laurey—promptly dies at Curly's hand. Jud must be eradicated because he is a threat not only to Laurey and Curly's future happiness but also to the area's new fellowship with the United States and its citizens. Curly is promptly acquitted, and he and his bride are hurried off to consummate their marriage while the newly minted Americans continue to make merry.[46]

Green Grow the Lilacs does not provide such a hasty and neat conclusion. After Jeeter's death, Curly is sent to "the cooler" in Claremore. He escapes and returns to Aunt Eller's house to comfort Laurey on what was to have been their wedding night. The men of the community track Curly there with the intention of returning him to the jail to await his trial. Aunt Eller, however, chastises them:

> I thought you was a fine bunch of neighbors. Now I see you're jist a gang of fools. Tryin' to take a bridegroom away from his bride! Why, the way you're sidin' with the federal marshal, you'd think us people out here lived in the United States! Why, we're territory folks—we ort to hang together. I don't mean hang—I mean *stick*. Whut's the United States? It's jist a furrin country to me. And you supportin' it! Jist dirty ole furriners, ever last one of you![47]

The men vehemently deny they are "furriners." One proclaims, "My pappy and mammy was both borned in Indian Territory! Why, I'm jist plumb full of Indian blood myself."[48] Another identifies himself as a mixed-blood Indian. In Riggs's original script, then, Eden exists outside of the physical United States and before statehood. A finely spun thread of golden Indian blood connects the fair-skinned denizens of Eden to one another; their Indian ancestry is a key component of their wholeness as fully realized individuals and, more important, as a people who love and nurture each other in the spirit of community. It can be argued that there are no white people at all in *Green Grow the Lilacs*, only mixed-bloods seemingly unaware of the politics of racial purity and blood quantum. The situation is much different in *The Cherokee Night*, where dilution of Indian blood alienates its possessors from their cultural center and tosses them into a void of nonexistence. If in that play the flawed mixed-blood stands as a metaphor for the unwelcomed and closeted homosexual, the celebrated mixed-blood who shuns unwholesome expressions of sexuality in *Green Grow the Lilacs* lends a kind of pro-queer irony to Riggs's vision of B.S. Oklahoma.

Why did Rodgers and Hammerstein change this last scene? Their alterations to the plot did more than just facilitate a commercially palatable happy ending. On another level, their new ending modifies Riggs's cosmogony to fit a much wider—and whiter—audience. While Riggs sought his own psychic escape from a homophobic society by mythologizing a queer pre-statehood Oklahoma, Rodgers and Hammerstein sought to unify a nation at war by providing a patriotic myth of an America (or of a part of it that stood in for the whole) at its inception, surrounded by a "bright golden haze" to which audiences could return through performed reenactment. Eliade identifies this desire to return to paradise, to a time glorious and ordered, as a universal human longing. The eternal myth of return—retold both by Riggs and by Rodgers and Hammerstein—is, for the culture that retells it, a "precious possession because it is sacred, exemplary, significant."[49] Myths supply "models for human behavior and, by that very fact, [give] meaning and value to life."[50] To Eliade, a myth is a creation story, relating how things came into existence—the cosmos, or some portion of it—through the deeds of exemplary beings or heroes.[51] By reenacting through myth sacred and creative acts, cultures align themselves with a sacred reality, rather than with a chaotic and profane one. The performance of the myth most importantly speaks of mankind's desire to abolish history and its terror, to rediscover paradise, and to satisfy a deep longing "to be brought close to the gods [and to] return to the realm of the supernatural."[52] In Eliade's view, a return to paradise makes time cyclical, annulling its irreversibility in favor of a new chronology that "constantly maintains the world in the same auroral instant of the beginnings."[53]

Whereas Riggs ontologically restored himself by creating his B.S. Oklahoma in *Green Grow the Lilacs*, *Oklahoma!* restores a different kind of order for its audience, and by extension for the nation, by turning away from the chaos of a country at war and enacting a ritual return to a moment of creation. By returning to its version of paradise, the forward march of historical time is abolished and, as described above, becomes cyclical and repetitive. Reviewing the musical in 1946 for the *Los Angeles Examiner*, critic Patterson Greene wrote:

> Throughout the performance, there is a certain tidal pull of nostalgia. The show presents an era that, like the Wild West of the films, has become a racial memory in the American mind, a mythical period before world wars, before the idea of One World was neatly counter-balanced by the idea of One Bomb. An era of incredible peace, all of 40 years ago. My, my—we have come a long way since then![54]

Green Grow the Lilacs and *Oklahoma!* are both valentines to a time and place that never existed. The former is a romantic myth that allowed Riggs to escape himself and to critique the Oklahoma that at once seduced and rejected him; the latter enabled Rodgers and Hammerstein to reach the pinnacles of success and musical theatre immortality by giving a war-weary America its own version of the Garden of Eden. Sadly, the voice of Riggs—forced to talk in code by the proscriptions of his own time—has been overshadowed by six decades of applause bestowed upon a white-washed patriotic revision of his work. This fate is unbefitting for the man (and the play) that Oscar Hammerstein himself proclaimed to be "the very soul of *Oklahoma!*"[55]

Though Riggs was pessimistic about the prospect for an inclusive and egalitarian America that might fully embrace outsiders like himself, he nonetheless exults in the fertile margins of democratic society, where the misfits can thrive and flourish. In his two profoundly American plays, Riggs creates a dramatic space for marginalized Others—specifically the mixed-blood American Indian, as a metaphor for the closeted homosexual—even as these groups face dehumanization, ostracism, assimilation, or annihilation. As Smith-Rosenberg asserts, such national habits are in fact "truly American."[56] By depicting the Oklahoma of the mixed-blood, with its twilight hours Before Statehood and with its Night, illuminated by the oppressive midnight sun of an American day, Riggs illustrates how the United States has kept its own gate. But, as Smith-Rosenberg also reminds us:

> The nation's Others cannot be so easily expelled. They are [its] own fantasized creations, [its] discursive and psychological doubles, projections of [its] most feared and hated qualities. . . . At the same time, figures of the forbidden and dangerous, they fascinate and intrigue [the nation]. A tortured ambivalence thus lies at the heart of America's relation to its Others. To keep [them] at bay, to maintain "the foreclosures . . . we prematurely call identities," requires the increasingly enraged enactments of their exclusion, enactments that have found expression through the United States' long history of racism, xenophobia, and sexism.[57]

In a letter to author and editor Barrett Clark, his longtime friend, Riggs wrote, "These people [these Others], human, were victims of a special and touching disinclination, and even inability, to publish their humanity. That's what I'm trying to do for them, and for their descendants . . . in the plays."[58] Publishing their humanity moves these misfits from the margins into the consciousness of the exclusionary mainstream, hopefully integrating them as essential characters in the sacred story of America, compelling the democracy to greater inclusion and understanding.

Notes

1. Patterson Greene, review of *Oklahoma!*, by Richard Rodgers and Oscar Hammerstein II, *Los Angeles Examiner*, 7 May 1946, quoted in Phyllis Braunlich, *Haunted by Home* (Norman: University of Oklahoma Press, 1988), 184.

2. Braunlich, *Haunted by Home*, 21. Riggs's father was white and of Appalachian stock and had come from Missouri to Indian Territory in the 1870s.

3. Russell Thornton, *The Cherokees: A Population History* (Lincoln: University of Nebraska Press, 1990), 128.

4. Ibid., 129–30.

5. "Oklahoma" means "red men" in the Choctaw language.

6. Quoted in Braunlich, *Haunted by Home*, 89.

7. Craig S. Womack, *Red on Red: Native American Literary Separatism* (Minneapolis: University of Minnesota Press, 1999). See chapter 8, "Lynn Riggs as Code Talker: Toward a Queer Oklahomo Theory and the Radicalization of Native American Studies," 271–310. Womack's analysis will be discussed in more detail later in this chapter.

8. Julie Little Thunder, "Mixedbloods and Bloodlust in *Cherokee Night*," *Midwest Quarterly* 43 (Summer 2002): 355.

9. Ibid., 356.

10. John Gassner and Edward Quinn, eds., *The Reader's Encyclopedia of World Drama* (Mineola, N.Y.: Dover, 2002), 257.

11. Lynn Riggs, *"Russet Mantle" and "The Cherokee Night": Two Plays* (New York: Samuel French, 1936), 215.

12. Ibid., 131.

13. Ibid., 201–2.

14. Oscar G. Brockett and Robert Findlay, *Century of Innovation: A History of European and American Theatre and Drama since the Late Nineteenth Century*, 2nd ed. (Boston: Allyn and Bacon, 1991), 149–50.

15. Mircea Eliade, *The Sacred and the Profane: The Nature of Religion*, trans. Willard R. Trask (San Diego: Harcourt Brace, 1959), 11.

16. Daniel L. Pals, *Seven Theories of Religion* (Oxford: Oxford University Press, 1996), 164.

17. Ibid., 163–64.

18. Eliade, *Sacred and the Profane*, 12–13.

19. Mircea Eliade, *Cosmos and History: The Myth of the Eternal Return*, trans. Willard R. Trask (New York: Harper and Row, 1959), 18.

20. Lynn Riggs, program note for *The Cherokee Night*, quoted in J. Brooks Atkinson, "Country Drama," *New York Times*, 28 June 1932, sec. 9, p. 11.

21. Burl Donald Grose, *"Here Come the Indians": An Historical Study of the Representations of the Native American upon the North American Stage, 1808–1969* (Ann Arbor: UMI, 1997). These two stereotypes, the red devil and the noble savage, and others are discussed in great detail in this doctoral dissertation.

22. This pattern recapitulates a tradition spanning more than a century of American dramas in which Indian characters are subject to manifest destiny. The tradition begins with James Nelson Barker's Pocahontas play, *The Indian Princess, or, La Belle Sauvage*, in 1804, regarded as the first American play about American Indians. The first play featuring American Indian characters was William Davenant's *The Cruelty of the Spaniards in Peru*, written in 1658. See Eugene H. Jones, *Native Americans as Shown on the Stage, 1753–1916* (Metuchen, N.J.: Scarecrow Press, 1988).

23. Riggs, *"Russet Mantle" and "The Cherokee Night,"* 258.

24. Ibid., 258–59.

25. Ibid., 258.

26. Ibid., 261–62.

27. Ibid., 262.

28. Ibid., 257.

29. Charles Hudson, *The Southeastern Indians* (Knoxville: University of Tennessee Press, 1976), 472.

30. Circe Sturm, *Blood Politics: Race, Culture, and Identity in the Cherokee Nation of Oklahoma* (Berkeley: University of California Press, 2002).

31. It should be noted that the other two federally recognized Cherokee Nations are less inclusive: the Eastern Band of Cherokee requires lineal descent from an ancestor on the 1924 Baker Roll and possession of at least one-sixteenth Cherokee blood. The United Keetoowah Band of Cherokee Indians in Oklahoma, considered the most culturally traditional, requires at least one-quarter blood quantum. For more, see "Eastern Band of Cherokee Enrollment Application," Eastern Band of Cherokee, http://nc-cherokee.com/enrollment/files/ . . . /enrollment-application.pdf, accessed 12 February 2014; and "Enrollment," United Keetoowah Band of Cherokee Indians in Oklahoma, http://www.keetoowahcherokee.org/government/78-enrollment, accessed 12 February 2014.

32. Braunlich, *Haunted by Home*, 191.

33. Ibid., 128–29. Riggs's confidantes about his homosexuality included actresses Bette Davis and Joan Crawford. See ibid., 127–33, 144.

34. Womack, *Red on Red*, 274–75.

35. Quoted in Braunlich, *Haunted by Home*, 71.

36. Womack, *Red on Red*, 275.

37. Quoted in Braunlich, *Haunted by Home*, 71–72.

38. The prize went, however, to Susan Glaspell's *Alison's House*, a drama inspired by the life of poet Emily Dickinson.

39. Andrew Lamb, *150 Years of Popular Musical Theatre* (New Haven, Conn.: Yale University Press, 2000), 258.

40. Quoted in Braunlich, *Haunted by Home*, 78–79.

41. Womack, *Red on Red*, 277.

42. Carroll Smith-Rosenberg, *This Violent Empire: The Birth of an American National Identity* (Chapel Hill: University of North Carolina Press, 2010), x–xi.

43. Frank G. Speck and Leonard Broom in collaboration with Will West Long, *Cherokee Dance and Drama* (Norman: University of Oklahoma Press, 1983). Anthropologist Frank G. Speck observed the Booger Dance among the Eastern Band of Cherokee in the 1930s.

44. Quoted in Braunlich, *Haunted by Home*, 183–84.

45. This phrasing appears both in *Green Grow the Lilacs* and *Oklahoma!* It derives from the real-life source for this dramatic villain, Jetar Davis—a contemporary of Riggs who was a farmhand in Claremore and known as the town drunk and the meanest man in town. See Albert Borowitz, "'Pore Jud Is Daid': Violence and Lawlessness in the Plays of Lynn Riggs," *Legal Studies Forum* 27.1 (2003): 178–79.

46. Richard Rodgers and Oscar Hammerstein II, *Oklahoma!*, in *6 Plays by Rodgers and Hammerstein* (New York: Modern Library, 1959), 82–83.

47. Lynn Riggs, *Green Grow the Lilacs*, in *Best American Plays: Supplementary Volume, 1918–1958*, ed. John Gassner (New York: Crown, 1961), 167.

48. Ibid.

49. Mircea Eliade, *Myth and Reality*, trans. Willard R. Trask (New York: Harper and Row, 1963), 1.

50. Ibid., 2.

51. Ibid., 5–6.

52. Daniel L. Pals, *Seven Theories of Religion* (Oxford: Oxford University Press, 1996), 168.

53. Eliade, *Myth of the Eternal Return*, 89–90.

54. Patterson Greene, review of *Oklahoma!*, quoted in Braunlich, *Haunted by Home*, 184.

55. Oscar Hammerstein II quoted in Braunlich, *Haunted by Home*, 180.

56. Smith-Rosenberg, *This Violent Empire*, x.

57. Ibid., xi.

58. Quoted in Braunlich, *Haunted by Home*, 71–72.

5. Moving the World toward Brotherhood

Representations of Cultural "Otherness" in the Theatre Union's *Black Pit* (1935)

Cheryl Black and Anne Fletcher

The Theatre Union, a professional workers theatre operating in New York City from 1933 to 1937, was part of the radical left that emerged during the tumultuous 1930s to challenge the conflation of "democracy" and "capitalism." With a collective organizational structure that reflected direct democracy; radically inclusive policies related to audiences, casting, and producing; and a repertory presenting wide-ranging critiques of undemocratic practices within American society as well as abroad, the Theatre Union may be fruitfully examined as a notable "experiment in democracy."[1] As promised in its foundational manifesto, the Theatre Union was primarily concerned with bringing working-class experience from the margins to the center of America's cultural life to produce plays that dealt "boldly with . . . the economic, emotional and cultural problems that confront the majority of the people . . . whose lives usually are caricatured or ignored on the stage."[2] During its four-year existence, the group produced eight plays: five set in America, three in Europe. With one exception, its plays featured working-class protagonists—dockworkers, factory workers, farmers, sailors, and miners—who also represented multiple races, ethnicities, and cultures.[3]

Arguably, the Theatre Union (following Marxist philosophy) perpetuated an oversimplified narrative that saw class difference as the most significant distinction between human beings. Such a narrative considered sexism, racism, and other forms of oppression as stemming from and ineluctably tied to economic injustice. With its second production, Paul Peters and George Sklar's *Stevedore*, the group set out to affirm the belief that the "Negro Question" was "not a racial issue at all, but an economic one."[4] As we have argued elsewhere, however, that perspective was challenged by response to the production that highlighted the significance of race as a profoundly meaningful category of identity: one related to, and yet explicitly distinct from, class hierarchies.[5] The Theatre Union's commitment to depictions of current social conditions brought a wide range of marginalized and denigrated cultural "Others" to the stage, including various immigrant groups specifically targeted as racially inferior in the exclusionary 1924 Immigration Act (particularly southern, central, and eastern Europeans). Additionally, Theatre Union plays feature "disabled" bodies that, through injury or illness, manifest the consequences of unsafe working conditions and poverty. These diverse characters share a common class identification forged through economic exploitation; an unequivocal critique of those economic conditions undergirds all Theatre Union plays. Because America's exploited working classes included individuals who were also racial, ethnic, or religious "Others," however, bringing their experiences center stage illuminated how various forms of oppression intersected to dehumanize, disenfranchise, and marginalize these groups.

Among the Theatre Union's American plays, Albert Maltz's *Black Pit* (1935) provides a striking example of this phenomenon. Set in a contemporary coal mining camp in West Virginia, *Black Pit*'s twenty-seven characters include Italian, German, and Slavic immigrants and first-generation Americans. The play's protagonist, Joe Kovarsky, is a Slovakian immigrant. Other central characters include Joe's "American" wife, Iola; his sister, Mary, and her Croatian-born husband, Tony Lakavich (who is wheelchair-bound from a mining accident); two Polish Americans named Anetsky and Bakovchen; and an Italian American named Barolla.[6] This chapter investigates the representations of economic, ethnic, and cultural "Others" in the Theatre Union's performance of *Black Pit*. As eastern European immigrants, the Kovarskys and Lakaviches are subject to a particularly vicious ethnic and cultural stereotype: the "bohunk." Our analysis particularly focuses on the ways that Maltz's characterizations relate to prevailing cultural assumptions regarding Slavic immigrants. Such an inquiry is aided by a remarkable historical coincidence: just weeks after *Black Pit* opened, a Hollywood film titled *Black Fury* debuted. It, too, was set in an American mining camp and featured a Slavic protagonist. Maltz's theatrical challenge to current thinking regarding American workers in general and the "bohunk" stereotype in particular is sharply illuminated by comparing these two contemporary works.

As Jonathan Shandell's introduction points out, at the time of the Theatre Union's inception, there was little doubt that the "homogenized Americanness" produced by the alleged melting pot was English-speaking, able-bodied, upwardly mobile, individualist, Protestant, and white.[7] In his cogent analysis of race and races *as* American history, Matthew Jacobson stresses the enduring rhetorical power of the Constitution's 1790 offering of naturalized citizenship to "free white persons"—a phrase that forever tied the concept of "freedom" (and American citizenship) with "whiteness"—and traces the ways in which various nineteenth- and early twentieth-century immigrant groups "became Caucasians only over time."[8] A relatively short amount of time seemed sufficient to "whiten" immigrating Germans and Scandinavians; even the once-marginalized Irish seemed assimilable by the early twentieth century. But a surge of migrants from southern and eastern Europe triggered a fresh wave of nativist xenophobia and racism in the 1910s through the 1930s.

Presenting authentic depictions of the conditions faced by American working classes was paramount among the Theatre Union's goals. Maltz's dramatization of a Slavic immigrant family accurately reflected current employment conditions in the mining industry. As early as 1904, labor writer Frank Julian Warne wrote of "the great conflict of races" between the Slavic immigrants who had "invaded" the mining industry and the "better citizen type of English speaking mine-workers" being forced out of the coalfields by this "Slav invasion."[9] In 1910, 82 percent of Slovak males worked as miners or in iron and steel mills. By 1930, Slavic immigrants—derisively known as "bohunks" and considered mentally and morally inferior to northern or western Europeans—still dominated the industry.[10]

According to historian Karel D. Bicha, the epithet "bohunk" or "hunky" probably originated in the Pennsylvania anthracite region in the late nineteenth century as a conflation of the terms "Bohemian" and "Hungarian" and was used to describe all "unskilled laborers of eastern European origins." The "entirely derogatory" term implied "physical strength and mental insufficiency. . . . Dangerous, unskilled jobs came to be known as 'hunky' jobs."[11] Slavs were viewed as temperamentally volatile: "submissive yet explosive" and given to sudden outbursts of violence,[12] traits that were vividly manifest in Philip Yordan's depiction of a "barbaric" and "miserable" Polish immigrant family in "Anna Lukasca," as discussed by Jonathan Shandell in chapter 12. Slavic men were characterized as chauvinistic (even "brutish" to women) and prone to drunkenness.[13] Henry Cabot Lodge denied Slavs both "whiteness" (they interfered with a "civilized laborer earning a 'white' laborer's wage") and "freedom" (they were "not a good acquisition for us to make, since they appear to have so many items in common with the Chinese")—declaring them a race "most alien to the body of the American people."[14]

In his study of rhetorical cultural expression in 1930s America, Michael E. Staub identifies the decade's "unprecedented concern with recording the speech of disinherited and marginalized Americans for persuasive purposes to encourage social change and foster political and cultural awareness."[15] Although Staub's textual analyses do not include dramatic literature, the Theatre Union's commitment to truthful portrayals of working men and women was in keeping with this concern. Like those writers Staub considers (including John Dos Passos, Zora Neale Hurston, and Tillie Olsen), the Theatre's Union playwrights seem to have been particularly conscious of problems of representation that continue to engage cultural critics today, including the "contestedness of historical truth" and the difficulty in attempting to represent "reality" without being "complicitous in its distortion."[16] Their determination to "deal boldly" with current social conflicts led them to experiment with various strategies for representing the experiences and perspectives of others authentically. Just before *Black Pit* opened, in the spring of 1935, the Theatre Union released a manifesto articulating members' collaborative and inclusive principles: "In the Theatre Union, a democracy prevails [representing] the collective thought of all departments." During *Black Pit*'s development, according to this record, two miners reviewed the script and advised playwright Albert Maltz on "the reality of situations, dialogue, and so on." Additionally, a stagehand from eastern Europe stepped in to coach actor Martin Wolfson (who portrayed Tony Lakavich) in creating a Slavic accent.[17]

The quest for authenticity in *Black Pit* was augmented by extensive research and fieldwork conducted by the playwright, Theatre Union artists, and fellow travelers into the era's mining industry. They were well aware of investigative exposés into the subject, including journalist Anna Rochester's *Labor and Coal* in 1931 (quoted in *Black Pit*'s preface) and Lauren Gilfillan's *I Went to Pit College* (1934). Maltz and other Theatre Union leaders and supporters visited Harlan County, Kentucky, during coal mining strikes—practicing what we might now call embedded journalism or ethnographic research.[18] Writer David C. Duke has discerned an "essentialist" tendency among these investigative researchers to "envision mining people as ourselves with dirty faces, 'others' who would rather be more like us":

> The "otherness" of race, class, ethnicity, professionalism, location, and culture often served as barriers between writers and the people they were trying to help to creatively engage. Many of the writers who wrote about miners admired the people they were working with or writing about; they

especially praised their courage, work ethic, and endurance. But even in the glow of their admiration, the writers had a tendency to speak about rather than to mining communities.[19]

Although Maltz's elite education (he held degrees from Columbia and Yale) accorded him some degree of privilege, his experience as the son of Jewish emigrants from Lithuania and Poland[20] gave him a firsthand understanding of economic and cultural "otherness" and may have helped him avoid the essentializing tendencies Duke notes. Maltz was seven in 1916, when nativist author Madison Grant lamented that in cities like New York, the prototypical "old stock" American was being "literally driven off the streets" by "swarms" of immigrants—primarily Polish Jews—who "adopt the language of the native American. . . . They wear his clothes . . . they steal his name . . . they are beginning to take his women, but they seldom adopt his religion or understand his ideals."[21] Maltz's working-class credentials were heightened by the fact that he had already written two successful Marxist plays (including the Theatre Union's premiere work, *Peace on Earth*) and had joined the Communist Party in 1935.

This playwright's dramaturgical method included four months of ethnographic research while living in mining camps in Ohio, Pennsylvania, and West Virginia. There he observed firsthand the appalling working and living conditions he later portrayed onstage: low wages; unsafe practices that led to injuries and deaths; and the intimidation, blacklisting, evictions, and abuse used to prevent labor organizing. During a sojourn in the coalfields of West Virginia in 1934, he picked up a hitchhiker who told him about a local mine tragedy in which hundreds of miners perished from silicosis brought on by inhaling rock dust (the company did not furnish workers with masks) while drilling a water-power tunnel for a Union Carbide subsidiary.[22] Maltz gave this information to New York journalists and then wrote a short story based on the man's account. According to a feature on Maltz in *Cineaste*, his story titled "Man on the Road" "appeared in more labor publications in its day than any other piece of American fiction"[23] and was praised for its "full realization of . . . social implications and simple dignity."[24] The publicity surrounding the story sparked a 1936 congressional investigation of mining practices.[25]

During his time at the mining camps, Maltz also heard a story about a militant young miner who was falsely accused and imprisoned for dynamiting a coal tipple (a structure in which mine cars were "tipped" and emptied of their coal, which was then cleaned and loaded into railroad cars). That story became the genesis of *Black Pit*. Maltz's preface to the play, also printed in the production program, includes the epigraph from *Labor and Coal* and a quotation, written in dialect, from a miner named Steve Kristoff—who, shortly after Maltz met with him, was killed on the job.[26] The play's preface also details the sights and sounds of a coal camp, called a patch. Designer Tom Adrian Cracraft, who faithfully reproduced those details on stage, also brought impressive "authenticity" credentials to the project (duly noted by Theatre Union press releases). Before moving to New York and beginning a notable career in scenic design, Cracraft had worked for two years in a coal mine in Kenilworth, Utah. His knowledge of mining informed his realistic choices for settings and props, including his insistence on ordering special helmets worn by the actors playing miners.[27] Newspaper reviewers invariably praised Cracraft's detailed settings. According to one press release, a miner who saw the production asserted that "it actually smells of the mine!"[28] Another recounted how the technical staff garnered suitably shabby, worn clothes for "realistic" costuming and described their methods for distressing costumes and set furnishings.[29] Maltz's and Cracraft's firsthand experiences most clearly manifest in the play's explication of the day-to-day operations of mining—its various jobs (loaders, fire boss, pit boss, and the like), pay scales, scrip system, dead work (that is, work that has to be done before coal can be extracted and for which miners are not paid), economics, safety hazards, labor practices (including blacklisting), and the complex network of economic and political relationships among mining, steel, and railroad companies and state legislatures.

Black Pit programs also included a glossary of fourteen specialized mining terms, including "hot mine," "fire boss," and "tipple." During the play's run (in May 1935), Maltz published an article in *New Masses* recounting additional anecdotes and stories from miners he had met during his field research in coal country.[30] Additional authenticity came from the backgrounds and experiences of several cast members. Actor Harry Bellaver, who played the militant union organizer Barolla, was the son of Italian immigrants; he was born in a mine camp in Illinois and worked as a loader in the mines at the age of sixteen. According to a Theatre Union press release, Bellaver was known to mine bosses as a scrapper for his rights and for the union. His character is the union organizer who challenges Joe's loyalty, precipitating the play's climax. Martin Wolfson, who played Tony Lakavich, spent six months in western mines during his youth.[31] Actress Millicent Green, née Manja Grynszpan, was a Polish immigrant—although she played a southern Appalachian "American" (Joe Kovarsky's bride).

Hester Sondergaard, who played Tony's wife and Joe's sister, was the child of Danish immigrants.[32]

Maltz renders Joe Kovarsky as a tragic protagonist of considerable psychological complexity, challenging to some degree the Marxist aesthetic mandate to privilege social over psychological character motivations. Director Michael Blankfort, writing in collaboration with Nathaniel Buchwald, defended Maltz's dramaturgy as a new movement in revolutionary drama toward "an effective balance between inner conflict and outer events, between the drama of the individual and the drama of his class. . . . In *Black Pit*, not only are the hero's actions dramatized but also the inner moral and psychological conflicts."[33] Joe is a former militant union man, falsely accused and imprisoned for blowing up a mine tipple. Blacklisted, with a pregnant wife and his sister's family to provide for, he finds work in Pennsylvania under an assumed name. There his sobriety and faithfulness, in direct contrast to stereotypical "bohunk" behavior, perplexes his fellow boarders: "What be matt'r wit' you? You young feller, all time you no play card, no get drunk, no look for lil' bit whore in town—what's matt'r?"[34] When his true identity is discovered, Kovarsky is fired. Facing perpetual unemployment, he commits an unpardonable sin. In dire need to provide medical assistance for his pregnant wife, he agrees in exchange for a job to inform on his fellow miners, who are secretly trying to form an independent union. Despite horrendous pressure brought to bear on Kovarsky (if he does not agree to the boss's scheme, his family and his sister's family will be turned out on the street to starve), his fateful choice destroys him. His betrayal is discovered, and he is forced to leave the community, alone and friendless, with no hope of redemption. Although he will never see his beloved wife and infant son again, he leaves with the recognition of his tragic error—his placing of individual needs ahead of those of the community: "What good get t'ings by be false to odern miner? . . . Bett'r be starve, Iola, bett'r be live in hole lak animal" (105).

Maltz described the play as "psychological-social" and as a "modern treatment of the Judas story . . . man's betrayal of his friends and his cause." The playwright explained to audiences his increasing attention to "inner motives—to nuances of character" to "make the traitor understandable in human terms. . . . I think you will love Joe Kovarsky, the blacklisted miner who can't get a doctor for his baby. And when he capitulates—forgets the first commandment to be loyal to his fellow workers, I think you will hate him."[35] Just before the play's opening, an article in *New Theatre* described the play as "an ethical struggle in a man's soul."[36] Although several leftist critics objected to featuring a "stool pigeon" as the protagonist of a proletarian play, none could deny his humanity and dramatic stature. *New Masses*' critic Joseph North, in fact, refused to accept that this "picture of proletarian vigor" could have "turned stool."[37] Although critics John Mason Brown and Burns Mantle both identified Kovarsky as a "Polack,"[38] a lapse suggesting something about dominant cultural tendencies to generalize about eastern Europeans, descriptions used by mainstream critics regarding Joe Kovarsky (as performed by Alan Baxter) suggest none of the negative traits associated with the "bohunk" stereotype. These descriptors included terms and phrases like "virile";[39] "fine";[40] "a damn fine figure of a man";[41] "a forthright and vigorous young foreigner";[42] "manly, obdurate and authoritative";[43] "handsome and affectionate";[44] "innocent and industrious";[45] and "honest" with a "fine sense of righteous indignation against mine bosses."[46]

Joe Kovarsky's brother-in-law, Tony Lakavich, is a representation not only of a cultural "Other," a Croatian (aka "bohunk"), but also of a "disabled" individual, paralyzed by a mining accident and restricted to a wheelchair. Scholars have recently critiqued dramatic representations of disability that foster misconceptions of the disabled as either victims or villains or as "metaphorical devices" lacking human complexity.[47] Although Tony may be said to symbolize the injustices of America's class system (specifically unsafe working conditions), the character is too complex and too engaged in the action to be reduced to a metaphor. Although unable to work in the mines, he remains actively engaged in secret plans to form an independent union. He is also the play's *raissoneur* who first articulates the militant workers' creed: "Wurkingman wan' t'ings he got fight for t'ings, Joe. Nobuddy gone geev heem. He got tak" (35). Indeed, Tony's undisputed role as head of household, despite his "disability," manifests a trace of the chauvinism attributed to Slavic masculinity. However, his patronizing attitude toward the women in the family (he ridicules them for reading romance magazines) falls far short of brutality. It is Tony who ultimately articulates moral outrage at Joe's betrayal, declaring that his brother-in-law should have let his wife and baby starve rather than betray his fellow workers. It is Tony who sends Joe into exile: "You be dead man here" (107). And it is Tony who concludes the play on a note of militant and hopeful resistance. As Joe exits into exile, the three o'clock siren blows, heralding the beginning of a strike: "Holler out loud! Jesus Chris' miner got blow whistle . . . not boss blow . . . miner blow . . . Jesus Chris' I nevair gone die . . . I gone sit here wait for dat time!" (108). Critics applauded Wolfson's performance, recognizing the character's significance. Recurring descriptors include "steadfast"[48] and "forceful."[49] Thomas R. Dash described Tony as "idealistic and uncompromising," Joe's "harshest judge," and "the eloquent and passionate miners' spiritual leader."[50] *New Masses* critic Joseph North hailed Tony as "a splendid sample of proletarian courage. Here is the working class hero; though paralyzed in an industrial accident, he is fearless; he would rather have the slag hill his bed and coal his supper than turn traitor."[51]

Although the Kovarskys and Lakaviches seem to have been in America for at least ten years, and Mary and Tony have two children born in the United States, no one seems to consider them "Americans." Joe refers to his wife as an "American," specifically stating that he himself is "no 'merikan feller" but an "ol' co'ntry feller"—to which his wife responds, "Ah don' care that you're not an American fellah!" (22). In this context, Joe and Iola have an interracial marriage, precisely the kind of alliance that xenophobic alarmists like Edward A. Ross claimed was slowly polluting pure "American Blood [by] injecting sub-human blood" into the veins of "our people."[52] These sentiments were echoed by South Carolina senator Ellison DuRant Smith in support of the 1924 immigration restrictions: "I think we now have sufficient population in our country for us to shut the door and to breed up a pure, unadulterated American citizenship."[53] Despite their apparent acceptance of permanent "foreign" status, both Tony and Joe articulate their hopes for the "American dream," that is, to make money and have a nice house and children.[54] Here Maltz may be subtly critiquing the notion of "getting on" as a fundamental sign of "Americanness" or highlighting the empty rhetoric that promises equal access to the American dream to "all men."

Presumably seeking "truthful" depiction, Maltz renders the speech of the Kovarskys and Lakaviches in dialect, as in these lines where Mary Lakavich scolds her daughter: "Anna, I no like dis. All day long I wurk for you—night time come I wan' hear Iola read leely bit nice story—" (9). A few critics mentioned the dialogue as contributing to the play's "realism." Burns Mantle noted with approval Baxter's employment of "what I assume to be a perfect Polish American speech."[55] Thomas R. Dash, who promoted *Black Pit* as a Pulitzer contender (infinitely more important, according to Dash, than its nearest contender *The Children's Hour*) also praised "the foreign jargon of some Slovak dialect," asserting that this "materially aids [the drama's] realism," giving it "surprising crispness and vitality."[56] All evidence suggests that "realism" was Maltz's goal in reproducing the dialect *as he heard it*. As New York–born Maltz presumably did not speak Croatian or Slovakian, the miners he encountered were forced to speak to him in broken English. Maltz's reproductions of this speech prevent an audience from hearing his characters' thoughts expressed with their full power and eloquence and stand as a reminder that "broken English" has provided nativist ammunition for ridicule of "foreigners." Of course, "realistically," the Lakaviches would not speak broken English in their homes but their native language. That ten years after their arrival their English is still "broken" speaks to the cultural segregation of the era and leaves these characters vulnerable to stereotyping. Maltz does include fleeting moments when characters speak their native languages—when Mary greets Joe for the first time after his release from prison[57] and when the men play an Italian counting game *in* Italian. The play also calls attention to religious diversity, such as when Joe responds to Mary's question about the presence of priests in prison: "No have our priest, Mary [presumably Eastern Orthodox]. Jus' Roman priest" (16). These fleeting moments reveal a progressive, if imperfect, reflection of cultural pluralism within an expanded, multicultural concept of American identity.

A few mainstream reviewers criticized Maltz's portrayal of conditions, particularly the villainy of the mine superintendent, as "overdrawn." *Newark Evening News* writer John Whitney, who made his own claim to authenticity as a former coal miner, denied ever witnessing any of the abuses depicted in *Black Pit*.[58] Ever vigilant in its quest for corroborating evidence, the Theatre Union solicited and published testimonials from miners and union leaders who attended the performance, defending the play's authenticity in terms of events, characterizations, and physical conditions. The theatre sent to the New York press a signed note from President Clarence Irwin of the District 6 Amalgamated Association Iron Steel and Tin Workers Union of Pittsburgh, Pennsylvania, who praised the play as "remarkable for accuracy."[59] Tom Adrian Cracraft also penned a letter to the dramatic editor of the *New York Times* testifying (based on his own mining experiences) that Maltz's depiction was "entirely authentic."[60] Subsequent studies have corroborated Maltz's depictions. Historian John Hevener has documented similar conditions in the early 1930s at Black Mountain Coal Corporation in Harlan County, Kentucky, where one thousand workers were dismissed or struck in solidarity with those who were fired and three hundred nonunion workers, "scabs," took their place in the mine. Starving mining families found themselves ineligible for Red Cross assistance, as their situation was precipitated by a voluntary walkout and assistance from the local mine union was denied.[61] A 1935 commission, appointed by Kentucky governor Ruby Laffoon, described Harlan County mining conditions as "unbelievable . . . a virtual reign of terror, financed by a group of coal mine operators in collusion with certain public officials."[62]

The question of authenticity in Maltz's portrayal of working-class conditions in America, including his representation of Slavic masculinity, was thrown into sharp relief by the simultaneous appearance of a competing portrayal from one of America's most popular cultural platforms—the Hollywood film industry. Warner Brothers' *Black Fury* (based in part on a short story, "Jan Volkanik," by Judge M. A. Musmanno and a play by Harry R. Irving titled *Bohunk*) was also inspired by an actual incident in which a striking coal miner was beaten to death by company detectives. The film starred Austrian-born Paul Muni as Slovakian protagonist Joe Radek. As an Austrian Jewish immigrant, Muni was arguably a more authentic casting choice for an eastern European miner than Ohio native Alan Baxter, the son of a Cleveland Trust Company vice president. Authenticity in representation of conditions and character, however, was another issue.

The conditions of the workers in *Black Fury* are decidedly better than those depicted in *Black Pit*. Joe is a boarder with the Shemanski family; their cabin is simple but comfortable and reasonably spacious. Joe has his own bedroom; the family has a pet dog and a car. The miners go to work joking and laughing; Joe is especially jolly, singing as he works. He has saved enough money to marry his girlfriend, buy a farm, and settle down to raising pigs and children—his American dream approaching fulfillment after an apparently brief time in the land of opportunity. Joe's girlfriend, Anna Novak (played by Karen Morley), is presumably the first-generation child of eastern European immigrants, but she looks, dresses, and sounds like a Hollywood starlet. Most tellingly, *Black Fury*'s miners have recently negotiated a contract that seems to have improved working and living conditions.[63]

Still, rumblings of discontent come from a few miners who are later revealed to be planted troublemakers paid to stir up the workers so that the company might hire professional strikebreakers and bring in law enforcement. When Anna leaves Joe for another man (his dream deferred not by social injustice but by female infidelity), he drowns his heartbreak in drink and becomes a gullible tool for the pseudomilitants. Egged on by the "radicals," a drunken Joe spurs his fellow workers to form an independent union and to strike. The mine closes, throwing everyone out of work, and scabs are brought in. Joe's former friends, who believe he was paid to start trouble, reject him; the closest of these companions, Mike Shemanski, asks Joe to leave his home. Again, Joe drowns his sorrows in drink until Mike is killed by one of the company cops, an event that spurs Joe to desperate action. He steals dynamite and holes up in the mine, threatening to blow it up unless the owners reopen the operation and rehire his friends. This improbable tactic works; after five days, a Washington, D.C., investigating committee discovers the chicanery of the professional strikebreakers and intervenes, settling the strike to everyone's satisfaction. Joe's demands are met, the miners return to work under their previous contract, and the "bad guys" are prosecuted. Instead of facing prosecution, Joe is hailed as a hero, and he and his newly restored girlfriend exit on the shoulders of a wildly cheering crowd. In stark contrast to *Black Pit*'s insistence on communal activism, *Black Fury* glorifies the individual action of its protagonist.

Paul Muni was universally praised for his performance in the film (for which he won his third Oscar nomination), but the character Joe Radek (described in promotional copy as "simple")[64] aligns with many "bohunk" stereotypes: he is clownish and gullible; his girlfriend cheats on him with a cop; he is easily duped by his bosses, who outwit him. Radek's betrayal is unwitting; he suffers none of the internal conflict that tortures Maltz's Kovarsky. As the *New York Times* critic sums it up:

> Mr. Muni is the ignorant and jovial Hunky miner, Joe Radek, whose popularity with his comrades causes him to be singled out as the dupe of the strike-breaking gangsters. Joe is an innocent among the wolves. Having lost his girl, he drowns his sorrows in the whisky bottle. Without understanding the issues involved, he makes a drunken appearance at a union meeting at the psychological moment to cause a split between the conservative and the radical factions.[65]

Recurring descriptive phrases of Joe include "burly," "bewildered," "easy prey,"[66] "slow-witted,"[67] "dull but pleasant hunky,"[68] and a "blundering bohunk."[69] In an interview, Muni himself describes the character as a "poor ignorant bohunk . . . a groping fool of a fellow, trying to do something too big for him. He is heroic through his emotions. His head was never any good anyhow."[70] Many reviewers also note his drunkenness and volatile temper. A Warner Brothers ad describes him as a "savage lover," and the movie trailer promised audiences "Violence! Savagery! Terror!," identifying Radek as "an untamed brute!"[71]

Marxist critics—especially Albert Maltz and the Theatre Union Executive Board—were outraged and immediately took on *Black Fury* in the press. On 18 April 1935, Maltz published a letter to the editor of the *New York Evening Post* that decried the press's tendency to label *Black Pit* "pro-labor" propaganda. Maltz insisted that *Black Fury* was also propaganda—but of the "anti-labor" variety. He objected to the film's distortion of miners' working conditions, its depiction of miners as drunkards and dupes, its denial of the usefulness of strikes, and its "phony climax."[72] The following day the *Post* published a response from Harry R. Irving, *Black Fury* coauthor, defending his work. Irving wrote that, unlike Maltz and the "theatre movement with which he is connected," he and Warner Brothers believed that the stage was for "entertainment and enlightenment" and had not intended to depict the general condition of miners but only to tell the story of one individual miner. Irving defended the accuracy of "outlaw strikes" fomented by charlatans to "shake down" owners.[73] Maltz refused to give in, however, responding with another letter in which he insisted that

> Mr. Irving, whether he likes it or not, is giving us a general picture of a miner's life. And it is my contention that from first to last the impression of a miner's life and work which Mr. Irving has given is incredibly false and distorted. It makes no difference what he intended to do. This is what he has done. An Author is a propagandist by what he says or fails to say. He is a propagandist for one cause or another, directly or indirectly.[74]

In addition to his editorials, Maltz also published a lengthy and passionate critique of the film in *New Theatre* that condemned *Black Fury*'s values as "viciously anti-labor" and a "subtle, vicious blow at militant trade-unionism." Maltz criticized the "prettified" portrayal of the life and work of miners and, especially, the "absurdly heroic" way Joe Radek wins: "We are led to believe that the miners as a whole have no strength, [and] require a terroristic act to win their strike." Maltz railed against the film's conclusion as "a ridiculous, impossible, terroristic solution. This is the *Black Fury* version of the class struggle!"[75] This extended debate between Theatre Union defenders and the filmmaker underscores the aesthetic battle across the 1930s over the efficacy of theatre as "art" versus "propaganda," illustrated by the titles of Maltz's and Irving's dueling articles, "Which Play Is Propaganda?" and "It's Art, Not Propaganda." The Theatre Union continued the debate in a *Black Pit* versus *Black Fury* symposium hosted by the Belasco Theatre on 1 May. More than twelve hundred people attended the program, featuring Maltz; Pennsylvania governor Gifford Pinchot's wife, Cornelia; Judge M. A. Musmanno (author of the original short story on which *Black Fury* was based); film critic Andre Sennwald; actress Rose Hobart; *New Masses* editor Mike Gold; and Fred Siders of the Montour 10 Mine of Library, Pennsylvania.[76] The *Partisan Review* hosted a second "controversial symposium" at the Civic Repertory Theatre on 5 May with

Maltz, Gold, *Daily Worker* drama critic Leon Alexander, designer Mordecai Gorelik, Soviet historian Joshua Kunitz, and trade union activist Clarence Hathaway. Additional symposia on the topic were held at the Bronx Cooperative House (with Executive Secretary Margaret Larkin as Theatre Union representative) and the Plymouth Friendship League of the Brooklyn Community Temple, with Maryn Myers, Theatre Union assistant director, as the chair.[77]

While Maltz and his Theatre Union cohorts were hardly unbiased critics, his assessment of *Black Fury* is largely borne out by comparison: the film specifically challenges the need for working-class unity or working-class activism, suggesting that either individual heroism or benevolent federal intervention will solve labor's problems. Moreover, Maltz's critiques are largely confirmed by critical response from mainstream writers, who also questioned the film's political substance. John Reddington of the *Brooklyn Daily Eagle* averred that

> at no point in the film are the grievances of the miners stated—we are increasingly in doubt as to whether they want shorter hours, more pay per load, better working conditions, less dead time, schools for their children, etc. . . . They are a peaceful and contented lot trooping off to the mines with a song on their lips.[78]

Martin Dickstein, while praising the film as "vigorous" and "exciting," similarly noted that "*Black Fury* evades the real issues between the miners and the coal barons. . . . It is not the courageous sociological drama its producers claim it to be."[79] Although *New York Times* critic Andre Sennwald named *Black Fury* the "most notable American experiment in social drama since 'Our Daily Bread,'" he also pointed out that "far from being radical, 'Black Fury' is a rousing defense of the conservative viewpoint in labor-employer relations."[80]

Maltz's indignation, like that of his Marxist colleagues in the Theatre Union, was aimed at *Black Fury*'s depiction of *workers*—an economic, rather than a racial or cultural, group. But once again (as with *Stevedore*'s depiction of workers who are also African Americans), its depiction of workers who are also ethnic and cultural Others illuminates how structural institutions of racism, nativism, and xenophobia intersected with capitalism to shape the distinctive experiences of eastern European immigrants in America, revealing how dehumanization facilitates exploitation and oppression. Representation of Otherness is always fraught with danger, and for all its earnest intentions to depict workers' lives "boldly" and "truthfully," the Theatre Union's optimistic blind faith in militant unionism (evident in all of its plays) is subject to question. To Maltz's credit, however, *Black Pit*'s conclusion, though ending on a high note of worker solidarity and rebellion that was typical for the Theatre Union, contains the organization's bleakest and arguably most "realistic" resolution. The play's protagonist neither dies a martyr's death nor leads his comrades into militant resistance. Instead, he succumbs to the unbearable pressures of his oppressive condition. Joe Kovarsky may be seen as a prototypical "common man" tragic protagonist who would later be theorized by Arthur Miller in 1949: a hero whose struggles illustrate "the indestructible will of man to achieve his humanity" and whose "destruction in the attempt posits a wrong or an evil in his environment."[81] Although Maltz may have hoped his audience would see capitalism as that evil, his play also reveals how institutional racism and other oppressive structures have intersected with capitalism to deny democracy and equality in America. In presenting Slovakian Joe Kovarsky as a mentally and morally complex human being; in portraying Croatian (and wheelchair-bound) Tony Lakavich as imminently "able," strong, and courageous; and in bringing their experience as American workers struggling to provide for their families to the forefront of public consciousness, Maltz posed a serious challenge to the prevailing stereotypes of brutish "hunkies" unfit for full participation in American citizenship. Its comparison to *Black Fury* reveals how Hollywood and similar cultural institutions have worked to simultaneously romanticize and infantilize cultural Others.

Albert Maltz continued to advocate for disenfranchised groups through art long after the dissolution of the Theatre Union in 1937, as an author of short stories, novels, and screenplays. In 1939 Maltz contributed an essay to *We Hold These Truths . . . : Statements on Anti-Semitism by 54 Leading American Writers, Statesmen, Educators, Clergymen and Trade-Unionists*, written in response to Father Charles E. Coughlin's bigoted radio broadcasts and magazine. To further counteract Father Coughlin's impact with the general public, Maltz propelled the inaugural issue of a new journal, *Equality*.[82] Employing ethnographic research once again in 1936 by traveling to Detroit, Maltz published *The Underground Stream*, a novel set in the world of a sit-down strike that explored the theme of sacrifice for one's principles.[83] He spent the 1940s writing for film in Hollywood. During this time, he also crafted what has been hailed as his greatest literary achievement, *The Cross and the Arrow* (1944), a novel that denounces racism and fascism, revisiting the belief (explored earlier in *Black Pit*) that one "is born neither good nor evil, but can, by circumstance or pressures, be led in varied directions."[84] Maltz, along with fellow Theatre Union playwright John Howard Lawson, suffered the consequences of blacklisting as a member of the Hollywood Ten. For more than two decades he worked under a pseudonym; by the time he could safely write under his own name in the late 1960s, he was forgotten.

In an interview from the 1970s, Maltz revealed that his literary heroes were the "citizen writers" of history—Zola, Gorky, Thoreau, Whitman—"those who plunged into the turbulent affairs of their day." Of his own "citizen writing" during the 1930s and 1940s, Maltz recalled, "I felt that I had attached myself to a movement that was going to bring about human brotherhood, and an end to all discrimination in the world." Classic Marxist literature, Maltz affirmed, is

> the noblest body of literature that has ever been penned by man. Because it speaks of moving the world into brotherhood, of moving it into true democracy, of ending all exploitation in every area—wage exploitation, exploitation of colonies by imperial powers, of women by men, of colored people by white people. There is no area of exploitation that it doesn't say, "We will abolish it. We will arrive at true equality." Now that's a marvelous dream! And a *moral* dream, in my code. And I do not feel embarrassed today that I adhered to it. I felt that my greatest dignity as a human being was that I did adhere to it.[85]

Notes

1. Research for this chapter has been funded in part by the University of Missouri Research Council and the University of Missouri Center for Arts and Humanities. In keeping with the book's general usage, the terms "America /American" throughout refer to the United States of America.

2. Margaret Larkin, "Building a Social Theatre," Margaret Larkin Papers within the Albert Maltz Papers (hereafter Larkin/Maltz Papers), Wisconsin Center for Film and Theatre Research (WCFTR), Madison.

3. The company's five American plays include George Sklar and Albert Maltz's *Peace on Earth* (1933–34), Paul Peters and George Sklar's *Stevedore* (1934), Albert Maltz's *Black Pit* (1935), Albert Bein's *Let Freedom Ring* (1935–36), and John Howard Lawson's *Marching Song* (1937). Plays with European settings were Friedrich Wolf's *Sailors of Cattaro* (1934–35), Bertolt Brecht's *The Mother* (1935), and Victor Wolfson's *Bitter Stream* (1936). The protagonist of *Peace on Earth* is a college professor, and another central character is a journalist; striking dockworkers, however, figure prominently in the action.

4. Quoted in John Anderson, "Wharf Nigger vs. Stevedore: Collaborators Act upon Theory That 'Problem' in South Is Economic, Not Racial," *New York Evening Journal*, 19 April 1934, Theatre Union Scrapbook, Billy Rose Theatre Division, New York Public Library for the Performing Arts.

5. See Anne Fletcher and Cheryl Black, "The Color of Revolution: Race Trumps Class in the Theatre Union's *Stevedore*, 1934," *New England Theatre Journal* 22 (2011): 23–51. Following *Stevedore*, the Theatre Union's repertory further dramatized anti-black prejudice within the working classes in subsequent plays, particularly *Let Freedom Ring* and *Marching Song*.

6. The term "Slavic" is used to refer to peoples from eastern and central Europe, including Russians, Poles, Czechs, Serbs, Slovaks, Croats, and Bosnians.

7. In "Democracy Versus the Melting Pot," Horace Kallen describes the representative American as "individualist, English-speaking, interested in getting on, kind, neighborly, not too scrupulous in business, indulgent to his women, optimistically devoted to laissez-faire in economics and politics, very respectable in private life, tending to liberalism and mysticism in religion." *Nation*, 25 February 1915, http://www.expo98.msu.edu/people/kallen.htm, accessed 12 October 2013.

8. Matthew Frye Jacobson, *Whiteness of a Different Color: European Immigrants and the Alchemy of Race* (Cambridge, Mass.: Harvard University Press, 1998), 4. The act of 1790 restricted naturalized citizenship to "free white persons" of "good character." See "First Congress Statutes at Large," http://rs6.loc.gov/ll/llsl/001/0200/02270103.tif, accessed 15 November 2013.

9. Frank Julian Warne, *The Slav Invasion and the Mine Workers: A Study in Immigration* (New York: Young People's Missionary Movement, 1904), 6.

10. See Michael Novak, *The Rise of the Unmeltable Ethnics* (New York: Macmillan, 1972).

11. Karel D. Bicha, "Hunkies: Stereotyping the Slavic Immigrants, 1890–1920," *Journal of American Ethnic History* 2.1 (Fall 1982): 19.

12. Ibid., 22–23. See also Jacobson, *Whiteness of a Different Color*, 80.

13. Bicha, "Hunkies," 27.

14. Quoted in Jacobson, *Whiteness of a Different Color*, 77.

15. Michael E. Staub, *Voices of Persuasion: Politics of Representation in 1930s America* (London: Cambridge University Press, 1994), x.

16. Ibid.

17. Theatre Union press release, March 1935, "On Selecting and Producing Plays: Collaborative Method," Larkin/Maltz Papers, WCFTR.

18. See William Stott, *Documentary Expression and 1930s America* (New York: Oxford University Press, 1973), 242.

19. David C. Duke, *Writers and Miners: Activism and Imagery in America* (Lexington: University Press of Kentucky, 2002), 4.

20. In his 1942 biographical sketch for *Twentieth-Century Authors*, Maltz noted that his father "went to a comparatively early grave, worn out, carrying with him a love for America and painter's lead poisoning." His mother worked as a seamstress in a sweatshop where she contracted trachoma. See Stanley J. Kunitz and Howard Haycraft, eds., *Twentieth Century Authors: A Biographical Dictionary of Modern Literature* (New York: H. W. Wilson Co., 1942), 899.

21. Madison Grant, *Passing of the Great Race* (c. 1916; New York: Arno Press, 1970), 80–81.

22. See, for example, Waldemar C. Dressen and R. R. Jones, "Anthraco-silicosis," *Journal of the American Medical Association* 107.15 (October 1936): 1179–85.

23. "Albert Maltz: Portrait of a Hollywood Dissident," *Cineaste* 8.3 (1977–78): 3–15.

24. Edward J. O'Brien, ed., *Best Short Stories 1936* (Boston: Houghton Mifflin, 1936), xxiii.

25. "Investigation Relating to Health Conditions of Workers Employed in the Construction and Maintenance of Public Utilities," *Transcript of a 1936 Report of the House of Representatives Subcommittee on Labor*, http://www.english.illinois.edu/maps/poets/m_r/rukeyser/investigation.htm, accessed 1 January 2014.

26. *Black Pit* program, *Black Pit* file, Billy Rose Theatre Division.

27. "Mining Experience," press release, n.d., Larkin/Maltz Papers, WCFTR.

28. Press release, Larkin/Maltz Papers, WCFTR. Reviews from the New York City papers in Theatre Union Scrapbook, Billy Rose Theatre Division.

29. Transcript of press release, marked "to *Sun* and *Eagle*," WCFTR.

30. Albert Maltz, "Dramatist in the Coalfields," *New Masses*, 14 May 1935, 27–28.

31. "Mining experience," press release, n.d., WCFTR. Wolfson (1904–73) had previously appeared in Theatre Union's *Stevedore* and *Sailors of Cattaro* and would later perform in its *The Mother* and *Marching Song*. He enjoyed a fairly substantial Broadway career until 1970, despite being blacklisted during the McCarthy era.

32. Martin Wolfson and Hester Sondergaard were blacklisted during the McCarthy era.

33. Quoted in Malcolm Goldstein, *The Political Stage: American Drama and Theater of the Great Depression* (New York: Oxford University Press, 1974), 133–34.

34. Albert Maltz, *Black Pit* (New York: G. P. Putnam's Sons, 1935), 27. Subsequent citations are indicated parenthetically in text.

35. Transcript of unedited interview with Maltz, "Black Pit Is a Modern Treatment of the Judas Story," *New York Post*, 16 March 1935, in *Black Pit* file, WCFTR.

36. "Backstage," *New Theatre*, March 1935, 26.

37. Joseph North, "Theatre Union's Black Pit," *New Masses*, 2 April 1935, 42. See also Carl Reeve, "Despicable Role of Scab Portrayed in *Black Pit*," *Daily Worker*, 23 March 1935, 7. See Jack Stachen, *Daily Worker*, 29 April 1935, and North's response to Stachen, *Daily Worker*, 2 May 1935. Isadore Schneider defended the play against accusations of melodramatic excess and glorification of a "stoolie" by calling it a tragedy and "uniquely impressive" as a social document. *New York Times*, 12 May 1935, sec. 10, p. 5.

38. John Mason Brown, *New York Evening Post*, and Burns Mantle, *New York Daily News*, 21 March 1935 (all reviews are in Theatre Union Scrapbook, Billy Rose Theatre Division).

39. Grenville Vernon, *Commonweal*, 5 April 1935, 654.

40. Arthur Pollock, *Brooklyn Daily Eagle*, 27 March 1935.

41. R. P. Smith, *Columbia Spectator*, 17 April 1935.

42. Arthur Pollock, *Brooklyn Daily Eagle*, 21 March 1935.

43. Fragment in Theatre Union Scrapbook, Billy Rose Theatre Division.

44. See "The Drama," *Catholic World*, May 1935, 213. Edith Isaacs was one who considered Baxter too handsome, or too "drawing room" handsome, for the role. *Theatre Arts*, May 1935, 331–32.

45. Percy Hammond, *New York Herald Tribune*, 21 March 1935.

46. Burns Mantle, *New York Daily News*, 21 March 1935.

47. See David T. Mitchell and Sharon L. Snyder, *Narrative Prosthesis: Disability and the Dependencies of Discourse* (Ann Arbor: UMI Press, 2000), 47. See also Victoria Ann Lewis, *Beyond Victims and Villains: Contemporary Plays by Disabled Playwrights* (New York: Palgrave Macmillan, 2005).

48. Pollock, *Brooklyn Daily Eagle*, 21 March 1935.

49. Mantle, *New York Daily News*, 21 March 1935.

50. Thomas R. Dash, "Black Pit," *Women's Wear Daily*, 21 March 1935.

51. Joseph North, "Theatre Union's *Black Pit*," *New Masses*, 2 April 1935, 43.

52. Ross is quoted in E. Digby Baltzell, *The Protestant Establishment: Aristocracy and Caste in America* (New York: Random House, 1964), 105.

53. "Shut the Door" speech by Senator Ellison DuRant Smith, 9 April 1924, *Congressional Record* (Washington, D.C.: Government Printing Office, 1924), 65:5961–62. This act passed with only six dissenting votes.

54. For Tony's articulation, see Maltz, *Black Pit*, 12; for Joe's, 19.

55. Burns Mantle describes Joe as an "honest young Polish lad" in *Daily News*, 21 March 1935.

56. Thomas R. Dash, "Black Pit," *Women's Wear Daily*, 21 March 1935.

57. Maltz translates her repeated murmuring of "Matke Bozhia" as "Mother Virgin," a prayer of thanks. We have not been able to find this phrase in translation, but there seems to be a town named Matka Bozia in present-day Slovakia.

58. See Percy Hammond, *Herald Tribune*; Richard Lockridge, the *Sun*; and John Whitney, *Newark Evening News*, 21 March 1935, all in Theatre Union Scrapbook, Billy Rose Theatre Division.

59. Theatre Union press release transcript, marked "for Labor press," quotes from miners John Borsick and Aubrey Price, with an addendum from Clarence Irwin, WCFTR.

60. Tom Adrian Cracraft to Dramatic Editor, *New York Times*, 25 April 1935. Copy of letter in Maltz/Larkin Papers, WCFTR.

61. John W. Hevener, *Which Side Are You On? The Harlan County Coal Miners, 1931–39* (Urbana: University of Illinois Press, 2002), 34–39.

62. Quoted in F. Ray Marshall, *Labor in the South* (Cambridge, Mass.: Harvard University Press, 1967), 139, and in Hevener, *Which Side Are You On?*, 114.

63. *Black Pit* advocates for the kind of contract and universal working conditions proposed by the United Mine Workers Association (a national union) over smaller-scale agreements between independent miners and individual companies, whereas in many ways *Black Fury* demonizes the UMWA.

64. *Black Fury*, dir. Michael Curtiz, Warner Brothers, 1935, available on VHS and via Amazon Instant Video, http://www.amazon.com/gp/product/B007FO0AU4/ref=atv_feed_catalog?tag=weblab-treatment-20.

65. Andre Sennwald, "Paul Muni in the Coal-Mine Melodrama 'Black Fury,' at the Strand," *New York Times*, 14 April 1935.

66. "Paul Muni Has Leading Role in Black Fury," *Binghamton (N.Y.) Press*, 14 May 1935, 24, http://www.fultonhistory.com/Fulton.html, accessed 12 November 2013.

67. "Black Fury Opens at Valencia Today," *Jamaica Long Island Daily Press*, 17 May 1935, http://www.fultonhistory.com/Fulton.html, accessed 12 November 2013.

68. "Paul Muni, Karen Morley Star in Black Fury, "*Jamaica Long Island Daily Press*, 17 May 1935, http://www.fultonhistory.com/Fulton.html, accessed 12 November 2013.

69. Molly Marsh, "Muni Wins a Great Tribute—Censorship," *Screen and Radio Weekly*, 12 May 1935, http://www.fultonhistory.com/Fulton.html, accessed 12 November 2013.

70. Ibid.

71. Trailer available on DVD.

72. Albert Maltz, "*Black Pit* vs. *Black Fury*: Which Play Is Propaganda?" *New York Evening Post*, 18 April 1935, 10.

73. Harry R. Irving, "It's Art, Not Propaganda—Says Author of Black Fury," *New York Evening Post*, 19 April 1935, 7.

74. Albert Maltz, "What Is Propaganda?," *New York Times*, 28 April 1935.

75. Albert Maltz, "Coal Diggers of 1935," *New Theatre*, May 1935, 8–9.

76. *New York Evening Post*, 24 April 1935.

77. Margaret Larkin (?) to Leo Marsh, n.d., WCFTR. See also Cultural Committee of the New Masses Branch of the IWO to Miss Waldorf, 23 April 1935, and Margaret Larkin to Leo Marsh, 29 April 1935, WCFTR. The Civic Repertory was the Theatre Union performance space.

78. John Reddington, "Sound and Fury," *Brooklyn Daily Eagle*, 14 April 1935, http://www.fultonhistory.com/Fulton.html, accessed 12 November 2013.

79. Martin Dickstein, "The Screen," *Brooklyn Daily Eagle*, 20 April 1935, http://www.fultonhistory.com/Fulton.html, accessed 12 November 2013.

80. Sennwald, "Paul Muni in the Coal-Mine Melodrama."

81. Arthur Miller, "Tragedy and the Common Man," *New York Times*, 27 February 1949.

82. Maltz contributed few signed pieces to the journal but many unsigned editorials. *Equality* hired unemployed workers to aid in distribution. See Jack Salzman, *Albert Maltz* (Boston: Twayne, 1978), 47.

83. Ibid., 57.

84. Albert Maltz to Jack Salzman, 24 July 1969, as quoted in ibid., 75.

85. "Albert Maltz: Portrait of a Hollywood Dissident," 9.

6. (Re)Visioning Mexican Intellectual and Peasant Life

Josefina Niggli's Plays with the Carolina Playmakers (1936–38)

Elizabeth Coonrod Martínez

In Josefina Niggli's historical drama *The Cry of Dolores* (1936), the lead character, Josefa Domínguez, issues a passionate plea for freedom at any cost—a cry that personifies Mexican and female leadership in pursuit of democratic ideals:

> HIDALGO: The independence of New Spain must be bought at any price.
>
> ALLENDE: Mexicans must be aroused! And how easy it is, since the Spaniards see us only as degenerates, imbeciles, incapable of exerting the smallest sign of volition.
>
> DOÑA JOSEFA: . . . Now is the time to free our country: I dedicate myself to the revolution although it may cost all of us our lives.[1]

The theme and title of the drama relate to the 1810 beginnings of the Mexican struggle for independence, following three hundred years of European rule. The message of Niggli's play—the first creative work in English on this topic—in many ways parallels the mythos surrounding the Boston Tea Party rebellion against British rule. The drama is an expression of the principle that people on the American continent need to be free.

Another of Niggli's plays, *The Ring of General Macías* (1938), is based on the 1910 Mexican Revolution. Its main character is Raquel Macías, a federal general's wife whose Mexico City home is invaded one night by two revolutionaries. Her husband has been captured and is being held by rebels at their camp. In the ensuing dialogue, Raquel discovers in the resolve and ideals expressed by the rural peon Cleto the idealism behind the uprising that her husband is trying to quell:

RAQUEL: And you believe in the Revolutionary cause?

CLETO: Yes, señora. I am a poor peasant, that's true. But still I have a right to live like a man, with my own ground, and my own family, and my own future. . . .

RAQUEL: Has a woman less honor than a man, then?

CLETO: No, señora. Please, I don't know how to say it. The general is a soldier, he has a duty to his own cause. You are a woman. You have a duty to your husband. It is right that you should try to save him. It is not right that he should try to save himself.[2]

Raquel begins to understand the implications of the civil struggle waged by the vast and long-suffering underclass. By the end of the play, Raquel acknowledges that the revolution will succeed.

These historical plays and several of Josefina Niggli's "Mexican" comedies—first staged by the progressive ensemble the Carolina Playmakers in Chapel Hill, North Carolina, in the late 1930s—represented Mexicans both as citizens of America (in Texas and the Southwest) and as worthy neighbors to citizens of the United States. The story of how Niggli found her way from her birthplace in Mexico to Texas and finally to Chapel Hill and the legacy of what she expressed to an American[3] audience stand as a testament to the democratic potential of the American stage. Throughout her long yet underappreciated career as a playwright, Niggli worked from a steadfast commitment to dramatizing her own heritage as a vital and constituent part of a pluralistic American democracy. This chapter examines Niggli's writing for the stage, with particular emphasis on works created for the Carolina Playmakers and the cross-cultural resonance of her dramaturgy for predominantly Euro-American audiences in North Carolina and beyond.

In an era of fluid movement across the U.S.-Mexico border during the early twentieth century, Niggli lived the borderlands experience. Her primary culture and education was Mexican, but her adult life and career transpired in the United States. She wrote in English but spoke through her plays of democratic values rooted in early twentieth-century Mexican experience: values that promoted freedom from colonial hegemony and a restoration of indigenous Mexican roots native to the continent. Born in Monterrey, Nuevo León, in northern Mexico in 1910, Niggli relocated with her mother to San Antonio, Texas, in 1925. Her mother bought a house in the English-speaking downtown area, but as a girl Niggli attended a Spanish-language church on the Mexican side of town. Her father (born in Texas) spent his adult life working in Monterrey until his death in the mid-1940s. After completing high school and earning a college degree, Niggli worked in radio and community theatre in San Antonio, paying regular visits to her father's home in Monterrey. She then sought a specialized master's program in playwriting, selecting the University of North Carolina–Chapel Hill in 1935. Niggli chose this program because of its leader, Frederick H. Koch, and his particular emphasis on the folk play (as will be explored in more detail later in this chapter).

Niggli's ultimate goal as an artist was to return to Monterrey and set up her own theatre company. But once in North Carolina—where Koch encouraged her to write about Mexican life—Niggli sought to expand U.S. understanding about Mexican culture, to demonstrate Mexican resolve toward democracy, and to champion the plight of Mexico's common people. Her writing drew upon her own experiences as one of an estimated one million migrants to the United States following the disruptions of the 1910 revolution.[4] This civil struggle sought to bring rights to "those below" (as Niggli refers to the underclass in her second novel): a vast, near-slave population who had historically been denied access to education and other basic rights (following independence from Spain in 1821). Niggli's focus on populist Mexican concerns (a focus shared by many artists in post-revolution Mexico) came in an era when the United States was consolidating for itself a national identity and, as a result, mostly ignoring Mexican/Hispanic presence and cultural heritage within its borders. This conception of a national identity rooted in European origins had contributed to the geographic expansion of the United States while dismissing indigenous and Spanish-Mexican contributions to the national character.

As a region still in expansion and settlement, the U.S. Southwest sat at the margins of the national discourse at the turn of the century. New Mexico and Arizona achieved statehood only in 1912; although Texas had earned statehood in 1845, it was commonly known for its large ranches established by people of European origin rather than for the haciendas of earlier Spanish settlement.[5] Monuments in the state commemorated Stephen Austin and Sam Houston; folklore celebrated the heroism of Davy Crockett. Meanwhile, Juan Seguín's achievements in the movement for Texan independence and as a pioneer of Hispanic settlement of Texas remained obscure to most in the nation.[6] The late nineteenth century brought the arrival of the railroad and an expansion of a cattle ranching industry. These changes sparked political fluctuations. At one point, Hispanics born in Texas were declared "immigrants" so that they could vote, until an opposing political system used the same designation to prevent them from voting.[7] Eventually, the emerging Euro-American hegemony lumped "Mexicans" with American Indians, requiring their extraction.[8]

Manifest destiny (the process of occupying the North American continent while removing American Indians to reservations) extended its influence beyond the continent with the Spanish-American War. The U.S. victory in 1898 over the "Spanish brute" (as Spain was portrayed in political cartoons of the era) won for the United States the last colonial possessions of the Spanish monarchy: the Philippines and Spanish Caribbean islands. On the mainland, long-term Hispanic (Spanish colonial) residents of the United States and those who relocated for greater safety during the Mexican Revolution struggled to find voice in a Euro-oriented national culture. As noted by Juan González, "The job of justifying [North America's] frontier conquest fell to the dime-store novelists of frontier life, to the travel writers," whose accounts spoke only to non-Hispanic settlement.[9] This lore influenced the emerging Hollywood film industry, which often depicted Mexicans and American Indians as savages,[10] cementing an Anglicized explanation of the creation of the United States.

In the early twentieth century, an image of the sleeping—or lazy—Mexican based in late nineteenth-century travelogue interpretations of Mexican countryside life grew in popularity. This image depicted a *sarape*-clad figure seated with arms folded over his knees, reclining his head under a wide-brimmed sombrero.[11] In the 1930s and 1940s, as automobile tourism increased, tourists seemed eager to capture the nostalgia of a countryside era that was endangered by rapid modernization. The bright colors and representations of Mexican and Indian peasants fulfilled yearnings for romantic escape. But in the new national ideology, depictions became more stereotypical, especially as the hardships of the 1930 Depression set in.[12] By midcentury, the "sleeping Mexican" had joined a parade of Euro-American ethnic cartoons: Chinamen with long braids, cigar store Indians, southern "mammies," and black jokester Cubans and Filipinos.

As a self-declared "bi-national" who reached adulthood in this fervent era, Niggli was acutely aware of the marginalization of the "Mexican" subject in American society. Many of her characters are peasants, with folk qualities common to rural areas of Mexico and the United States at the turn of the century. Others are urban intellectuals who want to help find rights for all and to change colonial society through revolution. In addition to revealing diverse personalities and human interactions, Niggli's plays dramatize some of the complexities of Mexican history, including the contributions of women as leaders. Niggli sought to teach American audiences about the mestizo ideology of the newly victorious revolution and its celebration of indigenous Mexican culture. Her dramaturgy valorizes the campesino (or peasant, a figure also visible in the murals of Diego Rivera) as the personification of that ideology. Decades before the proliferation of a Chicano movement in the 1960s, Niggli's plays brought Mexican culture and democratic principles into focus within the United States. Most Mexican American authors of her era wrote in Spanish, which restricted their access to mainstream publishers and producers and thus limited the visibility of their work. Niggli made a considered choice to write in English so as to gain a wider audience for her writing. In her view, the English-speaking public "needed it more."[13]

After the First World War, popular interest in various forms of "Latino" art and culture surged. Mambo and other Afro-Caribbean rhythms infiltrated commercial "big band" orchestrations; Mexican muralists gained notoriety and employment in the United States; film star Dolores del Río began her career in Hollywood; and soon the group Trio Los Panchos would soar in popularity with its romantic Mexican melodies. Author Anita Brenner explored Mexican art and revolutionary politics in her writings for an English-speaking readership;[14] English translations of anthropologist Antonio Mediz Bolio's readings on Mayan culture (available in Spanish in the 1920s) circulated in the early 1940s. Positioned at the forefront of this creative and scholarly activity, Niggli stands out as the only playwright whose work sought to connect English-speaking audiences with Latino creative influences, as well as with the impact and social meaning of the 1910 Mexican Revolution.

In the years following the First World War, greater accessibility to transportation and to stage technologies created new opportunities for the American theatre. These developments helped propel a new emphasis among dramatists on more nuanced regional cultures and social concerns. One who spearheaded the movement toward a new regional "folk" drama was Frederick H. Koch, professor at the University of North Carolina and founder of the Carolina Playmakers. Koch recruited students to Chapel Hill in a spirit of democratic idealism and inclusion. His goal was to train a new generation of playwrights to portray the folk life of diverse regions and rural populations, collaborating in creating what he called a "People's Theatre."[15]

Koch's emphasis on folk plays had "nothing to do with the folk play of medieval times." He wanted students to interpret authentic American experience. "For many years," Koch wrote in 1939, "our playwrights were imitative, content with reproducing the outlived formulas of the old world.

There was nothing really *native* about them. Whenever they did write of American life, the treatment was superficial and innocuous."[16] Thus he launched his experimental program in 1919 at the university's Forest Theatre. He soon took the Carolina Playmakers' productions of folk drama on the road throughout North Carolina and to other states. His company's new plays were published in drama magazines and made accessible through the Samuel French agency. In 1922, Koch published the first of his many collections of student work, titled *Carolina Folk Plays*. Based on his success, Koch was named regional adviser for the South by the Federal Theatre Project (FTP)—a position that boosted his recruitment efforts for the Playmakers. Students who had completed his program were hired to run FTP projects in several states, while Koch continued to receive new students at Chapel Hill.[17] While there, Niggli explored the folk play as a vehicle to describe Mexican social and cultural practices. Just as many Mexican writers were doing in their home country, Niggli sought to articulate the ideals of the 1910 Mexican Revolution through the ethos of the peasant. Her strategy was a natural fit within Koch's program. Even so, Niggli was the only member of the Carolina Playmakers—during the 1930s and afterward—whose work depicts the Mexican community.[18]

Niggli's writing for the Carolina Playmakers shows the imprint of her time spent in San Antonio and reflects the vibrant traditions of Spanish-language performance that spanned the U.S.-Mexico border. Building on a rich heritage of Spanish-language theatre in the Southwest and Los Angeles (where new plays were being produced) during the nineteenth century, San Antonio saw new theatrical companies established during the early twentieth century, including the prominent Teatro Nacional and the Carpa Cubana, both of which toured throughout the United States (including the prominent Spanish-language theatre locations of Los Angeles and Tampa) and into Mexico.[19] The repertoire of these and other companies ranged from vaudevillian acts to traditional Spanish *zarzuelas*, older-style melodramas, and comedies. In addition to these permanent theatres were the *carpa* (big tent) traveling companies that flourished during the Depression era, when English-language theatres struggled financially. Nicolás Kanellos describes the *carpas* as "havens for vaudeville acts, [though] some also included circus acts, slapstick comedy, a 10-piece band, and performers speaking in urban Mexican-American dialect, or *caló*."[20] Nicolás Kanellos cites San Antonio as a center for the rise of vaudevillian performances of national and international acclaim, as well as of tent theatres "that served an exclusively working-class audience."[21]

Niggli's investment in transnational performance traditions becomes clear in a letter she wrote to *Theatre Arts Monthly* shortly after her arrival in North Carolina. Her account (quoted at length below) describes a popular performance in "a small town of about 500 people, some thirty-five kilometers from Monterrey." She paints a vivid picture of popular Mexican theatre and speculates about the potential for translating that tradition to a new language and cultural context:

> A traveling stock company arrived there, and presented *Madame X*. Their stage was a few wooden planks supported on sawhorses, their costumes ranging from Stuart England to a very modern French maid. But Mexicans love the theatre, and when the great night arrived, the little square was packed. The play proceeded in a most magnificent manner until the fatal speech of the young lawyer in defense of his mother. The public was so still that the gnawing of a rat would have seemed a thunderclap. The young actor had been speaking for almost two minutes, the tears raining down his face, his arms flailing the air, and then—he stamped his foot. The stage began to rock slowly from side to side, Madame X gave a most undignified scream, and wooden planks, sawhorses, furniture and actors collapsed.
>
> The audience picked them up, put them all back in their proper places, there was a general handshaking all around—then the public returned to rocking chairs and benches, the young actor went on with his speech from the exact place where he had left off, and the play was considered the grand success of the repertoire. That is the true spirit of the Spanish theatre. Do you wonder that it cannot be reproduced successfully in English?[22]

The performance of comic drama for working-class audiences is a longstanding tradition in Mexican (and indigenous) culture. As noted by Judith Weiss, such performances "can serve as a safety valve or as a conduit for complaints"; in such a way "different cultures have found a space for traditional expression."[23] Niggli's ultimate goal was to share with American spectators the legacy and the innovations of Latino drama and folklore as she witnessed them in the early twentieth century—particularly the *género chico* (brief comic pieces and musical one-act plays) from the Mexico of Niggli's childhood that centered on the lives of peasants. Writing in English, she imported the new genre into the United States, incorporating this style of Mexican "folk" play into Koch's "People's Theatre" program.

Niggli's comedies highlight the essence of village life and its rural economies (goat farming, cheese production, and other trades practiced in villages), local courtship customs, and entertainment traditions. Her peasant characters, immortalized in Mexican revolutionary ideology, also reflect an American nostalgia for a rural experience quickly disappearing due to technological change. Although the setting for her comic writings is "Mexico," her depictions of village life seem just as appropriate to the southwestern United States. Though charming and lighthearted, Niggli's comedies deliver subtle, between-the-lines social commentaries.[24] They juxtapose peasants against urban elites, bringing focus to entrenched class disparities. Her writing defies these social imbalances within village communities by demonstrating that, despite differences in personality and socioeconomic status, all classes of society share a common humanity. Additionally, by exploring what Koch termed "the legends, superstitions, customs, environmental differences, even the vernacular of the common people,"[25] Niggli sought to raise the visibility of this *other* culture of North America and to expand the breadth of American representation. In a manner that echoes the Cuban American theatre in Florida's engagement with discourses of racial identity (as discussed in chapter 3), Niggli's folk plays draw attention to Mexican issues of social inequality, which were couched not in notions of black-white racial difference (as manifested in the Hispanic Caribbean) but in terms of peasant and indigenous cultural identity. In her comedies, Niggli brings attention to the plight of the lower class—much like other Mexican writers of the early twentieth century did in Spanish.

In the early months of her studies at North Carolina, Niggli wrote the one-act comedy *Tooth or Shave?* Its setting is a village street with two side-by-side home businesses; one house contains the workshop of the town carpenter, with the local barber/"tooth-puller" immediately next door. The play's four characters are the husband and wife of each abode. As the women emerge for the daily routine of sweeping their front porches, the carpenter's wife brags to her neighbor that she will soon be the first in town to own a phonograph—a luxury item that cost ten silver pesos and was arriving that day by train. Anxious to reveal her own skills in saving, the barber's wife responds that she too has saved ten silver pesos, secured in her trunk for a nice burial and casket someday. Overhearing their conversation, the carpenter concocts an elaborate plan to recover the cost of the phonograph (which he had secretly spent on a lottery ticket). He coerces the barber into taking his wife's savings so that they can meet the train and pay for the phonograph. The men return to find that the barber's wife has discovered that her money is missing; she soon learns the purpose to which it has been used and declares her ownership of the phonograph. When the carpenter objects, the barber solves the disagreement and resolves the comic plot by offering to pull his neighbor's teeth for free. As a snapshot of village life, Niggli's comedy juxtaposes rural occupations and ways of life with an emerging fascination with modern technology and consumerism (a familiar trend within U.S. society in the early decades of the twentieth century). Thus Niggli's comedy suggests an implicit linkage between the experience of "Mexican" life in the countryside and the aspirations of modern urban existence. The laughter evoked by her comedy is the means through which her messages of inclusivity and her celebration of lower-class experience may be heard.

Scene from *Tooth or Shave?* by Josefina Niggli. *Josefina Niggli materials used courtesy of the Western Carolina University Foundation, Cullowhee, N.C.*

Another comedy titled *This Bull Ate Nutmeg* (1938), also set in a rural milieu, is more distinctively "Mexican" in its depiction of bullfighting. The comedy sets up a play-within-a-play structure, as two male characters prepare to enact the roles of bull and bullfighter for a Sunday performance in their village corral. These two men are also rivals for the attention of the same young woman. The day before their bullfighting performance, a traveling peddler arrives selling what he calls a "love potion" (which is, in fact, merely nutmeg). The man playing the bull falls for the scheme and takes the "potion" to enhance his romantic prospects. The comic twist comes when his ingesting the nutmeg causes him to sneeze and snort uncontrollably—enhancing his performance of the bull. Thus, ironically, the love potion works, with his superior performance winning him the affections of the girl. With its mix of a comic courtship story and depictions of traditional Spanish customs, *This Bull Ate Nutmeg* offered another dramatic linkage between American rural experience and Spanish heritage.[26]

Another of Niggli's comedies, *The Red Velvet Goat* (1936), also employs a metatheatrical device. Its protagonist is a man who needs money to buy himself a goat (an economic commodity among rural peasants). To do so, he decides to create a play for paying customers, to be performed on his front porch. As he builds props, his wife becomes annoyed with his preparations. When he surreptitiously cuts a large swath of cloth from her red velvet dress (a garment she seldom wears) for his central character's costume, she becomes furious. She ultimately gets revenge by using her husband's earnings from the performance to purchase herself a new dress. Engaging with identifiable themes of gender difference, marital tension, and revenge in a lighthearted manner, this folk play was popular both in U.S. and London productions. Two years after its debut in Chapel Hill, the comedy was selected by the One-Act Repertory Theatre in New York City for its opening season (1938) and critically hailed as the season highlight.[27]

Scene from *The Red Velvet Goat* by Josefina Niggli. *Josefina Niggli materials used courtesy of the Western Carolina University Foundation, Cullowhee, N.C.*

Gender issues are even more front-and-center in the Niggli comedy *Sunday Costs Five Pesos* (1936). Based on a Mexican courtship custom, the play centers on the insecure bride-to-be Berta, who spies her fiancé, Fidel, walking around the plaza with another young woman. Fidel pleads his innocence to Berta from her porch, trying to get her to open the door, while prying neighbors listen in. Fidel explains that the woman is not a romantic interest but the daughter of a potential client (from another town) for his carpentry business. In rural Mexican custom, however, a walk around the plaza between a man and woman signifies romantic interest. After Berta sends Fidel away, neighboring girls gather on the porch next door to torment her and to stoke her insecurities about Fidel. The threat of a fight ensues between Berta and another girl. At a moment of tension, one member of the group remembers the day of the week—Sunday—which carries by law a fine of five pesos for public rowdiness. (Niggli's foreword to the play explains the derivation of the law referenced in the play's title.) The comedy resolves when, later that same day, Fidel returns to announce his securing of the out-of-town carpentry job—which will require him to relocate immediately. He asks Berta to marry him that very day so that she might join him. Berta accepts happily, supplying the play's comic reconciliation between the lovers as well as Berta's escape from the threat of physical harm. *Sunday Costs Five Pesos*, with an added musical score, was selected in 1950 by the Charlotte

Scene from *Sunday Costs Five Pesos* by Josefina Niggli. *Josefina Niggli materials used courtesy of the Western Carolina University Foundation, Cullowhee, N.C.*

(North Carolina) Opera Foundation for participation in a Metropolitan Opera one-act contest.[28] The performance was highly acclaimed by New York critics and tapped for the award as an "all-American" opera. In 1956 it was selected as an instructional text for secondary school plays (which continues to be reissued), and in 1972 the script was included in the first anthology of Mexican American authors.[29] Likewise, *The Red Velvet Goat* has enjoyed frequent revivals, attesting to the wide appeal of Niggli's comic story among many different types of audiences. As with all the short plays discussed here, Niggli successfully articulates universal cultural values within settings that emphasize a Mexican cultural identity. Her comedies attest to the notion that, even for white English-speaking audiences, Mexican culture stood as a viable presence within the American experience.

As she was writing her comedies, Niggli also worked in a different dramatic genre: the history play. In keeping with the objective of the Carolina Playmakers to dramatize the experiences of diverse cultures and regions, Niggli's history plays highlight the emergence of Mexican democratic ideals through key historic moments and personalities. The first one-act play she wrote as a Carolina Playmaker, *The Cry of Dolores* (1936), centers on the now historic inception of Mexico's war for independence from colonial Spain. In Mexican history, midnight of 15 September marks an observance called the *grito*: the call to arms issued by the priest Miguel Hidalgo in the village of Dolores in 1810, summoning villagers to launch their rebellion. The lead character of Niggli's dramatization is the historic figure Doña Josefa Domínguez, who led the plans for the rebellion through disguised "literary group" meetings in her home. Other historic characters in the play include the priest Hidalgo and the military hero Ignacio Allende; an invented character is Josefa's daughter, betrothed to Allende.[30] Hidalgo and Allende's names are today called out at midnight in community celebrations throughout Mexico and the United States. The name of Josefa Domínguez has more recently gained recognition within accounts of this revolutionary history. Thus Niggli's championing of this female revolutionary hero onstage was a gesture that was decades ahead of its time.

Another of Niggli's history plays brought the more recent Mexican Revolution into focus: *This Is Villa!* (1938) is a one-act drama centered on the close relationship that revolutionary general Pancho Villa sustained with his men. In the United States, Villa was simply known as a bandit: an outlaw pursued into Mexico by the U.S. Army after he crossed the border and raided the town of Columbus, New Mexico, in 1916. Among residents of northern Mexico, and to Niggli herself, Villa stood as a revolutionary hero. The play humanizes Villa, demonstrating not only his leadership skills among his men but also the bad qualities of his nature. The antagonist in this play is a professor from Mexico City who purports to be writing an article about Villa but is in fact a traitor to the revolutionary cause. A young man in Villa's troop, Antonio, arrives during the interview, wearing a red hat that he purchased for his wedding that afternoon. Villa wants the hat and bullies him into handing it over. Later, Villa finds himself smitten by Antonio's shy young bride-to-be and advances on her when Antonio is out of the room. She resists and falls backward, hitting her head and dying instantly. Villa asks the professor to use his "pretty words" to break the news to Antonio. Instead, the professor persuades Antonio to kill Villa in revenge. But Villa turns the tables by convincing Antonio to forgive him and discovering the professor's plot against him. In the end, Antonio kills himself (rather than harm his general), and the professor is to be executed by firing squad.

Niggli's dramatic portrayal of Villa as an infamous womanizer is true to his historic reputation. The play adds nuance to Villa's character, however, by emphasizing his excellent leadership skills. In her foreword, Niggli explains: "The most important thing about Villa was that he came from the people, the Mexican peasant. [He had] a connection to the land and simplicity of life which gave him an essential child-likeness, not childishness, that people forget."[31] In this—as in all of her historically inspired dramas—Niggli strove to depict not only Mexican history but also the human complexity of her Mexican subjects. Her characters were three-dimensional and philosophical. As Chicana critic Tey Diana Rebolledo has observed, Niggli was "eager to portray Mexico and its people in a complex manner so they would be better understood by Americans."[32] Indeed, we can link Niggli's portrayal of the Mexican peasant class with other contemporaneous efforts in U.S. drama to reveal the "American" essence of regional ethnic identities, such as Lynn Riggs's *Cherokee Night*, as discussed by W. Douglas Powers in chapter 4. If the 1930s was a decade that redefined U.S. government–American Indian relations (discussed by Elizabeth A. Osborne in chapter 9), it also might have been an auspicious moment for reconsideration of the "Hispanic" role within U.S. history, but that did not take place in any sustained or transformative manner. Mexican writers of the early twentieth century, including Niggli, highlighted democracy initiatives connected to practices and philosophy native to the American continent. Niggli's history plays, for example, specifically championed the inclusive democratic values sought by Mexicans.

Among those values was the strong role women could play in society. Niggli's one-act historical drama *Soldadera* (1936), produced in her first year with the Carolina Playmakers, featured a nearly all-female cast. This play's setting is historic, but its protagonist is a fictional composite inspired by one of the most popular folk songs to emerge from the 1910 revolution: a ballad titled "Adelita." In popular lore, the song articulated a longing by Mexican revolutionaries for a woman soldier who was both a beautiful object of male desire and an inspiring emblem of the heroic values of those women participating in the struggle. Adelita became an archetype for the woman warrior within Mexican culture. Niggli's play is an important contribution to the creation of this archetype; it is, in fact, the first theatrical work to dramatize an Adelita figure. Today, the term "Adelita" is used interchangeably with *soldadera* to refer to a woman revolutionary; in Chicano culture, the term has a wider connotation of any woman engaged in a struggle for human rights.[33] Niggli portrays her Adelita as the youngest of a group of women peasant revolutionaries stationed at a lookout post in the hills who hold as prisoner a high-ranking government official called "The Rich One" (the lone male character in the play). After exploiting the women's naïveté with compliments, "The Rich One" asks for a hand mirror, ostensibly to make himself more presentable, which he uses to signal the federal army. When his captors discover what he has done, Adelita martyrs herself in response; she stops the advance of the federal soldiers by walking toward them, concealing a grenade.[34]

Scene from *Soldadera* by Josefina Niggli. *Josefina Niggli materials used courtesy of the Western Carolina University Foundation, Cullowhee, N.C.*

A final example, Niggli's one-act historic play *The Ring of General Macías*, mentioned earlier in the chapter, uses the historical context of the 1910 revolution to contrast male cowardice with female valor. The two rebel soldiers who invade Raquel Macías's house late one night present her with her husband's wedding ring, which he had offered in negotiation for his release. As Raquel engages them in conversation and learns personal details of their lives, she comes to understand the motivations behind the civil war and why these men seek to overthrow Mexico's dictatorial government. Raquel has lived a life of privilege as an aristocratic woman married to a military leader. She has otherwise stayed uninvolved in politics. Through her encounter with these peasant revolutionaries, she comes to see her husband's role in a new light. Raquel's eyes are opened to the stark realities of her society and to the injustices of a system that jails hungry children for many years merely for stealing an orange. In debating the two sides of the conflict, the play's focus remains on Raquel's decision; although she sees the reasons for the revolution, she chooses to kill the rebels (putting poison in the wine) to defend her husband's honor. Raquel knows he will be killed when the rebels do not return, but she also understands that through her choice, he will die with honor rather than be known as a coward. Through this encounter, Niggli advocates for the underlying idealism of the revolutionary struggle and for the rights of peasants and the underclass and brings to the forefront the valor and reasoning ability of a woman (in contrast to that of her spouse).[35]

From a twenty-first-century critical perspective, Niggli's plays may appear as simple folklore from a fading era. But considering American cultural politics and the historic marginalization of Mexican-American voices, Niggli's work stands out in the pre–civil rights era. As noted by Chicano critic Raymund Paredes, this dramatist's "greatest achievement was to delineate an important aspect of Mexican-American experience and to create a distinctive ambience for its presentation. . . . Niggli suggests that few Mexican-Americans are truly detached from their origins. Their cultural memories . . . reside in the back of their minds, ready to emerge."[36] Thus Niggli's creative work preceded and paved the way for the pursuit of similar objectives by the Teatro Campesino and other Chicano artists of the 1970s. More than a theatrical ambassador for foreign Mexicans, Niggli used the stage to communicate the authentic roots of a distinctly Mexican ethos and culture through the social conscience of the 1910 Mexican Revolution, which is similar to the ethos of "American democracy." Working in North Carolina, she created plays for diverse audiences that not only entertained but also reflected her values and heritage. Had she remained in Texas or published in Spanish, opportunities for a wider dissemination of her creative voice would have been much more limited.

After completing her master's degree in 1937, Niggli continued to work with the Carolina Playmakers into the 1940s and wrote several radio plays that aired in New York. She left North Carolina in 1943 and returned to San Antonio, where she composed two historically based novels: *Mexican Village* (1945) and *Step Down, Elder Brother* (1947). In a 1949 lecture to historians in Monterrey, she reflected on her greatest satisfaction as a writer:

> I think my proudest moment was when the reviewers of *Step Down, Elder Brother* pointed out that although the story was set in Monterrey, it could have been laid in Minneapolis, Montreal, or Manchester. I had told my readers that Mexico was not a strange, exotic land, a romantic Banana Republic, but a country whose beliefs, ideals and desires were identical with human problems everywhere. A woman in Durham, North Carolina, said to me after one of my lectures: "After I went to Mexico last summer I read one of your books, and you know, I realized that the people I saw down there were human." Believe me, this is not a laughing matter. It is extremely serious. . . . You have met the people as individuals. Listen to their history as a nation.[37]

As a pioneer in the genre of Latino drama, and as an innovator in bringing understanding of Mexican culture to an English-language public, Niggli's imprint on Mexican American drama has been sizable. Without directly confronting Anglo-centrist notions, her work subtly and continuously opens awareness of Mexican (American) values. Assessing her legacy, Paredes describes her as a singular writer in bringing Mexican culture/presence to light. "After Niggli," he says, "Mexican-American writing changed significantly" (due largely to institutionalized racism and accelerating urbanization that sidelined people of color), contributing to an emerging literature of protest.[38]

Koch describes drama as "not a solitary but a social art," through which the student must recognize that "he, himself—his own view of life—should be his first consideration," which then must be subjected to a collaborative process working with actors and audience.[39] Koch's male-centric language notwithstanding, Josefina Niggli succeeded in putting Koch's ideals into action: bringing her own experience in Mexican culture, and her distinctive awareness of social inequality and the peasant class, into greater social currency for English-speaking American audiences. Within the social experiment of the early Carolina Playmakers, Niggli alone interpreted Mexican culture for a U.S. audience and demonstrated Mexican struggles for democracy in a way that modeled a vision of greater social justice for marginalized Mexican Americans and for all segments of society. Niggli's dramatizing of rural peasant experience and the roots of Mexican democracy was a noble and valuable contribution to the cause of *American* democracy.

Notes

1. Josefina Niggli, *The Cry of Dolores*, in Elizabeth Coonrod Martínez, *Josefina Niggli, Mexican American Writer: A Critical Biography* (Albuquerque: University of New Mexico Press, 2007), 79.

2. Josefina Niggli, *The Ring of General Macías*, in Martinez, *Josefina Niggli*, 106–7.

3. Although "America" for Niggli and Latin American intellectuals refers to the continent—where freedom from European control was desired—here "American" will be used as a descriptor of the United States and not for the continent or hemisphere.

4. Those nearest the border relocated temporarily for greater safety, some never returning. Those farther away arrived to recreate their businesses, such as the grandfather of Henry Cisneros (former mayor of San Antonio), who left Mexico City in 1926 after federal raids on his printing press offices. As a teenager, Henry worked in his grandfather's printing press in San Antonio.

5. Long-standing Spanish colonial haciendas had been taken by force by new settlers. From 1836 to 1860, new population in Texas soared from the thirty thousand Hispanic and Anglo settlers prior to 1836 to more than six hundred thousand (not counting Indians or Hispanics). Indians, estimated at fifteen thousand in the 1830s, decreased to eight thousand. After the annexation of Texas and other regions acquired from Mexico in 1848, the original Spanish-language settlers lost out: their land grant deeds were declared invalid, their cattle were stolen, and established businesses (such as the commerce of salt from lakes near El Paso—an Indian-Mexican venture) were taken over. In rural regions people were lynched. See William Carrigan, "The Lynching of Persons of Mexican Origin or Descent in the United States, 1848–1928," *Journal of Social History* 37.2 (Winter 2003): 411–38; see also William Carrigan and Clive Webb, *Forgotten Dead: Mob Violence against Mexicans in the United States, 1848–1928* (New York: Oxford University Press, 2013).

6. Juan Seguín's grandparents were among the original Spanish colonial settlers in 1712. After Mexican independence, Seguín—born in San Antonio in 1806—served on several electoral boards and briefly became mayor of San Antonio in 1834 but was openly critical of the new president, Antonio López de Santa Anna (who disbanded the Congress, becoming dictator in 1824). He

was a member of the group that would declare its independence from Mexico and became a key member of the new republic's army. Present at the Alamo under siege, he was sent out as a courier (because of his knowledge of Spanish) prior to the final battle. Seguín served as elected senator from Texas from 1837 to 1840 and worked closely with Congressman Juan Antonio Navarro to introduce and support legislation to support the interests of the native citizenry of Texas. Having won a second term as mayor of San Antonio in 1841, Seguín had to leave Texas due to threats on his life by incoming residents (and lost all of his properties). After the war of 1846–48 he returned to Texas and served two terms as justice of the peace of Bexar County, where he founded a chapter of the Democratic Party. Later he served a term as judge in Wilson County before being forced to flee Texas again, due to increasing murder rates and the burning of properties by incoming migrants from the U.S. Southeast. He died in Nuevo Laredo; decades later his remains were removed to Seguin, Texas.

7. On the changes to voting status, see Alwyn Barr, "Late Nineteenth-Century Texas," *Handbook of Texas Online* (Austin: Texas State Historical Association), uploaded June 15, 2010, http://www.tshaonline.org/handbook/online/articles/npl01, accessed 23 June 2013. See also Spencer Overton, *Stealing Democracy: The New Politics of Voter Suppression* (New York: W. W. Norton, 2006), for its frequent references to Texas voter suppression.

8. See Gary Anderson, *The Conquest of Texas: Ethnic Cleansing in the Promised Land, 1820–1875* (Norman: University of Oklahoma Press, 2005). In this anthology, we use the term "American Indians" to refer to the nations, tribes, and individuals native to the territory of the continental United States. For an explanation, please see chapter 9, n. 4.

9. Juan González, *Harvest of Empire: A History of Latinos in America* (New York: Penguin, 2011), 236.

10. No differentiation was made between the two: in rural areas both spoke Spanish (the native indigenous had learned Spanish in order to trade with Santa Fe), and both were indigenous in appearance. For example, a newspaper in Austin in 1870 described the Comanches as both "Mexican tiger[s]" and "rattlesnake[s]." See Stanley Noyes, *Los Comanches: The Horse People, 1751–1845* (Albuquerque: University of New Mexico Press, 1993).

11. The "sleeping Mexican" was an artistic rendering depicted on the pink glass ornaments of the early century (now valued by collectors). During the 1930s a Tucson café made it a classic Arizona emblem, producing matchbook covers with the figure resting under the shade of a tall saguaro cactus. By the 1950s the image proliferated on a variety of souvenir emblems (some made in Mexico), furniture, and statuary, popular with the growth of automobile tourism. Despite signifying rest from work or a long journey during the heat

of day, the figure later took on an allusion to mañana and laziness and became the *only* image applied to the Mexican.

12. Mexicans (some born in the United States) were rounded up and deported en masse during the hardships of the Depression and again after the Second World War, including those recruited to cities such as Detroit, Chicago, and Kansas City in the 1920s, during worker strikes at meat packing plants and automobile assembly lines.

13. Elizabeth Coonrod Martínez, *Josefina Niggli, Mexican American Writer: A Critical Biography* (Albuquerque: University of New Mexico Press, 2007), 282.

14. Brenner's experience is similar to Niggli's, having being born in Aguascalientes, Mexico, but arriving in Texas during the revolutionary struggle and completing college there. She also wrote and published in English about Mexico.

15. Walter Spearman, *The Carolina Playmakers: The First Fifty Years* (Chapel Hill: University of North Carolina Press, 1970), 36.

16. Frederick Koch, *American Folk Plays* (New York: Appleton-Century, 1939), xvi–xvii. Emphasis in original.

17. Spearman, *Carolina Playmakers*, 52.

18. One other "Latino" example depicts a cigar-making plant based in the Cuban community in Ybor City (a neighborhood of Tampa), Florida. This play was not written by a member of the Carolina Playmakers but was produced by the Southeast FTP (which Koch supervised) and was included in Koch's 1939 collection, *American Folk Plays*, under the category "Spanish Florida."

19. Nicolás Kanellos argues that San Antonio was not large enough, or politically powerful enough, to attract or support productions of new plays (*A History of Hispanic Theatre in the United States: Origins to 1940* [Austin: University of Texas Press, 1990], 71). This may also explain why Niggli left San Antonio.

20. Nicolás Kanellos, *A History of Hispanic Theatre in the United States: Origins to 1940* (Austin: University of Texas Press, 1990), 100–103.

21. Ibid., 73.

22. Newspaper article in Josefina Niggli Archives, Western Carolina University, Cullowhee, N.C. Also see Martínez, *Josefina Niggli*, 48–49. Although Niggli likely meant "Mexican" theatre, she uses "Spanish" as the more prevalent term for any Spanish-speaking person of that era.

23. Judith A. Weiss, *Latin American Popular Theatre: The First Five Centuries* (Albuquerque: University of New Mexico Press, 1993), 21–22.

24. Direct, overt messages were more difficult to stage. An FTP-sponsored play in Boston, *Created Equal* (1938), sought to reframe U.S. history from the

perspective of the masses, challenging viewers to reconsider events and minimize veneration of "founding father" figures and crediting working-class and African American participation in the nation's formation. But due to pressures from local political authorities, the script was never produced as originally written. Elizabeth Osborne, *Staging the People: Community and Identity in the Federal Theatre Project* (New York: Palgrave Macmillan, 2011), 54–57.

25. Quote from Koch, *American Folk Plays*, xxvi. Niggli demonstrated correct as well as erroneous usage of terms in Western lore that are derived from Spanish vocabulary in her instructional book, *Pointers for Playwriting* (1945).

26. Due to its popularity, this play was collected that year for *Contemporary One-Act Plays* (New York: Scribner) and a few years later in *Plays without Footlights* (New York: Harcourt Brace, 1945).

27. Martínez, *Josefina Niggli*, 40.

28. Ibid., 122.

29. Américo Paredes, ed., *Mexican American Authors* (Boston: Houghton Mifflin, 1972).

30. All of these revolutionary heroes paid dearly for their heroism. Allende and Hidalgo were soon captured by royal troops and beheaded; their heads hung in the central plaza for weeks. Josefa Domínguez spent many years in jail and lost her home and all her possessions.

31. Quoted in Martínez, *Josefina Niggli*, 51. On the other hand, her former professor, Walter Spearman, who apparently neglected to read her foreword to this play, trivialized Niggli's portrayals in his own introduction, calling her characters "childlike, but intensely alive" (Spearman, *Carolina Playmakers*, 71).

32. Tey Diana Rebolledo, *Women Singing in the Snow* (Tucson: University of Arizona Press, 1995), 25–26.

33. For more on theatrical treatments of the Adelita archetype, see Alicia Arrizón, "Soldaderas and the Staging of the Mexican Revolution," *TDR: The Drama Review; A Journal of Performance Studies* 42.1 (Spring 1998): 90–112. Tey Diana Rebolledo also discusses literary treatment of the Adelita image in *Women Singing in the Snow*.

34. Niggli acted as one of the supporting characters in the premiere performance of *Soldadera*. The play was selected for *The Best One-Act Plays of 1937*. *This Is Villa!* earned the same distinction in 1938 and was also published the following year in *One-Act Play Magazine*.

35. *The Ring of General Macías* was published in *Twenty Prize-Winning, Non Royalty One-Act Plays* (1943) and later in *Close-Up: A Collection of Short Plays* (1970), a scholastic series published by Glencoe/McGraw-Hill. It continues to be performed and taught by drama instructors and has been translated to Spanish.

36. Raymund Paredes, "Early Mexican American Literature," in *A Literary History of the American West*, ed. J. Golden Taylor and Thomas J. Lyon (Fort Worth: Texas Christian University Press, 1987), 1093–94.

37. From her talk included in the *Proceedings of the First Congress of Historians of Mexico and United States* (convened September 1949), published 1950; the Congress's notes are included in such journals as *Cuadernos mexicanos*, *Revista de Historia de México*, and *Library of Congress Information Bulletin*. Also see Martínez, *Josefina Niggli*, 151–52.

38. R. Paredes, "Early Mexican American Literature," 1093.

39. Koch, *American Folk Plays*, xxii–xxiii.

7. The Politics of Black Masculinity in Theodore Browne's *Natural Man* (1937)

Harry J. Elam Jr.

African American playwright Theodore Browne's expressionistic play *Natural Man*, written in 1937, reverberates with continuing relevance into more recent periods in American history in how it considers the meanings and possibilities of black masculinity. In the wake of the nationally broadcast and widely discussed 2013 Trayvon Martin trial—in which a Florida jury acquitted George Zimmerman, a white Hispanic man, of second degree murder in the killing of Trayvon Martin, a black teenager—many pondered over the social roles and limitations placed on black males in America, much as Browne did more than seventy-five years earlier in *Natural Man*. In fact, Browne's 1937 play offers a telling rejoinder to the recurring patterns of what James Baldwin called the "menacing" of black men.

Historical race-driven perceptions have affected and continue to inform every facet of the lives of the black male, as evidenced through contemporary statistics on racial profiling by police and the disproportionate numbers of black men in America's prisons. Responding to the protests that both preceded the Trayvon Martin trial and followed its conclusion in July 2013, the first black American president, Barack Obama, addressed the nation on the need for a renewed focus on African American males:

> This is a long-term project—we need to spend some time in thinking about how do we bolster and reinforce our African American boys. And this is something that Michelle and I talk a lot about. There are a lot of kids out there who need help who are getting a lot of negative reinforcement. And is there more that we can do to give them the sense that their country cares about them and values them and is willing to invest in them?[1]

Obama's call for new attention to the issues around black male identity in the United States references a painful legacy and its lingering effects, one that

Browne also seeks to address in *Natural Man*. Noting the powerful impact of representations of black men emanating from slavery and still playing out on the national landscape, black novelist and columnist Trey Ellis observed in 1995, "We [black men] have become the international symbol for rape, murder, robbery, and uncontrolled libido."[2] The staying power of these representations of black masculinity informed the public responses to the Trayvon Martin case—from the initial outrage at Martin's shooting, to the racially tinged social media posts of Zimmerman's brother, to the verdict of the jury, just as it contributes to scenarios within Browne's *Natural Man*.

On 9 August 2014, the fatal shooting of Michael Brown, an eighteen-year-old black man, by a white police officer in Ferguson, Missouri, further exacerbated the continuing crises surrounding the tenuous position of young black men in America. Unrest soon ensued in Ferguson. Notably, the local police department overacted in its attempts to quell the demonstrations by assembling 150 heavily armed officers in riot gear. The cause in Ferguson immediately gained national attention and outrage and eventually became an international movement highlighting the need for more focus on and response to the police's unequal and often overly violent involvement with black communities. This movement emphasizes and operates under the banner "Black Lives Matter." Tellingly, in his prescient essay written in 1962 as a letter of warning to his nephew and published later in *The Fire Next Time*, James Baldwin bemoans his nephew's fate as a black man in America: "You were born where you were born and faced the future you faced because you were black and for *no other reason*."[3] Baldwin's words reflect not only the situation of his nephew in the 1960s but also that of Trayvon Martin in Florida and Michael Brown in Ferguson in the new millennium. The context for and the condition of their existence as black men in America made them inherently at risk.

Writing about black men in the coal mines of West Virginia in the 1930s, Theodore Browne in *Natural Man* picks up this tragic and all too familiar theme. The fate of the black hero, John Henry, has been predetermined even before the start of the play and even prior to his agreement to race against the steam drill. As a black man in his particular time and circumstances, John Henry has few options. His employment, his social mobility, and his welfare are all restricted by race. Thus, both symbolically and literally, John Henry yearns to escape to a place where "natural men" like himself are no longer persecuted and where he can be free.

And yet, despite the precarious nature of black manhood, in contemporary American culture as well as in Browne's Depression-era construction of *Natural Man*, the representations and perceptions of black masculinity are replete with complexity. The image of the black man as brute-thug exists paradoxically alongside that of the black man as athletic paragon. Henry Louis Gates Jr., in *Thirteen Ways of Looking at a Black Man*—rephrasing W. E. B. Du Bois's famous, incendiary earlier question from *The Souls of Black Folk* "How does it feel to be a problem?"[4]—asks, "How does it feel to be a paradox?"[5] A most notable embodiment of this contradiction is the 2014 Super Bowl–winning Seattle Seahawks star cornerback Richard Sherman. Following the National Football Conference Championship game, Sherman, the dreadlock-wearing honors graduate from Stanford University, was vilified in the media and called a "thug" for his physical play and bravado outburst and at the same time celebrated for eloquence and intelligence in interviews. Sherman parlayed his notoriety into lucrative television endorsements as well as a football contract worth more than $40 million. This paradox embodied by Sherman enables the black male to be at once "all that is dangerous" and "the envy of the world," as journalist-author Ellis Cose proposed in a 2002 treatise "on being a black man in America."[6]

Similarly, in *Natural Man*, the legend of John Henry, a black male figure now of mythical status, becomes the site for exploration of this paradoxical positioning of black masculinity. Historically, the representation of John Henry as popular superhero has worked in concert with the negative stereotypes of black deviance. Like larger-than-life black sports stars in the twenty-first century, such as basketball players Kobe Bryant and LeBron James with their international fame and following, Browne's John Henry competes at the highest physical level and exceeds expectations. This steel-driving man battles against a steam drill and wins. Within *Natural Man*, Browne employs the legend of John Henry as an impetus for a complex and progressive reconsideration of the historical conditions and more contemporary perceptions of black masculinity.

Equally complex as its representations of black masculinity are the play's attempts at cross-cultural exchange. The play originally debuted as part of the Federal Theatre Project, an ultimately failed effort at federally subsidized and imperfectly integrated theatre. White directors mounted the play with its majority-black cast. Browne effectively uses the white European–derived aesthetics of expressionism to tell the story of African American folk hero John Henry. While the legend of John Henry has had a particular resonance for African Americans, he equally has become a figure of national significance and folklore. Thus interracial communion informs the play, even as Browne speaks particularly about African American experience. In consort with the underlying themes of this anthology, *Natural Man* offers the hope of a more pluralistic democracy.

Natural Man interrogates the image of black masculinity and reveals the challenge of black masculine achievement under the repressive racial conditions of Depression-era America. Because of the familiarity of the legend, John Henry's fate is never in doubt from the outset of *Natural Man*. Thus, the questions become how Browne uses and interprets this tale, how he shapes its action to comment on race, and how he reimagines the legend and situates it meanings. Rather than just existing as a passive mythic figure, Browne's John Henry is aware of the racism around him and angered by it. He speaks out. He fights back. He is a symbol of unyielding African American determination to persevere and survive against seemingly overwhelming odds. In Browne's episodic telling, John Henry wanders the American South desperately searching for a place for the "natural man." This concept of the "natural man" defines not only the way John Henry understands his own identity but also how he imagines other black men like himself. Ultimately, after finding some sense of respite digging tunnels on the railroad lines, John Henry dies after victoriously fighting with the steam drill. As it chronicles the life of John Henry, the play explores the relation between a racialized workforce (in this case, the convict lease system) and urbanization and between lingering racism and advancing technology.

As the title of his play suggests, Browne riffs on what is "natural" or essentialized in terms of race. Historically, in televised and written sports commentary, white announcers have repeatedly defined black athletes as "naturally gifted" and in so doing have denied their hard work, intelligence, and knowledge of the game. Accordingly, the title *Natural Man* plays on such existent stereotypes of black naturalness. It repeats and revises the conventional, patronizing meanings of what is "natural." John Henry—the prototypical black buck, black criminal, larger-than-life heroic figure, a specimen possessing superhuman strength—seemingly reinforces the notions of "the natural" as inbred black difference, as a sexualized, racialized, and primitivized animalistic prowess. Browne, rather than reaffirm such notions, shows the natural not to be ontological or essential but to be "man-made," constructed even. Such a notion of the "natural man" stands in opposition to the all-consuming power of technology and the all-too-oppressive connotations of black masculinity. The "natural" becomes a site of freedom, black self-determination, and difference, as it purposefully offers a point of liberatory resistance.

Moreover, the play does not traffic in the idea of the hypersexualized, hyperathleticized black male body. Significantly, there are few scenes of John Henry flexing his might. The play does not depict John Henry just as a black body. In fact, his black body is not always visible. The battle with the steam engine occurs offstage, inside the tunnel. The flashback moments show him struggling to fit in a society that has no space for the natural man. The sense of the natural in this play is not fixed but subject to different articulations. It most particularly speaks to the ability of black men to move toward self-definition: to stand in the face of white oppression and to exercise resistance and assert self in the face of a white patriarchy that limits black male access to the tools of social progress, as exemplified by the steam drill.

Musical and Historical Contexts

Through eight expressionistic scenes that reimagine the John Henry legend, Browne's play conjoins issues of racial liberation and class with questions of mechanization and modernity. Stylistically and thematically, Browne's appropriation of the principally European genre of expressionism links *Natural Man* to earlier significant white American experiments in expressionism of the 1920s. Plays such as *The Hairy Ape* by Eugene O'Neill (1922), *The Adding Machine* by Elmer Rice (1923), and *Machinal* by Sophie Treadwell (1928) pit a singular alienated human protagonist against the forces of expanding industrialization. In these plays, central figures struggle for belonging in a world where they just cannot fit until they ultimately succumb to death. Their deaths serve as moments of symbolic martyrdom with wider social ramifications. Similarly, Theodore Browne takes his protagonist on a journey—returning John Henry to his past through flashbacks and resurrecting key flashpoints in his life that contribute to his present predicament. Socially estranged and alone, John Henry feels "like a giant in a strait jacket,"[7] constrained by a world that does not recognize his strength or his greatness. Desperately, John Henry searches for a place where he fits; however, the white-controlled social order, with its confining limits placed on black existence, offers no safe harbor. Notably, the expressionist aesthetics underscore the cultural politics of the content, as Browne equates the ominous technological capacity of the steam engine to the suffocating authority of white hegemony. Thus, even as John Henry's victory over the steam engine leads to his demise, it still functions as a strategic triumph over white oppression, a reaffirmation of black masculinity and a harbinger of revolutionary actions to come.

Browne's prominent use of music further separates *Natural Man* from those earlier American adaptations of expressionism and serves to underscore his interrogation of black masculinity. First staged as a "folk opera" in 1937, *Natural Man* in its published form is more a play with music than a "musical." The play features blues and gospel performed by a live ensemble. Thus, music helps to position the play within a black vernacular tradition as it draws on the folk stature of the central character. The music in *Natural Man* repeats and revises the folk music associated with the mythic figure of John Henry as it also sets the mood, heightens the emotional context, and reinforces the meanings of the episodic scenes. In the first episode, set at the entrance to Big Ben Tunnel in West Virginia on the day preceding the "great contest between John Henry and the steam drill," John Henry hammers and sings:

> Ain't no hammer—huh!
> In these mountains—huh!
> Rings like mine, boys—huh
> Rings like mine—huh!
> (344)

The exuberance of the song and its lyrics points to John Henry's self-assuredness and his assertion of his difference from others. The repeated "huhs" not only buttress the thunderous rhythms of the hammering but also establish the inexorable rhythm of the piece, culminating in the battle with the steam engine and John Henry's ultimate death. The musical moments within the play feature predominantly male voices, principally that of John Henry. Through these lyrical interludes, Browne foregrounds prevalent and conventional representations of black manhood while showing John Henry's resistance to such limiting definitions of his own identity. The music of *Natural Man*, then, is not merely entertaining but also functional and political. It supports the mythic nature of the folk hero John Henry even as it underscores the real context of racial subjugation and social alienation that the protagonist endures.

The original production of *Natural Man* occurred during the tenure of an important racial, theatrical, and cultural undertaking: the Federal Theatre Project (FTP). The Seattle Negro unit of the FTP first staged *Natural Man* on 28 January 1937. Under the direction of Hallie Flanagan, the FTP (which ran from 1935 to 1939) reflects the only time the United States has operated a fully federally subsidized national theatre program. As a part of the Works Progress Administration's New Deal Arts Projects, the objective of the Negro Federal Theatre Project was to put black theatre practitioners, actors, directors, designers, and technicians back to work after the Great Depression. More than twenty black FTP units sprang up in thirteen cities across the country, including New York, Boston, and Seattle.[8]

As noted by Rena Fraden in *Blueprints for a Black Federal Theatre*, the Negro unit in Seattle put on "some of the most experimental productions of any Negro unit, partly due to the direction of white theatre practitioners Florence and Burton James, who taught at the University of Washington."[9] Elizabeth A. Osborne's analysis in chapter 9 of the often problematic representations of Native Americans offered by the FTP and Margaret F. Savilonis's study in chapter 8 of Myra Kinch's work with the Los Angeles Dance Unit reveal a recurring pattern within the FTP of representations that slipped at times into stereotypes. This tendency could also be seen within the Negro units and their representation of black characters. In Seattle, the black actors needed to educate their white directors about cultural archetypes and to inform their understandings of black dialect. Burton and Florence James had also previously founded the Seattle Repertory Playhouse; consequently, they were familiar with fledgling theatrical ventures. As Fraden goes on to point out, Seattle possessed a talented pool of professional black actors. It was this combination of circumstances that informed the expressionistic production of *Natural Man*.[10] According to Barry Witham, the Seattle Negro unit's production of *Natural Man*, which ran for nearly one month in 1937,

> exhibited all their strengths: Theodore Browne's lyric writing; [Joseph] Staton's powerful performance as the steel-driving "natural man"; a superb chorus to carry the audience from one scene to the next and to underscore the tragedy of this legendary black folk hero; an excellent supporting cast and original music by the young Howard Biggs, a composer in the raw whom they had discovered in their midst.[11]

Witham's description of Biggs as a "composer in the raw" strikes an ironic parallel to the notion of the "natural" espoused in the play, activating also the stereotypical notion of black performers as naturally gifted rather than professionally trained.

Theodore Browne, who served as the associate director and resident playwright for the Seattle Negro unit and also acted in two productions, believed in the activist potential of black theatre. He maintained, "I've always felt strongly about a Negro Peoples Theatre that emphasizes the heroic aspects of the black experience—the Exemplars who triumphed over the odds."[12] In addition to *Natural Man*—originally titled "This Ole Hammer"—the Seattle unit mounted three other plays: an adaptation of Aristophanes's *Lysistrata* set in Ethiopia; *A Black Woman Called Moses*, a play about Harriet Tubman; and a musical revue, *Swing, Gates, Swing.* In 1940, Browne left Seattle for New York and the American Negro Theatre (ANT). The ANT staged *Natural Man* as its second production in 1941 at the 135th Street Library Theatre in Harlem. The cast included noted African American actors Stanley Greene (as John Henry), Alvin and Alice Childress, and Ruby Wallace (soon to change her name to Ruby Dee). According to Doris Abramson and Henry D. Miller, the ANT's production featured nine episodes, rather than the eight in the Seattle production and the published script.[13] The ninth scene, an additional flashback, features John Henry in the North as a strikebreaking scab worker confronting white union workers for equal rights to employment:

> FIRST: We white workers can't get a living wage scale for you goddamned niggers!
>
> JOHN HENRY: Colored folks entitled to live the same as you whites.
>
> SECOND: They ain't entitled to buck no union.
>
> JOHN HENRY: We ain't aiming to buck no union.
>
> FIRST: No, you ain't! Not much!
>
> JOHN HENRY: We just doing what we got a right to do—work.[14]

This scene exhibits the same demands for black equality expressed in the other scenes but now situates them in the context of northern job markets rather than in the South. In addition, Abramson points to a different ending for the ANT production from the ending to the published version, to be discussed later. According to Abramson, John Henry emerges in the final episode from the tunnel drained from battle:

> There is a robot on a landing, a "full sized mechanical man." John Henry, weary to the point of utter exhaustion, wrestles with it. He throws the mechanical creature into the blackness of the tunnel, then staggers and falls from the landing to the floor. John Henry dies in his wife's arms. The robot can be heard, the steam drill at work in the tunnel.[15]

While this ending described by Abramson does emphasize the battle of man against machine and the mechanization of society, it does not foreground the triumph of John Henry over oppression, nor does it augur a vision of transcendent masculinity, as the published ending does.

In keeping with most myths, the story of John Henry is certainly based—at least in part—on historical circumstance. In the late 1800s, as the country recovered from the Civil War, railroad tracks began to stitch the nation together. The legend of John Henry embodies the spirit of American expansion evident at that time. In order to build the new railroad lines, companies hired workers to dig through rock and other impediments to prepare the land for the laying of track. "Steel-drivin' men" like John Henry hammered holes in those rocks and then used explosives to blast cavities into the mountains. This was also a story of interracial relations, interdependence, and exploitation. Cheap black labor in the postwar South as part of the convict lease system—a morally bankrupt system of indentured servitude, where white railroad owners bought the service of black convicts and compelled them to labor on the railroad, without compensation, to pay off a debt to society—became a critical component of the railroad construction process across the South. Railroad engineers of the 1880s, desiring a method to speed up the process and cut down on human labor—like the wealthy northern carpetbagger Browne also introduces into the play—invested in the steam drill as a more efficient method to blast through the rock.

Natural Man underscores the historic black indentured servitude on the railroad as symbolic of an oppressive social system that constrained the mobility of black men. In chapter 5, Cheryl Black and Anne Fletcher show how playwright Albert Maltz connects institutional racism to the class struggle in the mines of West Virginia. Browne similarly explores the connections between race and class. Writing in the shadow of the Great Depression, playwrights Maltz and Browne both sought to use their plays as means to express social ends. Just before the steel-driving contest in the second episode of *Natural Man*, the white railroad boss Captain Tommy boasts, "Most of my boys are handpicked. I do the hiring and firing around here. I get most of them off the chain gang. Pay their fines, give them a chance to work it off. Some of them boys were up for life. I buy their freedom and give them a new start" (348). Despite Captain Tommy's stated gestures toward benevolence, this convict lease system amounted to another form of slavery that victimized black men. As such, black male laborers had no chance for freedom or escape from their peonage. John Henry's only opportunity for liberation comes through death after his victory over the steam drill.

Historians dispute where the legend and the story of the battle with the steam drill originate. As country musician Merle Travis notes, "There's been dozens and dozens of different tales about where John Henry comes from."[16] Some have placed John Henry's epic battle in 1887 in Alabama; a strong local tradition maintains that John Henry raced a steam drill and died just outside the east portal of Oak Mountain Tunnel. In some versions of the folk song "John Henry," there are lines consistent with the Alabama location. However, at least two pre-1930 versions of the folk ballad "John Henry" place him on "the Georgia line" or on "the Central Georgia Rail Road." Still, many versions of the legend, including Browne's *Natural Man* and the 2002 novel by Colson Whitehead called *John Henry Days*, place John Henry's battle with the steam drill at the Big Bend Tunnel near the town of Talcott in Summers County, West Virginia.

Whatever the locale or the origin of the tale, the legend of John Henry has come to symbolize the triumph of the underdog and the power of perseverance against overwhelming odds—for Americans generally, and for black Americans specifically. In superhuman fashion, John Henry stood up to the steam drill and in so doing championed the power of the human spirit and of black resistance. John Henry's epic battle with the steam engine became celebrated in children's stories, postage stamps, film, and of course theatre, but above all through song. "John Henry" remains the single most well known and often recorded American folk ballad, popular with audiences regardless of their race. The enduring and ever-evolving myth of John Henry points to the symbolic power of this heroic icon. Indeed, John Henry has made his way into not only cultural but also medical vernacular. As Claude Steele notes, "The social psychologist Sherman James uses the term 'John Henryism' to describe a psychological syndrome that he found to be in association with hypertension in several samples of North Carolina blacks: holding too rigidly to the faith that discrimination and disadvantage can be overcome with hard work and persistence."[17] Even within this potentially deleterious psychological condition, John Henry signifies black obstinacy and opposition in the face of white oppression.

Complexities of Black Masculinity

From the outset of the play, John Henry must confront white oppression as well as battle conventional perceptions of black masculinity. Browne sets the first episode before the entrance to the Big Ben Tunnel at noon, lunchtime. Accordingly, this worksite lunch hour provides the optimal locale to present the stereotypical images of black male appetites. Whether in terms of food, sex, or deviant behaviors, black masculine physical desire has been noted for its overdetermination and excess. The black men lounging around the front of the tunnel sing a song in homage to their yearning for the proper, manly sustenance: "*Celery, lettuce—that's rabbit food / Bring me some sow-belly and beans*" (344). The song is humorous, and yet the representation of a chorus of black men singing it suggests that they too have ingested the stereotype. As Patricia Hill Collins writes:

> Definitions of black masculinity in the United States reflect a narrow cluster of controlling images situated within a broader framework that grants varying value to racially distinctive forms of masculinity. Arrayed along a continuum, virtually all of the representations of black masculinity pivot on questions of weakness, whether it is a weakness associated with inability to control violent impulses, sexual urges, or their black female heterosexual partners or weakness attributed to men whose lack of education, employment patterns or criminal records relegate them to inferior social spaces.[18]

Collins's notion of pivoting on "questions of weakness" informs the images that Browne constructs of John Henry's compatriots. Relegated to "inferior social spaces," they laze around, joke, and eat. They operate within the limited definitions of black manhood available to them. Thus, when John Henry's girlfriend, Polly Ann, arrives with his lunch, the other men led by Hard Tack jokingly come on to her in song:

> Well I ain't no lover,
> No lover's son,
> But, Baby, I can do your loving
> Till your lover come. (345)

Their inability or unwillingness as black men to regulate their appetites is comically on display.

John Henry stands in stark contrast to these images of weakness as he represents a figure of black male assuredness. While the other men lounge about over their lunches, John Henry continues to work in the tunnel. He wants to keep practicing in preparation for the battle with the steam drill the following day. Yet his preparations are not simply about brute strength and physical dominance; the mind must play a critical role. John Henry relates, "Can hardly wait. Studying how I'm going beat that old steam drill down, figuring it out this kind of stroke, and figuring some other till my brains whirl like a spinning top" (346). Moreover, John Henry argues that he has a historic right to the victory and primacy over the steam drill because of his pioneering work on the railroad. "Now, who come first? Me or this man-made steam drill? Who fixed it so locomotive engine can have a track to run on? Who? Well, it was me, that's who! I come first" (346). Positioning himself as the first, as a forerunner and innovator, John Henry contrasts himself with the man-made steam drill. In his vision, the battle is not simply about the future but about the ability to remember the past and the achievement of black steel drivers like Henry himself. He reflects and remembers past achievement even as he structures an alternative path for the present.

Still, John Henry in *Natural Man* is a black man who is, according to Mark Anthony Neal, "bound to and bound by [his] legibility."[19] Neal points out that the legibility of black masculinity marks black men and constrains them while justifying "the lynching of black male bodies after emancipation or the maintenance of anti-miscegenation laws and Black Codes."[20] The legibility and hypervisibility of black males as criminal and deviant justified the construction of laws that sought to contain, control, and punish such legibility. One could argue that for George Zimmerman, Trayvon Martin was "bound to and bound by [his] legibility," and this compelled Zimmerman to follow Trayvon on that fateful night. Most certainly in *Natural Man*, John Henry's white railroad boss, Captain Tommy, seeks to reinforce John Henry's boundedness and his legibility; just before the epic battle, Captain Tommy threatens to return John Henry to the chain gang if he does not win against the steam engine. John Henry's desire to escape such boundedness and controlling legibility plays out repeatedly in the scenes that flash back to critical moments of his earlier life. In these remembrances, Browne posits John Henry in spaces—a bar, a prison cell, a church revival meeting—that inhibit his expression of difference and prove decidedly unsympathetic to a natural man. John Henry's restlessness in and impatience with these environs stand as a critique of black subjugation but also as an indictment of black complacency within these conditions. Whether he sits at a bar or in his prison cell, due to his lack of understanding of and belonging in the world around him, John Henry remains caught within a system that constrains him and does not allow for exploration of self-determination or agency. This world does not see him as he want to be seen but rather constrains him and his freedom.

A black troubadour character known as Creeper introduces the flashback scenes and their significance to both the audience and to John Henry. The appearance of Creeper in the first episode foregrounds the inevitability of John Henry's fate. Creeper foreshadows the end of the play at the beginning by promising John Henry that he will "be with you to the end" and by informing John Henry's fellow steel drivers that, while he is unable to play for them today, he will surely play and sing something for them on the day of the competition: "Play something for you. Something special. Song I make up bout John Henry. I has a heap of songs, and they's all about John Henry, too" (348). Browne's stage directions describe Creeper as a "*small, nondescript Negro . . . in mismatched garish attire. A black troubadour, he carries a canvas-covered guitar case. [He] is to be a one-man Chorus to underscore the legend-in-the making charisma of John Henry*" (347). These stage directions point to Creeper's metatheatrical function as chorus and commentator. Creeper's garish dress and broken-down guitar case signify his folk roots and his existence as a fellow traveler along the roads that John Henry has traversed. John Henry acknowledges their long relationship: "And you like a buzzard waiting 'round for something to heave its last breath" (347). Yet representing the chorus as solely one voice, that of Creeper, eliminates the excess "noise" of different versions and interpretations and presents a commentary that foregrounds a certain appreciation of this particular John Henry, his odyssey, and his struggle for freedom.

A Liberatory Black Masculinity

The concept of freedom is critical in these flashback moments and more generally to John Henry's quest to find a space where he can belong as a natural man. The third episode of *Natural Man* finds John Henry drinking in a Beale Street bar with a prostitute. The denizens of this urban environment, described by Browne as "*characters out of the Negro underworld*," provide a telling contrast to the "natural" John Henry. They experience a distinctive type of freedom as they survive outside of the mainstream rules and expectations. They thrive within the seedy underbelly of the city, while John Henry feels himself trapped within the very same environment. John Henry seeks to break out of his confines through drink, but the liquor only reminds him of his exploits on the railroad and his inability to escape the system of white oppression.

The Beale Street inhabitants of the black underworld represent an alternative site of black resistance. Street hustling—with its denial of conventional wage labor, its defiance of black subservience, its distrust for and clever abuse of white authority, as well as its strategic location on the margins of society—was an explicitly resistant lifestyle. For black men (both past and present) who find the system stacked against them, "hustling," breaking the law, and attempting to beat that system can become significant declarations of black manhood. And yet this episode of *Natural Man* shows the limitation of such strategies of black criminality, which not only express but also repress black opposition. The system is parasitic, not progressive, as Beale Street's "Sweet" men and women feed off their exploitation of each other. The Sweet men sing,

> You know a man's fool to work,
> When women are so free.
> Gonna always have a sweet mama
> Doing my work for me. (352)

Due to his naïveté regarding street culture, John Henry succumbs to the cunning of a pickpocket and ends up being thrown in jail.

Browne similarly critiques the conventional and historic faith in black religion as a means of hope and potential liberation. The play's sixth episode, set at a church camp revival, opens with a black preacher urging his congregation to accept Jesus before they die. He offers Christian faith as a salve for sins and an escape for the trials and tribulations of earthly life. "Open up your troubled hearts to Jesus. Don't wait till you sick and afflicted on your dying-bed to call to Him" (358). Consequently, the preacher suggests to his congregation that Jesus represents the ultimate support, the answer to all problems. Belief in the afterlife, the preacher urges, will allow the congregation to persevere and survive. Implicit is the message that the black parishioners, through faith in the savior Jesus Christ, can break free of the racial limitations placed on them. Religion can serve as opiate. Yet Browne points to the hypocrisy in the preacher's practice and spiritual belief system. For when John Henry presents himself before the preacher and his gathered flock as a sinner in need of spiritual sustenance, they reject him. After he confesses that he has killed a white guard on a chain gang and has run away (as depicted in the fifth episode), John Henry expects that the congregation will understand, accept him, and pray with him. Instead, they move away, fearful of how his actions might reflect upon all of them. "You ain't oughta come here," the preacher warns (359). Similarly, the congregation castigates him, "Us cain't help no convict! We's God-fearing people. . . . Man, you stay here, you bring trouble to all us colored folks" (360). Rather than extend "Christian charity" and acceptance, the preacher and his flock feel threatened by John Henry's perceived criminality and expression of black masculinity.

The preacher offers a bleak view of Christian charity and the place for the natural man within conventional Christianity. "The world, my Brother, ain't made for the natural man. God ain't around to protect you no more. God's turnt his back on this sinful world. Washed his hands clean of this abomination. I say woe unto the natural man. Woe unto the high and the mighty" (360). The preacher suggests that the image of black masculinity offered by John Henry is not compatible with the society around him. There is no place to be a proud and strong black man. Moreover, the natural man cannot expect the safety and succor of God as his politics are not in line with conservatism and the reactionary stance espoused by the preacher. Not only does the preacher urge John Henry to return to the chain gang and be judged by "the law of man," but he also instructs him to "turn the other cheek" and "git humble" before the Lord (360). He warns that the activist stance that John Henry has taken in the face of white oppression is one that he cannot condone. Rather, it should be replaced by subordination.

In contrast, Browne uses John Henry to project a more liberatory or radical theology. Unmoved by the calls of the preacher to "git down low," John Henry stands tall and rebuffs the pleas for complacency. "Oh, Lord, I ain't got nothing ginst your mighty laws and rulings but I ain't going to allow no man-made laws to rule over me!" (360). John Henry points to the injustice of certain laws and the need to rebel against such conditions. Certainly, at key moments in African American history, lawbreaking has proven justified as a means of resisting unjust rules and mistreatment. Accordingly, with the laws of property that governed black lives in slavery or during the imposition of Jim Crow laws in the nineteenth century, black lawbreaking constituted acts of rebellion in the name of freedom. Similarly, John Henry now understands his act in the previous episode of saving a sickly black convict from being abused by a white prison guard to be justified by a higher law and code of righteousness. No longer willing to watch this mistreatment, John Henry uses his massive strength to strike against the guard and kill him.

John Henry also critiques the preacher's dogma in the advice he provides to an older woman who had asked for prayers of forgiveness for her purportedly wayward son. "Why don't you just tell him that his old mammy loves the ground he walks on and she ain't caring what he do. Maybe, he ain't bad like you think. Maybe he's just natural born like me. Cain't live like you and the preacher want him to. Maybe he cain't bow his head and walk humble" (360). In contrast to her black preacher's restrictive Christianity, John Henry offers the old woman a spirituality of loving acceptance that appreciates her son's "naturalness" and difference as a progressive expression of black manhood. Such a position reflects what Gay L. Byron terms a "true" black manhood that cultivates a genuine spiritual life, where an "emphasis on spiritual formation will enable African American men to recognize their own humanity and the humanity of others and would lead to building much more intimate and humane relationships while building coalitions to fight against various forms of oppression."[21]

In the fourth episode, John Henry, while in jail, goes a step further when ridiculed and taunted by a trio of white prisoners and preaches a radical apocalyptic vision of racial retribution:

> Going walk and walk, till the whole earth is destroyed by fire, like the Good Book say it will on the Day of Judgment. And all your goddamned laws and man-made steam engines and gadgets'll be melted like wax! Then the spirit's going to take on his natural flesh again, and wait till the earth cools off. The Almighty's going to put a ten-pound hammer in his hand. Tell him, go back to earth and see what he can do. (355)

John Henry prophesies not only an end to white oppression but also the rebirth or second coming of the natural man as God's chosen son who will undertake the task of earthly re-creation. He juxtaposes natural unrealized power, racialized power, in relation to the white Other and locates a spirit of transcendence and resistance in the natural.

In prison, John Henry asserts his difference, defiantly eschews black subservience, and defines the natural man as a powerful groundbreaker. When his white tormentors say, "Tell us, Sambo, how it feels to be like you," John Henry replies, "Like a giant in a strait jacket! . . . Like a great king without a throne to sit on!" (355). John Henry recognizes himself as outsized in relation to the limitations placed upon him. The straitjacket of stereotypes binds him and renders him legible. Yet, even within these constraints, he proclaims his greatness. Diminished and dehumanized by the white prisoners and the racially biased prison system that infantilizes black convicts, John Henry still maintains his dignity and determination. The natural man, then, exists as yet-unrealized potential, a "king without a throne."

Browne uses the chain gang scene, in the fifth episode that follows, to express most explicitly the natural as a point of black male resistance. The episode begins with the black convicts along the chain gang swinging their hammers and singing:

> Like a natural man,
> Swing that hammer—huh
> Like a natural man.
> Guard behind you
> Rifle in his hand. . . .
> This chain gang, Babe,
> Be the death of me. (356)

This work song indicates that the convicts' movement is "like" a natural man, not yet free but aspiring to be "natural"—that is, to exist beyond the confines of the chain gang. Moreover, the fact that these black convicts sing this song under the watchful presence of the guards speaks to its function as nascent revolt. In these lyrics, natural masculinity involves the agency to talk back to authority, as the constrained violence of the natural man's hammer operates directly under the threat and gaze of the guards and their guns. The line "This chain gang, Babe, / Be the death of me," addressed to an absent female, conveys the futility of their situation that they will probably never escape their current conditions, will never marry or see this lost lover, and will die in captivity.

John Henry asks that the men move from unrealized revolt to active resistance. When one convict argues that the prisoners cannot fight against the guards' guns because "a man ain't nothing but a man," John Henry responds, "Buddy, you said something! That's my kind of preaching. A man ain't nothing but a man. Ain't they more of us put together then they is guards holding we-all here in slavery . . . !" (356–57). The line "a man ain't nothing but a man" has become an important phrase within the lexicon and mythology of John Henry, as it has been repeated in John Henry folk songs, as well as in books and scholarly articles on the folk legend, to express how John Henry pushed the limits of manhood in his battle against the machine.[22] Here in *Natural Man*, Browne's John Henry offers what Henry Louis Gates terms a "signifyin(g) revision" on this adage.[23] In his reading of "a man ain't nothing but a man," manhood is something that the guards, despite their authority, cannot take from the convicts. Manhood for John Henry means declaring one's humanity while under conditions set to deny that very humanity entirely. This vision of manhood endures and escapes from the fact that the guards can render the black prisoners impotent with their uses of guns. In Browne's play, John Henry asserts a radical, "natural" manhood for those who appear completely incapacitated and rendered useless. Unfortunately, the other prisoners do not take up John Henry's call to action. When a suffering black convict collapses, unable to endure the intense pressure of the chain gang, only John Henry comes to his aid. Defending his fallen comrade, John Henry kills a white guard and is forced to flee. At this dire moment, the others do respond as a collective, in unison urging him to run, "Hurry John Henry! Get way fast as you can! Hurry! Them other guards is coming this way!" (358).

The Final Apocalypse

All of these flashback scenes point to the inability of John Henry, the natural man, to exist with the current limitations placed on him by society and thus underscore the need for him to carve out an alternative space. The play's final episode returns to the tunnel with John Henry inside combating the steam engine. Determined to win, but also troubled by memories of his problematic past and seemingly desperate future, John Henry chooses to define his own end. He resolves to fight and die on his own terms. John Henry battles on with such an increasing intensity and fervor that he sets the rocks in the tunnel aflame. Amazed and afraid, the crowd witnessing from the tunnel's entrance exclaim: "The mountain is going to burn to ashes . . . John Henry done hammer till he set the rocks on fire!" (361–62). This vision of a smoldering mountain is at once absurd and mythical. It is an apocalyptic vision, the realization of the image of judgment day that John Henry shared with the white prisoners in which "the whole earth is destroyed by fire" and "all your goddamned laws and man-made steam engines and gadgets'll be melted like wax!" (355). With this final act, John Henry not only punctuates his victory over the steam engine but also signals his symbolic transcendence over the earthly constraints that have limited his potential.

Gesturing toward divine judgment as well as racial equality, John Henry strikes out for black self-determination and a black liberatory masculinity. In episode eight, as he comes out of the tunnel physically exhausted and mentally prepared for his impending death, John Henry declares, "I come out peaceful" (362). Accordingly, he defies conventional expectation as he does not spew venom at Captain Tommy nor at white society more generally. He is not the "angry black man"—that legible stereotype of black masculinity. Rather, he presents an alternative vision of black masculinity, one that is unconstrained, one no longer bounded by its legibility but now natural and free: "I am as free now as the Blueridge Mountain, the Mississippi River, the Tall Lonesome Pine!" (362). John Henry is going to a better place. As he walks off into a glowing white light, he becomes symbolically linked to a higher cause of black social consciousness and resistance. For John Henry, the key to defining a new liberatory vision of black masculinity is in the steps he takes toward self-determination. Within the process of struggling with his own past, John Henry comes to a new understanding of himself in relationship to structures of power and systems of privilege. Creeper watches John Henry's final procession and strums a song that underscores this new understanding. "A man ain't nothing but a man," Creeper sings in the first verse. This lyric is the first line in the well-known folk ballad "John Henry." Here, however, it functions as repetition with revision, thereby referencing its earlier usage by John Henry in the play's chain gang scene. The familiar phrase not only evokes man's ultimate humanity in the face of the mechanized steam drill but also asserts the need for black men to exist as free men outside the stereotypes and conventional representations of blackness, ultimately because "a man ain't nothing but a man."

Theodore Browne presents this dynamic of black male empowerment through the notion of the natural man and his struggle against the mechanization of society. Yet the portrait of the natural is not a static one. Rather, it is one that recognizes the limits on the abilities of black men in this period to control the systems of power and technology and the tools of progress like the steam drill that relegated them to what August Wilson terms in his play *Ma Rainey's Black Bottom* "leftovers from history."[24] Elsewhere, Wilson writes, "reduced to its most fundamental truth, black men are a commodity of flesh and muscle which has lost its value in the marketplace. We are left over from history."[25] For playwright Theodore Browne, self-determination and collective resistance require a recognition of what he terms "natural," which rescues black men from the status of leftovers, articulates the connections between the personal and the political, and constitutes an alternative vision of black masculinity still relevant in the more contemporary period. In fact, the messages in Browne's play underscore the fact that "Black Lives Matter." First staged by white producers within a nationwide theatrical experiment in multiracial democracy, articulated in a European-derived stylistic milieu, and placed in conversation with the other works of the era (including many discussed in this anthology), *Natural Man* now becomes part of a larger dialogue across race and class on the enduring power of images of manhood and masculinity in America.

Notes

Special thanks to Rohin Deb for his assistance with this essay.

1. "President Obama Talks Trayvon, Being an African American Man in America," *Uptown Magazine*, http://uptownmagazine.com/2013/07/president-obama-video-transcript/3, accessed 5 March 2014.

2. Trey Ellis, "How Does It Feel to Be a Problem?," in *Speak My Name: Black Men on Masculinity and the American Dream*, ed. Don Belton (Boston: Beacon Press, 1995), 10.

3. James Baldwin, "My Dungeon Shook," *The Fire Next Time* (1962; New York: Vintage International, 1993), 7.

4. W. E. B. Du Bois, *The Souls of Black Folk* (1903; New York: Alfred A. Knopf, 1993), 7.

5. Henry Louis Gates Jr., *Thirteen Ways of Looking at a Black Man* (New York: Random House Value Publishing, 1999), xvi.

6. Ellis Cose, *The Envy of the World: On Being a Black Man in America* (New York: Washington Square Press, 2002).

7. Theodore Browne, "Natural Man," in *Black Theatre USA: Plays by African Americans*, vol. 1, *The Early Period, 1847–1938*, rev. and expanded ed., ed. James V. Hatch and Ted Shine (New York: Free Press, 1996), 355. All subsequent references to this play will appear parenthetically in the text.

8. There is some uncertainty around the precise number of Negro units that were established, depending on how the total is calculated. James V. Hatch writes of an "initial sixteen and later nineteen or even twenty-two Negro units, depending on how smaller projects are counted." James V. Hatch, "The Great Depression and Federal Theatre," in *A History of African American Theatre*, ed. Errol G. Hill and James V. Hatch (New York: Cambridge University Press, 2003), 315.

9. Rena Fraden, *Blueprints for a Black Federal Theatre, 1935–1939* (New York: Cambridge University Press, 1996), 177.

10. Ibid.

11. Barry Witham, *The Federal Theatre Project: A Case Study* (New York: Cambridge University Press, 2003), 75–76.

12. Quoted in Henry D. Miller, *Theorizing Black Theatre: Art Versus Protest in Critical Writings, 1898–1965* (New York: McFarland, 2010), 132.

13. Ibid.; Doris Abramson, *Negro Playwrights in the American Theatre, 1925–1959* (New York: Columbia University Press, 1969), 106.

14. Abramson, *Negro Playwrights*, 106.

15. Ibid., 108.

16. Quoted in *John Henry: Present at the Creation*, National Public Radio, http://www.npr.org/programs/morning/features/patc/johnhenry/index.html, accessed 4 March 2014.

17. Claude Steele, "Thin Ice: 'Stereotype Threat' and Black College Students," *Atlantic Monthly*, August 1999, 51.

18. Patricia Hill Collins, "A Telling Difference: Dominance, Strength, and Black Masculinity," in *Progressive Black Masculinities*, ed. Athena D. Mutua (New York: Routledge, 2006), 75.

19. Mark Anthony Neal, *Looking for Leroy: Illegible Black Masculinities* (New York: New York University Press, 2013), 6.

20. Ibid., 4.

21. Gay L. Byron, "Images of Masculinity in the Pauline Epistles," in *Progressive Black Masculinities*, ed. Athena D. Mutua (New York: Routledge, 2006), 112.

22. See, for example, Eric D. Carlson, *A Man Ain't Nothin' but a Man* (Columbia: University of Missouri Press, 2007); and Scott Reynolds Nelson, with Marc Aronson, *Ain't Nothing but a Man: My Quest to Find the Real John Henry* (Washington, D.C.: National Geographic Books, 2007).

23. Henry Louis Gates, *The Signifying Monkey: A Theory of African-American Literary Criticism* (New York: Oxford University Press, 1988), 64.

24. August Wilson, *Ma Rainey's Black Bottom* (New York: New American Library, 1985), 47.

25. August Wilson, "Foreword," in *Speak My Name: Black Men on Masculinity and the American Dream*, ed. Don Belton (Boston: Beacon Press, 1995), xi.

8. Choreographing Diversity and American Experience

Myra Kinch and Group, Federal Theatre Project (1937–39)

Margaret F. Savilonis

Housed in the archives of the Federal Theatre Project (FTP) at the National Archives in College Park, Maryland, is a striking photograph of a provocative moment in the history of modern dance in America. The photo records an instant from *Let My People Go*, a work choreographed by Myra Kinch, director of the Los Angeles Dance Unit of the FTP, as part of the Concert of Modern Dance (1938). The image displays a wall of bodies, mostly female, frozen in a pose that simultaneously evokes shock, grief, and supplication. Eighteen dancers stand in a semicircle, their arms raised, elbows bent at right angles, palms facing outward with fingers spread wide. With bare feet planted firmly, shoulder-width apart, their bodies lurch forward at the waist, their gaze directed toward the floor. Beneath them, lying face-up and inert, are three male bodies—each with a noose around his neck. This image—especially when considering the work's title, *Let My People Go*—seems to offer a powerful condemnation of a specific social injustice: lynching. At the same time, the photograph is striking for its absence of black bodies among the company of dancers. Kinch's most acclaimed composition for the FTP was *Theme of Expansion (An American Exodus)*, part of the Festival of American Dance (1937), a work FTP director Hallie Flanagan praised as "dancing which was theatre and . . . theatre which was America."[1] Reflecting the FTP's stated "desire to stimulate an interest in current social problems,"[2] this photograph is one indication of how *Let My People Go* was also "theatre which was America," employing the idiom of modern dance to examine—critically, but also imperfectly—issues of racial injustice and national identity.

Scene from *Let My People Go*, Los Angeles Dance Unit of the Federal Theatre Project, 1938. *Courtesy of the National Archives and Records Administration, photo no. 69-TC-SCA-9-1.*

This chapter examines how *Let My People Go* and other works composed by Kinch engaged with the FTP's mission to create theatre that aimed to "reflect our country, its history, its present problems, [and] its diverse regions and population."[3] This analysis begins with the understanding (also operative in chapters 7 and 9 of this anthology) that the FTP was itself an "experiment in democracy," "national in scope, regional in emphasis, and democratic in allowing each local unit freedom" to operate under a common set of principles.[4] At a time when modern dance was often described as an art form "aligned with communism" within public discourse,[5] Kinch promoted her project of "working toward group expression, a blending of individual personalities and techniques into a modern medium of expression," as an inherently American endeavor.[6] Kinch's staging of American experience foregrounded the nation's multiracial diversity in both its themes and its aesthetics in a way that parallels the innovations of the Jerome Kern and Oscar Hammerstein musical *Show Boat* (see chapter 2). Her dance vocabulary, coupled with the subjects she explored—from snapshots of American national holidays, to a narrative about the pioneer experience, to a condemnation of racial oppression—emphasized the importance of diversity within community. Yet her quest for an inclusive, democratic vision of America articulated through modern dance was complicated by politics, public perception, and administrative policies that circumscribed the FTP's democratic ideals.

Despite the democratic aspirations of the FTP, creative freedom for the artists working within it was not wholly unfettered. As part of the Works Progress Administration (WPA), a federally funded work-relief project, the FTP was subject to regulations that governed its operations: from the hiring of personnel to securing funding for costumes and scenery. Additionally, the project had an explicitly articulated mission to produce work that was entertaining and informative but neutral in regard to "any controversy be it social, political, or otherwise."[7] As Barry B. Witham notes,

> Censorship, from the very beginning, was a continuous battle. . . . In looking back it is important to understand that the sources of censorship were multiple and complex. They involved fear of federalized welfare, W.P.A. jealousies and egos, racial politics and the Catholic Church—to name only the most visible sources. All of these contributed to a climate where there was almost always resistance to the project somewhere in the country on a daily basis.[8]

Furthermore, despite the FTP's commitment to cultural diversity, evident in foreign language units that produced plays in Italian, German, Spanish, and Yiddish, as well as in the "special program for Negro companies,"[9] racial segregation in performance was common.[10] Susan Manning maintains that "segregation was more de facto than de jure,"[11] but integration varied by region. Los Angeles seems to have maintained a de facto policy of racial division, particularly in the early days of the project. Regarding black actors in LA's FTP units, stage manager Dale Wasserman asserted that "in general they were kept rather segregated and did their own material. . . . They were, in general, kept as segregated as the Yiddish unit."[12] Of the three major dance units—including those in New York and Chicago—the Los Angeles unit was the only one that did not at any time include black dancers.[13]

While all of the FTP's units were subject to varying degrees of scrutiny, resistance, and red tape, the dance units had an especially embattled existence, thanks in part to perceptions about the radical nature of modern dance. At the behest of the Dancers' Association, a committee that included dancer-choreographers Helen Tamiris and Gluck Sandor, the Federal Dance Theatre (FDT)[14] was created as an independent WPA unit under the direction of Don Oscar Becque in January 1936, but it suffered almost immediately from internal conflict and external criticism. One source of tension was its dancers' activism, including their advocacy of cultural pluralism. Among the resolutions passed at the first National Dance Congress in 1936 was one that advocated "foster[ing] Negro dance culture."[15] FDT dancers spoke out publicly against "fascist trends" that in Europe discriminated against those who were not of "so-called 'pure-Aryan' blood"—trends that they felt were emerging in the United States.[16] Becque resigned his position in December 1936,[17] and while internal strife subsided as the New York–based group produced several critically acclaimed works in 1937, public controversy persisted. Modern dance aroused suspicion and even outrage, with many complaints against the unit decrying the art form's threats to the status quo, its disregard for classical dance seen as one step on the road toward social disorder. In July 1937, the Dancing Teachers' Business Association declared that the FDT was presenting "political and propagandistic drivel," resulting in a "lack of respect for taxpayers' money on the part of the majority of persons connected with the dance project."[18] By October, when project-wide personnel cuts were made, the dance unit was absorbed back into the FTP,[19] its independent existence coming to an end just as the dance units in Los Angeles and Chicago were beginning to develop and produce original works.[20]

While much of the FDT controversy was specific to New York City, the dance unit in Los Angeles contended with similar challenges. Administrative policies, such as those restricting hiring and training, as well as bureaucratic oversight of operations, directly affected artistic output. Kinch became head of the LA unit in early 1937 on the recommendation of Martha Deane, with whom she had studied at UCLA. Because she was obligated to "have a certain percentage of those who were on relief" within the company, the thirty or forty dancers had varying levels of training and expertise, making devising a coherent program difficult.[21] In her official report on the festival, Kinch wrote that she needed to work with the company to "achieve a group sense before actual rehearsals of the dances began." That endeavor was complicated by time constraints and by the difficulties inherent in helping dancers trained only in ballet adjust to the "complete and unified use of the body" demanded by modern dance.[22] In addition to outlining her artistic process, Kinch devoted considerable attention to defining modern dance in the report, suggesting that she felt a need to justify her aesthetic choices to WPA administrators. As James R. Ullman observed after resigning from the project in 1939,[23]

> The greatest strength and greatest weakness of the Federal Theatre flow from the same source: its purely democratic form of operation. . . . It is a people's theatre, both in its relationship to its several thousand workers and its several million patrons, and its operation at all times has been

determined by what those several thousand and several million want. In theory, and occasionally in practice, this is a sound and laudable principle. The difficulty is that very few of those thousands and millions ever want the same thing at the same time. . . . So susceptible is the project to pressure from both within and without that its entire personnel could be . . . kept fully occupied for months on end with problems of labor, public relations, politics, and general policy without even coming close to putting on a play.[24]

For artists in Southern California, internal pressure meant answering to their local WPA director, Colonel Donald H. Connolly, whose primary objective for the theatre during his tenure was to keep the local FTP activities "out of the papers."[25] External pressure came from ordinary citizens who were concerned about "communistic plays and the moral life of the players."[26] Thus Kinch faced the challenges of pursuing experimental aesthetics and communicating her social vision of American justice and democracy without aggravating the resistances inherent within the vast and unwieldy democratic project in which she worked.

Carving out a space in which modern dance could provide a vocabulary for articulating American experience for an audience unfamiliar with the form was no easy task. In addition to the technical challenges Kinch faced in training her company, she had to navigate existing perceptions of modern dance held by audiences, critics, and FTP administrators. In October 1937, critic Isabel Morse Jones observed, "The modern dance and modern dancers have been under admiring and also acrimonious discussion [for] several seasons."[27] For some, modern dance was bewildering, not entertaining; for others, it offered "daring innovations."[28] Additionally, according to dance scholar Mark Franko, the genre of modern dance was "associated with political radicalism in the public mind."[29] Kinch, who made her solo debut in 1932 at the Max Reinhardt Theatre in Berlin, Germany, where she became familiar with different schools of modern dance, was deeply committed to the form. Her reports demonstrate her awareness of the need to overcome prevailing prejudices against modern dance as a form of creative expression:

> Los Angeles has far too little opportunity to view, and consequently, little chance to understand what American dancers are achieving and have achieved during the past ten years. Serious choreographers have had a struggle to make the country at large understand or to accept what they are doing. All of us are apt to be alarmed at anything other than the traditional form in art, and the sponsors for the newer modes must fight prejudice wherever they go.[30]

With these sentiments from her director's report on the Concert of Modern Dance, Kinch responded both to public suspicions about experimental dance and, more important, to the skepticism of those government officials overseeing her work, who very well might have harbored similar prejudices.

Modern dance in the 1930s included many adaptations of Native American, African American, and non-Western dance vocabularies. Such influences on the aesthetics of modern dance may have also contributed to anxieties about the form. Discussing the incorporation of these traditions by American choreographers such as Katherine Dunham and Martha Graham, Ramsay Burt argues, "To acknowledge a community of thought with other peoples is to recognize sameness across difference."[31] Like many of her peers, Kinch sometimes borrowed from other cultures in her choreography. Her concert work in the early 1930s was informed by sources such as "ancient Greek, Egyptian, and Mayan sculpture and painting," as well as by Portuguese art that she encountered while touring Mexico City in 1933.[32] Kinch continued to draw upon these sources of inspiration in her work for the FTP. In response, several critics seemed intent on describing Kinch's work in terms of its inherent Americanness, calling direct attention to her status as a native Californian, perhaps to quell anxieties about the foreign and "primitive" character of modern dance.[33] Kinch addressed such concerns in program notes she wrote for the FTP by describing the aesthetic contrasts between ballet and modern dance:

> Ballet gives spectacular technical feats. Modern dance aspires to complete and unified use of the body. . . . The ballet is traditional. The modern dance, unfettered by tradition, permits individual expression. . . . Modern dance is evolutionary. . . . These contrasts between modern dance and the older forms are mentioned, not to insist on any superiority of one dance form over the other, but to clarify the principal points of difference.[34]

Here Kinch constructs a narrative that implicitly plays on American values. By linking modern dance to "evolutionary" progress and to individualism, she makes the form seem less threatening; indeed, she describes it as a platform for that most-honored of American ideals: freedom of expression. Freedom in modern dance applied not only to its technical elements but also to its thematic concerns and its diverse cultural influences. Kinch argues that within modern dance, the old and the new can peacefully coexist; its panhistorical and cross-cultural pluralism is something to embrace.

Myra Kinch and dancers, Los Angeles Dance Unit of the Federal Theatre Project, 1938. *Courtesy of the National Archives and Records Administration, photo no. 69-N-19648.*

Determining precisely how the dances Kinch choreographed for the FTP related to "themes of American life"[35] is difficult, given the challenges of ephemerality faced by all performance scholars. Yet, as Burt notes, "The situation for the dance historian is even less certain," especially for those studying work from the 1930s, as archival traces are so scarce.[36] Extant materials documenting Kinch's work include still photographs, costume renderings, synopses written by Kinch and the composer Manuel Galea, programs, performance reviews, newspaper articles, interviews, and one brief (silent) film segment of *An American Exodus*. Although they provide an incomplete picture, these materials offer a compelling glimpse into

Kinch's representations of American experience from diverse perspectives and reveal the significant role her choreography played in the brief but vibrant life of the FTP.

The Los Angeles Dance Unit's first offering, an event titled A Festival of American Dance, premiered at the Hollywood Playhouse in July 1937. This performance, designed as a celebration of the diversity of American life, transferred to San Francisco's Alcazar Theatre in September. Described as "ultra modernistic, brilliantly original, and revealing a wide scope of moods,"[37] the program was well received by critics and audiences, drawing "many curtain calls at the end of each performance."[38] Although critic Marjory M. Fisher failed to detect "anything outstandingly 'American' about the dances or the dancers,"[39] the Festival of American Dance—from its title to its closing number, in both style and content—imagined both the past and the future of the nation. The program resonated with social theorist Randolph S. Bourne's suggestion that "American cultural tradition lies in the future. It will be what we all together make out of this incomparable opportunity of attacking the future with a new key."[40] Comprised of three parts—*Divertissements*, *Dance Satires*, and *Theme of Expansion (An American Exodus)*—the concert constructed a clear narrative. Its opening section was an introduction to dance forms and styles; its middle section was a comic interlude that doubled as a history lesson about dance; and the evening's dramatically choreographed finale valorized the pioneer spirit. Thus, the program built upon itself, synthesizing past and present to envision the future.

In part 1, *Divertissements*, dance functioned not only as a mode of expression but also as a subject of historical inquiry, with diverse roots that contributed to the richness of American culture. Wearing brightly colored, streamlined costumes designed by Robert Tyler Lee and performing in front of a black velour cyclorama, the troupe opened with "Three Dances of Presentation," preludes that "were expressive of abstract moods and movement."[41] They next moved into a series of dances that explored the creation of patterns, as well as interpretations of ethnic dances such as the traditional Mexican zapateado[42] and the South American tango. Singled out as a highlight by several critics was "Song of Judea," described by critic Johanna Lawrence as "a strong, sincere theme of Hebrew inspiration."[43] A commentator for the *Daily News* observed, "The 'Festival,' which includes examples of almost every form of dance, illustrates Miss Kinch's theory that a typically American technique of the dance may evolve from a combination of the old forms."[44] This diversity and combination of forms was also reflected in the musical accompaniment. While Kinch's collaborator and future husband, Manuel Galea, composed original music for most of the dances, works by Alexandre Tansman, Alois Hába, Meyer Lutz, Jaromir Weinberger, and Dmitri Shostakovich—composers of Polish, Czech, German, and Russian descent—rounded out the program. This arrangement of music and movement, informed by various histories and traditions, embodied Bourne's notion of "cultures [that] have not been melted down or run together . . . but have remained distinct but cooperating to the greater glory and benefit not only of themselves but of all the native 'Americanism' around them."[45]

Metatheatrical reflection and emphasis on cross-cultural exchange continued in part 2, *Dance Satires*. Kinch was renowned for choreographing lighthearted comic takes on various dance forms: from ballet to modern to fandango. Here the satires traced a path from "Ballet—1840" to "Modern Dance (Coronation)—1937," with stops at "Spanish—1890," "Skirt Dance —1900," and "Greek (Aesthetic)—1914" along the way. Providing a comic interlude before the evening's serious and reflective final movement, these satires also served as a reminder of the dance as historical practice and drew particular attention to the present moment, with an episode titled "Modern Dance" set in 1937. As a result, the dancers themselves became part of Kinch's historiography, one expressing her artistic philosophy that "choreography requires as its background a thorough knowledge of all that has been developed along terpsichorean lines in the past from ballet to folk dance."[46]

The final segment, *Theme of Expansion (An American Exodus)*, functioned as a multilayered history, one that was simultaneously about past, present, and future. Program notes describe the piece as "the tale of the early pioneers . . . , against a thudding background of percussion instruments, [portraying] the long trek to new lands, the establishment of new homes, the burdens of frontier life, nostalgia for the loved ones left behind, and the festal rhythms of the successful march of civilization."[47] This seven-part dance reflected the American experience in celebratory fashion. For Fisher, the dance evoked "moods and manners more human than national, and universally effective."[48] A familiar story told in a new language, one that the audience had come to learn throughout the program, *An American Exodus* folds dance history into this pioneer story, modern dance ushering in a new frontier.

Indeed, aesthetic form is one means through which *An American Exodus* inserts itself into conversations about American identity and democratic ideals. According to one critic, the concert's choreography was "based on the theory of director Kinch that the modern dance trend is toward emphasis upon groups and group movement."[49] By deemphasizing solos and privileging group patterns, the piece reminds viewers that progress and celebration are dependent on community. While traditional frontier narratives sometimes emphasize individuals singled out for their particular achievements, this frontier narrative provides a broader view. Still photographs, as well as a short film clip of the work as it was performed during the Golden Gate International Exposition in 1939, confirm how the group takes precedence over the individual in Kinch's vision. Its choreographic style reinforces its thematic focus on a collective American identity.

The extant film clip shows mid- to up-tempo choreography, in which the dancers (both male and female) employ sweeping gestures and focused movements that suggest a difficult though inspiring progress. The final tableau suggests a moment of ecstasy, as different groups of dancers converge but also maintain a sense of distinct units. The pattern reflects Deborah Jowitt's analysis of American dance in the 1930s: "Being an American dancer meant conveying a sense of immense frontiers and the pioneer hardihood that conquered them . . . expansiveness of gesture, a sharpness of outline; figures onstage appeared clearly set apart from each other, as if more virtual space than actual space separated them."[50] After reaching their final tableau, the dancers simultaneously turn their attention upward, as if following the sun as it charts the sky. They look over their shoulders and then sweep back out toward the audience, drawing their focus to their destination. This concluding moment generates a sense of awe and ecstasy, as some dancers kneel, one stretches his arms upward and outward, and another arches her back and extends her arms to the side, while others stand rigidly, arms by their sides, chins thrust upward. The dancers admire the glorious dawn, looking skyward in hope and wonder at the light that shines on them in this promised land.

An American Exodus addresses questions of diversity within American experience. In a program note, Kinch dedicates the piece "to the pioneers who had a dream . . . of a far challenge called California. . . . Spanish and Yankee, from their epochal struggle was born the spirit called American."[51] This emphasis on diverse perspectives is borne out in embodied practice; the cast for the 1937 debut included dancers of various ethnicities, including Russian, French, and Mexican: Grace Adelphi, Renaldo Alarcon, Janna Bolle, Patrice Brooks, Rose Marie Carter, Milton Chisholm, Clay Dalton, Eleanor Flaig, Luba Fox, Clarice Ganon, Eileen Hamilton, Kinch, Nathan Kirkpatrick, Madeleine Lazard, Maria Lentino, Bella Lewitzky, Maria Morales, Lysle Olston, Margaret Rees, Albert de Ruiz, Senta Stephany, Chris Velcoff, and Minerva Woolley. Also in the cast was Teru Izumida, a first-generation American of Japanese descent, who garnered special mention in reviews of the Festival of American Dance on the San Francisco leg of the tour.[52] Thus, the troupe's ethnic diversity added potency to the dance's themes of migration, suggesting a wide range of national and ethnic experiences within this ostensibly familiar vision of pioneer life and the pursuit of the American dream. At the same time, such inclusivity made the absence of African American dancers even more pronounced.

The Los Angeles unit continued to explore the diversity of American experience the following year, in a three-part program called the Concert of Modern Dance. Though not as enthusiastically received as the Festival of American Dance, Kinch's second major offering for the FTP tackled vital social issues—class consciousness, the effects of war, and racial inequity—more directly. Through this performance, Kinch's focus on the more troublesome aspects of American experience became more pronounced. Her perspective on American history was less romanticized and more sharply focused on the contradictions within the history of a nation whose venerated ideals of freedom and equality were never fully realized in practice. Much of the company and creative team remained intact from the previous year's Festival of American Dance.

A four-part suite titled *Anthem (American Holidays)* anchored part 1 of the program. It was a piece that attempted "to bring out in dance movement the feeling of the American people; the spirit and regard held in American consciousness and possible attitudes behind many years of celebration."[53] Its four segments were "First Monday in September: Expression of Unity," "December Twenty-Fifth: The Birth of Him Who Is the Spirit," "May Thirtieth: The Supreme Sacrifice—Youth and the Heroes' Graves," and "July Fourth: Our Priceless Heritage—Freedom of Expression." Overall, the suite was both celebratory and reflective. "First Monday," representing the "organization of the working classes and the development of their class consciousness,"[54] received only cursory mentions in most reviews. Critic Viola Hegyi Swisher dismissed the piece as having "most of the futile gestures usually found in the choreographic vocabulary of the dancer eager to express the concept of the worker."[55] "July Fourth," on the other hand, garnered more consistently positive responses; Mollie Prager assessed this segment as "a fresh, brief picture to which the audience responded enthusiastically."[56] However, "May Thirtieth" resonated most strongly with audiences and critics alike. The dance underscores the irony of honoring the dead in a time of rebirth: "Beginning of Spring. Re-decoration of graves and its evident futility. The disaster of War unfinished."[57] The score, expressing "romanticism . . . but couched in a minor key" and ending in the "eloquence of complete silence,"[58] informs the narrative, including a moment in which a "youth is pulled from his sweetheart's arms to join a silent procession of marchers to the grave."[59] Reviewer Carl Kondo noted that "the simplicity of expression and economy of movement in [this dance] brought out the great possibilities of the Modern Dance as a medium to create social consciousness."[60] Throughout *American Holidays*, Kinch strategically employs the modern dance idiom to reflect on both the longevity and the fluidity of traditions; by distilling "American consciousness" down to concepts such as unity, faith, respect, and independence and presenting those familiar ideals in an unfamiliar language, Kinch encourages viewers to consider what they are actually celebrating on these four holidays. Her choreographic aesthetic, balancing group patterns and individual characters, such as a mother giving birth or a young woman losing her beloved to war, emphasizes the value of unity while challenging the notion of uniform experience.

The boldest stroke of the concert was its finale, the symbolic dance drama *Let My People Go*, which addressed one of the most egregious crimes against humanity that was an all-too-common reality of American life: lynching. Between 1930 and 1937 alone, at least 111 black men and women were lynched in the United States (compared with approximately 8 white people lynched during that same period).[61] In a nation that espoused notions of equality for all its citizens, such a paradox demanded attention and action. Kinch was not alone in addressing the subject through dance. Her Los Angeles contemporary Lester Horton did so in *Chronicle* in 1937, as did Helen Tamiris in *How Long, Brethren?* (1937), an FTP production.[62] Confronting this social ill within a program that emphasized American freedoms demonstrates Kinch's ambitions for using dance to explore the "present problems" of U.S. society.

A synopsis of *Let My People Go* offers the following concerning its two distinct parts:

> PART I
>
> The misfortunes visited upon the dark races culminate in an Act of Abomination—lynching. Black Mother—a symbol of the soul of the race, finds release in her primitive grief. Her emotion spent, the Heavenly Host descends upon her in a vision. The trumpet sounds within her soul and she goes forth with the singing sword of religion in her hand.
>
> PART II
>
> In the overwhelming tide of religious ecstasy, those who walk the earth in sorrow are redeemed through the blood of the lamb.[63]

Most notable about this dance were its complex representations of American racial identity. As has been noted, Kinch's troupe included no African American dancers. Thus, as Tamiris and Horton did in their earlier explorations of lynching,[64] Kinch (who danced the role of the Black Mother) took a risk by performing the (perceived) experience of ethnic others. It is critical to note that these dancers did not employ blackface—thus manifesting Susan Manning's definition of "*metaphorical minstrelsy*, a convention whereby white dancers' bodies made reference to nonwhite subjects . . . not [to] mimic others but [to] present an abstraction or personification of others—Oriental, Indian, Negro." Manning argues that "metaphorical minstrelsy demonstrates how a convention that appears simply racist from the perspective of the early twenty-first century carried diverse ideological implications in its own time."[65] Franko describes the practice with a different term, "cultural cross-dressing"; he argues, "However out of date it [cultural cross-dressing] would appear by today's standards, it served a progressive purpose [in the 1930s]."[66] Kinch recognized the ramifications of her choice, directly addressing issues of race in her "Director's Report":

> Our third American suite, "Let My People Go," a symbolic dance drama depicting certain tragic phases in the lives of many American Negroes, might well be described in the words of one of our finest Negro directors and actors. He was very appreciative of all that had been accomplished choreographically as well as musically. He felt that both had allowed the white dancer freedom to convey an emotional force illustrative of the Negro but that no foolish attempt was made to give a photographic interpretation.[67]

Yet the representation of "Negro suffering" without black performers affected the reception of the piece and the ideas it communicated. Some audiences found the piece comic,[68] and several critics judged the piece's representation of African American experience in relation to the concurrent FTP offering of Hall Johnson's *Run Little Chillun'*, a joint production between the music and Negro units.[69]

Burt argues that it "is not the act of appropriation . . . but the underlying ethics of the act" that should be considered when assessing modern dance in the 1930s.[70] While Kinch was lauded for her "progressive activities" in the project,[71] and while it seems clear that her work was animated by a sincere desire to condemn racial inequality and oppression, production materials reveal a more ambiguous picture, including portrayals of African American identity that employed what bell hooks calls "recognizable forms . . . [that rely] on stereotypes of the 'primitive.'"[72] Robert Tyler Lee's costumes evoked

African American identity primarily through headscarves worn by the female dancers. The male figures' anatomical features and posture resonate with Jim Crow imagery, suggesting the pervasiveness of such visual caricatures. And while it is difficult to discern completely from still photographs, Kinch's movement vocabulary seems to play with existing stereotypes in the "dynamic yet frequently incomprehensible exploration of Negro grief and regeneration, symbolic, [and] stylized."[73] Because Galea composed his music simultaneously with or after Kinch's setting of movement, hints about choreographic style can be found in his "Composer's Report":

> The [dance] dealt with that portion of the Negro race victimized by poverty and adverse social conditions, and their release from these conditions through the medium of religious exhortation. Musically, the melodic material required the primitive character which remains in spite of the employment of the occidental tonal structure upon which it was built. The other indispensable quality is the savage syncopation of tempo so cleverly allied to the pulsation of movement emanating from the Negro's physical structure.[74]

Costume renderings by Robert Tyler Lee for *Let My People Go. Production bulletin, Concert of Modern Dance, 1938, box 993, Federal Theatre Project Collection, Music Division, Library of Congress, Washington, D.C., 19–20.*

T. D. Rice as Jim Crow. *MS Thr 556 (156), Harvard Theatre Collection, Houghton Library, Harvard University, Cambridge, Mass.*

This description reveals an investment in addressing inequity but also the maintenance of a social and cultural hierarchy that denigrates African Americans as "primitive" and "savage."

Furthermore, while attempting to use the theatre as a vehicle for expanding the conversation about American experience, the work perpetuates the marginalization of African Americans through erasure. Such erasure may have played a role in the piece's lukewarm critical reception. As Manning suggests, "Until the late 1930s white critics seemed to take for granted that white bodies could reference black subjects. But after 1938 white critics became more aware of the asymmetry between white bodies and black subjects that constituted metaphorical minstrelsy."[75] Although several reviewers commended *Let My People Go* for being impressive and well executed in terms of technique,[76] many were disappointed by its characterization of its subject. W. E. Oliver wrote, "The conventional treatment of Negro suffering and primitive mysticism . . . falls under the blight of white man's notions."[77] Prager lamented the ending that in her view reverted "to the old hackneyed conception of Negro grief drowning itself in jazzy religious ecstasy."[78] Such responses suggest that the piece did invoke stereotypes and that doing so diminished the impact of the statement Kinch was trying to make about American racial injustice.

Yet these same critics were also participants in the erasure of black bodies and the perpetuation of racial hierarchies. Prager claimed that Kinch "failed to take cognizance of the fact that a note of protest or defiance against [African Americans'] persecution would have presented a sharper, truer picture."[79] Her call for a "sharper, truer" picture seems curious in a review of modern dance; the demand is at odds with the art form's aesthetics. Additionally, her assumptions about what would have been an accurate portrayal are linked to disdain for the "religious ecstasy" of the ending. Such a reaction reflected tensions within the African American community itself, where some "blacks argued for a more dignified worship experience" as part of a wider project of racial uplift.[80] This same rhetoric of difference and class stratification infuses Galea's discussion of the work as well:

> In reply to the criticism that we should have portrayed the educated Negro's desire for emancipation from the religious hysteria and ignorance of their [*sic*] less fortunate brethren, I wish to say that it was not our aim nor presumption to visualize a solution to such a problem. Rather, we have tried to achieve a stylization of the distinctive qualities of emotional release which remains an important characteristic of the race, and to do this best it was necessary to depict that portion of the race in which this characteristic is still predominate.[81]

Such sentiments undercut the work's progressive aims by revealing latent class biases within both the work and its reception.

Yet the most problematic effect of the erasure of black bodies from the narrative was that this absence encouraged some spectators to perceive the work as comic. Arnold Gran, reviewing a 1939 performance in Oakland, found comedy in the work's racial signifiers: "The tragedy of the theme was both thrown into relief and mercifully attenuated by excellent comedy when, angels, fluttering in to save the erring mortals, appeared in the guise of Harlem bucks and wenches."[82] The scenario Gran describes directly references the costumes, making special note of the male dancers' top hats, tails, and haloes. Yet the following synopsis, a variation presented in programs for some performances, suggests no comic intent:

> Misfortunes visited upon the dark races culminate in an Act of Abomination. The Black Mother mourns her dead. She seeks recourse of prayer. To her comes a Celestial Vision, a literal translation of her spiritual life. The Heavenly Hosts descend. The Black Mother rises and goes among her children to regenerate the sinners and implore salvation for the innocent who have fallen. Through her comes a Resurrection of the Sinners and the sinned against. In the overwhelming tide of a new life she is released from earth bondage.[83]

While this description suggests a positive ending of redemption, resurrection, and eternal life, presented sincerely, not satirically, Lee's renderings are more ambiguous in their intent. The bright colors and depictions of accoutrements (such as hats, gloves, and tails) could suggest an elevation of character status; on the other hand, these markers might also be evocations of the "urban dandy" Zip Coon stereotype familiar from blackface minstrelsy.[84] Gran's connecting the characters to Harlem, as well as the derogatory and sexualized language he employs, strips them of their social efficacy. Certainly, the absence of black dancers in these roles exacerbated a disconnect between intent and reception.

Gran's review of *Let My People Go* was of a special one-night-only performance at the Oakland Auditorium on 25 May 1939 with the Federal Symphony Orchestra, conducted by Nathan Abas, and the Northern California Negro Chorus, directed by Elmer Keeton. This performance occurred about one month before Congress shut down the FTP. This joint production, given almost one year after the dance's Los Angeles premiere, introduced several key variations within the piece, changes that point to an implicit critique of the FTP and its failure to live up to its own ideals. In January 1939, as the FTP was experiencing significant cuts in funding and personnel, *New York Times* dance critic John Martin noted that the

> wiping out of the dance project altogether was at first considered essential in order that the theatre project, of which the dance is a minor department in the present set-up, might be saved from serious injury by the cuts ordered from on high. Happily, there were certain members of the production board who are said to have opposed the idea . . . [and] its essential validity has won a sufficient number of convinced friends to save it from extinction.[85]

The entire project was doomed to extinction, however, thanks to an act of Congress on 30 June. In February, the Golden Gate International Exposition opened at Treasure Island in Northern California, and several FTP units presented work there over the next several months. Among those units, Myra Kinch and the Modern Dance Group performed almost daily.

Costume renderings by Robert Tyler Lee for *Let My People Go. Production bulletin, Concert of Modern Dance, 1938, box 993, Federal Theatre Project Collection, Music Division, Library of Congress, Washington, D.C., 17–18, 22.*

The works the company performed at the Golden Gate Exposition—including *An American Exodus*, *American Holidays*, and *Comedy Dances*—were the least political works in its repertoire. Thus by comparison, the presentation of the more controversial *Let My People Go* on 25 May suggests a different level of political investment from Kinch and her company.[86] As a preface to this special performance, the chorus sang "Go Down, Moses," the spiritual from which the title of Kinch's piece comes. Keeton had arranged a rendition that Leta Miller describes as "more akin to opera than to spiritual arrangements."[87] Galea's score, originally for two pianos, was performed by a full orchestra, with Viola Lee (a singer in the chorus) serving as a narrator

Broadsheet advertising "a program of symphony and modern dance" and the Federal Theatre Modern Dance Group with the Federal Symphony Orchestra, 1939. *Courtesy of the Broward County Library, Bienes Museum of the Modern Book, Fort Lauderdale, Fla.*

by introducing "each episode of the dance with excerpts" from the book of Amos.[88] Although the dance unit still did not feature black dancers, the creation of this more inclusive hybrid performance foregrounded African American experience and musicality through song. At the same time, the evening made even more visible the erasure of African American presence within the dance itself.

The work of Myra Kinch and the Modern Dance Group illuminates the intersection between the actual and the ideal within the national experiment that was the Federal Theatre Project. As noted in other chapters in this anthology, works produced under the auspices of the FTP provided room for diverse voices and offered a wide range of representations of American life but sometimes simultaneously relied on, and perhaps perpetuated, stereotypes in doing so. Seeking to articulate American experience in the idiom of modern dance, Kinch crafted pieces that sought to celebrate the many voices woven within the fabric of U.S. society. Yet, ironically, her most socially conscious work, *Let My People Go*, mirrored some of the very same patterns of inequality it was critiquing. Even while taking a step forward in the 1939 collaboration among the Modern Dance Group, the Federal Symphony Orchestra, and the Negro Chorus, the FTP marginalized the African American artists who contributed to that event; publicity materials for the Program of Symphony and Modern Dance make no mention of the crucial role Keeton and the chorus played in the performance. Despite these shortcomings, the Los Angeles Dance Unit of the FTP engaged with the project's larger mission and, over the course of its brief existence, staged compelling visions of democracy that explored diversity, unity, and the spirit of progress, critiquing racial injustice and linking cultural diversity and racial equality with "modernism," pointing to a more just, democratic future in America.

Notes

1. Hallie Flanagan, *Arena: The History of the Federal Theatre* (1940; New York: Benjamin Blom, 1965), 283.

2. "The Federal Theatre—Recorder of History," 27 February 1937, quoted in Elizabeth Cooper, "Dances about Spain: Censorship at the Federal Theatre Project," *Theatre Research International* 29.3 (2004): 232.

3. Flanagan, *Arena*, 45.

4. Ibid.

5. Mark Franko, *The Work of Dance: Labor, Movement, and Identity in the 1930s* (Middletown, Conn.: Wesleyan University Press, 2002), 17.

6. Myra Kinch quoted in John O'Connor and Lorraine Brown, *The Federal Theatre Project: "Free, Adult, Uncensored"* (London: Eyre Methuen, 1980), 222.

7. "The Federal Theatre—Recorder of History," quoted in Cooper, "Dances about Spain," 232.

8. Barry B. Witham, "Censorship in the Federal Theatre," *Theatre History Studies* 17 (1997): 13. See also Cooper, "Dances about Spain," 232–46.

9. Flanagan, *Arena*, 45.

10. See Susan Manning, "Black Voices, White Bodies: The Performance of Race and Gender in *How Long Brethren*," *American Quarterly* 50.1 (March 1998): 24–46; Rena Fraden, *Blueprints for a Black Federal Theatre, 1935–1939* (Cambridge: Cambridge University Press, 1994); Barry B. Witham, *The Federal Theatre Project: A Case Study* (Cambridge: Cambridge University Press, 2003); and Franko, *Work of Dance*.

11. Manning, "Black Voices," 41.

12. Quoted in Fraden, *Blueprints*, 178.

13. The first Chicago offering, *Ballet Fedre* (1938), featured the critically acclaimed *L'Ag'Ya*, choreographed by Katherine Dunham and performed by an all-black company. Although the individual dances were segregated, the overall program featured a mixed cast. In New York, Charles Weidman cast African American dancer Add Bates in the Federal Dance Theatre's production of *Candide* in 1937.

14. Also called the Federal Dance Project, the Federal Dance Group, and the Federal Theatre Dance Project in newspaper accounts and WPA documents.

15. "Dance Congress In Retrospect," *Federal Theatre Dance Project Bulletin* 1.3 (c. 1936), gift of Lea Wallace, FTP personal folder, box 8, folder 9, p. 1, Special Collections and Archives, George Mason University, Fairfax, Va.

16. "Fascism: Its Meaning for Dancers," *Federal Theatre Dance Project Bulletin* 1.3 (c. 1936): 2.

17. "Quits WPA Dance Group," *New York Times*, 7 February 1937, 52.

18. "Decry Radicalism in Dance Project," *New York Times*, 21 July 1937, 17.

19. O'Connor and Brown, *Federal Theatre Project*, 215.

20. The first concert by the Los Angeles unit was in July 1937; the first in Chicago was in January 1938.

21. Myra Kinch, interview with D. Bowers, 21 February 1976, Works Progress Administration Oral Histories Collection, Collection #C0153, box 6, folder 11, tape 1, side 1, 3, 6–7, Special Collections and Archives, George Mason University.

22. Myra Kinch, "Director's Report," production bulletin, A Festival of American Dance, 1937, box 1008, Federal Theatre Project Collection, Music Division, Library of Congress, Washington, D.C.

23. Ullman was the assistant director of the New York FTP for fifteen months and the regional director for Southern California for three months before resigning in March 1939.

24. James R. Ullman, "Report on Democracy versus the Theatre," *New York Times*, 12 March 1939, 150.

25. Flanagan, *Arena*, 274.

26. Ibid., 284.

27. Isabel Morse Jones, "New Dance Explained as Evolution," *Los Angeles Times*, 24 October 1937, C5.

28. "Myra Kinch to Give Recital of Her Dances," *San Bernardino Daily Sun*, 15 December 1934, 7.

29. Franko, *Work of Dance*, 7. See also Ellen Graff, *Stepping Left: Dance and Politics, 1928–1942* (Durham, N.C.: Duke University Press, 1997).

30. Myra Kinch, "Director's Report," production bulletin, Concert of Modern Dance, 1938, box 993, Federal Theatre Project Collection, 4a.

31. Ramsay Burt, *Alien Bodies: Representations of Modernity, "Race" and Nation in Early Modern Dance* (London: Routledge, 1998), 194.

32. "Myra Kinch Finds Dance Inspiration in Mexico City," *Los Angeles Times*, 23 December 1934, A6.

33. Marjory M. Fisher, "American Dancer Heads WPA Ballet Group," *San Francisco News*, 15 September 1937, Kinch Scrapbooks, Jerome Robbins Dance Division, New York Public Library; "Myra Kinch Searches for U.S. Dance," October 1938, Kinch Scrapbooks; "Myra Kinch Ballet Will Dance Here," *Oakland Tribune*, 21 May 1939, 19. This pattern of establishing Kinch's American identity is evident in reviews of her pre-FTP work as well: "Myra Kinch Finds Dance Inspiration," A6; "European Dance Debut Proves Exacting Test," *Los Angeles Times*, 7 August 1932, B14. Of note is that Kinch's cross-cultural experience is highlighted, but her American citizenship is reinforced. Interestingly, in July 1932 a notice in the *Los Angeles Times* for Kinch's upcoming performance at Griffith Park refers to Kinch as a German dancer, a point that was amended the following week.

34. Myra Kinch, program notes, Festival of Modern Dance, L.D.S. Auditorium, 25 March 1938, Records of the Federal Theatre Project, Record Group 69, National Archives, College Park, Md.

35. Hallie Flanagan, "A Brief Delivered by Hallie Flanagan, Director, Federal Theatre Project, Works Progress Administration before the Committee on Patents, House of Representatives, Washington, D.C., February 8, 1938," Federal Theatre Collection, National Archives, 6.

36. Burt, *Alien Bodies*, 8.

37. "Dance Festival Scores Success on Hollywood Stage," Kinch Scrapbooks.

38. The Rialtan, "Federals' Dance Bill Applauded," *Los Angeles Evening Herald and Express*, July 1937, Kinch Scrapbooks.

39. Fisher, "American Dancer Heads WPA Ballet Group."

40. Randolph S. Bourne, "Trans-national America," *Atlantic Monthly*, July 1916, http://www.theatlantic.com/ideastour/idealism/bourne-full.html, accessed 9 January 2014.

41. Kinch, "Director's Report," production bulletin, 1937, 2.

42. A traditional Mexican dance; Kinch describes the one performed in "Tocatta" (*sic*) as a "modern Zapateado, with the beat of the feet in counterpoint with the music"; see ibid.

43. Johanna Lawrence, "American Dance Sponsored by Uncle Sam," 28 July 1937, Kinch Scrapbooks.

44. "Dance Group in Recital," *Daily News*, 1937, Records of the Federal Theatre Project, Record Group 69, National Archives.

45. Bourne, "Trans-national America."

46. "The Knave Week-Day Column," *Oakland Tribune*, 1 March 1939, 17.

47. Kinch, program notes, Festival of Modern Dance, 25 March 1938.

48. Fisher, "American Dancer Heads WPA Ballet Group."

49. "Federal Group Gives Festival of U.S. Dance," 1937, Kinch Scrapbooks.

50. Deborah Jowitt, *Time and the Dancing Image* (Berkeley: University of California Press, 1988), 177.

51. Myra Kinch, program notes, Festival of American Dance, 1937, Kinch Scrapbooks.

52. See Carl Kondo, "Cursory Comments," 1938, and "Federal Group Gives Festival of U.S. Dance," Kinch Scrapbooks. Ironically, Teru Izumida was relocated to Manzanar during World War II. See Bella Lewitzky, interview with Lorraine Brown, 12 March 1979, Works Progress Administration Oral Histories Collection, Collection #C0153, box 7, folder 6, Special Collections and Archives, George Mason University; and http://www.japaneserelocation.org.

53. Myra Kinch, "Synopsis," production bulletin, Concert of Modern Dance, 1938, box 993, Federal Theatre Project Collection, 1.

54. Ibid., 1.

55. Viola Hegyi Swisher, "Dancers Give Program at Belasco," *Hollywood-Citizen News*, 30 September 1938, Kinch Scrapbooks.

56. Mollie Prager, "Myra Kinch Concert," *Jewish Community Press*, 1938, Kinch Scrapbooks.

57. Kinch, "Synopsis," 1.

58. Manuel Galea, "Composer's Report," production bulletin, Concert of Modern Dance, 1938, box 993, Federal Theatre Project Collection, 5.

59. W. E. Oliver, "Style Fragments Appear in 'Concert of Modern Dance,'" *Herald Express*, 1938, Kinch Scrapbooks.

60. Kondo, "Cursory Comments."

61. "Lynching, Whites & Negroes, 1882–1968," Tuskegee University Online Repository, http://192.203.127.197/archive/bitstream/handle/123456789/511/Lynching%201882%201968.pdf?sequence=1, accessed 5 January 2015.

62. Additionally, choreographer Charles Weidman premiered "Lynchtown" as part of his three-part work *Atavisms* in New York in 1936.

63. Kinch, "Synopsis," 2.

64. Helen Tamiris's *How Long, Brethren?*, first produced in May 1937, was derived from *Negro Songs of Protest*, a collection compiled by Lawrence Gellert and Eli Siegmeister, culled from material Gellert had collected by interviewing and recording songs sung by black Americans while traveling in the southern United States. The racial implications of the production are complicated by the fact that the dancers were all female and white; the songs, arranged by Genevieve Pitot, were sung live by the Federal Theatre Negro chorus, part of the FTP's Negro unit (a rare collaboration). Scholars such as Ellen Graff, Susan Manning, and Mark Franko have addressed the potential meanings engendered by these choices and the difficulty of assessing the ways in which the juxtaposition of bodies and voices informs the messages of the piece. Horton's company featured black dancers by the 1940s, but photographs of *Chronicle* at the Library of Congress show no black dancers in the production. The lynching victim in the piece was danced by Bella Lewitzky, who danced for both Horton and Kinch.

65. Susan Manning, *Modern Dance, Negro Dance: Race in Motion* (Minneapolis: University of Minnesota Press, 2004), 10.

66. Franko, *Work of Dance*, 99.

67. Kinch, "Director's Report," production bulletin, 1938, 4–4a.

68. "Myra Kinch Wins More Praise with New Dance Program," *San Bernardino County Sun*, 16 July 1938, 13.

69. Leo Simon, "Modern Dance," *Daily News*, 1938, 9, Kinch Scrapbooks; Richard Sheridan Ames, "Stage and Screen: Run Little Kinchillun," c. 1938, Kinch Scrapbooks; Oliver, "Style Fragments."

70. Burt, *Alien Bodies*, 189.

71. Harry Mines, "Miss Kinch and the Dance," *Daily News*, 30 September 1938, Kinch Scrapbooks.

72. bell hooks, *Black Looks: Race and Representation* (Boston: South End Press, 1992), 26.

73. Ames, "Stage and Screen."

74. Galea, "Composer's Report," 6.

75. Manning, *Modern Dance*, 19.

76. See "Myra Kinch Program Wins Favor," and Harry Mines, "Miss Kinch and the Dance," Kinch Scrapbooks.

77. Oliver, "Style Fragments."

78. Prager, "Myra Kinch Concert."

79. Ibid.

80. Calvin White Jr., *The Rise of Respectability: Race, Religion, and the Church of God in Christ* (Fayetteville: University of Arkansas Press, 2012), ix.

81. Galea, "Composer's Report," 6.

82. Arnold Gran, "Applause for Myra Kinch's Dancing Group," *Oakland Post-Enquirer*, 26 May 1939, 9.

83. Myra Kinch, program notes, Festival of Modern Dance, UCLA, Monday, 1 August 1938, National Archives.

84. Eric Lott, *Love and Theft: Blackface Minstrelsy and the American Working Class* (Oxford: Oxford University Press, 1993), 23.

85. John Martin, "The Dance: WPA Troubles," *New York Times*, 8 January 1939, 130.

86. Kinch believed *Let My People Go* "was one of the things that [made WPA officials decide she] was doing propaganda"; quoted in O'Connor and Brown, *Federal Theatre Project*, 223.

87. Leta E. Miller, "Elmer Keeton and His Bay Area Negro Chorus," *Black Music Research Journal* 30.2 (Fall 2010): 315–16.

88. Gran, "Applause for Myra Kinch's Dancing Group," 9.

9. Imagined Democracy

The Federal Theatre Project Performs (Native) America (1938–39)

Elizabeth A. Osborne

> The reforms of the Indian New Deal failed to endure because, in the last analysis, they were imposed upon the Indians, who did not see these elaborate proposals as answers to their own wants and needs.
>
> —Graham Taylor, *The New Deal and American Indian Tribalism*

The Federal Theatre Project (1935–39) operated at an uneasy crossroads when it came to representations of American Indians. National director Hallie Flanagan took pride in the Federal Theatre Project's (FTP) diversity, particularly with the progressive Negro and foreign language units that populated cities throughout the nation. Less widely known but equally important, the Oklahoma unit employed a number of American Indians, and much of the material it researched, created, and produced centered "on the rich folklore of the Southwest—simple stories of pioneers, cowboys, Indians . . . people who made history."[1] The work that emerged from these units played a vital role in restoring agency and prominence to writers, actors, directors, and other theatre professionals from marginalized groups, as well as in drawing attention to the stories, myths, and plights of groups who were all too easily forgotten in the hard times of the Great Depression. Moreover, in taking this work to a national audience the FTP became a visible and public institution that shaped popular opinion. For American Indians, this opportunity for representation arose during a turbulent decade that had the potential to rewrite their relationship with the U.S. government.

One example of the FTP's Native American programming was the 1936 production of Lynn Riggs's groundbreaking *Cherokee Night* (1932), which dealt with the devastating effects of the U.S. government's nineteenth-century policies of eradication as a "lost" generation of American Indian children transitioned to adulthood. Through the FTP, Riggs's complex representation of Cherokee culture, history, and memory (as explored by W. Douglas Powers in chapter 4) had the potential to reach an unprecedented working-class audience in New York City. Yet the FTP used the production as a vehicle to train directors participating in its community drama training school rather than as a venue for widespread public consumption, thus limiting this important production's exposure.

In contrast, a series of radio dramas produced by the FTP titled *First Americans* played to thousands of Americans for fourteen weeks in 1938 and 1939. Created by the Los Angeles FTP and sponsored by the Board of Education of the City Schools of Los Angeles, the series was designed to appeal to students and focused on historical rather than contemporaneous events. These programs aired in the afternoons on the widely available station KECA, a local ABC AM-radio affiliate, in the midst of an almost meteoric rise in the popularity of radio programming. By 1938, 83 percent of American households owned at least one radio, enabling widespread consumption of radio programming across diverse groups.[2] As FDR's famous fireside chats demonstrated, this democratic medium could and often did attract listeners across lines of race, gender, class, and ethnicity. The fourteen episodes in the *First Americans* series dramatized stories of the Hopi, Zuni, Iroquois, Cherokee, Navajo, Dakota, Ojibway, and Tolowa tribes, as well as a smattering of other tribes categorized under broader titles like the "Southeast Indians" and the "California Indians."[3] Each fifteen-minute broadcast delved into the history, myth, and customs of a particular tribe, often by imagining an episode connected with a specific historical moment or tradition.[4] As Margaret F. Savilonis argues in chapter 8, the FTP was indeed an "experiment in democracy" dedicated to engaging with and stimulating interest in contemporaneous social issues. With *First Americans*, the FTP drew the attention of the American public to the unique histories and cultural identities of American Indians. The radio series was one important initiative within the FTP's larger project of using performance to jumpstart a dialogue about cultural and racial difference.

Like many other marginalized groups during the Great Depression, American Indians experienced extraordinary hardship, but their difficulties did not begin with the stock market crash in 1929. As documented in the 1928 Meriam Report—long considered to be one of the most influential accounts of U.S./Indian relations in this era—American Indians faced a profoundly demoralizing array of social maladies.[5] Of particular concern were radical inequities in household income (American Indian households averaged some of the lowest per capita income in the country); insufficient, incomplete, and abusive education practices that mandated the removal of children from their family and tribal homes; widespread health concerns, including a dearth of quality health care facilities, alarming infant mortality rates, and distrust in white medicine; inadequate land allocation and inheritance laws; and the utter dependence of many tribes on the U.S. government and the Bureau of Indian Affairs (BIA) for matters of survival.

The 1934 Indian Reorganization Act (IRA) marked a turning point in U.S. government policy. Described by some as the "only bright spot in the [Roosevelt] administration's treatment of minorities,"[6] the IRA (aka the Wheeler-Howard Act or the "Indian New Deal") has been deemed "the most important general statute after the General Allotment Act of 1887 and probably the most important single statute affecting Indians during the two-thirds of a century since its passage."[7] The IRA instituted wide-ranging social reforms, including the prohibition of further land allotments and the regulation of those allotments that were already in place, expansion of the reservation system, and increased attention to education, housing, and health initiatives. These reforms would boost American Indian quality of life and begin a process of political and cultural recognition.[8] Yet in March 1937, Senator Burton K. Wheeler of Montana, one of the act's original sponsors, publicly called for its repeal—arguing that its enactment had been too slow and that it relied too heavily on "herding" the Indians into reservations.[9] Volatile debates over the IRA's future raged through much of 1937, leaving confusion and concern over exactly how the U.S. government could best approach the many facets of its troubled relationship with American Indians. The FTP's *First Americans* series took up the task of publicly representing American Indians during this turbulent social and political moment.

This chapter examines the *First Americans* radio series with an eye toward the FTP's ambiguous and at times contradictory negotiation of American Indian representations during a decade that would redefine relations between the federal government and Indians. The radio plays situate American Indians within a mythologized past and rely on nineteenth-century melodrama types like the old "Indian" dialect; they simultaneously reimagine the "noble savage" archetype by focusing on the "noble" elements and justifying, distracting from, or altogether ignoring the "savage." The plays avoid discussion of current social issues but gently remind listeners of the many past wrongs the U.S. government enacted upon the continent's "first Americans." They draw attention to American Indians' rich history, mythology, and spiritual belief systems and highlight the potential cultural and social value of their contributions to the nation while overlooking less amenable customs. Above all, the series espouses the desire to respectfully assimilate the American Indians into the American social fabric while maintaining select facets of their distinct identities; American Indians are thus reimagined as Americans in pursuit of the American dream. In these ways, the *First Americans* radio plays strike a careful balance between the evocation of sympathy for the nineteenth-century plights of the American Indian and a desire to marshal popular support for the major governmental reforms that began with the IRA. My analysis will consider how these representations demonstrated the long-standing racial tensions that haunted the public imagination and the formation of a unique American identity. I argue that these broadcasted performances of "Others" both promoted and undermined the progressive model of self-governance and democratic inclusion—a historic "experiment in democracy"—forwarded by the IRA and the Roosevelt administration. Thus, the *First Americans* educational radio programs, created for a very specific audience in California, experimented with potential strategies in an ongoing national search for viable models of cross-cultural dialogue.

Investigating the wide-ranging and complex historical implications of *First Americans* requires not only close readings of the radio plays themselves but also a reconsideration of the contemporaneous social and cultural histories of American Indians onstage and throughout U.S. culture. The nation has a long history of dramatizing American Indians onstage. In performances ranging from James Nelson Barker's portrayal of the romance between Captain John Smith and Pocahontas in *The Indian Princess* (1808) to Buffalo Bill's wildly popular and internationally renowned Wild West show (1893–1908), American Indians have played a prominent role in representations of the frontier and manifest destiny, and thus in the fundamental creation and representation of American identity. Just as these and other theatrical precedents functioned in multiple ways, so too did the *First Americans* radio plays educate the public in matters related to American Indians, even as they carefully ascribe idealized characteristics to the Indians by performing an unthreatening and thoroughly domesticated American identity. This delicate balance emphasizes the historical and cultural value of American Indians by embracing their legends and art forms and by focusing on events from the nineteenth century or before (rather than on a more troubling recent history). Such a portrayal minimizes the direct representation of violence, emphasizes the (real or imagined) American Indians' desire and capacity to live culturally rich and peaceful lives, and articulates a deep desire for the mythic American dream. Indeed, these dramatized "First Americans" yearn to assimilate peacefully into American society; they settle into nuclear families, work hard to contribute to society, and (in a nod to the Christian practice of "turning the other cheek") resolve conflicts through collaboration and compromise rather than with arrows or tomahawks. In a historical moment that had turned the relationship between the government and the American Indian on its head—a moment in which the passing of the IRA had reversed decades-long federal policies designed to systematically destroy the Indians' heritage and tribal communities—these new representations of American Indians had the potential to reverberate widely through America's political, social, and cultural spheres.

In his landmark book *Playing Indian*, Philip J. Deloria connects the real-life experiences of American Indians to the ways in which that identity is constructed within a wider American imaginary. He argues that the American Indians have played an integral role in the construction of a uniquely American identity (or the lack thereof) since the first white pioneers arrived on these shores. Since the American Revolution, Deloria asserts, Americans have articulated themselves in opposition to others (Europeans, British, American Indians, and so on); in other words, American identity has been defined by what it is *not* rather than by what it *is*:

> Whereas Euro-Americans had imprisoned themselves in the logical mind and the social order, Indians represented instinct and freedom. They spoke for the "spirit of the continent." Whites desperately desired that spirit, yet they invariably failed to become aboriginal and thus "finished." Savage Indians served Americans as oppositional figures against whom one might imagine a civilized national Self. Coded as freedom, however, wild Indianness proved equally attractive, setting up a "have-the-cake-and-eat-it-too" dialectic of simultaneous desire and repulsion.[10]

This "simultaneous desire and repulsion" led to a situation in which the formation of American identity required either the assimilation or eradication of American Indian populations. U.S. policy regarding American Indians vacillated between these poles for two centuries prior to the sweeping changes that would arise under cultural pluralist John Collier's 1933–45 reign as commissioner for the Bureau of Indian Affairs. This back-and-forth policy was clear both to experts and to the general population. A 1940 *Survey Graphic* article speaks to the U.S. government's policies of eradication:

> Since the beginning of white occupation of the North American continent the Indian has been trampled upon and exploited. . . . Every effort was made, over a long period of time, to get rid of the Indian; to kill him off, starve him and discourage him into race suicide, in an effort to solve the Indian problem by eliminating the Indian.[11]

The article goes on to discuss the implementation of the IRA, noting that it offered American Indians the chance to exercise some degree of democratic authority over their own lives as they assimilated into the U.S. "melting pot." Despite reactions from tribal leaders ranging from wary acceptance to outright rejection, the IRA passed into law on 18 June 1934; it was a day that advocates of the act would dub "Indian Independence Day."[12] With the IRA, the U.S. government literally thrust an experimental democracy upon those nations that agreed to accept its terms.[13]

The passage of the IRA came within a decade marked by surging public interest in the affairs of the American Indian. Between 1930 and 1940, more than forty-five thousand articles related to Indians appeared in the *New York Times* alone, including informational articles about various nations or individuals and diverse commentaries about native cultures, arts, and rituals. This rising tide of fascination shows through in a 26 September 1937 report on an "Indian Day Fete" in New York City's Prospect Park. The article describes how representatives from twenty-four tribal families—resplendent in the costumes of traditional Indian regalia and carrying weapons of historic value such as a hundred-year-old tomahawk used in the Indian Wars—performed "authentic" rituals including a christening, a "peace-pipe ceremonial, the kindling of the council fire and [an] invocation ritual."[14] The author specifies that the performance of these authentic rituals attracted an estimated two thousand spectators. A similar spectacle at the Brooklyn Museum culminated in an elaborate dance performed by American Indian men, each "well above six feet and built proportionally. Their thickly beaded war shirts, buckskin leggings and caps were heirlooms."[15] Yet it was the appearance of the half dozen papooses ("young children") that the three-thousand-person audience applauded most vigorously. Again, the article emphasizes the historic value—the "authenticity"—of the performers, their props, their costumes, and their bodies.

The "Indian Day Fete" article, and many others like it, demonstrates a desire to return to a "traditional" notion of the American Indian who speaks little or broken English, lives proudly off the land, and personifies an authentic connection to the past, the land, and an imagined "spirit of

America." That these American Indians gathered in New York City parks to perform this role in 1937—the same year that political opponents attacked the viability of the IRA—is of paramount importance. After the celebration, these "authentic Indians" may well have returned to their homes in Brooklyn and to their roles as members of the vast army of unemployed and relief workers that permeated the Great Depression. In this way, these American Indians consciously performed the identities that many white Americans anticipated, without allowing the contemporaneous social issues faced by tribes to complicate that expectation. They played the kinder, gentler version of the historical "Indian," rather than a community in need of redress for injustices suffered and of social, political, or economic aid.

First Americans, the FTP radio series, operated along similar lines. As with the Indian Day Fete, the *First Americans* series occupied an ephemeral space and operated in an imagined past that defied any connection to the present while resisting the nineteenth-century stereotype of the noble savage. Vital to the underlying function of the series (and to the celebration reported upon in the newspaper), this in-between space and time allowed for the possibility that American Indians might maintain some aspects of their tribal identities even as they assimilated into U.S. society. The series was based on an extensive anthropological and sociological history of American Indians researched by and written for the FTP, which highlighted the legends, customs, ideology, and accomplishments of the individual and united nations. The resulting text, *First Americans*, came in the form of a 363-page document that served as source material for the complete series of radio plays. At least four of the radio plays in the *First Americans* series contain extensive passages of narration lifted nearly verbatim from this report.

Like the Indian Day Fete, the *First Americans* series revealed a fascination with American Indian history and myth and the complex notion of authenticity. Both sets of performances carefully documented rituals, traditions, and the "facts" of an American Indian way of life that had, for most practical purposes, disappeared because of U.S. government policies of eradication. Rather than fusing presentations of the past with examinations of the present, both sets of performances avoided contentious public debates surrounding the future of the IRA and the place of the American Indian in U.S. society. On the surface, the *First Americans* radio plays dramatized a history that was already written. Like the FTP's famous Living Newspapers, the extensive research provided documentation that supported the production choices to those who would accuse the FTP of advocating a political agenda. Because of this focus, the plays drew attention to the recorded past of the American Indians in very specific and strategic ways.

Designed to appeal to Americans as an educational program, the *First Americans* radio series capitalized on the public's growing interest in American Indian culture. Set in an imagined historical moment, the series invited Depression-era listeners to escape their own troubles for a brief moment by delving into American Indian history, myths, or culture, with special emphasis on the most widely familiar art forms and tribes. For example, episodes 8 and 9 examined the history and symbols related to Navajo blanket weaving, while episode 10 portrayed the relationship between the Dakotas and buffalo hunting. Situated in the midst of the debates over the future of the IRA and of the tenuous budding relationship between the U.S. government and American Indians, the *First Americans* radio series oscillated between assimilation and extermination, signaling a need to reinvent a romanticized past in order to integrate the American Indians into the present. Though many potential topics emerge, a focused examination on the radio dramas' portrayals of war and the potential for violence reveals that balancing act most vividly. In attempting to integrate the American Indian into the myth of the American dream, these radio plays carefully revised existing notions of the culture and history of American Indians so as to find common ground between American Indians and the dominant white culture.

As Thomas Postlewait deftly explains, the connection between American Indians and violence had solidified in the stage portrayals of the late nineteenth century:

> Before the Civil War some plays, such as *Metamora*, presented "Indians" as noble savages. But the western expansion and the Indian wars of the 1870s and 1880s changed the popular idea of Indians. In the mind of the general public Indians became ruthless savages: they killed General Custer, they attacked wagon trains and stagecoaches, they burned the homes of settlers, and they scalped innocent women and children. Accordingly, the American theatre provided an outpouring of plays set in the West that featured the struggle of civilization against the savage Indians.[16]

Postlewait's description is particularly useful here because the majority of the *First Americans* radio plays are set in a reimagined late-nineteenth century when representations of "savage Indians" abounded on U.S. stages. Yet acts of violence rarely appear in the *First Americans* series. Instead, allusions to violence emerge as historical reference points, as external threats to the tribe, or as a response of absolute last resort to imminent peril.

Consider this exchange from the first episode between a tribal elder and a young Hopi brave:

> YOUNG BRAVE: Oh Chief Wikyatiwa, the numbers of our dead are many. Our Braves untutored in the ways of war, have again fallen victims to the bloodthirsty Apaches. The maidens wail and weep for their lovers and husbands.
>
> WIKYATIWA: Ours have been the ways of peace: So have our Gods decreed. So must we live.
>
> YOUNG BRAVE: This time come but the Apaches. Soon the Navajo will join them and perchance the Piutes.[17]

Here, the Young Brave laments the deaths of the Hopis, who are "untutored in the ways of war," and attributes their fall to the "bloodthirsty Apaches." In the face of this devastation, Chief Wikyatiwa counsels peace and patience. Even with the greater threat of invasion by the Apaches, Navajos, and Piutes, the elders refuse to mount a violent defense. Instead they join together and pray to the gods for protection, which arrives in the form of the Tewas, a tribe of "born fighters." The script describes how the Tewas drive the Apaches, Navajos, and Piutes away in a single sentence of spare, factual narration that discloses few details: "Before the marauding tribes of Apaches, Navajos and Piutes had learned not to kidnap and steal, 180 of their hostile numbers were killed."[18] The play thus establishes that the Hopis are a peaceful tribe with neither a history of warmongering nor a desire to train warriors and suggests that they are incapable of mounting a defense against a single invading tribe. The narration emphasizes how the attacking tribes suffered severe losses to their ranks of "hostile" warriors and implies that civilians were left in peace. Finally, by implying that the attacking tribes "learned not to kidnap and steal," the text suggests that the Tewas' defense effectively taught the inciting tribes the civilizing lesson that kidnapping and stealing are punishable offenses. This brief, refined discussion of warfare then shifts quickly into the domestication of the Tewas via a young maiden named Nampeyo and her wholesome love affair with the Hopi brave White Cloud. The remainder of the episode—eight of its ten manuscript pages—centers on the courtship of Nampeyo and White Cloud and on the ways in which they consciously bridge cultural barriers in order to live out their days as husband and wife, father and mother.

The Hopi episode set the stage for a series of dramas in which violence is consistently present but also largely removed from the action. *First Americans*' depiction of the Hopis—a vulnerable tribe living in fear of the bloodthirsty Apaches, praying to their gods for help and determined to live in peace—sets up a parallel between the Hopis and many white settlers. Returning to Postlewait's description of the public perception of the American Indian in the late nineteenth century, here the Hopis are resituated as the victims of "ruthless savages" who attack peaceful settlers and scalp innocent women and children. Moreover, the Tewas—"born warriors" who answer the Hopis' prayers and defeat the Apaches and Navajos—become symbolically domesticated through the romance of Nampeyo and White Cloud. Their courtship, punctuated by frequent swells of a musical "love song," demonstrates gentle customs of hair combing, sewing wedding apparel, making piki bread, and eventually the christening of their first child, Whirlwind. By the conclusion of the episode, Nampeyo and White Cloud appear to be living out a version of the American dream. Surrounded by friends and family, they work hard, build a home for their children, and contribute to their society as citizens. In this way, the inaugural episode of the *First Americans* series repositions the Hopis as a sympathetic community, forced to battle bloodthirsty opposition while struggling to survive and thrive.

This characterization of violence vilifies the violent Apache and Navajo tribes while championing the peaceful Hopis in a way that is both progressive and troubling. While the FTP's desire to show specificity in terms of individual tribes rather than to group all American Indians into a homogeneous "noble savage" is commendable, the *First Americans* series frequently creates conflict by pitting one tribe against another. Each tribe comes to represent a common melodramatic type. The Hopis emerge as the ingenues, desperately in need of audience sympathy and strong fighters who will rise to their defense. The Tewas play the heroes, powerful fighters who battle unknowable odds and rescue the Hopis. By reversing these tribal representations with the Tewa maiden Nampeyo and Hopi brave White Cloud, who fall in love and live out their days in domestic bliss, the play effectively domesticates both the Hopis and the Tewas. The Navajos and Apaches portray the faceless villains who threaten to annihilate the Hopis and, in so doing, unwittingly bring together the couple to live out the American dream. These representations both trade on and manipulate the nineteenth-century stage stereotypes that Postlewait describes in a way that simultaneously refutes those categories for some tribes and reinforces them for others. Indeed, when the *First Americans* series ultimately takes on the Navajos in the eighth and ninth episodes, it focuses exclusively on the mythologized stories of Navajo women weaving blankets and desiring freedom from their regimented social structures rather than on the men who hunt or fight for the tribe. Thus the stereotype of faceless warriors who attack the Hopis in the first episode remains untroubled and reinforces the FTP's fraught representations of American Indians.

Similar themes arise in other episodes as well. In the second installment, the Zunis face a terrible drought and rampant starvation in a historical migration that parallels that of the "Okies" during the Dust Bowl;[19] their flight to the neighboring Acoma tribe garners willing aid and culminates with the wish that "no season go by that one of your young men, comes not to court one of our young women. . . . Let our blood flow together that some day we may be as one people."[20] Episode 4 follows the romance of white explorer John Trimble and the Iroquois woman Cries for Spring. Before the couple can come together, however, Trimble must embrace the traditions of the Iroquois. The fifth episode, depicting the Five Civilized Tribes of the Southeast—the Cherokee, Chickasaw, Choctaw, Creek, and Seminole—dramatizes a young man's choice between a future as a warrior and one as a medicine man; he eventually opts for the path of the medicine man, giving up his way of life as a warrior and his young wife to pursue a higher calling. The twelfth episode follows the romance of the Ojibway maiden Red Feather and Brave Heart, a young Ojibway brave who saves his peace-loving people with a medicine bag made from a sawbill duck; his faith and his medicine bag's magic imbue his people with the speed to flee their enemies. The Ojibways bring their tribe's peace pipe to the leaders of the neighboring tribe and return home to their loving families.

Each of these episodes recalls a nineteenth-century American Indian type not defined by violence. When violence is present, it is enacted *upon*—rather than enacted *by*—the American Indian tribe depicted in the episode. Each drama's protagonists are the victims rather than the perpetrators. Inverting the pattern identified by Postlewait, *First Americans* situates American Indians within a role traditionally occupied by white settlers: as a population fearing attacks on their homes and families, beset by poverty and starvation, praying to their gods for help, and struggling futilely against the terror and violence of the Other. This refiguring of the "noble savage" is all "noble" and no "savage." When combined with the efforts to "Americanize" the Indians by having them live out the American dream, this dramaturgical strategy aligns the American Indian with the radio audience. Reaching across differences of culture and race, this choice offers the audience the seemingly paradoxical ability to learn about and remember the history, culture, and beliefs of the American Indian, even as the drama actively erases contemporaneous social concerns. The American

Indian thus exists simultaneously across time and space, captured in an imagined past, purged from the present, and projected into an idealized future of assimilation into mainstream U.S. society.

The notable exception to this pattern occurs in the eleventh episode. The second of a two-part special on the Dakota tribe, this episode stands out as unique in several ways. It is the only one in the series that contains an extended discussion of violence, it directs that violence explicitly toward white men, and it reverses the perspective so that white men become characters in the piece. The first of the two-part special examines the Dakotas' dependence on the buffalo, focusing on the tribe's desperate circumstances and their increasingly frantic search for the white buffalo that the gods required as a sacrifice. This portrayal lays the groundwork for the violence that follows in the next installment of the series.[21]

As the eleventh episode begins, a narrator succinctly explains the conflict: "In the later years of the history of the Dakotas, the white man figures with a certain deadly prominence, for it was through the lands of the Dakotas that he laid the tracks of that monster of fire, steam and deafening roar."[22] The encroachment of the railroad throws the Dakotas into chaos; it destroys the buffalo herds that sustain the tribe, devastates their land with deep scars that can never heal, and anticipates the influx of white settlers. The railroad heralds the destruction of their way of life, and their peaceful efforts to deter it are for naught. The medicine man's rousing speech functions as both a call to action and foreshadowing:

> If we can wipe out the pale face and destroy the iron monster, tear up the tracks they have laid down, it will be years before they will have the courage again to come into the lands of the Dakotas. We must not wait—now is the time. Let us muster all our braves—send the word to all the tribes. In the dead of the night we must fall upon the whites and kill them. Restring the bows, fill the guns with powder and shot, sharpen the tomahawk and hunting knife. Be ready to fall upon the invaders of the prairie and wreak our vengeance upon them.[23]

This speech both recalls the late nineteenth-century Indian archetype of the bloodthirsty savage and signals the gravity of the situation: "We must not wait—now is the time." The medicine man realizes that the railroad portends the end of his nation's way of life. He calls for all of the braves and all of the tribe's allies to act. "If the buffalo is lost to the prairie," he says, "so will be the Indian."[24] Their actions in this moment will either defeat the white man (and the railroad) or mean the end of the Dakotas.

With this reference to the end of the tribe, the medicine man in the radio play invokes a history that has not yet transpired in the play's timeline. The Dakotas, as part of the Great Sioux Nation, refused to bend to the government's rule in the late nineteenth century. Vicious combat occurred during the Dakota War (1862), the Great Sioux War (1876–77), the Battle of Little Bighorn (1877), and the Wounded Knee Massacre (1890), and many Sioux fled to Canada rather than adhere to U.S. law.[25] With these battles floating in the consciousness of the 1930s audience, it is notable that the radio play deliberately refrains from identifying the Dakotas as Sioux; they are simply the Dakota, a tribe with allies in the area, to be sure, but not able to call upon the resources of the Great Sioux Nation. In other installments, the *First Americans* series emphasizes specific tribal names, customs, and objects. The omission of the more commonly known "Sioux" as a framing device for the Dakotas' struggles situates the Dakotas as isolated and under-resourced and suggests a political and social agenda to garner greater support for the plight of the American Indian.

This predisposition becomes clear in the following scene, set in a camp of white railroad workers. Prior to the attack, the workers quietly doze around their fire, weaving a relaxed conversation of home, girlfriends, and patriotic songs by Stephen Foster. In an exchange that parallels the numerous American Indian superstitions explored in previous episodes, a railroad worker gifted with premonition senses the impending arrival of the Dakota warriors. He first says that he is "hearing things in the wind" and that the voice is "harsh and loud, filled with a warnin'." The others mock him, suggesting that he has awakened from a bad dream, has seen the headless horseman, or is being haunted by a witch. When he perseveres, claiming that his mother "had the gift of forebodings and warnings," the others decide to fire a shot off into the plains. The shot reveals the Dakota war party, poised for attack.[26]

War whoops, gunshots, and screams of terror disrupt the quiet conversation around the campfire. Yet even in the midst of battle, several white men (while frantically searching for reinforcements) take the time to sympathize with the plight of the Dakotas:

> VOICE FOUR: If somethin' ain't done soon, we'll all be wiped out. This is their home, this prairie, and we're just chasin' 'em out. Scarin' away the buffalo which is their food.
>
> VOICE TWO: They're fightin' for their very lives and I can't say as I blame 'em but now we're fightin' for ours.

VOICE THREE: Cover me, boys, and I'll make a run for the locomotive. Keep the Indians away from her until I can get up steam and we've all got a chance.[27]

The workers here understand that the stakes for the Dakotas are a matter of life and death. Even as arrows and fire rain down upon them, they credit the Dakotas' need to defend their way of life. The workers want to survive, though. When they successfully send the train for reinforcements, the Dakota braves surrender and send word to the women and children to begin "the first retreat in the history of the Dakotas. . . . Forever and ever, the Indian will be pushed farther back, until the day will come when he will not be master of all his eyes can see, but only the smallest portion."[28] Again, this narration references a history of which these characters would not be aware; the Dawes Act of 1887 (aka the General Allotment Act) served as the cornerstone of the federal assimilationist policy toward American Indians until the passage of the IRA in 1934. In addition to extending legal authority to the reservations, requiring children to attend a "universal" school system, and breaking up tribal lands by allotting plots to individuals and selling off unused portions, the Dawes Act awarded U.S. citizenship to those American Indians who accepted property allotments and separated from their tribes. By pushing the American Indians into smaller and smaller parcels of land, the Dawes Act intentionally fractured the tribal reservations so as to force American Indians to assimilate into Euro-American institutions. Between 1887 and 1934, the Dawes Act reduced American Indian reservations from 138 million acres to 48 million acres.[29] This statement regarding the "smallest portion" of land reminds the audience of one of the most well known and uncontroversial elements of the IRA—its repeal of the Dawes Act and emphasis on recovering land for the American Indians.

This rhetorical strategy of dramatizing white men considering the American Indians' plight—used only once in the entire radio series—offers a way to portray the violence associated with American Indians in the public mind while actively refuting its larger meaning. The dramaturgical shift in perspective from the Dakotas to the white men empowers white characters to speak on behalf of American Indian subjects. By acknowledging the Dakotas' motives in going to battle, the railroad workers affirm that the Dakotas were more than bloodthirsty "savages." Instead, the episode portrays the Dakotas as individuals fighting honorably to protect their identities, their families, and their way of life.

Perhaps the most powerful parallel drawn between the American Indians and the early American settlers is in the almost mythologized ways both groups battle for their own freedom. From the days when the United States was nothing more than a loose collection of upstart colonies, Americans have declared their independence through such famous phrases as Patrick Henry's "Give me liberty or give me death!" Similar rhetorical flourishes pepper the *First Americans* series. In episode 6, when confronted with the directive to forsake his position as warrior and become a medicine man, the heroic Strong-as-a-Panther declares, "Among our peoples I am free to choose that which I will."[30] Episode 8 features a Navajo woman proclaiming, in a manner that evokes Patrick Henry, "I will roam the mountains, plains and mesas, I will live even as the wild mountain goat—on whatever the Great Spirit offers him—whether it be life, or death, but I will be free—!"[31] This drive for freedom—for the ability to enjoy "life, liberty, and the pursuit of happiness"—similarly propels the Dakotas to sacrifice all in their last-ditch battle against the railroad. In this way, the *First Americans* series taps into the American identity crisis that Philip Deloria identifies in *Playing Indian*; it aligns Euro-Americans' desperate desire for the instinct, freedom, and "spirit of the continent" that the Indians represent with performances of American Indians that mesh these potentialities with the American dream. The "noble savage" becomes a "noble American freedom-fighter."

During a decade in which the government struggled to redefine its relationship to American Indians, the *First Americans* series simultaneously dramatized both the assimilation and the eradication of the American Indian. The series strategically employed and shaped nineteenth-century archetypes so as to create a new "authentic" Indian. This American Indian valued family, peaceful resolution, and freedom in a way that corresponded to the ideals of Euro-Americans. In doing so, it appealed to Americans' fascination with American Indian culture and heritage in the 1930s while ensuring that any "savage" behavior was filtered out or justified. Effectively, this choice assimilated the American Indians through their desire to live out the American dream and become contributing members of society even as it eradicated their individuality by falling back on nineteenth-century archetypes and refusing to engage with the many difficulties of the present. With this strategy, the FTP troubled the ways in which government policies of assimilation and eradication could be enacted in the 1930s, negotiated complex public identities and perceptions of American Indians, and made the American Indian safe for mass public consumption and acceptance. Thus, the reimagined American Indian joined the many immigrant populations that took on the mantle of U.S. citizenship, at a cost.

Notes

1. The Oklahoma Federal Theatre Project conducted oral history interviews and research, supplied scripts to more than two hundred dramatic clubs, supervised dozens of community theatre programs, encouraged local dramas, and created a popular marionette unit that toured Civilian Conservation Corps camps. Hallie Flanagan, *Arena* (New York: Duell, Sloan, and Pearce, 1940), 97–100; John Dunn, "Foreword," quoted in Flanagan, *Arena*, 98–99.

2. Though I have not been able to locate audience information for this particular series, the FTP's Radio Division enjoyed extraordinary success, estimating its weekly national audience at 10 million. In comparison, FTP national director Hallie Flanagan documented an audience of 30.4 million nationally for all FTP stage shows between June 1935 and March 1939. By this estimate, in a single month the Radio Division would have had more listeners than the rest of the FTP had in four years of operation. For more information, see Alan Kreizenbeck, "The Radio Division of the Federal Theatre Project," *New England Theatre Journal* 2.1 (1991): 27–37; and Flanagan, *Arena*, 434–35.

3. The episode on the Iroquois included the Five Nations (Mohawk, Seneca, Oneida, Onondaga, and Cayuga). Those nations included in the "California Tribes" designation are not explicitly noted; the geographic area that is now California contained dozens of tribes, many of which varied widely depending on their own customs and local geography.

4. The use of the terms "Native American," "Indian," "American Indian," and others has spurred much scholarly conversation. Complicating this issue is the fact that "Native American" is understood to include Indians, native Hawaiians, Inuit people of Alaska, and other peoples and cultures that were native to the geographical space that is now the United States before the arrival of European explorers. More informally, a number of colleagues report conversations with individuals who prefer the term "American Indian" because many early treaties with the U.S. government refer to "Indians," and they fear jeopardizing those treaty rights in exchange for a politically correct name. Thus, I have chosen to follow the conventions of anthropology and archeology and refer to the nations, tribes, and individuals that are my focus here as "American Indians."

5. *The Problem of Indian Administration* (aka the "Meriam Report") was an 872-page document overseen by Lewis Meriam and the staff of the Institute for Government Research in response to the widespread call for an independent investigation of the Bureau of Indian Affairs. The result of a year-long study, the Meriam Report addressed eight primary areas: (1) general government policies related to American Indians; (2) health; (3) education; (4) economic condition (of people and property); (5) family and community life (including a special section on the activities of women); (6) migration (including a discussion on

the colonization of some tribes and individuals, and not of others); (7) laws pertaining to American Indians and the related issues; and (8) religion and missionary activities. The report's objective was to "look to the future and insofar as possible to indicate what remains to be done to adjust the Indians to the prevailing civilization so that they may maintain themselves in the presence of that civilization according at least to a minimum standard of health and decency." W. F. Willoughby, "Letter of Transmittal," in *The Problem of Indian Administration* (Baltimore, Md.: Johns Hopkins Press, 1928), viii.

6. The Digital History site describes the IRA in this way, and many websites have taken that description to heart in subsequent discussions of the Roosevelt administration's policies regarding minorities. While it is true that Roosevelt's policies rarely specifically addressed issues of civil rights, an enormous range of U.S. citizens and immigrants benefited from the New Deal policies, including many otherwise marginalized groups seeking work or relief such as African Americans, Latinos/Latinas, American Indians, women, Jews, and many non-English-speaking immigrants. S. Mintz and S. McNeil, "Native Americans," Digital History, http://www.digitalhistory.uh.edu/disp_textbook.cfm?smtID=2&psid=3449, accessed 30 May 2012.

7. Elmer Rusco, *A Fateful Time: The Background and Legislative History of the Indian Reorganization Act*, Wilbur S. Shepperson Series in History and Humanities (Reno: University of Nevada Press, 2000), ix.

8. Charles Wilkinson, *Blood Struggle: The Rise of Modern Indian Nations* (New York: W. W. Norton, 2005), 60.

9. John Collier, commissioner of the Bureau of Indian Affairs, contended that the transition required careful planning because most American Indians were "not ready to be thrown into modern society without the guardianship of the government." John H. Crider, "Two Camps Form over Indian Law," *New York Times*, 28 March 1937, 63.

10. At this point Deloria is building on the writing of author D. H. Lawrence, who struggled with the crisis he saw in an unfinished American identity and seemed ultimately unable to articulate the complex role that Indians played in the formation of national identity. Philip Deloria, *Playing Indian* (New Haven, Conn.: Yale University Press, 1999), 3.

11. Alden Stevens, "Whither the American Indian?," *Survey Graphic* 29.3 (1940): 168+, http://newdeal.feri.org/survey/40b09.htm, accessed 30 May 2012.

12. Quoted in Joel Pfister, *Individuality Incorporated: Indians and the Multicultural Modern* (Dunham, N.C.: Duke University Press, 2004), 199; Deborah Welch, "Gertrude Simmons Bonnin (Zitkala-Ša) / Dakota," in *The New Warriors: Native American Leaders since 1900*, ed. R. David Edmunds (Lincoln: University of Nebraska Press, 2004), 51.

13. By 1945, 181 tribes had accepted the terms of the IRA, though only 96 ultimately developed tribal constitutions and 73 received corporate business charters. The 77 tribes that rejected the IRA included the Klamath (Oregon), the Crow (Montana), and the Navajo. "Indian Reorganization Act," ABC-CLIO, http://www.historyandtheheadlines.abc-clio.com/ContentPages/ContentPage.aspx?entryId=1171806, accessed 6 October 2014.

14. "Indian Tribesmen Revive Old Ritual," *New York Times*, 26 September 1937, 45.

15. Ibid.

16. Thomas Postlewait, "The Hieroglyphic Stage: American Theatre and Society, Post–Civil War to 1945," in *The Cambridge History of American Theatre, Volume II: 1870–1945*, ed. Don B. Wilmeth and Christopher Bigsby (New York: Cambridge University Press, 1999), 139.

17. Edward Lynn, "The First Americans, No. 1," NARA, E1008, box 369, "*The First Americans*—1," 3. All NARA citations refer to the National Archives and Records Administration, Works Progress Administration Collection, Record Group 69, College Park, Md.

18. Ibid.

19. During the Great Depression, large numbers of farmers, the highest percentage of which came from Oklahoma, fled their homes and fields in an effort to escape the Dust Bowl.

20. Edward Lynn, "The First Americans, No. 2," NARA, E1008, box 369, "*The First Americans*—2," 8.

21. The story of the white buffalo remains one of the foundational legends of the Dakota tribe. Even today, the birth of a white buffalo is a symbol of hope and the coming together of humanity in body, mind, and spirit for the Great Plains tribes. Mark Memmott, "One White Buffalo to Get Sacred Name; Death of Another Still Stirs Anger," National Public Radio, last modified 27 July 2012, http://www.npr.org/blogs/thetwo-way/2012/07/27/157489542/one-white-buffalo-to-get-sacred-name-death-of-another-still-stirs-anger, accessed 21 June 2013.

22. Edward Lynn, "The First Americans, No. 11," NARA, E1008, box 369, "*The First Americans*—11," 2.

23. Ibid., 5–6.

24. Ibid., 5.

25. Even after defeat, many Sioux refused to surrender. The famous Sitting Bull was often asked to give speeches in his native language and is said to have engaged in some truly inspired performances of resistance as he performed respect while cursing his white audience in his native language.

26. Lynn, "First Americans, No. 11," 7.

27. Ibid., 8–9.

28. Ibid., 10.

29. "Dawes Act," *Encyclopedia of the American West*, ed. Charles Phillips and Alan Axelrod (New York: Macmillan Reference, 1996).

30. Edward Lynn, "The First Americans, No. 6," NARA, E1008, box 369, "*The First Americans*—6," 4.

31. Punctuation preserved from the original. Edward Lynn, "The First Americans, No. 8," NARA, E1008, box 369, "*The First Americans*—8," 6.

10. "Ethnic Americanism" versus Isolationism

Pluralistic Antifascism in "Fun to Be Free" (1941)

Garrett Eisler

From Adolf Hitler's ascendancy to power in January 1933 through the Pearl Harbor attack of 7 December 1941, the United States remained officially neutral toward Nazi Germany and its allies. This position was driven largely by popular opinion; while many Americans may have objected to totalitarian dictatorship in principle, a long national mythology of "splendid isolation" encouraged a more self-interested stance.[1] Other factors were the lingering embitterment over World War I (the United States' first direct military engagement on the European continent) and the woes of the Great Depression. For some, the more the economy suffered, the greater the appeal of the Fascist nations' authoritarian efficiency and ethnic scapegoating became. Many prominent Americans initially welcomed the rise of Nazism out of express support for its social Darwinist racial philosophies—beliefs that still held sway in many American universities and cultured circles. Such history reveals that the war now mythologized as "The Good War" hardly seemed like a good idea to many Americans even throughout most of that fateful year of 1941. Decades later, even after the cultural schisms over McCarthyism and the Vietnam War, historian Arthur Schlesinger Jr. recalled the national argument over entering World War II as "the most savage political debate of my lifetime."[2]

After 7 December 1941, antifascism, of course, became national policy; but before then, it was potentially subversive. While opposition to Nazism may seem utterly uncontroversial in hindsight, actively organizing against it in the United States during the time of official "neutrality" could draw scrutiny. (Hence the wartime classification "premature antifascist" used by military draft boards to exclude suspected Communists from service.) As long as the U.S. Congress continued to pass "Neutrality Acts"—as they did four times between 1935 and 1939, to block President Franklin Roosevelt from aiding U.S. allies in any way—the full power of the state buttressed the isolationist position, as did a de facto white Christian supremacy that still pervaded American media, academia, and business institutions. As a result, American antifascists of the 1930s and early 1940s—in order to motivate and mobilize like-minded citizens throughout the country—had no choice but to reach across partisan, ethnic, and class divides to find strength in numbers. Such mobilization was enabled by the Popular Front, an international coalition forged between leftists and liberals in the mid-thirties precisely for the purpose of forming a bulwark against fascism.[3] Under the umbrella of this broader movement, fighting against dictatorship abroad could more easily be limned with classic homegrown "patriot" narratives of liberty combatting tyranny.

A highpoint of the prewar antifascist campaign of the Popular Front was the rally "Fun to Be Free," held at New York's Madison Square Garden on 5 October 1941—just two months before Pearl Harbor. Seventeen thousand spectators filled the hall that night to support American intervention in World War II, and they did so expressly in the name of civil liberties and cultural pluralism. The three segments of this self-proclaimed "mammoth revue" (a classical music program, an all-star variety show, and a thirty-minute "patriotic pageant" by Ben Hecht and Charles MacArthur) all countered Nazi ideals of "Aryan" supremacy and racial "purity" with a celebration of American diversity that extolled racial and religious tolerance as the natural antidote to fascism. The "fun" promised in the evening's title could be had only within the "freedom" made possible by a pluralistic democratic society.

Framed in these terms, the event echoed the "cultural pluralism" of early twentieth-century Progressive intellectuals (particularly Randolph Bourne and Horace Kallen) that Jonathan Shandell discusses in his introduction to this volume. In the Popular Front, this creed manifested in what Michael Denning identifies as an "ethnic Americanism"—a coupling of traditional patriotic discourse about the nation's founding ideals with a distinctly modern embrace of immigration, diversity, and civil rights. In his definitive study *The Cultural Front*, Denning highlights how, "under the sign of the 'people,'" the Popular Front "sought to forge ethnic and racial alliances, mediating between Anglo American culture, the culture of the ethnic workers, and African American culture, in part by reclaiming the figure of 'America' itself."[4] However, such flag-waving displays "were not the sentimental invocations of a people without race or ethnicity, nor were they 'politics of patriotism,' resolving all conflicts in the harmony

Official Fight for Freedom poster advertising the premiere performance of the "Fun to Be Free" program, including Billy Rose's variety show and the Hecht-MacArthur pageant. *Collection of Garrett Eisler.*

of 'Americanism.' Rather, they were attempts to imagine a new culture, a new way of life, a revolution."[5] Unlike the jingoistic nationalism of Fascist nations (and of American isolationism), "both the Americanism and the nationalism of the Popular Front was inflected with a popular *internationalism* . . . [a] pan-ethnic appeal to a federation of nationalities both within the United States and around the globe."[6] Such "pan-ethnic Americanism" emerged as “a paradoxical synthesis of competing nationalisms and internationalism—pride in ethnic heritage and identity combined with an assertive Americanism.”[7]

Where this “Americanism” and “internationalism” most potently converged was in antifascism. In the Popular Front mindset, the struggles against fascism abroad and racism at home were one and the same fight. This sentiment was most succinctly expressed in the widespread African American “Double V Campaign” (as discussed both in the introduction and in chapter 11). By reclaiming and redefining patriotism for a racially diverse America amid a prevailing isolationism, “Fun to Be Free” demonstrated the centrality of “ethnic” and “pan-ethnic Americanism” in prewar interventionist discourse. Revisiting this forgotten performance also reveals how important antifascism was to the era’s civil rights coalitions, with opposition to the external threat of a common enemy bringing progressives of different colors, classes, and religions together.

“Fun to Be Free” was presented by Fight for Freedom, a pro-intervention advocacy group that had been launched just six months earlier (in April 1941) on the premise that—given Germany’s initial victories in Europe and its stated ambitions of world domination—America was already at war, “whether declared or undeclared.”[8] The organization vowed to do “whatever [is] necessary to insure a Hitler defeat” and thereupon help bring about for all peoples “a new order in which political, social, and economic democracy may develop its full meaning.”[9] The statesmen, university presidents, business executives, clerics, and newspaper editors who founded Fight for Freedom were hardly political radicals; but, in typical Popular Front spirit, they built a broad coalition of antifascist allies that included special outreach to labor (through their “Labor Division”), African Americans (“Harlem Division”), and Jewish organizations (including the Jewish War Veterans of the United States).[10] They also sought the participation of stars from Broadway and Hollywood, where Popular Front antifascism was already effectively mobilized through highly visible organizations like the Hollywood Anti-Nazi League. In expanding its activities beyond editorials and lectures to radio broadcasts and live performances, Fight for Freedom joined not only the broader Popular Front movement but also the “cultural front” within it—the artistic spheres in which “the Popular Front social movement met the cultural apparatus.”[11]

This “cultural front” was especially important to antifascist activists in the entertainment industry frustrated with Hollywood’s squeamishness about addressing the Nazi threat—and particularly to the many Jewish immigrants and first-generation Jewish Americans working there.[12] American Jews risked special stigmatization when entering the interventionist/isolationist debate, since isolationists often accused them of prodding America into another foreign war solely out of "narrow" racial interests. (According to such logic, Hitler purportedly posed no danger to American security as a whole.) Given their minority status, plus fears of anti-Semitic backlash for drawing attention to Jewish issues, Jewish Americans faced especially formidable obstacles to mobilizing against fascism.[13]

Moreover, by the late summer of 1941 (when Fight for Freedom was preparing "Fun to Be Free"), isolationist discourse had become openly and routinely anti-Semitic. The America First Committee, founded in September 1940, explicitly accused what it identified as Jewish media outlets (like Hollywood movie studios and New York newspapers) of fanning the flames of intervention. Just one month before "Fun to Be Free," in September 1941, the organization's most famous spokesman, aviator Charles Lindbergh, identified the Roosevelt administration, Great Britain, and immigrant Jews as the three driving forces of pro-war "agitation." Implying that American Jews represented as foreign and as monolithic an entity as the British government, Lindbergh accused "both *races*" (as he tellingly put it) of trying to drag the country into war "for reasons that are not American."[14] Isolationists in Congress apparently agreed. In the fall of 1941, a special Senate committee began investigating Hollywood "warmongering" and anti-German "propaganda" in hearings that frequently drew attention to the ethnicity of the studio heads and moviemakers involved.[15]

"Fun to Be Free" addressed these congressional hearings, and their implicit anti-Semitism, head on. In the days and weeks preceding the rally, Fight for Freedom waged a publicity campaign denouncing the hearings as "the most barefaced attempt at censorship and racial persecution which has ever been tried in this country" and condemning their "racial and religious attacks" on antifascist filmmakers.[16] Among the opening speakers at "Fun to Be Free" was 1940 Republican presidential candidate Wendell Willkie, who had just broken with many in his party by serving at the hearings as counsel for the Hollywood studios. Willkie came to Madison Square Garden that night to accuse isolationists and their congressional allies of "resorting to one of the basest arguments to divide the United States on the basis of race and religion."[17] He also contributed a written program note that pointedly contrasted the divisive motivations of the committee with the racial equality promoted by the evening's event:

> During the past few weeks the American people have watched a sorry performance by a number of prominent citizens who, now that the tide has turned against them, have seen fit to inject religious and racial issues into the great debate on foreign policy. Tonight's meeting is the peoples' reply to them. . . .
>
> On the stage and in the audience Jew and Gentile, Protestant and Catholic, native and foreign born, we join together renewing our faith in the democratic way. This method is a basic principle of American life, as we have known it for over 150 years. Because of our loyalty to it we despise the racial discrimination of Nazism.[18]

Following Willkie's speech, actor Burgess Meredith (one of the event's emcees) put to a symbolic "vote" a resolution drafted by Actors Equity Association alleging that the Senate hearings were "designed to breed religious and racial discord."[19] Here "Fun to Be Free" declared its own versions of a "Double V" agenda—fighting not just foreign fascism but domestic isolationism and advocating not just for military intervention abroad but also for political intervention into anti-Semitic discourse at home.

Fight for Freedom was headed by Protestant and Catholic elites, and "Fun to Be Free" was never identified as a "Jewish" event. But, given the anti-Semitic tenor of the times, the evening as a whole could not help but communicate—often subtextually and, at times, openly—something about the plight of world Jewry and the targeting of American Jews. This certainly would have been on the minds of the many Jewish American show business figures involved in the rally's planning. Its coproducers were impresario Billy Rose and the Labor Stage unit of the International Ladies' Garment Workers' Union (which produced the 1937 hit labor musical *Pins and Needles*). The lead writer of the evening was playwright/screenwriter Ben Hecht.[20] A celebrated Broadway and Hollywood craftsman, Hecht composed many scripts-for-hire during the 1930s that were not known for being outwardly political. But behind the scenes, he was one of the American media's earliest anti-Nazi activists and one of the first to explicitly self-identify as Jewish. (He later wrote that he "turned into a Jew in 1939" in reaction to the Nazi threat.)[21] A former Chicago beat reporter, Hecht made his greatest contribution to the prewar antifascist cause as a columnist for Ralph Ingersoll's progressive daily paper *PM*, "perhaps the most successful organ of the New York Popular Front."[22] During the year leading up to Pearl Harbor, *PM* readers could take in Hecht's moving accounts of the plight of European Jews, his derisive dissections of isolationist spokesmen, and his proud declarations of his own Jewish identity. As he later wrote of his time at *PM*, "I was as much Jew as reporter."[23]

The "revue" components of the three-hour performance of "Fun to Be Free" worked together to characterize all "non-Aryans" and antifascism itself as distinctly "American." The evening opened with a musical program featuring performers and songs emphasizing solidarity across boundaries of race, class, and nationality in the fight against fascism. The opening number, "Arms for the Love of America," had been written by Irving Berlin earlier that year on commission from the U.S. Army to bolster support for munitions factories.[24] Next, selections from George Gershwin's 1935 "Negro opera" *Porgy and Bess*—sung by original African American cast members Anne Wiggins Brown and Edward Matthews—alluded to the collaboration between Jews and African Americans in the American Popular Front. (Such creative exchanges between black and Jewish artists are discussed at length by Stuart J. Hecht in chapter 2.) Flamenco guitarist Vicente Gómez represented the fallen Spanish Republic, just as tenor Jan Kiepura, a part-Jewish Polish refugee, embodied the suffering of his native land.[25] Closing the musical segment was "I Hear America Singing," a setting of Walt Whitman poems by Jewish American composer George Kleinsinger, performed by the International Ladies' Garment Workers' Union chorus and orchestra. The piece was performed under the direction of Lazar Weiner—founder of the ILGWU chorus, conductor of the Yiddish-singing Workmen's Circle Chorus, and a leading composer and champion of Yiddish art songs. "A great company of Americans from all walks of life are here," boasted a radio announcer for a live broadcast of the evening, "to voice their thrilled desire to participate in the struggle for freedom for all men."[26] The broadcast aired on WEVD, a network owned by the *Jewish Daily Forward*, whose call letters stood for the name of the late Socialist Party leader Eugene V. Debs.

The cast assembled for the "variety show" portion of the bill also pointedly displayed American diversity. Billy Rose, a nightclub owner as well as a producer, enlisted George Jessel to host, while Jack Benny and a cross-dressing Eddie Cantor parodied Irving Berlin's "Easter Parade." Singing her hit signature song, "South American Way," Carmen Miranda (known as "The Brazilian Bombshell") embodied the Roosevelt "Good Neighbor Policy"—which was of special importance as fears grew of German encroachment into Central and South America. But the most racially charged moment occurred when Bill "Bojangles" Robinson danced to another Irving Berlin song, the explicitly anti-Hitler "When That Man Is Dead and Gone," written earlier that year. Robinson dramatized the vengeful glee of the song by literally dancing on Hitler's grave. A *New York Times* reporter described the moment:

> Bill Robinson, no Aryan, tap-danced on Adolf Hitler's coffin in Madison Square Garden last night before 17,000 persons, as the band played "When That Man Is Dead and Gone." . . . Down one of the aisles paraded a funeral procession—a big black coffin, with silver-painted handles, borne on the shoulders of "storm troopers," and guarded by "Nazi soldiers" in iron helmets. Before and behind the swastika was carried. With stiff ceremony the coffin was placed on the stage, and then Bill appeared, wearing the stupendous costume he made famous in "The Hot Mikado" a few years back, it being chiefly gold and ermine. With a smile of satisfaction he stepped to the top of the coffin and, to the guffaws of the audience, tapped gingerly with left foot and right, and then really went to town . . . with an abbreviated version of his stair-step dance from the coffin to the stage floor and, finishing his best grin, tap-tapped out of sight. When he had disappeared a group of jitterbugs grabbed the stage and put on a demonstration of hilarity and acrobatics that looked like the celebration of the end of the war.[27]

Robinson had already had a great success with the song in the 1939 Broadway hit *The Hot Mikado*—a Harlem-set, jazz update of Gilbert and Sullivan in which Robinson played the Mikado figure himself. At "Fun to Be Free" he once again wore the glittery, winged costume from that role, which now made him look like an avenging angel, treating Hitler's coffin as mere "groundwork" (as one press release said) for the "stair-step dance" he had done in the show.[28] Moreover, the "jitterbugs" (also from *The Hot Mikado*) were billed in the program as "Lindy Hoppers," referring to an acrobatic dance then popular in African American clubs that had been named—ironically—in honor of the aeronautical feat of Charles "Lucky Lindy" Lindbergh.[29] The contrast between "Aryan" and "no Aryan" could not have been clearer in such a carnivalesque upending of multiple racial hierarchies: a black authority figure (literally, a "Mikado") travesties highbrow operetta while burying (alive) a Nazi white supremacist as Harlem dancers appropriate the name of America's leading isolationist and Hitler apologist—all to the bluesy melody and defiant lyrics of America's most famous Jewish songwriter.

After Robinson's number opened the variety show, the racial rebellion became more expressly Jewish when the orchestra began what was called a "Verboten Overture," a medley of Jewish composers comically interrupted in caricatured Prussian style: "As each renowned tune composed by a 'non-Aryan' composer was played, a burly gent in a Nazi storm trooper's uniform stepped forward and apoplectically bellowed, '*Verboten.*' Mendelssohn's 'Spring Song' and 'Wedding March,' Strauss's 'Waltz,' Jerome Kern's 'Smoke Gets in Your Eyes,' among others, were thus treated and the crowd roared."[30] So well acquainted was the audience with the Jewishness of the composers—even in the tenuous case of Johann Strauss—that no further explication was required for the joke.[31] These musical references added to an overall celebration of Jewish composers throughout the evening. Along with music by Berlin, Gershwin, George Kleinsinger, and, later, Kurt Weill, they powerfully illustrated the true meaning of the words "Fun to Be Free"; at the same moment that the Third Reich was ruling these melodies "degenerate" (and thus "verboten"), their performance delighted thousands of American listeners in Madison Square Garden.

Following the variety show was Ben Hecht and Charles MacArthur's "patriotic pageant" *It's Fun to Be Free.*[32] Like earlier Progressive Era civic pageants, Hecht and MacArthur's featured reverential enactments of such iconic scenes from American history as the signing of the Declaration of Independence and Lincoln's Gettysburg Address. But this history play was at its core a revisionist one, reframing these familiar scenes as conflicts between militant liberalism and corrupt "appeasement." Moreover, given that Hecht appears to have been the primary author, *It's Fun to Be Free* can also be read as a Jewish American pageant—part of an already established practice of Jewish immigrants adopting the pageant genre as part of their acculturation to their new land.[33] Beth Wenger describes how patriotic pageantry provided Jews "occasions to write themselves into the narratives of American history and to make themselves and their culture pivotal actors in the most fundamental events of the American past. . . . When they honored America's heroes and joined in national observances, Jews conjured and performed myriad versions of American history and sketched a Jewish place within it."[34]

It's Fun to Be Free begins with the authors' extended paean to the country, a monologue asking, "What is America?" At first, various arbitrary definitions are dismissed—such as geographical markers ("Some people think it's a piece of map shaped like a wisdom tooth") and measures of material abundance ("the goldarndest collection of railroad ties, window panes, manhole covers, wheatfields, electric signs, apple pies and steel mills ever assembled within the boundaries of one nation") (238). After concluding that the nation cannot be defined by such worldly, incidental details, the text shifts to purely ideological terms, prioritizing its debt to the liberal humanist tradition. "We're here to tell you America is an idea," the speaker says, "the simplest and yet most difficult idea ever hatched by the human mind—the idea of Freedom." Celebrating "freedom" in the abstract, of course, has always been routine in American oratory, but a particularly antifascist point of view emerges in the concrete imagery provided of the obstacles facing freedom in 1941:

> America is an idea that people can live without having the wits scared out of them, without a gag in their mouths or a straitjacket on their spirits. The USA is the dream that a human being is better than a red ant and that the soul of man is a bigger flag than the biggest Swastika ever tacked up on a Nazi platform.

Then, claiming the mantle of the American Revolution itself, the speech announces the pageant's thesis that America's history is not one of isolation but engagement—and that the cause of fighting for freedom overseas is just as patriotic as defending it at home:

And, finally, calling out domestic "enemies" (that is, isolationists), Hecht and MacArthur align the cause of internationalism and ethnic liberation with the mission of the Founding Fathers:

> This, say our enemies, is democratic twaddle. This, say our enemies, is the cry of a war-monger. They lie. History proves they lie. History proves that our battlefront has never been the line of conquest but always, since the barefoot soldiers of Stony Point and Valley Forge—the frontiers of Freedom. Our history reveals that Americans have fought—and fought damned well—only for the defeat of things that tormented the soul of man—tyranny, slavery and intolerance. (238–39)

The phrase "tyranny, slavery and intolerance" pithily brings together under one flag the colonists' rebellion against George III, the Civil War, and the contemporary struggle against racial and religious discrimination. Linking these various campaigns constituted the overarching mission of the "Fun to Be Free" event.

As set to music by émigré composer Kurt Weill (himself a Jewish refugee from Hitler's Germany), the "What is America?" speech, in performance, resembled other "patriotic cantatas" by Popular Front composers of the era. The "patriotic cantata" was a form explicitly devoted to the search for American identity. The most widely known example of the genre was Earl Robinson and John LaTouche's "Ballad for Americans," which became an instant sensation on 5 November 1939 when Paul Robeson sang it on Norman Corwin's *Pursuit of Happiness* radio program.[35] In that song's cavalcade of American history (much like that of *It's Fun to Be Free*, even including many of the same highlights), a speaker walks the chorus through the progression of liberty and equality over time. Just as in Weill's arrangement of "What Is America?," the chorus in "Ballad" frequently interrupts the soloist, asking him, "Who are you, mister?," "What's your racket?," and (almost skeptically), "Are you an American?"—to which the soloist responds in all-embracing polyglot terms: "Am I an American? I'm just an Irish, Negro, Jewish, Italian, French and English, Spanish, Russian, Chinese, Polish, Scotch, Hungarian, Litvak, Swedish, Finnish, Canadian, Greek and Turk, and Czech and double Czech American."[36] "The song is a continual deferral and refusal of a single identification," notes Denning. "The drama of the cantata is the continual questioning."[37] Because the pluralism represented in these cantatas is not one of homogenized harmony, the musical language characterizing it in these pieces is that of the modernist dissonances and irregular meters of early twentieth-century classical music. Such was the difference between the older assimilationist, "melting pot" ideal and the "ethnic Americanism" of the thirties, which allowed for social "dissonances" within the national community in the interest of a richer collective whole.

Following the prologue of "What is America?," the nine historical episodes of *It's Fun to Be Free* illustrate the announced thesis that the United States has always been actively antifascist, even if avant la lettre. Proceeding chronologically from 1775 to 1941, the scenes feature iconographic tableaux with silent "super[numeraries] in colonial costume" impersonating historical figures, while celebrity narrators "worded their speeches over mikes from a box right-rear of the stage."[38] (The narrators listed in the program for the Madison Square Garden performance were Hollywood stars Burgess Meredith, Tallulah Bankhead, Melvyn Douglas, and Franchot Tone.)[39] The episodes retell familiar tales of patriotic lore in distinctly contemporary political terms. For instance, before Patrick Henry cries, "Give me liberty or give me death!," he is harassed by a mob that the stage directions label "a gallery of appeasers" who accuse him of "treason" and "rabble rousing"; Henry's answer—a conveniently authentic quotation—is: "Gentlemen may cry peace, peace—but there is no peace. The war is actually begun" (240). Next, Thomas Jefferson is shown triumphing over those in the Continental Congress who "yammered for appeasement" of King George (241). George Washington, though frequently cited by isolationists for his Farewell Address (with its warning against alliances and foreign wars), is here transformed into a spokesman for the interventionist cause via his more bellicose 1793 State of the Union speech: "If we desire to secure peace, it must be known we are at all times ready for war" (246). Even Lincoln is pitted against isolationist stand-ins like Clement Vallandigham, leader of the Northern pro-Confederate "Copperheads" who are heard advocating "acquiescence in the doctrine of secession"; Lincoln's answer echoes the Popular Front's universal, borderless application of "American" democratic ideals when he says (in the words of his 1861 Independence Hall speech), "The sentiment in the Declaration of Independence . . . gave liberty not alone to the people of this country, but hope to all the world, for all future time" (249). That the Copperheads, like 1941 "appeasers," were also countenancing racial persecution (in the form of slavery) made the implicit parallels between the Civil War and World War II even stronger.

It's Fun to Be Free explicitly links antifascism to Jewishness, as well, by including Haym Salomon among its pantheon of heroes. Long a footnote in American Revolution legend due to his financial assistance of Washington's Continental Army, Salomon was embraced by Jewish American groups of the early twentieth century as a symbol of Jewish patriotism. (He is even referenced in "Ballad for Americans.") In her study of the evolution of the Salomon myth during this era, Wenger posits, "The legend of Haym Salomon often took center stage as American Jews worked to establish Jewish institutions and construct an American communal self-definition. For Jews positioning themselves within American culture, Haym Salomon provided an ideal representative to demonstrate how thoroughly Jews belonged in the United States and how much they had contributed to their adopted homeland."[40] The figure of Salomon provided Hecht and MacArthur the perfect dramatic character through which to write Jews into the American origin story and to merge contemporary antifascism with the iconography of the American Revolution.

The pageant's narrator minces no words in introducing this forgotten hero, restoring Jews to the nation's founding legend and reclaiming that iconic moment of 1776 as a Jewish moment: "There were Jews in the American Revolution—thousands of them. They went without food, stood by shoeless, and with guns in their hands—and fought for the new idea for freedom and liberty for all. . . . Here is one of them—the Jewish warmonger of 1776, Colonial Soldier, the Paul Revere of the Jews" (244). Salomon thus took the stage as a stand-in not just for all American Jews but particularly for those advocating war in 1941—those sounding a Paul Revere–like alarm in the press, like Hecht, and other Hollywood artists defending themselves in the Senate against that same charge of "warmongering." In the scene, Salomon interrupts the holiest of all synagogue services, Yom Kippur, to collect funds from his community for General Washington. (The stage directions set the scene: "Synagogue—Jewish music playing. All Jews are in their praying shawls, and present is Rabbi leading them in their chanting.") The dialogue between the revolutionary and his rabbi encapsulates the oldest of Jewish American dilemmas—how to practice modern civic duty without interfering with ancient pious observance. "Forgive me, Rabbi," Solomon entreats, "but on this Sabbath we can do more than pray to God—we can fight for Him. . . . Jews, the world knows how you love God. Do you also love liberty?" (244–45).[41]

In its stagecraft, *It's Fun to Be Free* owed more to 1930s labor and agitprop theatre practices than to Progressive Era pageantry. Interpolations of verbatim historical texts (including extended speeches from Washington, Jefferson, and Lincoln) lent the piece a documentary theatre quality not unlike the "Living Newspaper" series popularized by the Federal Theatre Project. This link was especially clear in the final, contemporary scene in which Franklin Roosevelt was depicted as heir to the legacy of all the patriots seen preceding him. "On the same platform today stands another of our spokesmen," the narrator's part reads. "He isn't in the history books yet. But he is heading for them" (249–50). The Roosevelt text chosen was a "fireside chat" from only three weeks before the performance—an address that soon became known as the "shoot on sight" speech due to the president's authorization of U.S. vessels to attack any German submarines trespassing into American waters.[42] Instead of an actor reciting the text, a recording of the fireside chat itself (accompanied by a magnified projection of Roosevelt's face on-screen) was played over loudspeakers, filling the Madison Square Garden auditorium with Roosevelt's admonition to "repel Hitlerism" and his pronouncement that "the time for active defense is now." Use of electronic recordings (especially of political speeches) was one of the defining characteristics of the new documentary theatre (or "total theatre") pioneered by Erwin Piscator in 1920s Berlin and became a staple of Federal Theatre Project Living Newspaper stagings. While neither Hecht nor MacArthur had any direct involvement with the FTP, the director hired for the pageant, Brett Warren, was a veteran of the Living Newspaper series, having staged the premiere of Arthur Arent's *Power* in 1937.

The agitprop approach of *It's Fun to Be Free* was even more apparent in the "shock tactics" of its surprise ending: a simulated "air raid" announcing the sighting of German planes over New York City. Immediately following the Roosevelt recording—when the pageant was appearing to reach its conclusion—the narrator (Burgess Meredith in the Madison Square Garden performance) urged the audience to "hold your seats, hang on to your hats" for "a present of tomorrow—the tomorrow that rides on the Panzer tanks and on the dive bombers of the Luftwaffe" (250–51). At this point, sounds of planes (reportedly a recording of "the horrible noises of an actual air raid on London") began to crescendo as real-life journalists and known radio voices appeared at microphones as if broadcasting the incoming attack live.[43] With the loudspeaker noise intensifying, air raid sirens began to blare as another announcer alerted, "They're coming . . . guns and tanks out of the sky. An enemy out of the clouds. Stand by your posts . . . lights out. . . . Black out. The alert is sounding. . . . Here they are" (251–52). As the Madison Square Garden lights went out, plunging the audience into darkness, and the speakers continued to bombard them with sound effects, miniature parachutes were then released from the rafters, each carrying a small cardboard cutout of a German infantryman.

While the toy soldiers may have provided some comic relief as they dropped into spectators' laps, the two minutes of anxiety fomented in the hall leading up to the effect worked on the audience in many ways. Over the preceding year, live broadcasts of London air raids (like those of Edward R. Murrow for CBS) had already become familiar to American radio listeners. This simulated "New York blitz" thus established a visceral audience identification with the victims of the London Blitz at a time when aid to Britain was the most contentious issue of the day in the isolationist-interventionist debate.[44] Putting the Madison Square Garden audience at an imagined "ground zero" compelled these Americans to identify, for at least a few minutes, with the besieged Londoners—and, by extension, with all the other populations across the Atlantic currently under very real attack by German forces.[45] Press accounts testified to at least a momentary credulity within the hall of seventeen thousand. As *Life* magazine reported, "Searchlights flashed, gunfire sounded, women screamed."[46]

The "Fun to Be Free" enterprise continued to have a life well after the 5 October premiere and even for some time after the United States finally declared war. Fight for Freedom had originally planned a tour to several cities, initially announcing as many as "forty or fifty."[47] While that goal proved overly optimistic, a follow-up staging was mounted in Washington, D.C., on 4 November 1941. Even on 10 December, three days after Pearl Harbor, a planned performance in St. Louis went ahead as scheduled, with Humphrey Bogart among the Hollywood luminaries joining the cast of narrators. But entry into the war and the rapid fading of the isolationist cause effectively deprived Fight for Freedom of its raison d'être and its fund-raising momentum; scheduled remountings in Cleveland and Chicago for January and February were canceled, and Fight for Freedom ceased operations altogether by March 1942.

But even without Fight for Freedom's backing, the script of the Hecht-MacArthur pageant lived on, thanks to a quickly released Dramatists Play Service acting edition intended for amateur and school productions—for which the playwrights waived all royalty fees.[48] The edition's "Notes on Production" indicates the pageant's proselytizing intent:

> The authors who wrote this play for the purpose of stirring the American people to a sense of their national destiny by reminding them of the glories of their consistent struggle to attain freedom and preserve it, believe that *Fun to be Free* can and should be widely used by our schools, and that the easiest and quickest way for large numbers of our young people to see it is to act it out in classrooms and school auditoriums, without scenery or costumes.[49]

Excerpts from the pageant text were also published in a "souvenir program" sold to "Fun to Be Free" audiences and, in 1942, in the annual Dodd, Mead series *Best One-Act Plays*. Both the pageant's authors and producers were interested in circulating the text as widely as possible, for both reading and staging, even after the short-term objective of intervention was achieved.

Some of the involved artists made one last push in early 1942 for an expensive Broadway transfer of the entire "Fun to Be Free" program. This new version was to update and adapt the event into a wartime revue. (It was not "merely a benefit staged for a few performances only," reported gossip columnist Wilella Waldorf, but "a bang-up Broadway musical scheduled to run for months, perhaps even years.")[50] Hecht and MacArthur, Fight for Freedom claimed, had already "revised and elaborated" their pageant (though no revised script is extant), and other playwrights and composers were ready to join the project, including such formidable teams as Oscar Hammerstein II and Jerome Kern, George S. Kaufman and Moss Hart, and Howard Lindsay and Russel Crouse.[51] Songwriters Irving Berlin and Harold Rome agreed to contribute new material, as did Kurt Weill.[52] Groucho Marx, active in the Hollywood antifascist movement for many years, was tentatively slated to star. By the time that the project officially collapsed in late March, due to lack of funds, much material had been written; some of it would soon be recycled in other war-effort projects.

Billy Rose announced that he was purchasing the rights to some of Rome's and Kaufman and Hart's sketches for entertainment at his own Diamond Horseshoe nightclub. When Irving Berlin's morale-boosting show *This Is the Army* was announced to open on Broadway that summer, one press report speculated that "some of the material of the once planned 'Fun to be Free' may go into the revue."[53] The great success of *This Is the Army* offers a hint of what place a revived and revised "Fun to Be Free" might have occupied in the Broadway theatre of the early war years.[54]

Reflecting upon his forays into antifascist and pro-Jewish activism, Ben Hecht later wrote, "In addition to becoming a Jew in 1939 I became also an American."[55] One way he and others were able to feel equally "ethnic" and "American" was through the antifascist campaign of the Popular Front, of which the entire "Fun to Be Free" project was a culminating achievement. While rooted in its historical moment (and thus, perhaps, largely "dated" for twenty-first-century readers), this unusual work of political entertainment is notable today for how it reclaimed and recentered American history around the progressive politics of liberation and pluralism, rejecting the still-dominant and exclusively white Protestant narrative of the Pilgrims and the Puritans. In this respect, its vision mirrored that of Bourne, Kallen, and other earlier intellectual proponents of "cultural pluralism." As one such writer, Louis Adamic, posited in 1938, it was time for Ellis Island to supplant Plymouth Rock in the iconography of American origins.[56] While not explicitly about immigration, "Fun to Be Free" challenged origin stories built upon ideals of "splendid isolation" and white supremacy, substituting for them a pluralist declaration of solidarity with the world's oppressed. On a 1941 government-sponsored radio series (fittingly called *I'm an American*), Kurt Weill echoed this sentiment in boasting of his newly adopted national identity: "Those who come here seeking the freedom, justice, opportunity and human dignity they miss in their own countries are already Americans before they come."[57] By virtue of what Emma Lazarus dubbed their "yearning to breathe free," émigrés and refugees, Weill daringly implied, might be the most "American" Americans of all.

To take such an argument into the arena of Madison Square Garden in October 1941 was to invite accusations of "warmongering" for a cause "real" Americans supposedly had no stake in. Indeed, the revered place that World War II now holds in U.S. history belies the rancor and controversy that infused this prewar cultural moment. But the later legend of a world "liberated" by a (distinctly American) "Greatest Generation" owes much to such "experiments in democracy" as "Fun to Be Free." The vision enacted onstage that evening of a proudly "ethnic American" and culturally pluralistic society would later be embraced by wartime and postwar propaganda as representative of the very values worth sacrificing for. In this way, Popular Front antifascism supplied much of the idealistic language that proved so necessary in justifying "The Good War" as "good" after all.

Notes

1. "Beginning in early 1935, American isolationism hardened from mere indifference to the outside world into studied, active repudiation of anything that smacked of international political or military engagement." David Kennedy, *Freedom from Fear: The American People in Depression and War, 1929–1945* (New York: Oxford University Press, 2005), 393.

2. Quoted in Lynne Olson, *Those Angry Days: Roosevelt, Lindbergh and America's Fight over World War II, 1939–1941* (New York: Random House, 2013), xviii.

3. The ideal of a united "front" against Fascist nations was first advanced at the Seventh Congress of the Communist International in August 1935, when the Communist Party called for temporarily compromising doctrinal purity and setting aside more revolutionary goals (like the immediate overthrow of capitalism) in order to join forces not only with all workers but even with the bourgeois liberals of the Western democracies. But while the Communist Party may have sparked the impetus for the coalition building that ensued, the Popular Front (in the United States, at least) took on a life of its own as a broad progressive movement (or proliferation of movements) that was never centrally directed by any one entity.

4. Michael Denning, *The Cultural Front: The Laboring of American Culture* (London: Verso, 1997), 9.

5. Ibid., 132. Denning frames this argument in terms of Antonio Gramsci's formulation of the "national-popular," a popular culture in perpetual struggle against the hegemonic ideology of the ruling elite.

6. Ibid., 131–32.

7. Ibid., 130.

8. "U.S. Is Now at War, New Group Holds," *New York Times*, 20 April 1941. For more background on Fight for Freedom, see Olson, *Those Angry Days*, 323–25, 330–31; and "Finding Aid," Fight for Freedom, Inc. Records, Mudd Manuscript Library, Princeton University, Princeton, N.J., http://findingaids.princeton.edu/collections/MC025.pdf, accessed 13 October 2013.

9. "U.S. Is Now at War."

10. Fight for Freedom's most prominent leaders were Herbert Agar and Ulrich Bell of the *Louisville Courier-Journal*; *PM* publisher Marshall Field III;

Reverend Henry Hobson; Senator Carter Glass; Harvard president James B. Conant; and Allen Dulles. Hollywood was represented on the board of directors by 20th Century Fox president Spyros Skouras; many other movie moguls were listed among the organization's donors.

11. Denning, *Cultural Front*, 50. While many historians have claimed the Popular Front effectively ended with the August 1939 Hitler-Stalin pact (after which the Communist Party temporarily withdrew from the antifascist cause), Denning argues that this setback did not dissuade many non-Communist American leftists and liberals from continuing its agenda right up through the U.S. entry into the war and beyond.

12. For a recent account of how Hollywood studios did and did not engage with Hitler's Germany, see Thomas Doherty, *Hollywood and Hitler, 1933–1939* (New York: Columbia University Press, 2013). While Doherty highlights many attempts within the industry to protest Nazism, another recent study by Ben Urwand goes further in denouncing studio heads as virtual "collaborators." Ben Urwand, *The Collaboration: Hollywood's Pact with Hitler* (Cambridge, Mass.: Belknap Press of Harvard University Press, 2013).

13. Far from triggering an outpouring of sympathy for Jews from the American populace, the World War II years may have marked, according to Leonard Dinnerstein, a "high tide" of anti-Semitism in U.S. public discourse. Leonard Dinnerstein, *Anti-Semitism in America* (New York: Oxford University Press, 1995), 128–49.

14. While conceding that "the persecution [Jews] suffered in Germany would be sufficient to make bitter enemies of any race," Lindbergh still insisted that the "greatest danger to this country" posed by American Jews "lies in their large ownership and influence in our motion pictures, our press, our radio and our government." "Transcript of Charles Lindbergh Address to America First Committee Meeting," *American Experience*, Public Broadcasting Service, http://www.pbs.org/wgbh/amex/lindbergh/filmmore/reference/primary/desmoinesspeech.html, accessed 14 July 2013 (emphasis added).

15. Steven Alan Carr, *Hollywood and Anti-Semitism: A Cultural History up to World War II* (Cambridge: Cambridge University Press, 2001), 242–43.

16. Open letter, 8 September 1941, Fight for Freedom Records.

17. "Freedom Rally Thrills 17,000," *New York Times*, 6 October 1941. The article's subheading underscores "Willkie Scores Appeals to Bigotry."

18. "Fun to Be Free" souvenir program, Fight for Freedom Records.

19. "Resolution," Fight for Freedom Records.

20. Not only were he and longtime collaborator Charles MacArthur credited with the "patriotic pageant" that was the evening's centerpiece, but Hecht also appears to have been the uncredited author of much of the opening variety

show content. During rehearsals, Hecht wrote to his wife, "I had to write all the *spieler* stuff for Billy Rose's part of the shindig." Undated letter from Hecht to Rose Caylor Hecht, Ben Hecht Papers, Midwest Manuscript Collection, the Newberry Library, Chicago, Ill.

21. Ben Hecht, *A Child of the Century* (1954; New York: Primus, 1985), 517. This conversion actually appears to have happened at least four years earlier when, as a "guest columnist" for Walter Winchell, Hecht proclaimed himself both a Jew and an ardent antifascist in the pages of the *New York Daily Mirror*. "On Broadway," *New York Daily Mirror*, 31 July 1935.

22. Denning, *Cultural Front*, 16.

23. Hecht, *Child of the Century*, 520.

24. Berlin's "Arms for the Love of America" was soon adopted as the army's official "Ordnance Song." As with his other famous civic composition, "God Bless America," Berlin relinquished all rights, in this case to the Army Ordnance Department. Robert Kimball and Linda Emmet, eds., *The Complete Lyrics of Irving Berlin* (New York: Hal Leonard, 2005), 372.

25. On Kiepura's Jewish heritage, see James S. Pula, ed., *The Polish-American Encyclopedia* (Jefferson, S.C.: McFarland, 2010), 225. *Variety* reported that Kiepura sang a "Polish folk song" at "Fun to Be Free." "17,000 Turn Out at 'Fun to Be Free,'" *Variety*, 8 October 1941. For more on the significance of the Spanish Civil War to American antifascists, see chapter 11.

26. This announcer was James Waterman Wise (son of American Jewish Congress president Rabbi Stephen Wise). A recording of the WEVD broadcast of "Fun to Be Free" is at the Library of Congress Recorded Sound Reference Center. The broadcast is divided among several different tracks, listed under two different headings: "American Pageant" (LWO 5404 R5) and "Fun to Be Free" (LWO 5404 R6).

27. "Freedom Rally," *New York Times*, 6 October 1941.

28. Undated press release ("News from Fight for Freedom"), Fight for Freedom Records.

29. For a history of the Lindy Hop, see Lawrence McClellan, *The Later Swing Era, 1942–1955* (Westport, Conn.: Greenwood Press, 2004), 10.

30. "17,000 Turn Out at 'Fun to Be Free.'"

31. On the Strauss family's partial Jewish lineage, see Camille Crittenden, *Johann Strauss and Vienna: Operetta and the Politics of Popular Culture* (Cambridge: Cambridge University Press, 2006), 104.

32. Ben Hecht and Charles MacArthur, *It's Fun to Be Free*, in *Best One-Act Plays of 1941*, ed. Margaret Mayorga (New York: Dodd Mead, 1942). Both the pageant and the overall event are inconsistently referred to in contemporary documents as alternately "Fun to Be Free" or "It's Fun to Be Free." In order to

avoid confusion, I have chosen to call the rally as a whole "Fun to Be Free" and to use the title *It's Fun to Be Free* only for the Hecht-MacArthur pageant within it. In late 1941, an "acting edition" of the script was published by Dramatists Play Service under the title *Fun to Be Free*. But because the text of the pageant anthologized in the subsequent *Best One-Act Plays* collection appears to have been taken directly from the production script (as is evident from the typescript in the Fight for Freedom Records), all quotations from the play will be cited from this edition unless otherwise noted. Page numbers will appear in text.

33. According to Hecht biographer William MacAdams, by the 1940s, "despite the well-publicized legend of Hecht and MacArthur . . . the friendship became increasingly strained and sad." MacAdams, *Ben Hecht* (New York: Barricade Books, 1990), 267. Because much of the composition of the pageant entailed the editing and bridging of historical material, the only two passages requiring original content were the two that most bear Hecht's voice—a prologue and epilogue whose heightened prose-poetry and political stridency echoes Hecht's own contemporaneous *PM* columns. As Hecht's continued and escalating involvement in Jewish and antifascist pageantry throughout the war era attest, *It's Fun to Be Free*, as well as the whole rally itself, bears his stamp more indelibly than that of any other author on the bill.

34. Beth Wenger, *History Lessons: The Creation of American Jewish Heritage* (Princeton, N.J.: Princeton University Press, 2010), 59.

35. "Radio: Bravos," *Time*, 20 November 1939. "Ballad for Americans" actually originated in a short-lived Federal Theatre Project revue *Sing for Your Supper*, in which it was called "Ballad of Uncle Sam." For more on Robeson and his involvement in Popular Front causes, see chapter 11.

36. Quoted in Denning, *Cultural Front*, 128.

37. Ibid.

38. "17,000 Turn Out at 'Fun to Be Free.'"

39. "Fun to Be Free" souvenir program, Fight for Freedom Records.

40. Wenger, *History Lessons*, 186. Wenger extensively documents and analyzes this period's various tributes to Salomon in chapter 5 of her book.

41. This oft-repeated though apocryphal synagogue scene had been dramatized two years earlier in another, more prominent Popular Front tribute to Salomon: the 1939 Warner Brothers short film *Sons of Liberty*, directed by Jewish Hungarian immigrant Michael Curtiz and starring Claude Rains as Salomon.

42. Roosevelt's "shoot on sight" radio address was broadcast 11 September 1941.

43. "17,000 Turn Out at 'Fun to Be Free.'" The casting of the "guest-star" journalists changed with each performance of the pageant. Appearing in

the Madison Square Garden premiere were newspaper editor and foreign correspondent Wythe Williams; *Nation* columnist and German refugee Johannes Steele; and WHN commentator, and former congressman, George Hamilton Coombs.

44. Congress had finally passed Roosevelt's "Lend-Lease Act" providing such aid in February 1941 after much resistance.

45. This staging of mass panic under the cloud of war evoked another famous fictional air attack of the era's popular culture: the "hoax" Martian invasion of Orson Welles's 1938 *War of the Worlds* radio broadcast, which reportedly convinced many listeners that a real extraterrestrial attack was occurring. (Indeed, for someone tuning into WEVD's airing of "Fun to Be Free," in medias res, the effect might have been eerily similar.) In Michael Denning's reading, Welles's infamous stunt was not a prank but a deliberate political gesture in an emerging genre of "air raid" radio dramas: "*The War of the Worlds* did not have to be an explicit 'parable of fascism' because its very form was part of the anti-fascist aesthetic. . . . The use of the radio announcer as a character had been created in the experimental radio dramas depicting fascist invasions and air raids." Denning, *Cultural Front*, 382.

46. "Fight for Freedom Fun," *Life*, 20 October 1941, 38. The *New York Times* review similarly ascribed gullible reactions to women: "When it was all over one woman shouted: 'My God, I thought it was real!'" "Freedom Rally Thrills 17,000."

47. "Stars Will Join Patriotic Revue," *New York Times*, 20 September 1941.

48. The copyright date on the Dramatists Play Service edition (titled *Fun to Be Free*) is 1941 and was presumably after the 5 October performance.

49. Ben Hecht and Charles MacArthur, *Fun to Be Free* (New York: Dramatists Play Service, 1941).

50. "Forecasts and Postscripts," *New York Post*, 5 March 1942.

51. "Memo on Proposed 'Fun to Be Free'" (undated), Fight for Freedom Records.

52. Throughout February 1942, Weill frequently wrote to his wife, actress Lotte Lenya, mentioning "Fun to Be Free" planning meetings and even auditions. Lys Symonette and Kim H. Kowalke, eds., *Speak Low (When You Speak Love): The Letters of Kurt Weill and Lotte Lenya* (Berkeley: University of California Press, 1996), 287, 297, 303, 315.

53. "The 'Autumn Hill' Will Open Tonight," *New York Times*, 13 April 1942; "Gossip along the Rialto," *New York Times*, 5 April 1942. Among the more intriguing of these "lost" "Fun to Be Free" pieces is a musical sketch called "The Aryan Mikado" attributed to Kaufman and Rome. "Equity Grants Concessions," *New York Herald Tribune*, 4 March 1942.

54. Another possible offshoot of the "Fun to Be Free" Broadway development process was Weill's "Lunchtime Follies" series—a traveling cabaret beginning in April 1942 sponsored by the American Theatre Wing to entertain munitions factory workers, for which Weill wrote many topical self-described "propaganda songs" for the war effort.

55. Hecht, *Child of the Century*, 518.

56. Louis Adamic, "Ellis Island and Plymouth Rock," *My America* (1938; New York: Da Capo Press, 1976), 185–259.

57. "I'm an American!," Kurt Weill Foundation for Music, http://www.kwf.org/pages/wt-im-an-american.html, accessed 14 February 2011.

11. "Spain . . . Brought Me Back to America"

Ghostings of Other Races in Paul Robeson's Othello and José Ferrer's Iago (1943)

Lisa Jackson-Schebetta

> Lincoln Battalion,
> International Brigades,
> November Something, 1937.
> Dear Brother at home:
>
> We captured a wounded Moor today.
> He was just as dark as me.
> —Langston Hughes, "Letter from Spain"

> Every day I have more faith in our country (Puerto Rico) and I see the day coming when our people, like the people of Spain, will take arms to squash the tyrants (the United States) with the same valor and resolution that the people of Spain have taken against their military and political traitors.
> —Lieutenant Carmelo Delgado Delgado, Abraham Lincoln Brigade

Several scholars have examined Paul Robeson's 1943 Broadway production and subsequent tour of *Othello* as a powerful confrontation of black-white race relations in the United States.[1] Both in its historical moment and beyond, the production has been rightly hailed as remarkably progressive due to its casting of an African American in the title role and to the entire cast's refusal to play in segregated theatres on tour. These same commentators and historians have pointed out how the Broadway program note's comparison between Othello's service to Italy and the Allied powers' fight against fascism in World War II functioned as a savvy wedding of nationalist and antiracist politics, consonant with the "Double V Campaign" articulated by James G. Thompson in the *Pittsburgh Courier.* "Let colored Americans adopt the double VV," wrote Thompson in 1942. "The first V for victory over our enemies from without, the second V for victory over our enemies within. For surely those who perpetrate these ugly prejudices here are seeking to destroy our democratic form of government just as surely as the Axis forces."[2] Robeson's vision of Othello, performed just one year later, echoed Thompson's call. In rehearsal and production, *Othello* tested and promoted what Jonathan Shandell describes in the introduction to this collection as an "equitable model" of democracy in terms of black-white race relations in war and peace.

Yet there were other ways that this production functioned as an "experiment in democracy" with respect to the portrayal of race during wartime. Robeson's African American body was not the only racialized body on stage. Puerto Rican José Ferrer, a then up-and-coming young actor, played Iago. In the 1940s, "Puerto Rican," "Hispanic," and "Latino/a" were not easily delimited, identifiable, or legally constituted racial categories in the United States. Additionally, as Eric Mayer-García reminds us in chapter 3, diasporic Caribbean communities had to negotiate race, blackness, and whiteness as it was practiced and understood both in the United States and in their homeland. Puerto Ricans in the United States experienced widespread discrimination based not only on national origin and language but also on phenotypical characteristics and/or their presumedly mixed ancestry of indigenous, African, and peninsular Spanish extractions. Elizabeth Coonrod Martínez, in chapter 6, demonstrates how the "sleeping Mexican" had "joined a parade of Euro-American ethnic cartoons" by midcentury, along with "black jokester Cubans and Filipinos." Euro-American imaginations shaped the Puerto Rican as well, characterizing him (and her) alternately as infantile, sexually exotic, untrustworthy, and lazy. Ferrer, hailing from an economically comfortable background, did not share the experiences of the masses of non-English-speaking, working-class Puerto Ricans living in *la colonia*—the Puerto Rican community in East Harlem. Still, self-identified as "Puerto Rican by birth, Spanish by descent, American by devotion," Ferrer understood each of these affiliations as a distinct category of his public identity. Indeed, each category was charged with particular social and political significance by the wars of the era in the years leading up to *Othello*'s 1943 opening.[3] I use the plural "wars" because—although World War II was the conflict explicitly discussed in the *Othello* playbill—both Robeson and Ferrer found themselves haunted onstage by another overseas conflict: the 1936–39 Spanish Civil War.

Scene from *Othello*, with Paul Robeson (*left*) and José Ferrer, Theatre Guild production, Broadway, 1943–44. *Courtesy of the Library of Congress, Prints and Photographs Division, FSA/OWI Collection, LC-USW331-054941-ZC.*

The "present experience" of theatre performance, as Marvin Carlson writes, "is always ghosted by previous experiences and associations while these ghosts are simultaneously shifted and modified by the processes of recycling and recollection."[4] Robeson and Ferrer, as actors in *Othello*, functioned as what Carlson has termed "recycled bodies," performers who (through previous roles as well as through public offstage behavior) found themselves "entrapped by the memories" and expectations of their "public."[5] Robeson's and Ferrer's publics understood both actors' performances in relation to memories of these men's activism in response to the Spanish Civil War. Spain's democratic Republic, elected in 1931, was overthrown by General Francisco Franco's Nationalist rebels in 1939. Though American supporters of the Republic suffered explicit U.S. governmental persecution for decades after the Republic's fall, the ideological and imaginative power evoked by that bygone Spanish regime persisted in American consciousness. Both Robeson and Ferrer participated in pro-Republican performance on and off the stage into the early 1940s. During the run of *Othello*, Robeson declared Spain to be the "focal point" (still) of the global fight against fascism.[6] The Spanish Civil War had coalesced multiple strands of antifascist sentiment from 1936 to 1939, but it (and the 1943 *Othello*) also exposed *hemispheric* aspects of race relations in the United States and the Americas. By subtly evoking the Spanish Civil War through the presence of Robeson and Ferrer, the 1943 *Othello*'s "experiment in democracy" extended beyond black-white race relations in the United States. The production dramatized how a renegotiation of concepts of race-ethnicity-nation in the Americas—which were rooted in Spain and violently upended by the Spanish Civil War—presented viable opportunities for new global political alliances that could reconfigure hemispheric power relations.

Spain and Race in the Hemispheric Americas

In 1931, a left and left-center coalition succeeded in democratically and bloodlessly electing a Republican government in Spain. Deposed King Alfonso XIII left the country. Reforms stripped the military, monarchists, and the church of power. Five years of instability ensued. In July 1936, the Spanish military (with the support of monarchists and selected clergy) revolted against the Republic, and a civil war began. By August, western European states (with the exception of Switzerland), the United States, and Russia officially pledged to adhere to a nonintervention agreement in relation to the conflict. Though Germany signed the agreement, evidence demonstrates that the German state helped finance the Spanish generals' first forays in July. The noninterventionist agreement did not preclude Germany's dedication of troops, munitions, planes, and tanks to the Nationalist side. Italy followed suit. The Republic appealed to its fellow Western democracies for help but was denied. Despite the recalcitrance of European and American governments toward the Spanish government, citizens of these nations organized to send supplies and volunteers to the Republic's aid. Only Russia (also violating the nonintervention agreement) and Mexico officially sided with the Republic. Governmental aid arrived from these nations in the form of weapons, money, foodstuffs, and soldiers.

The Communist Party recruited more than thirty-five thousand volunteer soldiers from more than fifty countries worldwide, including twenty-eight hundred from the United States, to serve in the International Brigades on the side of the Republic. The volunteers saw themselves as fighting not only for Spain but also for a future free of fascism, racism, and imperialism. They and their supporters hailed the Republic as the first democracy to successfully make an armed stand against Fascist aggression. As Alun Kenwood writes, from November 1936 to March 1939, Madrid became "the center of the world" for Republican sympathizers, "the forge of a new humanity and new consciousness: a symbol of heroism, martyrdom and anti-fascist struggle."[7] Madrid's rise as a global focal point also decentered traditional ideas of the distribution of world power and, in doing so, enabled a series of geopolitical *hemispheric* imaginings.

In February 1939, Joseph North published the pamphlet *Why Spain Can Win* with Workers Library Publishers. North had worked for fourteen months in Spain as special correspondent for the *Daily Worker* on the Spanish Civil War. Like much of the writing around the conflict, North's narrative depicted Spain as a crucial battlefront in the war against fascism. Western democracies had yet to take action against the global rise of fascism. They had neglected Ethiopia's pleas for help. They had done nothing to avert Japan's bombing of China. Spain was the first nation to mount resistance. All antifascists, North wrote, were obligated to support the Republic's fight. North's pamphlet expressed derision for the Western democracies' noninterventionist stance on Spain, as would be expected, but it did so from a broader hemispheric perspective. A map of Europe, Africa, and the Americas used arrows to visualize how quickly fascism (if Nationalists prevailed) might spread: not *across* the Atlantic from Spain but *up* from the Caribbean, from Mexico, from Brazil.[8] The map argued that if Republican Spain fell, so too might U.S. democracy. This map inverted the north-to-south flow of power and influence that the United States had been shoring up in the Americas since 1898. A victory for Republican Spain could, the arrows suggested, reverse the flow of U.S hegemony in the American hemisphere. Democratic or Communist influence and power could travel the same channels as fascism. From 1936 to 1939, such sentiments were already circulating through the Americas and the Caribbean. Whether the Nationalists won or the Republicans emerged victorious, the Spanish Civil War repositioned the United States as a single nation within the Americas, as but one country/geography surrounded by many others—with no guarantee of economic, military, or political privilege over its neighbors. Such a (re)positioning carried particular implications for meanings of race in the United States.

In *The Idea of Latin America*, Walter Mignolo articulates race in the Americas as a concept formed in the sixteenth century, when Spanish Christians equated blood with "race" (an understanding taken from horse breeding).[9] From the Reconquista onward, Iberian Christians constructed themselves, Jews, and Muslims as "races" wherein ethnicity was wed to religion and borne by blood. The theopolitical triad, as Mignolo calls it, of Christian-Muslim-Jew (a construction of race) fell apart in the New World. As Mignolo writes, the people that Christian Spaniards confronted in the New World worshipped no recognizable god. This fact placed indigenous populations outside of the theopolitical (ethnic-racial) Iberian triad. Thus, the Spaniards *invented* "Indians" as *godless* beings. Located outside the hierarchy that positioned born Christians as superior to all others by blood, Indians could only be converted and/or used for labor. Simultaneously, African slaves transformed from Moors to "Ethiopians": exploitable bodies. In old Spain, categories of *converso* (a Jew converted to Christianity) and *morisco* (a Muslim converted to Christianity) persisted. In New Spain, categories of *mulattos* (people of African and Hispanic mixed ancestry) and *mestizos* (people of indigenous and Hispanic mixed ancestry) took hold. All four categories, along with their variants, connoted "race." Consequently, "race" became a nuanced and complex identity category, inclusive of colonial histories and bound up with language, ethnicity, nation, and religion as well as skin color. Driven by early capitalism, these sequences of invention wove a colonial-racial matrix, argues Mignolo, that wed the geographies of the Americas to origin stories bound up with Spain. With Spain's defeat in 1898, the United States effectively assumed the imperial lead in the American hemisphere during the early twentieth century to shore up a political and economic hegemony across the region, exercising particular might in Puerto Rico and Cuba. Spain's presence in the Americas, and its role in racial formations, was thus occluded. In 1931, a refigured Republican identity for "Spain" returned to the Americas as an imaginative force, exposing the hemispheric underpinnings not only of political anxiety in the Americas (as North's map intimated) but of racial discourse as well. This new hemispheric order, inextricably (in)formed by Spain and its sixteenth-century empire, configured race within a triad of race-nation-ethnicity. The Spanish Civil War (re)exposed these linkages in the United States in the 1930s and 1940s. Such concepts of race-nation-ethnicity ghosted the 1943 *Othello*.

"Other Wars, of Other Times": *Othello* on Broadway

When the Theatre Guild opened *Othello* on Broadway in 1943, audiences and the media discussed, protested, and lauded the casting of an African American actor in the title role. Yet the production framed itself first within the terms not of race but of war. Its program note stated:

> As this production of "Othello" begins, we are in the middle of a year and in the middle of a war: and when at war, it may not be out of place to keep other wars, of other times[,] in mind. For, by this means, patterns and directions may be the clearer.
>
> We are now engaged in a war to protect a way of life which we feel offers the greatest benefits to the greatest number of people. Venice in the Sixteenth Century was fighting too: her wars were to protect Christianity in the Eastern Mediterranean.
>
> In our conflict, all races are allied to fight for common ideals. The Negro pilot of the Army Air Corps may fly under the command of Chiang in China, just as other soldiers of other races fought with Venice for the protection of Christianity.[10]

Othello asked its audiences, as they observed the traffic on the stage before them, to view "race" through a lens of "war." In this context, "war" carried multiple meanings: Venice's war for Christianity as evoked in the play and World War II, to be sure, but also—given the previous performances and politics of its leading men the Spanish Civil War.

Because of their military superiority and the aid they received from both Germany and Italy, Spain's Nationalists expected a rapid victory in the summer of 1936. Yet the Republicans held out, famously stopping the Nationalist advance on Madrid in November 1936 with the help of Soviets and the first battalions of the International Brigades. Although Communist aid to the Republic has long since been exposed as a more corrupt than altruistic measure, the International Brigades fighting alongside the "People's Army" of the Spanish Republic stood as a united force against fascism. The brigades offered both blood and bodies to replace the assistance withheld by French, American, and British democracies under the nonintervention agreement. In Spain, individual battalions named themselves after national icons of ideal politics. U.S. volunteers named their battalions after Abraham Lincoln and George Washington.

Like the Moorish soldier Othello, like the "Negro pilots" flying under Chiang, the soldiers of the International Brigades lent their bodies to a nation other than their own. Ferrer as Iago and Robeson as Othello could have stood in for both Allied soldiers and volunteer soldiers for Spain. Abraham Lincoln Brigade (ALB)[11] volunteers and World War II soldiers were, in fact, often one and the same. As Peter Carroll details, the Lincoln vets, sent home from Spain in 1938, saw the United States' entry into World War II as but a continuation of their fight in Spain. Milton Wolff, the last ALB commander, wrote to President Roosevelt on 8 December 1941, "We who fought the Fascist Axis in Spain proudly volunteer to march shoulder to shoulder with our fellow Americans for the final crushing of this menace to the independence and democracy of America and all people."[12] The racial and ethnic makeup of the ALB also supported the reading of Ferrer's Iago and Robeson's Othello in a Spanish Civil War context. Of the twenty-eight hundred U.S. American volunteers in the ALB, eighty to one hundred identified as African Americans. Cuban, Puerto Rican, and other Latin American nationals fought alongside U.S. Americans in the ALB.[13]

Carlson argues that "directors and producers and of course actors themselves are also well aware as they have always been of the importance of an audience's previous experience with an actor in conditioning their reception of him or her in a new role."[14] Previous roles played and performances staged by both Ferrer and Robeson provided additional evocations of this "other war" context for the audiences of *Othello.* Significant portions of these artists' careers intersected with the Spanish Civil War—particularly with respect to the volunteer soldiers of the International Brigades. The Spanish Civil War haunted Ferrer through his previous stage roles. It also ghosted Robeson through his widely circulated public persona.

In December 1940, Ferrer (somewhat new to Broadway) played Victor d'Alcala in the twenty-five-page prologue of Maxwell Anderson's *Key Largo.* Set on a "hilltop in Spain, January 1939," the prologue tells the story of five Lincoln volunteers assigned to outpost duty. The men's leader, King McCloud, overhears that he and the other four have been left behind to cover a retreat while the Nationalist army advances. The five volunteers face certain death. McCloud orders the men to abandon the futile assignment and desert the brigade. Only Victor d'Alcala resists. D'Alcala—an American whose peninsular Spanish father fought Napoleon—grew up in Florida. He explains why he will not desert:

> If I die
> Then I will know men will never give in;
> Then I'll know there's something in the race
> Of men, because even I had it, that hates injustice

More than it wants to live. Because even I had it
And I'm no hero. And that means the Hitlers
and the Mussolinis always lose in the end—
force loses in the long run and the spirit wins
whatever spirit is.[15]

Three of the four men change their minds and opt to stay with Victor to die fighting. McCloud leaves them. The play that follows this prologue focuses on conflicts between U.S.-based gangsters and the d'Alcala family in Florida; but the prologue frames the entire drama within the haunting experience of Victor d'Alcala during the Spanish Civil War.[16] Ferrer's biography in the *Key Largo* program echoes that of his character, Victor. Ferrer describes himself as "Puerto Rican by birth, Spanish by descent, American by devotion," suggesting both a shared heritage and political affinities among the three identities.[17]

Two years later, Ferrer appeared in *Othello* as a soldier-in-arms alongside Robeson, an actor who was well known as a pro-Republican activist. Uta Hagen, Ferrer's wife in real life and playing Desdemona in *Othello*, had played Victor's sister Alegre in *Key Largo*. While Ferrer's biography for *Othello* made no mention of his part in *Key Largo*, Hagen's biography notes her performance in that show, "in which her husband, José Ferrer, also played."[18] The 1943 *Othello* was thus ghosted by the d'Alcala family. The family's convictions reverberated against Robeson and the "other wars" the production evoked.

Additionally, in 1943, Republican Spain persisted in the U.S. political consciousness. The veterans of the ALB—in coordination with countless other organizations, including the Spanish Refugee and Relief Association—turned their attention toward aiding the thousands of persons (Spanish and otherwise) displaced by Franco's victory. Ferrer was questioned about his own anti-Franco sympathies in front of the House Un-American Activities Committee (HUAC) in 1951. Ferrer consistently denied any knowledge of participating in events or organizations with any Communist sympathies. He hedged when asked why his name might have been used on publicity for actual and suspected Communist benefit events, including those for the Spanish Republic. Still, Ferrer would not back down in terms of his convictions against Franco, testifying that "anytime there was an opportunity to oppose him, I, for one, invariably did."[19] Although Ferrer was not as visible as Robeson in terms of pro–Spanish Republic activities, he admitted to regular involvement with the Joint Anti-Fascist Refugee

Committee, including appearances at a seventeen-thousand-person rally at Madison Square Garden and at regional events while on tour with *Othello.*[20] Theatregoers in any culture, Carlson reminds us, "are repeat theatre goers."[21] *Othello*'s audiences would have remembered Ferrer for his previous roles, including that of d'Alcala. Given that New York City functioned as a hub for pro-Republican organizing in the late 1930s and into the 1940s, likely some also would have known of Ferrer's anti-Franco politics. In tandem with Robeson's very public pro-Republican activities, those of Ferrer likely appeared quite significant.

Though Robeson had been invested in global politics through the 1920s and 1930s, his affinity for the Spanish Republic catapulted him into the public political eye more visibly than ever before. Through the fall of 1936 and into the spring of 1937, the London-based Robeson was in increasingly high demand to perform and speak at high-profile, pro-Republican events and fund-raisers, both in Russia and in England. As Robeson saw it, the battle being waged in Spain was no less than the linchpin in a global fight against all tyranny, fascism, imperialism, and racism—a position he would embrace and articulate long past Franco's 1939 victory in Spain. It was during this period, in 1937 or 1938, that Robeson approached Margaret Webster about directing him in *Othello. Othello* and Spain thus were not separate for Robeson, neither temporally nor ideologically. The International Brigades soldiers captured his heart and imagination. In January 1938, around the same time of his and Webster's first conversation, Robeson traveled to the Republican front lines. Top Communist Party officials hosted Robeson and his wife at dinners and parties, but Robeson was much more interested in the fighting and in visiting wounded soldiers than in attending party functions. He sang songs for the soldiers, gave autographs, and promised to carry messages home to relatives and loved ones. "In Spain," Robeson recalled in his autobiography, "I sang with my whole heart and soul for these gallant fighters of the International Brigade. A new, warm feeling for my homeland began to grow within me as I met the men of the Abraham Lincoln Brigade."[22] Upon his return from the front, Robeson continued his pro-Republican activities, including speaking on behalf of Spain to the British House of Commons.[23] He also moved forward with plans for his U.S. *Othello.* Robeson recalled, "Spain—the anti-fascist struggle and all that I learned in it—brought me back to America."[24]

From 1936 to 1939, Republican Spain and its civil war, in coordination with antiracist Communist Party support, became the place to take a stand against multiple global oppressions, including exploitative capitalism, fascism, anti-Semitism, and racism. As noted above, of the volunteers from the United States, between eighty and one hundred identified as African American. Though this seems perhaps a small number, their presence signified an extension of the fight against Mussolini in Ethiopia in 1935–36 and was representative of a larger activist base in the United States. Indeed, it is likely more African Americans would have joined the Lincoln ranks had there been time; but, in hopes of securing international aid, Spanish prime minister Juan Negrín sent the brigades home in 1938 and truncated recruitment efforts. The African Americans in Spain fought not only fascism globally but also racism at home. In service in Spain, many experienced a racial equality not present in the United States. The International Brigades did not segregate based on race. Men of African descent rose to officer positions; racist behavior was censured among the ranks. One of the many posters issued and distributed by the Republican Ministry of Propaganda depicted (with the triangular symbol of the International Brigades) the faces of three men in military helmets: one Caucasian, one Asian, and one black. The caption reads "Todos los pueblos del mundo estan en las Brigadas Internacionales al lado del pueblo español."[25] In a January 1938 article in the *Daily Worker*, Robeson proclaimed, "To me Spain is another homeland, because the people of this country are opposed to racial and class distinctions."[26]

Much discussion surrounded the 1943 production of *Othello* concerning the phenotypical characteristics envisioned by Shakespeare for the Moor. In February 1944, Kenneth Porter wrote to the *New York Times* mailbag to weigh in on just what he thought Othello should look like:

> It would be difficult to distinguish, racially, a considerable element of the Moorish population from a large part of the Negro population, so called, of the United States. . . . And, with apologies to Mr. Robeson for introducing Franco's Moors as evidence in this connection—anyone who has carefully observed the photographs of individual Moorish soldiers will have noted that, while many are of the bearded, aquiline, Arab type, others are obviously at least mulattos.[27]

On the one hand, Porter's letter supports the argument that the Spanish Civil War ghosted Robeson and the *Othello* production. Yet it also indicates how the Spanish Civil War challenged ideas of race. Porter suggests that audiences made broad connections between the production, Robeson, and the Spanish Civil War. His letter also indicated, if unintentionally, the idea of race as race-nation-ethnicity, a configuration rooted in Spain's history with

Multicultural poster distributed by the Republican Ministry of Propaganda. *Courtesy of the Rare Book and Manuscript Library, University of Illinois at Urbana-Champaign.*

Africa, the "East," and the Americas. The political implications of a United States of the *Americas* alluded to political alliances across global souths. Robeson and Ferrer brought both possibilities on to the stage with them.

Race-Nation-Ethnicity in Spain and the Americas

Mignolo contended in 2010, "In the United States, the specter of Islam on a global scale has been accompanied by the rising specter of Hispanophobia."[28] Mignolo's provocation that we consider contemporary Islamophobia and Hispanophobia as inextricably linked is part of his larger project. Mignolo challenges scholars to embrace a paradigmatic shift in the conceptualization of America and to think of the geography from the southern tip of Argentina to the northernmost point of Canada not as discovered nor imagined but as invented by a (Christian and capitalist) European worldview from *the* colonial moment of 1492. Such a formulation refigures contemporary ideas of race, racialization, and racism by positioning their origins temporally in the sixteenth century and geographically in the *souths* and *easts* of the globe.[29] Race, in Mignolo's formulation, thus becomes race-ethnicity-nation and functions as an underpinning of the relations between the United States, Latin America, Spain, and Africa from 1492 to the present. This origin story was both evoked (and invoked) by Robeson and Ferrer in *Othello*. Through their performance as fellow Lincoln volunteers and Allied soldiers, the two actors offered a revision of the racial and ethnic history of Spain, the United States, and the Americas.

Though soldiers of all heritages and skin colors could serve as officers in mixed battalions of the Spanish Republic, Republican supporters could not but bear witness to (and in some cases propagate) deep prejudices against Franco's so-called Army of Africa, battalions comprising the colonized citizens of Morocco. "Moors" occupied a conflicted position in Spain, one as new as the Rif War of 1926, as old as the thirteenth-century reign of Alfonso el Sabio, and as mythic as the fall of Granada in 1492. Anti-Nationalist, pro-Republican propaganda villainized the Moorish soldiers as bloodthirsty, lustful, and unfeeling. Christopher Othen describes pro-Republican efforts to portray Moroccans as "black caricatures rather than Arab or Berber."[30] Another poster issued by the *ministerio* of propaganda, captioned "Los Nacionales," included three white men (a German soldier, a Catholic priest, and an Italian businessman) and two black men. One of the latter wore a turban and the other the red hat of the Carlist. Both were dark-skinned with minstrel-like red lips and long noses. Such representations of the "Moorish soldier" resonate with the character of Othello, as described by Roderigo (and Iago) to Brabantio in act 1 as having "thick-lips" and as being "an old black ram" and "a Barbary horse."[31] International media shrouded tales of "Franco's Moorish militia" in racial slurs of brutish lasciviousness. Women were purportedly raped by whole firing squads of Moors before death. Journalist (and propagandist) John Whitaker reported that he saw two girls given to a Moroccan company and was told "calmly" that they "would not survive more than four hours."[32] Othen describes a pro-Republican cartoon of "a barely human looking Moroccan clutching the corpse of a young white woman."[33] Desdemona, Roderigo claims in *Othello*, is within the "gross clasps of a lascivious Moor," another potent echo of the characterization of Moors in the Spanish Civil War.[34]

Despite the integrated International Brigades, pro-Republican African Americans in the United States had to grapple with the conflicted place of African heritage in the propaganda and practices of the Spanish Civil War. Langston Hughes, fellow activist to Robeson, expressed the struggle with particular poignancy. In Hughes's poem "Letter from Spain," first published in the *Volunteer for Liberty*, an African American Lincoln soldier (Johnny) faces a wounded and dying Moor. Johnny questions the dying man—"I said, Boy, what you been doin' here / Fightin' against the free?"

> He answered something in a language
> I couldn't understand.
> But somebody told me he was sayin'
> They nabbed him in his land
>
> And made him join the fascist army
>
> . . . .
>
> He said he had a feelin'
> This whole thing wasn't right.[35]

Hughes projects his own political desires onto the Moor. The Moor, as Hughes characterizes him, could have desired to fight for the Republic. Hughes's Johnny looks "across to Africa":

> I looked across to Africa
> And seed foundations shakin'.
>
> Cause if a free Spain wins this war,
> The colonies, too, are free—
>
> . . . .
>
> I knelt down there beside him,
> And I took his hand—
> But the wounded Moor was dyin'
> And he didn't understand.

Johnny apprehends the larger fight being waged in the field of Spain, the global anticolonial, antiracist, antifascist fight Robeson found there as well.

In the Spanish Civil War, international propaganda figured "Moors" in terms of race, both as race had been hewn in the Iberian Peninsula (as race-nation-ethnicity) and as race had been phenotypically marked in the contemporary and post-Enlightenment world. Robeson, playing Othello and ghosted by the Spanish Civil War, carried these significations with him onto the stage to rewrite history. Robeson's Othello became a soldier for the International Brigades, a black Moor within the Republican army. He realized the hopes of Hughes's poem: the Moor understands. Hughes's Moor, through Robeson, joined African Americans in their fight for liberty and equality, likely in the Abraham Lincoln Brigade, enacting a political and transhistorical linkage of race-ethnicity-nation as well as of various *souths* from around the globe—the south of the United States, the south in Europe, the south of Europe.

Such linkages, as Mignolo reminds us, carry with them a hemispheric dimension as well. The 1943 *Othello* realized this dimension, too, through the presence of a Puerto Rican Iago in José Ferrer. In rehearsals for *Othello*, Webster envisioned Ferrer as an Iago inflected with a "Spanish quality," a "matador"-like figure, quick and mercurial. Ferrer held that his Spanish heritage, including his upbringing in Puerto Rico, provided him excellent access points into the Renaissance text.[36] These anecdotes demonstrate a certain slippage between the specific cultural characteristics of persons of Spanish language heritage (not unlike the category "Hispanic"), a slippage that elides the imperialist history of Spain in the Americas and homogenizes race in the Spanish-speaking Americas. Ferrer's heritage could be read as Anglo-Saxon, or, at the very least, as peninsular Spaniard, rather than as African, "Latin American," or indigenous—phenotypically, economically, and linguistically. A deeper analysis of the historical power dynamics of indigenous, European, and African heritage in the Caribbean is beyond the scope of this essay. But despite his evidently discrimination-free experience in *Othello* on Broadway and on tour, Ferrer repeatedly, publicly positioned himself as Puerto Rican—from *Key Largo* through his HUAC testimony and beyond. Ferrer's Puerto Rican identity, ghosted by the Spanish Civil War in *Othello*, directly challenged U.S. hegemony in another *south*: the Caribbean.

Twice in American history, emigration from Puerto Rico swelled: first in 1917 (when Puerto Ricans were granted American citizenship) and again in 1929 when, after the stock market crash, plantations and factories slashed their workforces in response to economic depression.[37] Transplants from Puerto Rico could affiliate quickly with their countrymen and countrywomen in New York through community organizations, Spanish-language newspapers, and public events. Yet Puerto Ricans in New York also had to contend with discrimination based on language, race, and ethnicity in a variety of combinations. Bernardo Vega recalls that in the 1920s, "hardly a day went by that a Puerto Rican child did not come home from school with a black eye," having been set upon by his non-Spanish-speaking neighbors.[38] Joaquín Colón López remembers that "once a building was occupied by our countrymen, no more maintenance was done on it. Garbage collection also became inadequate. . . . Men, women and children shared what little room they had with rats, cockroaches, and garbage."[39] Puerto Ricans who phenotypically appeared to be of indigenous or African descent suffered triply.

In the 1930s in the United States, persons from Mexican, Caribbean, or Central and South American geographies found themselves in a conflicted, confused position in terms of "race." As Richard Vázquez puts it, "Hispanic" populations in the United States into the 1930s "found themselves in a world that was centered on . . . *English-speaking Black and White*."[40] Due to the long history of indigenous, African, and European mixing (both coerced and voluntary), Puerto Rico sustained a racial hierarchy that was more nuanced (though no less charged) than a black-white dichotomy. If a Puerto Rican living in the United States "looked white," he or she could avoid certain race-based discriminatory practices. Yet language, as well as negative stereotypes of a "Hispanic" character inherited from centuries-old Black Legend propaganda, kept such a person from fully accessing the privileges of a "white" person. The Black Legend Spaniard—looming out of early modern geopolitical battles between England and Spain, resurrected as recently as the 1898 Spanish-Cuban-American War—was a greedy, fanatic, and barbaric racist caricature. Populations from Mexico, Cuba, and Puerto Rico could not escape the stereotype. Whether seen as "black" or "white," the "Puerto Rican" immigrant was treated as a racial Other in the United States throughout the 1930s. In 1932, *Time* magazine published Rockefeller Institute pathologist Cornelius Packard Rhoads's contention that "Puerto Ricans are beyond doubt the dirtiest, laziest, most degenerate and thievish race of men ever inhabiting the sphere." Rhoads went on to claim he had transplanted cancer into eight Puerto Ricans, doing his small part to help the extermination of the "race." A subsequent investigation by the Rockefeller Institute yielded no evidence; Rhoads insisted his letter was but a "parody on supposed attitudes of some American minds."[41] Yet debates in the U.S. government over the status of Puerto Rico (state, colony, or nation) centered on similar arguments.[42]

Spain and its struggle to defend its Republic captured particular passions in *la colonia*, the New York–based Puerto Rican community. Military occupation, aggressive economic restructuring, and ambitious Americanization campaigns made it clear to many Puerto Ricans that they had but traded one colonizer for another in 1898. In the 1930s, two distinct causes—the Spanish Republic and an independent Puerto Rico—layered onto each other. In August 1936, for instance, fliers advertised a rally at the Park Palace Theatre, "En apoyo al heróico frente popular español, ¡Por la liberación nacional de Puerto Rico! Lucha a muerte contra el Fascismo, la reacción y el Imperialismo!"[43] Lawrence Chenault's 1938 study of the Puerto Rican community in Harlem concluded that the majority of the frequent parades and marches in *el barrio* were organized in support of Puerto Rican independence or Loyalist Spain.[44] "If the grave situation in Puerto Rico in the middle of the 1930s stirred up the Puerto Rican community in New York, so did the events in Spain around the same time," wrote Bernardo Vega in his memoirs.[45] The Spanish Civil War and Republican Spain occupied a prominent place in *la colonia's* politics. A typescript report of the American Spanish Aid Committee reported that the Spanish Division's efforts toward Spain were remarkably organized and far-reaching. "In spite of the fact that 70% of the Spanish speaking population of New York is unemployed," the report states, "the fundraising activities of the Spanish section have intensified and produced startling results for the benefit of other compatriots."[46]

George Charney noted that despite widespread poverty, entire families in *la colonia* were involved in efforts to support Loyalist Spain. "I never knew a people or a community," he recalled in his memoirs, "so passionately involved in the Spanish Civil War. It was their cause; no group could cry out the slogan 'No Pasarán' as they could, or contribute as much as they did in dimes, quarters and dollars."[47] Bernardo Vega remembered with pride that Puerto Rican workers did not "scrimp" when it came to donating to the Loyalist cause, despite their own dire economic situations.[48] According to James Fernández's research, the Sociedades Hispanas Confederadas in New York was second only to the North American Committee to Aid Spanish Democracy in raising money.[49] Vega recalled that "around three thousand Latin Americans were fighting in Spain as volunteers, among them some three hundred Puerto Ricans, both from New York and from Puerto Rico itself."[50] If African Americans in the International Brigades felt they were fighting racism at home and imperialism abroad, Puerto Ricans similarly fought both racism and imperialism at home. Lieutenant Carmelo Delgado Delgado from Guayama joined the Lincoln Brigade while studying in Spain. He wrote to Puerto Rican Nationalist leader Carlos Carrera Beníte: "Every day

I have more faith in our country (Puerto Rico) and I see the day coming when our people, like the people of Spain, will take arms to squash the tyrants (the United States) with the same valor and resolution that the people of Spain have taken against their military and political traitors."[51] José Ferrer, ghosted by the Spanish Civil War through previous roles and political activities and explicitly self-identified as Puerto Rican in the volatile 1930s and 1940s, brought such associations onto the stage with him as Iago, adding another *Americas* south of Robeson's.

In Shakespeare's play, Othello is destroyed by Iago, and Iago is destroyed for his evil. Ferrer could have been read as a Black Legend Spaniard wielding his colonialist sword over Africa (and the Americas). Yet Ferrer adamantly identified himself as a Puerto Rican as well as a Spaniard, dislodging the possibility of an Imperialist peninsular Iago. In the play, a personal grievance tears Iago and Othello apart. In the 1943 production, Robeson's offstage affair with Ferrer's wife poisoned what might have been a friendship. Mirrors of personal life aside, the 1943 *Othello* confronted black-white race relations in the United States and linked nationalism and antiracism through World War II. It also reconfigured U.S. hemispheric hegemony by placing a Puerto Rican-American-Spaniard in the International Brigades of the Republican army alongside an African-American-Moor, enacting the south-to-north toppling posited by Joseph North's *Why Spain Can Win*. Though Republican Spain had lost to Franco, its imaginative force—the reconfiguration of race as race-nation-ethnicity and the resultant alliances such a reframing exposed as possible—persisted. While in Spain in 1937, Robeson's wife, Eslanda Robeson, experienced such a reconfiguration in an encounter with one International Brigades volunteer:

> As our car came to a standstill, I saw a young Negro soldier, who saw Paul and stopped dead and stared. . . . He said he recognized Paul at once, but simply could not believe his eyes. He is a Spanish Negro from Harlem, and his name is Roderigo. He has been here 11 months, fighting, and was wounded at Teruel last week but is much better now. He was delighted to talk about Harlem, and Negroes, knows Ford, etc. Speaks Spanish fluently.[52]

In confronting multiple races through multiple wars, the 1943 *Othello* presented a vision of an imaginary global order in which north-to-south hegemonies in both the Americas and Europe were inverted. It was a vision posited by the defense of the Second Republic in the Spanish Civil War. Though the Republic had been defeated, the battle continued.

Notes

1. See, for example, Lindsey Swindall, *The Politics of Paul Robeson's Othello* (Jackson: University of Mississippi Press, 2011); and Sheila Tully Boyle and Andrew Bunie, *Paul Robeson: The Years of Promise and Achievement* (Amherst: University of Massachusetts Press, 2001). These volumes also contain detailed production analyses and descriptions, which are not the purview of my chapter. For further production details, Janet Barton Carroll's close examination of Webster's promptbook and the critical contexts of the production is invaluable: Janet Barton Carroll, "A Promptbook Study of Margaret Webster's Production of *Othello*," PhD diss. (Louisiana State University and Agricultural and Mechanical College, 1977). Milly S. Barranger situates the production within Webster's career and aesthetics: Milly S. Barranger, *Margaret Webster: A Life in the Theater* (Ann Arbor: University of Michigan Press, 2004).

2. James G. Thompson, letter to the editor, *Pittsburgh Courier*, originally printed 21 January 1942, reprinted 11 April 1942, p. 5.

3. "The Playwright's Company presents *Key Largo* by Maxwell Anderson, Directed by Guthrie McClintic" (1940), *The Playbill* for the Ethel Barrymore Theatre, author's collection.

4. Marvin Carlson, *The Haunted Stage: The Theatre as Memory Machine* (Ann Arbor: University of Michigan Press, 2003), 2.

5. Ibid., 8–9.

6. Paul Robeson, *Paul Robeson Speaks: Writings, Speeches, Interviews, 1918–1974* (New York: Citadel Press, 1978), 146.

7. Alun Kenwood, "Art, Propaganda and Commitment: Hispanic Literature and the Spanish Civil War," in *The Spanish Civil War: A Cultural and Historical Reader*, ed. Alun Kenwood (Oxford: Berg, 1993), 33.

8. Joseph North, *Why Spain Can Win* (New York: Workers Library Publishers, 1939), unpaginated.

9. Walter Mignolo, *The Idea of Latin America* (London: Wiley Blackwell, 1991).

10. "Paul Robeson as Othello," The Theatre Guild Program for *Othello Moor of Venice*, directed by Margaret Webster (1943), 2, in author's possession.

11. Technically, the Abraham Lincoln volunteers were a battalion. However, the volunteers, their supporters, and their historians use the term "brigade."

12. Peter Carroll, *The Odyssey of the Abraham Lincoln Brigade: Americans in the Spanish Civil War* (Stanford: Stanford University Press, 1994), 249. Lincoln veterans found themselves discriminated against for their "premature antifascism," however.

13. Due to a number of factors, precise International Brigades numbers are difficult to ascertain; new information continues to be uncovered. Determining

the number of Puerto Rican volunteers is particularly challenging. The U.S. American Communist Party recruited from both the *colonia* in New York and on the island of Puerto Rico itself. Upon arriving in Spain, Spanish speakers from the Americas often passed into Spanish units rather than into U.S. American units.

14. Carlson, *Haunted Stage*, 72.

15. Maxwell Anderson, *Key Largo* (Washington, D.C.: Anderson House, 1939), 21.

16. Acts 1 and 2 take place a year and a half later, around and in the d'Alcalà family house in Key Largo, Florida. Although McCloud's fight is, ultimately, at home rather than in Europe, the play's structure implies that such a fight, if not borne in fields abroad, would soon be tested there again.

17. "Playwright's Company Presents *Key Largo*."

18. "Paul Robeson as Othello."

19. Eric Bentley, *Thirty Years of Treason: Excerpts from Hearings before the House Committee of Un-American Activities 1938–1968* (New York: Viking Press, 1971), 413. It was not, as Dennis Brown has said, Ferrer's "finest hour." Belying his inner turmoil over the testimony, Ferrer recalled in 1999 that it was "very personal and very very painful." Dennis Brown, "Cyrano: José Ferrer," in *Actors Talk: Profiles and Stories from the Acting Trade* (New York: Limelight Editions, 1999), 245.

20. Bentley, *Thirty Years*, 410–12. The rally referred to was sponsored by the Spanish Refugee Appeal of the Joint Anti-Fascist Refugee Committee and held on 24 September 1945. Attendance numbers reported vary from fifteen thousand to seventeen thousand. Ferrer was a featured speaker.

21. Carlson, *Haunted Stage*, 63.

22. Paul Robeson, *Here I Stand* (Boston: Beacon Press, 1958), 53.

23. Boyle and Bunie, *Paul Robeson*, 395.

24. Robeson, *Here I Stand*, 53.

25. In English: All the people of the world are in the International Brigades at the side of the Spanish people. "Todos los Pueblos del Mundo están en las Brigadas Internacionales al lado del Pueblo Español," Abraham Lincoln Brigade Archives, http://www.alba-valb.org/resources/media, accessed 28 April 2013.

26. Boyle and Bunie, *Paul Robeson*, 385.

27. Kenneth Porter, "Drama Mailbag: About Othello," *New York Times*, 27 February 1944, 27.

28. Walter Mignolo, "Islamophobia and Hispanophobia: How They Came Together in the Euro-American Imagination," *Arches* 4.7 (Winter 2010): 25.

29. For Mignolo, this configuration is in direct contrast to secular conceptualizations of "race as skin color." Mignolo reminds us that race as skin

color is a rather recent (eighteenth and nineteenth century) and geographically bound (central and northern Europe and North America) notion.

30. Christopher Othen, *Franco's International Brigades: Foreign Volunteers and Fascist Dictators in the Spanish Civil War* (London: Reportage Press, 2008), 194.

31. William Shakespeare, *Othello*, in *Mr. William Shakespeare's Comedies, Histories, and Tragedies: A Facsimile of the First Folio 1623* (London: Routledge, 1998). Act line references: as having "thick lips" (1.1.66), as being "an old black ram" (1.1.88), and as being "a Barbary horse" (1.1.113).

32. Anthony Beevor, *The Battle for Spain: The Spanish Civil War, 1936–1939* (New York: Penguin, 2006), 92.

33. Othen, *Franco's International Brigades*, 194–95.

34. Shakespeare, *Othello*, 1.1.44.

35. Langston Hughes, "Letter from Spain," in *Langston Hughes in the Hispanic World and Haiti*, ed. Edward J. Mullen (Hamden, Conn.: Archon Books, 1977) 156–57.

36. J. Carroll, "Promptbook Study," 125, 132.

37. In 1938, two hundred thousand Spanish speakers lived in New York City. Puerto Ricans made up the largest group, followed by Cubans. James R. Fernández, "Nueva York: The Spanish Speaking Community Responds," in *Facing Fascism: New York and the Spanish Civil War*, ed. Peter N. Carroll and James D. Fernández (New York: Museum of the City of New York and NYU Press, 2005), 88.

38. Bernardo Vega, *Memoirs of Bernardo Vega*, trans. Juan Flores (New York: Monthly Review Press, 1984), 151.

39. Joaquín Colón López, *Pioneros puertorriqueños en Nueva York, 1917–1947* (Houston: Arte Público Press, 2002), 155.

40. Richard Vázquez, "The Origin and Need for the Term Hispanic," *Las Culturas*, http://www.lasculturas.com/aa/aa051701a.htm, accessed 30 April 2013.

41. Susan E. Lederer, "Porto Ricochet: Joking about Germs, Cancer and Race Extermination in the 1930s," *American Literary History* 14.4 (Winter 2002): 720.

42. Hispanic, in terms of the U.S government, was defined in 1977 as an ethnicity, not a race, a category that denoted Spanish language heritage and/or origin in Mexican, Puerto Rican, Cuban, Central or South American, or peninsular nations. Vázquez, "Origin and Need for the Term Hispanic."

43. "In support of the heroic Popular Front of Spain. For the national liberation of Puerto Rico! Fight to the death against Fascism, Repression and Imperialism!" "Gran Mítin de Protesta," Erasmo Vando Collection, box 2,

folder 16, El Centro de Estudios Puertorriqueños, Hunter College, City University of New York.

44. Lawrence R. Chenault, *The Puerto Rican Migrant in New York City* (New York: Columbia University Press, 1938), 154.

45. Vega, *Memoirs*, 191.

46. United American Spanish Aid Committee, "Organizational Structure and Fundraising Techniques," ts., Jesus Colón Collection, box 20, folder 7, El Centro de Estudios Puertorriqueños, Hunter College, City University of New York.

47. Cited in Gerald Meyer, *Vito Marcantonio: Radical Politician, 1902–1954* (Albany: State University of New York Press, 1989), 151.

48. Vega, *Memoirs*, 197.

49. Fernández, *Nueva York*, 88.

50. Vega, *Memoirs*, 197.

51. "Carmelo Delgado Delgado Biography," Abraham Lincoln Brigade Archives, http://www.alba-valb.org/volunteers/carmelo-delgado-delgado/?searchterm=delgado%20delgado, accessed 4 January 2016.

52. Eslanda Robeson, "Diary of Mrs. Eslanda Robeson," ts., January 1938–February 1938, Veterans of the Abraham Lincoln Brigade Records, ALBA 019, box 3, folder 3, Tamiment Library/Robert F. Wagner Labor Archives, New York University, 9. *Ford* here refers to Henry Ford.

12. Turning "Negroes" into "People" Onstage

Anna Lucasta in Harlem and on Broadway (1944)

Jonathan Shandell

In Alice Childress's 1955 play *Trouble in Mind*, the protagonist, Wiletta Mayer, is an African American actress cast in a play called *Chaos in Belville*, a stilted melodrama about the lynching of a young African American man in the South. Conflict centers on Wiletta's interactions with the white director, Al Manners, who prods the veteran performer to "justify" the actions her character takes. Wiletta balks, because she can find no truth in the naive choice her character makes to surrender her son to the lynch mob. In pleading with Wiletta to take her character seriously, Manners issues a strange directive. "Don't think 'Negro,' think 'people,'"[1] he urges her—as if these two categories require some fundamentally different interpretive approach. What the director refuses or is unable to see is how Wiletta's character has been imbued with subhuman intelligence and how a conspiracy of white interests—playwrights, producers, directors like Manners, and audiences—have established this inhumanity as a norm for black characters on the commercial American stage.

Childress had worked as a professional actress before turning to playwriting out of dissatisfaction with the marginalization of African American women both onstage and off. Scholars have noted *Trouble in Mind*'s autobiographical dimensions, but no one has yet identified what I believe to be the source of this particular line of dialogue. In 1944, Childress played a supporting role in the ensemble cast of *Anna Lucasta*, which debuted at the American Negro Theatre in Harlem before transferring to Broadway. Critic Louis Kronenberger of the New York newspaper *PM* lauded that Broadway production with a curious bit of praise: "One of the real merits . . . of *Anna Lucasta* is that it is a play not about Negroes, but about people."[2] There's no proof that Childress deliberately placed a version of this unfortunate sentence into the mouth of her character, but the similarity seems too striking to be coincidental. Comparing Kronenberger's condescending praise with Manners's condescending direction illustrates how long and hard-fought the effort waged by Childress was, on both sides of the proscenium, to escape the obligation of convincing supposedly sympathetic white men of her own humanity.

There is nothing unusual about the white chauvinism in Kronenberger's review, but the play that elicited it merits closer investigation. *Anna Lucasta* was a revolutionary experiment with race on the American stage—one that challenged and intrigued both black and white audiences in its dramatization of African American identity. This play created a sensation in Harlem and on Broadway for its drastic departure from mainstream cultural practices of the 1940s. It featured African American actors embodying characters defined not by racialized assumptions, nor through familiar signifiers of racial difference, but only by their own humanity. The play and its public reception provide a glimpse into a nation's uneasy search for more equitable race relations during the pre–civil rights era and into how the stage helped facilitate that exploration. But for all of its synergy with race liberalism of the mid-1940s, *Anna Lucasta* also demonstrated the persistence of power imbalances along racial lines within the commercial theatre. To fully comprehend the American theatre's contradictory attitudes and problematic history on integration in the 1940s, we must wrestle with the paradoxical legacy of *Anna Lucasta*, which will be the purpose of this chapter. Here was a play that reflected in equal measure both democratic progress and persistent inequality. Its history typifies the larger machinations of a country increasingly willing to *think* and *talk* about justice, inclusion, and democracy but hesitant to travel the difficult path toward meaningful action on those ideals.

The American Negro Theatre (ANT) is now regarded as "the most important, self-contained black theatre troupe between the demise of the African Company in 1823 and the birth of the Negro Ensemble Company (NEC) in 1967."[3] Launched in 1940 by playwright Abram Hill and actor Frederick O'Neal in the basement of the Harlem Library, the ANT was the most influential African American ensemble of the 1940s. The group's mission, as outlined by its constitution, was to defy prevailing stereotypes of African Americans as "superstitious, spiritual-singing misfit[s] in a complex modern civilization . . . the comical, lazy, ignorant, carefree and not too bright offspring of the minstrel."[4] In a decade of activity, *Anna Lucasta* was by any measure the ANT's most influential and popular effort. Yet, for reasons explored in detail below, the production also initiated the company's demise just six years later. O'Neal once remarked, "Our greatest success was the cause of our greatest failure."[5] The full story of that successful failure begins years before the ANT was founded.

Anna Lucasta's journey to Harlem and Broadway began in Chicago in 1938, when Philip Yordan—an attorney of Polish descent with aspirations as a playwright—wrote a drama titled "Anna Lukasca." This was a domestic tragedy about a poor Polish American family in rural Pennsylvania. In Yordan's script, the Lukasca family attempts to pass off their daughter Anna (a Brooklyn prostitute and source of familial disgrace) on the unsuspecting Rudolf Slavick—the son of a family friend, just off the boat from Poland with a bankroll of $800 cash. For two years, Yordan shopped his play to New York producers but received rejection "from practically everybody who is anybody in the theater."[6] One obstacle was the play's too-obvious resemblance to Eugene O'Neill's *Anna Christie*. Even more distasteful to producers was the extreme pessimism and brutality that pervaded Yordan's dramaturgy. Though audiences never saw the original "Anna Lukasca," its contents are central to disputes over ownership and compensation that arose later when the ANT's adaptation became profitable. How significantly had the ANT altered Yordan's work in adapting it for African American actors? Whose creativity was *most responsible* for *Anna Lucasta*'s success? Did recognition and remuneration reach the proper parties? The original manuscript of "Anna Lukasca" reveals some answers.

As it shuttles between the Lukasca home and Anna's haunts in Brooklyn, "Anna Lukasca" paints a misanthropic portrait of miserable people. The play invests no nobility in the Lukasca family's economic struggles; their lives, like the furnishings of their living room, "merely evince the barbaric instinct to covet."[7] When paterfamilias Joe refuses to foist his disgraced daughter on the son of his good friend from Poland, sons Stanley and Frank pummel him into submission:

> STANLEY: You used to beat me when you was big and strong. You used to beat ma too. That was good, wasn't it? It's good to beat women. It makes men strong. It's good to hear them scream. It makes life real. . . . (*The old man looks up and smiles through his cut and bleeding face; like an old and blinded dog he scents something familiar in that which confronts him.*) . . . You want to learn the hard way. O.K. I'll teach you so you'll learn fast. (*Stanley cuffs the old man on the side of the head knocking his hat to the floor; the old man sits scratching his head.*) . . . You know who Anna is, don't you, pa? (*The old man looks up with a vague meaningless look which only serves to further antagonize Stanley.*) Don't pretend you don't understand or we'll lam you all over again. (*Stanley raises his arm*

in a threatening gesture and a spasm of life shakes the old man's frame. Then with trembling jowls he slides off the chair to the floor but Frank quickly jerks him up and props him back into the chair.) You yellow bastard, falling before I so much as touched you. You ain't as dumb as you're pretending. Now I'm askin' you for the last time. Are you gonna go get Anna? (*The old man sits mute; Stanley grabs him by the collar, choking off his breath.*) Say it! Say it!

JOE: (*nodding weakly; he drools*) Anna.[8]

Rudolf, an uncomprehending newcomer who speaks only broken English, is a particularly distasteful iteration of what Cheryl Black and Anne Fletcher identify in chapter 5 as that "vicious ethnic and cultural stereotype: the 'bohunk.'" He arrives from Poland and quickly surrenders his cash to Anna, despite her unrepentant warnings: "Sucker, you're being taken for a buggy ride. Don't you know nothin', you dumb mutt?" Comprehending nothing, Rudolf asks her, "Vat you say Anna? . . . Vy you laugh at me?" before forking over his money.[9] For three acts, the Lukascas snipe at, swindle, and victimize one another as they fight for the cash—culminating in the fracturing of the family, an accidental murder, the hasty deportation of an oblivious Rudolf back to Poland (minus his $800 in savings), and Anna's return to her old pimp's payroll in Brooklyn. The original "Anna Lukasca" offers no life raft of optimism or any hint of a larger psychological, moral, or metaphysical perspective that might elevate a tragedy. The contempt that its characters show for one another mirrors the contempt shown by the playwright for the entire world he dramatizes.

Despite its harsh texture, Yordan's script found an advocate in a playwrights' agent named Claire Leonard, who became enamored of what she called the play's "violent intensity in character."[10] Beginning in 1940, she shopped the play all over the theatre district but found no buyers. After years of rejections, she broadened her search by approaching Abram Hill (whom she also represented as a playwright) with the suggestion that "Anna Lukasca" "would make a good vehicle for black actors." Some time elapsed before the ANT seriously considered the play for production. Hill recounted:

> We read the script, and our feeling was that it was too close to Eugene O'Neill's *Anna Christie*. It dealt with the life of a prostitute, and we were trying to get away from that sort of thing. So we put it aside. . . . [The next year] we were desperate for a new play, and we didn't feel we had anything, so I reread "Anna Lukasca." And all of a sudden, I felt it had a tremendous possibility that I didn't see when I first read it.[11]

Hill secured Yordan's permission to rewrite the script. To direct the play, the ANT hired Harry Wagstaff Gribble (a British-born Broadway veteran), who worked with Hill on a first rewrite. Their revised version underwent many additional changes in rehearsals. Frederick O'Neal described the ANT's final version of the play as "a group action more or less."[12] Ruby Dee—not part of the original Harlem cast but a frequent observer of rehearsals—concurred with O'Neal's account. Her memoirs tell of Gribble working cooperatively with the actors as they "improvised on the script—making up dialogue on the spot, throwing out scenes, and creating new ones."[13] With so many artistic hands at work, Leonard later noted that "it was hard to tell who rewrote what" in *Anna Lucasta*[14] —an uncertainty that presented complications once the play started making money. Putting aside (for now) those concerns, it is worth noting the unconventional collaborative process that turned the toxic "Anna Lukasca" into the revolutionary and infectiously popular *Anna Lucasta*. This was an uncommon exercise in collaborative creation during an era when black and white artists rarely shared artistic autonomy as equitable partners.

Cosmetic changes were necessary in adapting Yordan's script for the ANT's actors. The family's Polish roots were replanted in Alabama, with the surnames "Lukasca" and "Slavick" changed to the less identifiable "Lucasta" and "Slocum." Most surprising to some observers was what Hill, Gribble, and the ANT did *not* do in their adapting work. Commercially popular precedents they might have followed—such as John Houseman and Orson Welles's "Voodoo" *Macbeth* (1935) or the jazzed-up Gilbert and Sullivan adaptations *Swing Mikado* (1938) and *Hot Mikado* (1939), for example—overflowed with racialized cultural allusions and dialect and traded upon blatant appeals to primitivism or exoticism. *Anna Lucasta* rejected that approach and included no mention of race, racial difference, or African American heritage whatsoever within its dialogue. To use the parlance of its time, there was nothing explicitly "Negroid" at all about the new text that the ANT crafted from Yordan's raw material. As one observer put it, this was refreshingly "not the usual . . . exploitation of the Negro as a shiftless, immoral, crap-shooting, dope-peddling, gin-drinking, 'colorful,' 'quaint,' or 'charming' character but . . . a serious story of average human beings (all highly individualized) who happen to have pigmented skins."[15]

The ANT's nonracialized rewrite also struck a much different tone from the original script.[16] Though the Lucastas remain antagonistic and occasionally violent toward one another in attempting to secure Rudolf's $800 endowment, their family squabblings become less depraved and more laughable. The confrontation between Joe and his sons (still tinged with aggression) is tempered and infused with a new psychological layer—a suggestion that Joe's resistance to bringing Anna back home stems from suppressed incestuous feelings:

> FRANK: So what was it that made you kick [Anna] out? Why won't you have her back?
>
> JOE: 'Cause I ain't goin' to let you steal Otis Slocum's money!
>
> FRANK: God! There ain't nothin' in this world I hate so much as a liar! . . .
>
> JOE: I don't know what you're talkin' about. There ain't no truth but what I've said!
>
> FRANK: Oh, yes, there is! You're afraid of her! That's what's eatin' your guts—you're scared of her!
>
> JOE: Afraid? What can she do to me?
>
> FRANK: I dunno! What does she do to you?
>
> JOE: Nothin'! Nothin'!
>
> FRANK: Nothin' but the mere mention of her name turns you into a tremblin' old fool—scared!
>
> JOE: You're a devil! You're a mean, wicked devil to say such things to me! They're lies! They're lies!
>
> FRANK: Then prove it by bringing her back—showing all of us that you can act like a father to her. A nice kind father, Joe.
>
> JOE: No! No!
>
> FRANK: Yellow, eh? Well, I'll just have to give you a little courage. This is where you need it, Joe. (*He gives him a vicious pummel in the gut.*)[17]

As this scene illustrates, the new *Anna Lucasta* (while distinctly less extreme in its depravity) did retain elements of sexuality, crudeness, and hyperemotionality from Yordan's original play. These qualities in the original likely informed to some degree Claire Leonard's impulse that "Anna Lukasca" "would make a good vehicle for black actors" and may have been at work in Abram Hill's sense of the play's "tremendous possibility" for the ANT. Despite mainstream critics' celebrations of the play's universalizing dramaturgy, some measure of its appeal to white spectators should be attributed to how the work subtly confirmed existing attitudes and expectations toward African Americans.

Still, the ANT worked to redirect those attitudes and expectations by adding an identifiable moral center to the drama, refining the two central characters into sympathetic romantic leads. Rudolf Slocum—no longer a "dumb mutt" like Rudolf Slavick—is a well-spoken college graduate too wise to be parted from his fortune. He is keen enough to see past Anna's tough, streetwise exterior to find wisdom and humanity:

RUDOLF: I sure never met anyone like you. I sure never did. So nice and pretty, and yet so understanding. . . . You seem to be looking right through people and reading their thoughts.

ANNA: According to you I don't always read them right.

RUDOLF: I think that's because you don't trust people. Someone must have hurt you.

ANNA: More than one, brother.[18]

Left to right: Hilda Simms (Anna), Georgia Burke (Theresa), and Earle Hyman (Rudolf) in a scene from the 1944 Broadway production of *Anna Lucasta. Photo: Eileen Darby/LIFE Images Collection/Getty Images.*

As the plot device of the disgraced daughter's return home to marry into Rudolf's money unfolds, the drama affords to Anna Lucasta a dignity and sensitivity that Yordan never gave to Anna Lukasca, making her a worthy match for the improved version of Rudolf. The romance of these two characters signifies the triumph of thoughtfulness and genuine feeling over the baseness and opportunism that surround them.

In that light, though it never explicitly addresses what America called "the Negro problem," *Anna Lucasta* articulates an unmistakable critique of social prejudice. Though some in the community denigrate Anna as a "class-A slut"[19] and others seek to exploit her marginal status for their own financial gain, the character proves worthy of respect. Her enlightened lover Rudolf (himself the target of misplaced derision as an Alabama "hick") shrugs off the narrow-mindedness around him and marries Anna—rejecting bias and opportunistic greed in favor of genuine affection. In this metaphoric way, *Anna Lucasta* spoke evocatively to an antiracist politics through what Harry J. Elam Jr. calls "the productive ambivalence of the black performer . . . to explore, expose and even explode definitions of blackness."[20] By removing the familiar cultural baggage that usually encumbers black bodies onstage, the play's black performers spoke against American prejudice in new ways.

Even as the production refrained from defining its characters specifically as "Negroes," there are moments where Harlem's cultural imprint is unmistakable. One is this flirtatious exchange:

> RUDOLF: Say, you aren't married, are you?
>
> ANNA: Don't see any ring on me, do you?
>
> RUDOLF: Thought you might be one of those fashionable divorcees.
>
> ANNA: You can do a little kiddin' yourself. What's fashionable about me?
>
> RUDOLF: I like your taste—that dress—nothing flashy, but real pretty. And you fill it out good.
>
> ANNA: Say! You have a line! Bet the girls in Alabama are just crying their hearts out for you.
>
> RUDOLF: Do we have to keep up this "jivin'"?
>
> ANNA: You seem to be gettin' groovy.
>
> RUDOLF: Do I look like a jitterbug?
>
> ANNA: No—And it don't suit you.
>
> RUDOLF: No more than "jive" talk suits you. Do you just put it on to let people know you've lived in Brooklyn?[21]

Here the dialogue captures the lively energy of "jive talk," a new dialect that had emerged from the ballrooms and back parlors of Harlem. Jervis Anderson provides this instructive account:

> In the late thirties and early forties, the term "jitterbug" referred not only to a popular dance form but the dancer, as well, and to almost anyone whose speech and manner of dress identified him as a "hep cat." . . . And almost anyone was accepted as a jitterbug or hep cat if he could talk "jive"—an in-group language that hardly any "square" could make sense of. The language was so esoteric that outsiders could appropriate it only by consulting textbooks like Cab Calloway's *Hepster's Dictionary.*[22]

Alongside Calloway's dictionary was *Dan Burley's Original Handbook of Harlem Jive*, published the same year as *Anna Lucasta*'s debut, which fed a growing cultural curiosity with this lively Harlem vernacular. Anna and Rudolf's repartee is never quite esoteric enough to need a reference for translation, but its language imbues these characters with a distinctively urban, cosmopolitan spirit. Such passages in the play demonstrate how *Anna Lucasta* was, for all of its mainstream marketability as a Broadway vehicle, a product with some distinctly uptown influences.

But even with its breezier tone, the ANT's version of *Anna Lucasta* ends tragically, with Anna's suicide following the rapid breakdown of her marriage with Rudolf. The script also introduced a darker context of World War II for its action (set in 1941) by "concocting a prologue and epilogue laid in 1944"[23] that made ominous reference to conflicts in Europe. Noting contrasts between its comic spirit and tragic framing, critics used labels like "comedy-drama" and "tragi-comedy" to characterize *Anna Lucasta* in its debut Harlem version. That mixture of moods did not survive the move to Broadway, where the production's innovations in depicting race on stage met a wider, and whiter, audience.

As Alice Childress remembered it, the ANT had placed no commercial designs behind their production: "*Anna Lucasta* was a surprise. . . . We were pleasing ourselves, having a community experience. We didn't expect [it] to go professional."[24] Though she was active within the company, it seems that Childress was unaware of what was happening behind the scenes of the production. Before *Anna Lucasta* opened in Harlem, Hill, Leonard, and Yordan had discussed the play's commercial prospects. "Abe has high hopes on it being sold," Leonard wrote to Yordan in May 1944.[25] Such hopes likely prompted the hiring of Gribble as director and then multiplied once critics lauded the Harlem opening. A column by Hill published in the

Amsterdam News quoted the most gushing praise from various newspapers and gleefully compared the play's success to other activities downtown: "Ironically, the four shows that did open on the Great White Way last week, representing an investment of approximately $15,000, received notices that contained for the most part all the synonyms for lousy. Yet, the ANT[,] with its vest pocket budget of $600 and the fearless fortitude of its 40-odd members, won the golden laurels of the week."[26] Though Hill had been angling for Broadway from the outset, he later explained why the ANT passed on the opportunity to produce the transfer themselves: "We [were] a tryout company. It would change our format if we became a first-class producer."[27] So commercial interests descended upon the Harlem Library theatre and made numerous entreaties to Hill, Gribble, and Leonard. Leonard advised her partners to favor the bid of John J. Wildberg, primarily because of his earlier success as coproducer of *Porgy and Bess*. Wildberg led a team of eighteen investors that won the rights to bring *Anna Lucasta* to Broadway.

The selling of the play's professional rights marked the end of the ANT's creative influence over the drama. Gribble and Yordan made additional rewrites for Broadway (without Hill and the cast at the table), giving *Anna Lucasta* an even broader comic feeling and a more positive outlook. The dark prologue and epilogue were discarded. A new ending offered the hopeful suggestion of a "happily ever after" reunion, with Rudolf following Anna back to Brooklyn to rescue her from a return to her old profession. Direction and acting style for Broadway veered toward the farcical. Reviewers who had seen the original Harlem production noted the changes with distaste:

> It is discouraging . . . to see what inevitably happens to a play from one of the city's workshop theatres when it is taken in hand by Times Square experts and revamped with a wary eye on the box office and possible movie rights. . . . [The play] has been hooked up, rendered more obvious and revamped to conform more closely to the regulation Broadway groove. . . . A happy ending that is also a sappy ending has lately been tacked on without the slightest regard for what might be termed artistic verisimilitude. "Anna Lucasta," though its earlier scenes are filled with a gusty comedy, is essentially a tragedy—or was before Mr. Wildberg and their [the ANT's] backers got to tinkering with the script.[28]

Kronenberger went so far as to trash this new staging as "a rather shameless bid for laughs . . . [that] commits every possible sin against art."[29] But the artistic sins committed by Yordan and Wildberg pale in comparison to the economic malfeasance that ensued.

Left to right: John Tate (Lester), Hilda Simms (Anna), Canada Lee (Danny), and Alvin Childress (Noah) in a scene from the 1944 Broadway production of *Anna Lucasta. Photo: Eileen Darby/LIFE Images Collection/Getty Images.*

Anna Lucasta opened at the Mansfield Theatre on 30 August 1944, less than three months after closing in Harlem. Lingering enthusiasm from the ANT production sparked a huge demand for tickets. Ruby Dee later reflected, "Broadway needed a lift, needed a laugh, needed to try to forget the war in Europe. *Anna Lucasta* was just the ticket."[30] The play also capitalized on a Broadway culture that had seen notable recent improvements in the acceptance of African American actors into serious dramatic roles—especially Paul Robeson's 1943 turn as Othello with the Theatre Guild (discussed in detail in chapter 11) and Canada Lee as Bigger Thomas in the Richard Wright/Paul Green adaptation of *Native Son* (1944). The popularity of *Anna Lucasta* was to many a hopeful sign of continuing reform of the Broadway status quo with respect to black performers. A profile in the NAACP's *Crisis* proclaimed, "A new star blazed across the Broadway horizon recently and left in her wake something new in the American theatre. New York's sophisticated audiences became conscious of the Negro actor as a serious, dramatic personage after the opening of 'Anna Lucasta.'"[31] The National Urban League's journal *Opportunity* foresaw as a result of this play's impact the breaking of "the rigid taboo against dramatic roles for Negro actors which are not stereotyped . . . Will Hilda Simms, Alice Childress, Earle Hyman, Frank O'Neal [*sic*] and others be forced eventually to join clown school in order to earn a living at their profession? The answer is, they won't, if *Anna Lucasta* is indicative of a new trend."[32]

Anna Lucasta ran for 947 performances at the Mansfield: a two-year engagement that still stands as the longest ever for a spoken drama with an entirely African American cast. The play's commercial life continued for years to come—through several national tours, an engagement in London's West End, and two feature film versions.[33] What accounts for *Anna Lucasta*'s widespread popularity with audiences beyond Harlem? How can we understand this fascination with a relatively ordinary play that used black actors in an out-of-the-ordinary fashion? To answer those questions, I want to offer a deeper structural argument about why and how this novel experiment with race on the stage resonated with the prevailing American political dialogue.

Carol A. Horton describes the mid-1940s as "an exceptionally receptive historical moment" for the ideology of white liberal antiracism.[34] Pseudoscientific theories of biologically innate racial difference had been thoroughly discredited by social scientists; the Great Migration had concentrated black voting power in northern urban centers in ways that white politicians found difficult to ignore. As Andrea Nouryeh details with respect to the Stage Door Canteens in chapter 13, the continuing fight against the Nazis had prompted a national reexamination of homegrown notions of racial superiority; leadership in the Allied campaign of World War II sparked new considerations of how American racism might compromise the country's global influence as a voice for freedom and justice. At the same time, growing militancy among black protest movements and a spate of race riots in Detroit, Los Angeles, and Harlem added urgency to the problem. These converging forces stirred a collective yearning for a new way forward that reached its apex precisely when *Anna Lucasta* arrived on the Broadway stage. Liberal publications like the *Nation*, the *New Republic*, and *Common Sense* frequently published commentary about ending white racism, appealing to the collective conscience of "a large passive group of white Americans who consider themselves loyal supporters of the principles of American democracy, and who have some actual sense of the meaning of the term."[35] The year 1944 also saw the publication of two seminal books: the anthology *What the Negro Wants*, in which historian Rayford Logan brought together leading black intellectuals to make a well-reasoned case for full equality; and Swedish sociologist Gunnar Myrdal's sweeping study *An American Dilemma*, an encyclopedic indictment of American racism that quickly became the definitive expression of a new liberalism on race. The effect of all of these publications was "to expose the moral gap between America's liberal precepts and racial practices" for the entire nation to see and to spark widespread dialogue among liberally minded whites about the need for solutions.[36]

Appearing at this propitious moment, *Anna Lucasta* transported audiences into a theatrical world within which the promises of liberalism were implicitly fulfilled. Audiences could encounter African Americans without insistent reminders of that group's status as an estranged and disadvantaged "other" or as an intractable social problem. The production employed black actors without fetishizing their blackness, in a manner that was aesthetically pleasing and fundamentally nonthreatening for the majority. Audiences could, for a time, test the experience of viewing African Americans outside of the contours of the "Negro problem," with no demands made for a permanent adjustment in attitudes and no material threat posed to white privilege. Real-world solutions to the American dilemma of racial inequality were distant and difficult. Achieving what the Negro wanted was a daunting prospect, requiring significant investment and sacrifice from white Americans. But attending *Anna Lucasta* was a safe, enticing opportunity to sample the experience of seeing Negroes as people, as fellow citizens in a democracy that was magically cured of its racial pathology. The play's popularity was, I believe, a function of its correspondence with white America's growing desire to escape the difficulties of the present and to glimpse a more democratic future.

The quest for "color blindness" in performance has met with rigorous and justified critical scrutiny in recent years. New scholarship allows us to consider *Anna Lucasta* with awareness of "the shortcomings of color blindness's emphasis on transcending racial discourse." As Brandi Wilkins Catanese concludes, any attempt at transcending racial categories onstage "exacts disavowal of our racially mediated reality as the price of progress toward resolving American society's racial conflicts."[37] Such a disavowal will—no matter the intentions of the artists—obscure the lived history of oppression and reinforce in subtle ways the white hegemony that it purports to challenge. Consequently, alongside the progressive liberal experimentalism of *Anna Lucasta* that both black and white audiences celebrated, a subtextual evasion of racism's material consequences and an unspoken reification of racial hierarchies played themselves out at the Mansfield Theatre.

Paradoxically, this production both resisted and reinforced the dilemma facing American democracy.

Though *Anna Lucasta*'s cultural politics were complicated, in terms of economics matters were less ambiguous. On one hand, John Wildberg and Philip Yordan parlayed the play's popularity into large personal fortunes for themselves. *Ebony* magazine reported in 1945 how Wildberg had managed to "clean up more than two million dollars" while paying his cast as little as he could get away with. "The talented troupe of *Anna Lucasta* gets the lowest wages on Broadway [while] Yordan with a 10 percent straight royalty makes more than the entire cast combined."[38] That Philip Yordan profited so handsomely from *Anna Lucasta* was a particularly cruel irony. As Frederick O'Neal reflected years later, "his play was as different from its original form as night and day. . . . It was nothing like what he'd written. [But] that very next year, Phil Yordan made a million dollars writing [in Hollywood, based] on what he didn't really do."[39] On the other hand, the ANT's contract with Wildberg and his partners brought the Harlem theatre company that created *Anna Lucasta* only 1.25 percent of the gross Broadway sales, or an income of "around $250 per week for about two years."[40] With standard industry agreements affording 2 to 10 percent of Broadway receipts to contributing parties (with additional considerations for other professional productions and film rights), there can be little doubt that this play perpetuated—and elevated to shameful new heights—an all-too-familiar pattern in American theatre history of opportunistic white power brokers exploiting the creativity of African American artists.

For the ANT's bottom line, a growth in expenses that followed *Anna Lucasta* quickly overshadowed the new income the group received. In June 1945 the New York Public Library's director, Franklin F. Hopper, wrote to Abram Hill expressing alarm about safety and fire hazards due to overcrowding of performances at the Harlem Library, now that the ANT had raised its visibility significantly. "I regret that I must write you that we must discontinue use of the 135th Street Branch by the American Negro Theatre. . . . We have been glad to have you operate there during the experimental period and while your group was trying to get recognition. However, that period has passed."[41] Evicted from their rent-free home, the company moved to the 126th Street Elks Lodge. A larger stage, new rent and utility bills, and the desire to satisfy public expectations for professional production values sent costs climbing. Compounding the financial challenges faced by the ANT were new strains on the group's spirit of ensemble collaboration and artistic experimentalism. With some

ANT actors winning acclaim on Broadway, others who did not get the same opportunity became, as Hill recounted, "very hostile, very negative, finding fault with everything that was being done because they felt they had been left out."[42]

Dissension and high turnover of personnel were commonplace within the ANT throughout the late 1940s. Broadway and touring casts of *Anna Lucasta* took many company members away from Harlem. With ANT actors having proven their mettle on Broadway, other producers increasingly hired from within the company's ranks. Hill recounted:

> We could be rehearsing with members of our company, and they'd get a Broadway opportunity, and go accept it, so we'd have to recast. We could not compete with Broadway, and a talented, ambitious person is in the market for an opportunity. If that opportunity showed up, we suffered by the loss. Sometimes, we'd open a show, and a few days later, an actor had gotten exposure and a nice write-up. As a result, some producer would send for them and want to cast them in a Broadway thing . . . and we'd lost them.[43]

Such opportunities were well deserved, but these talented and ambitious people were rarely compensated more fairly than those on Wildberg's payroll. Claude Sloane (chairman of the ANT's board of trustees) once railed in a letter to O'Neal against the exodus from the company for bargain-rate wages: "Fred, we are baffled at a solution to keep the kids from being exploited by Broadway, for the damn fools are suckers for making $60 a week."[44] Once these actors started working professionally, O'Neal explained, "a lot of them never went back. . . . [They] looked on returning to the American Negro Theatre as going backwards. They wanted to move on with their careers."[45] New members joining the company brought with them much different expectations and goals. According to Loften Mitchell, "The morning after *Anna Lucasta* was pronounced a hit, there were hundreds of applications from potential professional theatre people who sought to use A.N.T. as a stepping stone to Broadway."[46]

By its rhetoric, the ANT wanted to dispel this new reputation it had acquired through its commercial success. "We do not wish to ape conventional Broadway and Hollywood," Abram Hill declared in 1945. "Nor would we wish to imitate ourselves with the production of another 'Anna Lucasta.' We're in the market for new things that Broadway and Hollywood would hesitate to take a chance on."[47] But these statements were undercut by the group's own behavior. The very next ANT production was Hill's own play *Walk Hard*—an adaptation of Len Zinberg's novel about Jim Crow segregation in the world of professional boxing. After its Harlem engagement, the ANT sent this play to midtown as well, fueling speculation in Harlem that the ANT had "lost its original perspective and has turned into a feeder for Broadway. . . . If ANT has become too commercial-minded and 'gone Broadway,' it won't be the means of establishing the community theatre Harlem needs."[48] *Walk Hard* earned mostly negative reviews and closed after three performances at Forty-Second Street's Chanin Auditorium.

More telling was the impact on the company's repertoire. From its founding in 1940 until its 1944–45 season, the ANT had produced several new and experimental works by influential black playwrights, including a critically celebrated 1941 staging of Theodore Browne's expressionist drama *Natural Man* (which play is the subject of chapter 7) and other plays by Owen Dodson and Hill himself.[49] Developing such works for Harlem audiences furthered the group's avowed mission of "expressing . . . the refined and disciplined emotional experience of the Negro" and facilitating "an awakening of the dormant dramatic gifts of the Negro folk temperament."[50] After 1945, however, no works by black writers found their way to the ANT stage. Some of the plays the company presented were written originally for white actors and presented in a spirit of color-blind transcendence. Others dealt directly with racial themes and utilized all-black or integrated casts. None of these had an impact or a public response anywhere near that of *Anna Lucasta*. In the eyes of outside observers and several of the group's own members, the ANT's historic Broadway coup had dampened its experimental spirit and undercut its vitality as a Harlem cultural institution.

Aware of the problems and frustrations, the company organized a public forum in March 1947 to address certain vital questions and to seek a new path forward: "Has the A.N.T. lost sight of its goals? Is [the] A.N.T. too Broadway-conscious? Is the A.N.T. a force for unity in our community? Can a people's theatre maintain its independence?"[51] Definitive answers that might have helped recapture the company's bygone spirit and rebuild its reputation remained elusive. As the troubles mounted, Abram Hill became a convenient scapegoat—for a perceived mishandling of finances (including the commercial rights for *Anna Lucasta*) and for an increasingly abrasive leadership style. Hill resigned from the ANT in 1948, and in the spring of 1949 remaining leadership annulled the group's constitution and convened a reorganization committee—a last-ditch attempt to rekindle the company's vitality. As the committee discussed the ANT's future, the difficulties aroused by *Anna Lucasta* lingered. One faction of this group maintained that past failures arose from "the sudden success of *Anna Lucasta*, at which time the question of non-commercial theatre was forgotten and work was immediately focused on another Broadway production." A competing camp led by Frederick O'Neal felt that "the life of [the] organization itself could depend on whether ANT gets anything [else] on Broadway. *Anna Lucasta* . . . should have been a springboard for continued artistic growth. . . . Another lucky production could be that springboard."[52] Though the committee drafted a new constitution for the group, its records tell of no common understanding on this impasse. Though reorganized on paper, the ANT was not reenergized. Its 1949 staging of Kenneth White's one-act play *Freight* was the group's last theatrical effort. It played in Harlem for a few weeks and then transferred to the Fulton Theatre on Broadway but closed after only five performances.

Surveying what had become of the ANT in the wake of its Broadway triumph, Loften Mitchell pronounced *Anna Lucasta* to be "one of the great tragedies of the American Negro Theatre and the American theatre itself. . . . Money entered the picture and few people paid any attention to the aims and goals of the American Negro Theatre once the dollar sign appeared."[53] Cultural critic Harold Cruse agreed and blamed the ANT's leadership for getting "impaled on the horns of the integration dilemma" that (in his view) had perennially depleted Harlem of its cultural vitality:

> A conflict over aims was implicit in the ANT's institutional structure. In other words, characteristic of all Negro movements and groups, especially in the cultural field, there existed ideological conflicts over integration versus ethnic group identity. . . . It followed then, that once the greener-looking fields of "integration in the theater" downtown beckoned to the actors, ANT's all-Negro theatre idea would be undermined.[54]

These critiques illustrate how the New York theatre's experiments with integration during the 1940s—inspired by a crescendo of democratically minded race liberalism—were often subject to the undemocratic forces of American economics. For all its innovations with humanizing black characters, *Anna Lucasta* reaffirmed the disempowered position that African Americans occupied within the white-dominated theatre industry and set in motion the destruction of the Harlem theatre company that brought the play into being. The cynicism that fueled Mitchell's and Cruse's assessments of the ANT had much on which to feed.

But a different perspective can be found in Robert Károly Sarlós's biography of American avant-garde pioneer George Cram "Jig" Cook. When the Provincetown Players disbanded in the wake of the troupe's own Broadway triumph with Eugene O'Neill's *The Emperor Jones*, its idealistic founder, Cook, and wife, Susan Glaspell, left the country—disillusioned over the careerism that had overtaken their amateur collective. But, Sarlós argues,

> Cook's fundamental error was his unwillingness to accept popular success as an indication that the experiment had profitably been completed. He believed in a permanent state of revolution, in a continuous and ever-broadening ferment, without realizing that in such a process the original yeast cannot stay in one lump, but must dissolve and be absorbed beyond recognition for its work to be done.[55]

So, too, in this case did the wider American culture benefit by absorbing the results of a historic experiment. Its "yeast" would continue to circulate throughout American culture—as Childress, O'Neal, Hilda Simms, Earle Hyman, Ossie Davis, Ruby Dee, Sidney Poitier, and so many other African American actors who had appeared in different productions of *Anna Lucasta* continued the work of humanizing black characters on stages and screens. The project of dislodging racist stereotypes from the center of the American cultural imagination would continue long after *Anna Lucasta* appeared. The march toward fuller recognition of Negroes as people onstage and in society would remain sporadic and painfully slow. Nonetheless, *Anna Lucasta* was a problem-ridden but promising step forward in that journey.

Notes

1. Alice Childress, *Trouble in Mind*, in *Selected Plays*, ed. Kathy A. Perkins (Evanston, Ill.: Northwestern University Press, 2011), 98.

2. Louis Kronenberger, "Anna Lucasta Scores Again," review of *Anna Lucasta*, Mansfield Theatre, New York, *PM*, 31 August 1944, in *New York Theatre Critics Reviews*, vol. 5 (New York: New York Theatre Critics Reviews, 1944), 146.

3. James V. Hatch and Errol Hill, *A History of African American Theatre* (Cambridge: Cambridge University Press, 2003), 350.

4. "ANT Foreword," American Negro Theatre Records (1940–81), folder 1, Schomburg Center for Research in Black Culture, New York, N.Y.

5. Frederick O'Neal, interview by James Hatch, 8 February 1972, Hatch-Billops Archive, New York, N.Y.

6. "'Anna Lucasta's' Odyssey," *PM*, 27 August 1945, American Negro Theatre Scrapbook 1944–45, Schomburg Center for Research in Black Culture, New York, N.Y.

7. Philip Yordan, "Anna Lukasca," unpublished manuscript, 1.1.1, Claire Leonard Papers, *T-Mss 1992-008, Billy Rose Theatre Division, New York Public Library for the Performing Arts.

8. Ibid., 1.1.21–1.1.22.

9. Ibid., 2.1.15.

10. Claire Leonard, untitled and unpublished essay, n.d., Claire Leonard Papers.

11. Abram Hill, interview by Michelle Wallace, 19 January 1974, Hatch-Billops Archive, recording transcribed by author.

12. Frederick O'Neal, interview by Robert Wilson, 13 August 1973, Hatch-Billops Archive, recording transcribed by author.

13. Ossie Davis and Ruby Dee, *With Ossie and Ruby: In This Life Together* (New York: HarperCollins, 2000), 158.

14. Claire Leonard, "Comes Success . . . ," unpublished manuscript, III-134, Claire Leonard Papers.

15. Burton Rascoe, "'*Anna Lucasta*' Thrilling Drama of Negro Life," review of *Anna Lucasta*, directed by Harry Wagstaff Gribble, American Negro Theatre, *New York World-Telegram*, 19 June 1944, Theater Reviews Collection, Billy Rose Theatre Division, New York Public Library for the Performing Arts, Dorothy and Lewis B. Cullman Center.

16. The ANT's first version of *Anna Lucasta* has been lost. My discussion emerges through information gleaned from reviews and news articles on the Harlem and Broadway productions. Citations from the Random House edition are offered to suggest how the ANT transformed Yordan's original script. Though the actual dialogue may have been somewhat different on the Harlem stage, my research leads me to conclude that the essence of the ANT's adapting work remains in the passages I quote.

17. Philip Yordan, *Anna Lucasta* (New York: Random House, 1945), 30–32. Yordan was the only individual to ever receive authorial credit for *Anna Lucasta* in any of its forms. The others who contributed to the development of the play—Abram Hill, Harry Wagstaff Gribble, and members of the American Negro Theatre—should not be forgotten.

18. Ibid., 106.

19. Ibid., 21.

20. Harry J. Elam Jr., "The Black Performer and the Performance of Blackness: *The Escape; or, A Leap to Freedom* by William Wells Brown and *No Place to Be Somebody* by Charles Gordone," in *African American Performance and Theatre History: A Critical Reader*, ed. Harry J. Elam Jr. and David Krasner (Oxford: Oxford University Press, 2001), 289.

21. Yordan, *Anna Lucasta*, 110–11.

22. Jervis Anderson, *This Was Harlem, 1900–1950* (New York: Farrar Strauss and Giroux, 1981), 315.

23. Wilella Waldorf, "Harlem's American Negro Theatre Puts Vitality into 'Anna Lucasta,'" review of *Anna Lucasta*, directed by Harry Wagstaff Gribble, American Negro Theatre, *New York Post*, 19 June 1944, Theater Reviews Collection, Billy Rose Theatre Division.

24. Alice Childress, interview by James V. Hatch, 21 February 1972, Hatch-Billops Archive, recording transcribed by author.

25. Claire Leonard, letter to Philip Yordan, 24 May 1944, Claire Leonard Papers.

26. Abram Hill, "'Best Show since 1920' Says B'way Critic about 'Anna,' ANT Latest Show," *New York Amsterdam News*, 24 June 1944, 7B.

27. Abram Hill, quoted in Loften Mitchell, *Voices of the Black Theatre* (Clifton, N.J.: J. T. White, 1975), 137.

28. Wilella Waldorf, "'Anna Lucasta' No Great Shakes as a Play but the Acting Is Fine," review of *Anna Lucasta*, directed by Harry Wagstaff Gribble, Mansfield Theatre, New York, N.Y., *New York Post*, 31 August 1944, in *New York Theatre Critics Reviews*, vol. 5, 146.

29. Kronenberger, "Anna Lucasta Scores Again," 146.

30. Davis and Dee, *With Ossie and Ruby*, 158.

31. Constance Curtis and Adele Glasgow, "A Legitimate Theatre for Harlem," *Crisis* 51.2 (October 1944): 321.

32. Fanny McConnell, "A Broadway Taboo Is Lifted," *Opportunity* 22.4 (Fall 1944): 175.

33. The first film of *Anna Lucasta* (1949) was directed by Irving Rapper, with screenplay by Yordan and Arthur Laurents. Its all-white cast included Paulette Goddard and Broderick Crawford. A remade 1958 film version with African American actors was directed by Arnold Laven and starred Eartha Kitt, Sammy Davis Jr., and Frederick O'Neal.

34. Carol A. Horton, *Race and the Making of American Liberalism* (Oxford: Oxford University Press, 2005), 124.

35. "The Negro: His Future in America." *New Republic* 109.16 (1943): 535.

36. Horton, *Race and the Making of American Liberalism*, 125.

37. Brandi Wilkins Catanese, *The Problem of the Color[blind]* (Ann Arbor: University of Michigan Press, 2011), 18, 21. See pp. 9–22 for a critical overview of nontraditional casting.

38. "'Anna' Cast Draws High Profits, Gets Low Wages," *Ebony*, December 1945, 23.

39. O'Neal, interview by Wilson.

40. Hill, interview by Wallace. Abram Hill contended that contracts securing his and the ANT's interests were mysteriously "lost" both by Wildberg and the Dramatists Guild. Without those contracts, Hill and the ANT were forced to negotiate with Wildberg and Yordan after the fact and settled for the best arrangements they felt they could secure under such circumstances. Hill settled an individual suit privately with Wildberg and Leonard for $25,000.

41. Franklin F. Hopper, letter to Abram Hill, 29 June 1945, American Negro Theatre Records, folder 9.

42. Hill, interview by Wallace.

43. Ibid.

44. Claude Sloane, letter to Frederick O'Neal, 28 May 1946, American Negro Theatre Records, folder 12.

45. O'Neal, interview by Wilson.

46. Mitchell, *Voices of the Black Theatre*, 142.

47. Abram Hill quoted in Wilella Waldorf, "Two on the Aisle: American Negro Theatre Moves to a New Home," *New York Post*, 24 September 1945, 28.

48. "American Negro Theatre, Some Harlem Savants Feel, Has 'Gone Broadway,'" *Variety*, 22 August 1945, 45.

49. For more on the plays by African American playwrights staged by the ANT, see Jonathan Shandell, "Looking beyond Lucasta: The Black Dramas of the American Negro Theatre," *African American Review* 42 (2008): 533–47.

50. "Preamble," in "Constitution of the American Negro Theatre," American Negro Theatre Records, folder 1.

51. "Won't You Join Us at a Forum: Discussion on the Pros and Cons about A.N.T.," Schomburg Clipping File, Schomburg Center for Research in Black Culture, New York, N.Y.

52. Minutes from Reorganization Committee Meeting, 29 May 1949, American Negro Theatre Records, folder 20.

53. Mitchell, *Voices of the Black Theatre*, 142–43.

54. Harold Cruse, *Crisis of the Negro Intellectual* (New York: William Morrow, 1967), 528, 210.

55. Robert Károly Sarlós, *Jig Cook and the Provincetown Players: Theatre in Ferment* (Amherst: University of Massachusetts Press, 1982), 141.

13. The Stage Door Canteen

The American Theatre Wing's Experiment in Integration (1942–45)

Andrea Nouryeh

> Why do naval vessels advertise it, why is a song written about it, why a film? It is wrapped up in 1600 volunteer workers whose untiring efforts have combined to introduce to servicemen within this downstairs enclosure, an atmosphere of complete warmth and affection—informal and endless entertainment—excellent cuisine—wholesome companionship—dancing partners—gaiety—nightly holidays—mental relaxation. . . . Of major interest is the hobnobbing of our servicemen with British gobs, Canadian flying cadets, New Zealand soldiers, Free French marines, Dutch sailors, Chinese airmen and other allied fighting representatives. And thus you have an inevitable exchange of stories, trading of laughs and cigarettes, friendly jibes—a formation of friendships—call it a consummation of hands across the sea or call it a free league of nations herding together.[1]

These remarks, written on 24 February 1943 by Sergeant Sid Gray, an officer reporting for an army camp newspaper, were in praise of the Stage Door Canteen, a social venue that had opened its doors nearly a year earlier in the heart of the theatre district. He marveled at the ideals displayed in this community center where all were treated as brothers with equal worth, regardless of national, racial, religious, ethnic, or class differences. An experiment in social diversity and inclusivity, the Stage Door Canteen pursued a spirit of cooperation and volunteerism to which the United States aspired during the World War II years.

Conceived as a social club for American and Allied service men, the Stage Door Canteen was the creation of a group of women from the American Theatre Wing: Rachel Crothers, Theresa Helburn, Vera Allen, Antoinette Perry, and Gertrude Lawrence. Upon learning that Germany had attacked Czechoslovakia and Poland, these women reactivated the "Stage Women's War Relief Committee" (created during World War I) under the new name "American Theatre Wing of the Allied Relief Fund." After the bombing of Pearl Harbor on 7 December 1941, the "American Theatre Wing" became an independent entity devoted to supporting U.S. war efforts. Responding to the sight of servicemen milling aimlessly around Times Square, the committee established a venue in the theatre district where soldiers and sailors could be fed and entertained any day of the week. For two and a half years, the canteen became a haven for men on leave in New York, a home away from home. From 5:00 P.M. until midnight, uniformed servicemen indulged free of charge in coffee, milk, donuts, sandwiches, and cakes. They enjoyed Broadway-style entertainment: shows, opera, vaudeville, and jazz bands. A bevy of women served as companions with whom the soldiers could converse and dance away their homesickness, fear of the inevitable move into combat, or trauma after their return from battle. This chapter examines the legacy of the Stage Door Canteen, with emphasis on the historic efforts made by its creators—members of New York's theatre community—toward fulfillment of the promise of American democracy.

At the outset, the American Theatre Wing and its Canteen Committee (led by Selena Royle and Jane Cowl) knew that this effort would be the

Servicemen enjoying musical entertainment at the New York Stage Door Canteen. *Billy Rose Theatre Division, New York Public Library for the Performing Arts, Dorothy and Lewis B. Cullman Center.*

most direct way that they could give pride, gratitude, and goodwill to the men engaged in combat overseas.[2] The canteen became the entertainment industry's most potent contribution to the war effort. The committee's plan was to create an experience that would serve as a model of egalitarian principles across race, religion, and class divides to counter the injustices of Hitler's regime. In Crothers's words, the goal of the canteen was to "serve humanity in more ways than entertaining" and even to "save civilization."[3]

In one sense, this social venue (designed and managed by theatre professionals) can be seen as a theatrical space within which a carefully controlled experiment in democratic inclusion was staged each evening for an audience of soldiers who also played a role in the performance. As one soldier recalled:

> Colored couples jitterbug. A white girl dances by with a colored sailor but nobody pays much attention and the dancers chat. A Canadian soldier in hob-nailed shoes scuffs by taking his dancing very seriously and his little partner looks lost in his arms. A good-looking Marine with five ribbons including the Purple Heart (awarded to the wounded) and the insignia of Guadalcanal on his shoulder dances with a cute girl who looks at him cow-eyed. Five . . . Marines look on expressionlessly. A Scot in kilts and with the whiskbroom looking gadget in front walks across the floor and people look at his legs. Bored MPs doze in a corner.[4]

While Jim Crow, ghettoization, discriminatory housing, unfair employment practices, and segregation within the armed forces defined the status quo in the United States as World War II erupted, the Stage Door Canteen sought to provide an example of American democracy's more egalitarian possibilities on the home front. As a model of interracial and international harmony, it not only served as an effective grounding in American identity for the servicemen setting off across the Atlantic but also subtly proposed an alternative to the entrenched biases that they might have learned at home.

The New York theatre community had not always been so welcoming to African Americans; there were segregated casts, stereotypical roles (if any roles at all) for performers, rampant discrimination against black theatre artists, and segregated seating in theatres. However, throughout the 1920s and 1930s, serious dramas about African American life, miscegenation, and the exploitation of white and black workers had found their way onto New York stages. After a furor over Eugene O'Neill's depiction of interracial marriage in *All God's Chillun Got Wings* (1924), various other dramas depicting African American families or race relations appeared on Broadway: Paul Green's *In Abraham's Bosom* (1926), Jerome Kern and Oscar Hammerstein's *Show Boat* (whose complex engagements with race in America are discussed at length by Stuart J. Hecht in chapter 2), Frank Wilson's *Meek Mose* (1928), Garland Anderson's *Appearances* (1929), and Wallace Thurman's *Harlem* (1929), for example. By the 1930s, New York producers took more tentative chances with socially conscious plays that questioned exploitative and unfair social practices based on race and class: Paul Peters and George Sklar's *Stevedore* (1934), John Wexley's *They Shall Not Die* (1934), Langston Hughes's *Mulatto* (1935), Clifford Odets's *Waiting for Lefty* (1935), and Marc Blitzstein's *The Cradle Will Rock* (1937).[5] In chapter 12, Jonathan Shandell identifies "notable recent improvements in the acceptance of African American actors" on Broadway stages and discusses a climate of white liberal antiracism in the years leading up to the outbreak of World War II and the canteen's opening. Despite the fact that African Americans were denied the right to donate blood,[6] that Washington had failed to pass antilynching legislation, and that riots were resulting from executive orders to integrate war industry worksites, in the theatre district certain cultural trends had emerged to support the democratic objectives of the Stage Door Canteen.[7]

In light of the racist ideology at the heart of the Nazi regime, those in the American Theatre Wing were determined to foster values that separated the United States from its Fascist enemy and from the most undemocratic tendencies of their own nation. When riots broke out in Detroit at the shipyards on 22 June 1943, the prejudices that undergirded domestic resistance to integration seemed to strengthen the German and Japanese claims about American hypocrisy. Many lawmakers in Washington believed that segregation was the only way to promote peaceful coexistence and that the Fair Employment Practices Committee's policies for integration would lead to continued social unrest. Yet the nightly events at the canteen were orchestrated to send a message that fighting men on the same side in a battlefield were interdependent and could overcome their biases in the face of a common enemy.

The American Theatre Wing's vision of an egalitarian social club depended upon participation from the entire New York theatre community. The Shubert brothers provided the abandoned speakeasy in the basement of the Forty-Fourth Street Theatre for the purpose. Others donated materials and labor to convert the space into a nightclub/canteen. Volunteers from the unions that organized sign painters, engineers, teamsters and chauffeurs, locksmiths, and theatrical haulers cleaned up the space and constructed and furnished the venue. Designers, scenic artists, and members of the theatre photographers union decorated the walls with thirty-six murals. Union locals for theatrical agents and managers, box office treasurers and ticket sellers, entertainment and amusement service employees, theatre porters, wardrobe attendants, and costume workers marshaled volunteers to ensure that this entertainment enterprise would run smoothly. Supporting these massive efforts, food wholesalers and restaurants donated food and cakes, particularly for holiday meals and for canteen anniversaries and weekly birthday celebrations. New York City housewives used their sugar, butter, and flour rations to bake cookies and cakes, which they would deliver to the venue daily. The entire venture exemplified a spirit of collectivity that the war had engendered among many segments of the American public.

Once the infrastructure was in place, the American Theatre Wing sought workers to run the "soup kitchen" and nightclub and registered more than three thousand volunteers from among the entertainment industry. This collaborative effort of a united theatre industry garnered celebration in the leftist press:

> All of this, the spirit of camaraderie . . . was an important and democratic expression of the determination of the American people to unite among themselves and with the Allies to win the war. Here was trade union unity. And some people marveled about it. Why, the workers, the workers of the theatre, every single one of them, had taken the place over. . . . On the rock of workers' unity, a new kind of Broadway night club emerged. Here the stars and their public rub elbows, dance with one another, laugh and get acquainted—and it is all clean, all good fun.[8]

With the stage set, the props found, the mise-en-scène designed, and the administration in place, the Canteen Committee cast its production with a community center atmosphere in mind. Hosts and a large roster of hostesses were recruited to greet the clientele and to provide aid and companionship. The men would arrive together with pals, come alone, or even reunite with buddies they had thought had died on the battlefields. Activities included donut dunking contests, conga lines, Ping-Pong tournaments, sing-alongs, square dances, and a variety of party games. Those seeking more solitude could sit and write postcards (illustrated with sketches of canteen life) and have them mailed; they also might have artists draw caricatures or have photographs taken to be sent to their families. Canteen workers could help procure theatre tickets, arrange to reunite family members in the armed services, convey messages of love for the soldiers, and deliver flowers.[9] In a sense, each worker at the canteen played the part of a friend, a sister, an aunt, or a neighbor of the same all-American town.

Junior hostesses entertaining sailors from Dutch Guiana and Curaçao at the New York Stage Door Canteen. *Billy Rose Theatre Division, New York Public Library for the Performing Arts, Dorothy and Lewis B. Cullman Center.*

Not only did the canteen serve up food, activities, and female company, but it also offered the best of Broadway and New York culture. Singers, musicians, dancers, comics, performers from the vaudeville circuit (jugglers, magicians, acrobats), musical theatre artists, and dance bands volunteered to perform. For two and a half years, the Stage Door Canteen produced seven hours of entertainment each day. When the canteen opened, New York drama critics proclaimed it the biggest and most successful hit of the season, topping anything on Broadway.[10] John Anderson called it "the only opening that can be raved about sight unseen" and proclaimed his desire "to toss a column of bouquets to the Stage Door Canteen."[11] Richard Watt Jr. lauded the people of the stage and screen for their valiant performance in every branch of the war effort, writing,

> One of the most admirable of their accomplishments in the Army and Navy is the establishment of this canteen. If only one thing it would be a

> remarkable achievement. It reveals all of the combative unions that comprise the theater working together in free and unaccustomed harmony to make it a success. Fortunately, though, it has many other virtues. In truth, it is so attractive a place, so gay and friendly and charming, so capably and brightly managed, that even the crustiest of drama critics, judging it solely on its merits and not being moved by its fine intentions, must give it an enthusiastic notice.[12]

No serviceman of an Allied fighting force was denied access to the canteen; all a soldier or sailor needed for admission was his uniform and dog tag. When he entered, he was an honored guest of the theatre community and was treated royally. As one serviceman reported, "You can't help feeling like a king when everyone puts on fine entertainment for you, checks your outer clothing, fills your stomach and then washes the dishes—because you wear a uniform. I defy anyone to describe our feelings of awe, amazement and thanks . . . thanks and gratitude."[13] The personnel strove to accommodate each serviceman's needs while away from the comforts of home and family and to be sensitive to the changes the canteen's clientele had undergone because of their service.

As the war progressed, this "experiment in democracy" had to evolve to meet new challenges. By the summer of 1944, the canteen had initiated new practices for its workers to accommodate the growing number of servicemen who had experienced firsthand the horrors of the battlefield. Hosts and hostesses received new "scripts" and special training to manage their own responses to the physical and psychological effects of combat on the men. They were to exhibit no pity, no patronizing, nor excessive sentimentalizing; they were to treat combat veterans as people of whom they were proud, but also as those who were no different from others despite maiming, disfigurement, or psychological impairment.[14] Many canteen workers found that the young, innocent, and naive young men they had entertained months earlier often returned sobered, embittered, and filled with hatred. Their job was to help these men see that there was still the possibility for good in the world and to foster in them understanding and kindness despite the destruction and ugliness that they had witnessed in battle. One private on furlough wrote to the canteen:

> I entered the room buzzing with conversation and laughter. Music came from an orchestra—but most important was the spirit of warmth that permeated the air. Junior and Senior Hostesses were present, smiling—"Hello Soldier—have some food?"—"No, thank you, I'm not hungry—for food."—

> "Hello soldier—want to dance?"—"No, thanks, not now."—"Care to sit down, soldier?"—We sat at a corner table. We spoke—about little things—me, mostly. But I talked, I laughed. I was warm. And my heart cried—its tears flooding and washing away the unpleasantness within me. I was no longer alone. I was with people. I became me again—I BECAME ME![15]

In the spirit of inclusivity, the American Theatre Wing sought to provide this sense of individual worth to all "servicemen, of every rank of the service without ever the slightest discrimination on account of race, color or religion."[16]

The democratic vision that the New York theatre community enacted nightly won commendation in leftist and African American newspapers. Here was "one place where Negro boys need have no fear of feeling out of place or not wanted."[17] The Harlem newspaper the *New York Age* published a series of candid photos of real life in the United States where "color is only an incidental in the deeper and rewarding business of human relationships, in which friendship grows on the basis of mutuality, of like appreciations and a man's ideas."[18] Among these were photographs of American servicemen of all races socializing together at the canteen. Other reporters interviewed hosts and hostesses and wrote glowing reviews of their work. Radie Harris captured a particularly poignant story of how boys from Harlem reacted to their reception inside the canteen. Apparently, canteen cofounder Antoinette Perry extended her hand to one of these soldiers and asked, "Is there anything I can do for you?" Instead of answering, he put his hand up to his throat. "Oh, I'm sorry! Have you a sore throat?" Miss Perry wanted to know. "No," was his simple retort, "but I have such a lump in my throat from everyone being so wonderful here that I can hardly talk."[19]

The nightly performance of democracy got positive critical notices, and the staff also received testimonial letters. One African American corporal urged the canteen workers to keep up the good work because their nondiscriminatory practices were an example of the American principles that made him and his peers proud of their American heritage and, as a consequence, made the rigors and dangers of the battlefield easier to bear.[20] Another expressed how the Stage Door Canteen's hospitality bolstered his own unbiased response to an injured white soldier who had previously expressed racial hatred toward those African Americans serving alongside him:

> I am proud of the Stage Door Canteen and all that she stands for which is plentifully expressed. A day ago both white and colored went to battle side by side. . . . It was every man for his own life. Before we came up to

Actress Anne Seymour handing Sergeant Jimmie Daniels a half-pint of milk at the New York Stage Door Canteen. *Billy Rose Theatre Division, New York Public Library for the Performing Arts, Dorothy and Lewis B. Cullman Center.*

> the line a white fellow said, "I can't stand those darkies next to me—they are hard luck." Well . . . he was shot simply awful and the colored medical attachment was on duty. A few men said it serves him right and I said no, so I carried him over my shoulder for six miles in the heat of things, saw that he got to the medical attachment and he will live. We had a little chat today and he thanked me for saving his life.[21]

The experiences of many African American visitors to the canteen offered them an unfamiliar alternative to the status quo in American race relations and instilled new feelings of optimism that Americans might overcome the prejudices that habitually separated them.

The American Theatre Wing's efforts influenced white soldiers' attitudes as well. Rosetta Le Noir—veteran African American actress of stage and screen and a senior hostess at the canteen—recounted one occasion when she excused herself from the company of a white southern soldier after spying an African American soldier sitting alone. Although she was apprehensive, she brought this other soldier back over to the table where she had been sitting and introduced the two men. Fearful that these two southerners, one black and one white, might not appreciate being brought together, she was pleasantly surprised. Within seconds they had found out that they were from the same neighborhood in New Orleans. In fact, they had lived around the corner from each other before entering the service. Soon, they ignored her completely and eventually "left the Canteen together, arm in arm."[22]

Though powerful as a model of democracy, clearly the canteen had little power to undo the most deeply ingrained racial and religious prejudices. However, its policies could ensure that within its walls, such prejudices would be challenged. Virginia Kaye, cochair of the Junior Hostesses Committee, related a poignant story of a young white GI from a prominent southern family interacting with the canteen's hostess captain on duty: an educated African American woman. The white soldier froze before her and blurted out that he simply could not stomach the idea of a "Negro" being in charge. After returning to the front, however, this soldier wrote a personal letter to this hostess, who had remained calm during his outburst. His letter expressed regret for his unjust response to the social mixing of the races that he had witnessed. Finding himself on the bloody battlefields of Europe, the soldier realized that his encounter had left an impression:

> I am a heel for thinking that I am any better than they [African Americans] are. What reason have I to think this? Or to carry a hatred which for no sound reason I can back. I am not going to blame it on the South because I am a Southerner. It's because I am of the white race. Bad thought, is it not? . . . I will join your army any day in bringing better democracy back home.[23]

Having the opportunity to share the company of those from whom he had been segregated all of his life afforded this soldier the chance to reconsider the social scripts that he had been taught.

As the "war for democracy" raged across both oceans, the Canteen Committee knew that the blatant disparity between the ideals that men were fighting for abroad and the undemocratic realities at home must be confronted. That contradiction was particularly galling to those most victimized by segregation. African American author Countee Cullen illustrated this by contrasting the Stage Door Canteen with the outrageous policies of the Hillburn New York School Board. Hillburn was a rural school district that forced African American children to attend a small wooden schoolhouse with no gym, no library, and no indoor plumbing while white pupils attended a fully equipped modern building. Wrote Cullen:

> Coming home the other night from the Stage Door Canteen where democracy is being given a chance to prove itself with Negro and white service men fraternizing as brothers in arms should, I thought what a step backward the city of Hillburn has taken. I think of them in this way:
>
> God have pity
> On such a city
> Where parent teaches child to hate;
> God looks down
> On such a town
> Where Prejudice the Great
> Rules drunkenly and evilly
> What should be Liberty's estate.[24]

For Cullen and others who patronized the canteen, the vision of American democracy on view each night was one far removed from what most African Americans experienced on a daily basis.

Not everyone celebrated the Stage Door Canteen's success as an integrated space; some prominent citizens thought Harlem should have a canteen of its own. Over the course of the canteen's history, there was talk within the organization for creating a Harlem venue, particularly during the 1943 Detroit riots. But the canteen's public relations director, Isadora Bennett, repeatedly opposed such a move. Bennett stressed that the American Theatre Wing did not support any move toward dividing the canteen's clientele, as such a project "would be interpreted by many as a discriminatory act."[25]

Despite the accolades the canteen received for its inclusiveness, some racist incidents did occur. Writer Carl Van Vechten served as a busboy and captain of the kitchen at the canteen on Monday and Tuesday nights. In a letter to Langston Hughes dated 8 October 1942, he recounted that one African American serviceman questioned him about whether junior hostesses of color were kept out of the canteen. Apparently, none of the fifty black women volunteers had shown up that evening. When Van Vechten explained that African American women were actively recruited to serve as hostesses, the soldier replied, "Well I guess it doesn't matter anyway. When they do come, they always jump with the white boys."[26] Additionally, some white junior hostesses at the New York canteen were reluctant to talk to and dance with African American clients, despite the nondiscrimination policy. In response, Margaret Halsey—a writer and captain for the junior hostesses—wrote a long memorandum reminding the other hostesses that the canteen's policy was based upon principles from the Declaration of Independence and the Fourteenth and Fifteen Amendments to the U.S. Constitution.[27] She urged her colleagues to use their experiences at the canteen to overcome historic patterns of prejudice:

> Few outsiders realize, but all of us know, that being a Junior Hostess and entertaining unselected strangers for three and a half hours is difficult at best. You only make it more difficult when you artificially set aside a portion of these strangers as targets for unreasonable, unscientific, and undemocratic emotion. If you'd just relax and keep your pores open, there wouldn't be any "Negro problem."[28]

While the staff mostly adhered to nondiscriminatory policies toward U.S. and Allied servicemen, the Stage Door Canteen had a decided blind spot when it came to women. The courtesies afforded to men in uniform did not extend to the more than 150,000 American women who served in the army. Queries about allowing women soldiers into the canteen were regularly dismissed. The needs of servicewomen for companionship and solace after traveling away from home or serving overseas were hardly considered. Given the historical context, this omission is fairly predictable. Women were not accepted into the U.S. Army until May 1942, months after the canteen had already opened. Women served initially in auxiliary branches of service, mostly as nurses and office personnel. Most women in uniform performed noncombatant jobs that mirrored their work in civilian life, so as to free up more able-bodied men to perform essential and dangerous combat duties. Though Crothers and her committee members all were independent theatre women with successful careers, they too envisioned roles for women working at the canteen in extremely traditional terms. The senior hostesses were to be nurturing mother figures, while the junior hostesses acted as young, attractive dancing partners providing comfort and companionship. Thus the practices of the canteen echoed those of the branches of the military, where the presence of women posed the least threat to male power and privilege.[29]

Despite the lack of access for servicewomen, the Stage Door Canteen's enactment of acceptance, tolerance, and inclusion across racial barriers garnered widespread global attention. This social club for servicemen was hailed as "The Crossroads of the War."[30] News of the canteen spread across oceans; Allied ships would signal to each other, "When in New York visit Stage Door Canteen. West 44th Street. No liquor, but lots of fun."[31] Young sailors and soldiers from China, the British Commonwealth, and the liberated French colonies of Africa, South America, and the Caribbean all visited and were met with respect, gracious hospitality, and friendship. A Nigerian soldier sang the canteen's praises in a letter:

> That matchless serviceman's home of world renown stands like a lighthouse in my mind. . . . It is unfortunate that it took so much as a war to make mankind with all its races and creeds tune its life together, but if that lead upheld by the Stage Door Canteen today will go with us to the world that is to emerge after guns are silent, then I dare say America will indeed be a specimen of Democracy, where all men are free and happy, and she will not only receive the genuine respect of all other nations, but she will receive their adoration.[32]

Men from nearly every continent entered the space and shared with each other their national anthems, their folk cultures, and their holiday traditions. While many young American soldiers had never before fraternized with people from other parts of the world, they and their English and British Commonwealth counterparts would take their Greek-, Russian-, Chinese-, Brazilian-, and French-speaking peers down the food lines and ask the hostesses to find them companions who spoke their languages. As public relations director Isadora Bennett suggested, "A special kind of 'canteen Esperanto' was spoken" by all who came through the canteen's doors.[33]

For servicemen around the globe, the canteen became a symbol of freedom and unity. One soldier asked a junior hostess for her apron to use as the flag for his plane as he flew on his mission. Its red, white, and blue stripes would be the first sign of colors from the United States over enemy territory. He saw this apron as a talisman: "It has been the insignia worth fighting for—hospitality and humanity and true ideals of democracy for at the Stage Door Canteen I've seen ideals in practice—no race or creed prejudices."[34] On 13 October 1943 a navy ship built in the Baltimore shipyards was launched as the S.S. *Stage Door Canteen* and completed its maiden voyage about six months later. In May 1944 at a U.S. military base in England, a Flying Fortress was christened by its Army Air Corps B-17 bomber crew as the "Stage Door Canteen." The Forty-Fourth Street Theatre's basement became known even in enemy territory: "Dulag Luft," a prison camp near

Frankfurt, was dubbed the "Stage Door Canteen" by its Allied prisoners, a fact that surfaced only when the camp was liberated in April 1945.[35]

The success of the canteen exceeded the expectations of its founders; within months of its opening, there were plans to launch similar canteens across the United States. Like all Broadway smash hits, the show went on the road. From June 1942 through December 1943, new American Theatre Wing Stage Door Canteens opened in Philadelphia, Washington, Cleveland, San Francisco, Newark, and Boston. Inspired by what she saw in the basement of the Forty-Fourth Street Theatre, Bette Davis partnered with John Garfield to create the Hollywood Canteen, an independent film industry equivalent that opened in October 1942. On the other side of the Atlantic, by August 1944 a canteen was open for business in London's Piccadilly Circus; on 9 March 1945, after the Allied liberation of Paris, a canteen opened on the Champs-Élysées.

News of these canteens spread throughout the United States. As curiosity among civilians grew, CBS radio offered a new window for the public with its half-hour weekly show *The Stage Door Canteen Radio Broadcast*. The series, which began in June 1942, provided a sampling of the entertainment on offer for the servicemen. Military men and their families served as live audiences for these broadcasts. As the club's reputation grew, the American Theatre Wing entered into negotiations for rights to the story of the Stage Door Canteen and use of its name. These negotiations led to the June 1943 release of a feature-length movie, overseen by independent producer Sol Lesser and directed by Frank Borgaze. By the spring of 1944, the War Department had come to agree with President Roosevelt that the entertainment industry was "indispensable in war time."[36] Recognized as an important morale-building institution for soldiers going overseas and returning home through the port of New York, the Stage Door Canteen underwent renovations with help from Washington. Its space was enlarged, and its inadequate air conditioning system received enhancements (thanks to a special concession to use scarce and valuable steel). The canteen also added a precipitron, a machine to clear the air of cigarette smoke, usually available only to essential war industries. What had been a sweltering, smoky hotbox in the two preceding summers became a spacious and comfortable club, courtesy of the Pentagon.

The Stage Door Canteen officially remained a fixture on Broadway until 27 July 1945. After relocating for a fourteen-week run at the Diplomat Hotel's Crystal Room, the enterprise officially closed its doors on 1 November 1945. Over the course of its brief history, the canteen entertained more than

3.2 million servicemen from all of the Allied nations and served more than 720,000 sandwiches, 438,000 cups of milk, 5,000 pounds of candy, and 3.5 million cigarettes.[37] Its legacy is perhaps most familiar thanks to the Irving Berlin tune "I Left My Heart at the Stage Door Canteen" from his 1942 musical, *This Is the Army*, as well as from the eponymous 1943 Hollywood film. While the film recreated the physical space of the Forty-Fourth Street basement and showed a crowd dancing, watching shows, and lining up to be served food by celebrities, in truth the number of famous entertainers working at the canteen was never as large as the movie led audiences to believe.[38] Both the song and the film focus on a thwarted romance between a soldier and his "Eileen," a junior hostess. Officially, such romances were forbidden. Hostesses lost their passes allowing them to work at the canteen if they were found dating someone they had met. Even so, some engagements and weddings took place between several junior hostesses and the servicemen they had escorted and were even announced in the canteen newsletter or the local papers.

Once inside the canteen, each soldier became the protagonist of his own drama, supported by the ensemble of hosts, hostesses, entertainers, and celebrity kitchen staff in his journey away from home. Each individual soldier became the center of attention, his stature magnified above everyday experience. Here was a liminal space between home and the front lines where a soldier could reflect on his wartime circumstances. It served as a safe "launching pad" to motivate and sustain each soldier headed for battle. If he were fortunate enough to survive combat and return, the canteen provided the war veteran with a place of solace to process what he had witnessed, reintegrate his spirit, and get back in touch with the man he was and the life he had left behind. It offered a space for transition from the horrors of war toward the rediscovery of "gaiety, not grimness," in life.[39] It was a testament to the hope that envisioning our common humanity, rather than exercising inhumane treatment of others, was what the nation prized most. By presenting a utopian vision of how the country might live up to its founding principles, the American Theatre Wing's Stage Door Canteen illustrated to each man serving in the armed forces—and to the nation and the world at large—that the United States had the possibility of really being a democracy worth fighting to preserve.

Notes

1. Sergeant Sid Gray, "New York Stage Door Canteen Good Deal for Soldiers," *Camp David Barrage*, 24 February 1943.

2. "Door Stage Canteen Opens," *Brooklyn Citizen*, 3 March 1942.

3. Rachel Crothers, "Between Curtains," *Theatre Arts Monthly* 25 (April 1941): 317–18.

4. Staff Sergeant Burr Patten, *Glens Fall Post Star*, 27 November 1943.

5. Langston Hughes and Milton Meltzer, *Black Magic: A Pictorial History of the African-American in the Performing Arts* (Englewood Cliffs, N.J.: Prentice Hall, 1967), 113. In contrast, radio and film continued to give little opportunity for African American actors to appear in serious or important nonstereotypical roles.

6. "Navy Denies Negro Ban in Blood Service," *New York Herald Tribune*, 18 January 1942.

7. Joe William Trotter, "From Raw Deal to a New Deal," in *To Make Our World Anew: A History of African Americans from 1880*, vol. 2, ed. Robin D. G. Kelley and Earl Lewis (New York: Oxford University Press, 2000), 131–66.

8. Ralph Warner, "A People's Night Club for the Service Men," *Sunday Worker*, American Theatre Wing Scrapbooks, n.d., Billy Rose Theatre Division, New York Public Library for the Performing Arts.

9. See clippings in American Theatre Wing Scrapbooks.

10. Brooks Atkinson, "Curtain's Up at the Stage Door Canteen," *New York Times*, 3 March 1942; *Variety*, 4 March 1942; *Equity*, March 1942; Ward Morehouse, "Broadway after Dark," *New York Sun*, 16 March 1942.

11. John Anderson, "The Drama," *New York Journal American*, 1 March 1942.

12. Richard Watts Jr., "The Theater: The Canteen; A Stage Door without a Door Keeper," *New York Herald Tribune*, 15 March 1942.

13. Eugene Burr, "From Our Front," American Theatre Wing Scrapbooks, n.d., Billy Rose Theatre Division.

14. "Civilians to Learn Duty to Wounded," *New York Times*, 27 November 1944.

15. Harold Chessum PFC, *Canteen News*, 6 April 1944.

16. *New York Daily Worker*, 2 March 1943, American Theatre Wing Scrapbooks.

17. *People's Voice*, 26 June 1943, American Theatre Wing Scrapbooks.

18. "Common Ground Presents . . . ," *New York Age*, n.d., American Theatre Wing Scrapbooks.

19. Radie Harris, "Canteen Capers," *Variety*, 8 April 1942, 22.

20. John Meldon, "Bullets Don't Discriminate—Nor Does the Stage Door Canteen," *New York Daily Worker*, 7 May 1945.

21. Ibid.

22. "Headlines and Footlights by Fredi Washington," *People's Voice*, 29 May 1943.

23. Harold Preece, "The Living South: Dixie Writes to Dorothy," *Norfolk (Va.) Journal and Guide*, n.d., American Theatre Wing Scrapbooks.

24. Quoted in Margaret Perry, *A Bio-Bibliography of Countee P. Cullen, 1903–1946* (Santa Barbara, Calif.: ABC-CLIO, 1971), 16–17. In fact, this discrimination case was being fought in the courts by Thurgood Marshall, chief counsel for the NAACP, and was eventually won.

25. Morgen S. Jensen, "Deny Plans to Establish Harlem 'Stage Door Canteen,'" *Pittsburgh Courier*, 1 July 1944.

26. Emily Bernard, ed., *Remember Me to Harlem: The Letters of Langston Hughes and Carl Van Vechten, 1925–1964* (New York: Alfred A. Knopf, 2001), 211.

27. Margaret Halsey, "Memorandum to Junior Hostesses," in *Primer for White Folks*, ed. Bucklin Moon (Garden City, N.Y.: Doubleday, Doran and Co., 1945), 476.

28. Ibid., 475–78.

29. Judith L. Bellafaire, *The Women's Army Corps: A Commemoration of World War II Service* (Washington D.C.: Defense Department, Army Center of Military History, 2008). Eventually the Cleveland Stage Door Canteen did allow women in the service access to its facility but was the only canteen that did. It is my contention that denying women soldiers access to the Stage Door Canteen was a measure taken to minimize the potential for upsetting the canteen's carefully controlled atmosphere. The junior hostesses were not allowed to date the soldiers they danced with. They were to keep their personal information secret and not show preference for any man they met. Had uniformed women been admitted to the canteen, they could have become alternative dancing partners for the servicemen and potential objects of their romantic or sexual attentions.

30. Arthur "Bugs" Baer, "'Bugs' Baer Takes a Bearing in the Stage Door Canteen," *American Weekly*, 21 March 1943, 7.

31. American Theatre Wing press release, n.d., American Theatre Wing Scrapbooks.

32. Tai Solarin, RAF, letter to the manager, *Canteen News*, 16 November 1944.

33. Isadora Bennett, "And Start Again at the Beginning," *Equity* 30.8 (August 1945): 10.

34. Marjorie Barkentin, "Somewhere a Boy Keeps Stage Door Apron Flying," *Brooklyn Eagle*, 7 March 1943.

35. *Life*, 9 April 1945, American Theatre Wing Scrapbooks.

36. “President Praises Amusement World,” *New York Post*, 4 June 1943.

37. Douglas Gilbert, *World Telegram*, 2 November 1945.

38. Archer Winsten, “Movie Talk: Service Men Interviewed Like ‘This Is the Army,’” *New York Post*, 26 August 1943. Winsten quotes a cadet who said that “one should not confuse the movie stars seen with the real one [canteen] where famous stars do not appear as regularly as indicated.”

39. Bennett, “And Start Again at the Beginning,” 9–11.

Afterword

American Democracy—a Work in Progress

Cheryl Black

> O, let America be America again—
> The land that never has been yet—
> And yet must be—the land where every man is free.
> —Langston Hughes

> I live my life every day with a great deal of optimism for our future as a society. Optimism is a radical weapon.
> —American playwright John Belluso

American democracy is much in the news lately, and the news is frequently not good. Works documenting the demise of American democracy have proliferated in the past decade or so, with telling titles such as *America: Who Stole the Dream?*, *Categorically Unequal*, *Stealing Democracy*, *The Historic Unfulfilled Promise*, *Demanding Democracy*, *Plutocrats*, *Searching for the Spirit of American Democracy*, *The Case against Democracy*, *Dollarocracy*, *The Unheavenly Chorus: Unequal Political Voice and the Broken Promise of American Democracy*, and *The New Jim Crow*. Since 1996, *Democracy Now!*, an independently funded progressive news program, has aired its antiwar, anticorporate, antiracist, and antisexist broadcasts, demanding democracy from a nation that seems in short supply of it. In 2000, Green Party presidential candidate and consumer advocate Ralph Nader described American democracy as in crisis: "Big business has increasingly dominated our political economy. This control by the corporate government over our political government is creating a widening 'democracy gap.' This state of affairs is a world away from the legislative milestones in civil rights, the environment, and health and safety of worker and consumers seen in the sixties and seventies."[1] Nader and his vice presidential running mate, environmental activist Winona LaDuke, received less than 3 percent of the popular vote. His dire warnings, of course, have proved only too apt.

In the second decade of the twenty-first century, the nation is reeling from economic disaster, an apparently endless war against "terror," high unemployment rates, a stunningly dysfunctional Congress (with equally stunning incumbency rates), and conflicts surrounding immigration. Despite (or perhaps partially because of) the election and reelection of America's first biracial president—whose "Americanness" has been consistently challenged by opponents in coded racist terms—racial tensions have escalated. In 2014, the deaths of unarmed black men, including Michael Brown, Eric Garner, and twelve-year-old Tamir Rice at the hands of white police officers sparked protests and riots across the nation. In March 2015 white members of the University of Oklahoma chapter of Sigma Alpha Epsilon were filmed performing a racist chant they allegedly learned on a "leadership cruise."[2] In June 2015, a twenty-one-year-old white supremacist confessed to shooting nine members of a black church during a prayer service in Charleston, South Carolina.[3] Income inequality, which has reached its highest level since 1928,[4] looms large as a serious threat to the national health, prompting some writers to pronounce the expiration of American democracy:

> The switch from the America of the Great Compression [i.e., relative income equality characterizing the immediate post–World War II era] to the America of the 1 percent is still so recent that our intuitive beliefs about how capitalism works haven't caught up with the reality. In fact, surging income inequality is such a strong violation of our expectations that most of us don't realize it is happening.[5]

Race, ethnicity, and culture are demonstrated factors in income inequality. The 2010 U.S. census revealed that 15.1 percent of the population lived in poverty, with this startling racial breakdown: 9.9 percent of all non-Hispanic white persons, 12.1 percent of all Asian persons, 26.6 percent of all Hispanic persons (of any race), and 28.4 percent of all black persons qualified as poor. Some 39 percent of black children are from families with incomes below the poverty line, compared with 12 percent of white children.[6]

A recent report based on data gathered by the Economic Policy Institute proclaims that "on all socioeconomic measures, African Americans still lag white citizens by wide margins."[7] This same study documents an alarming regression in American society in terms of racial integration, reporting that public schools are more segregated now than they were forty years ago. This situation, unfolding because "most education policymakers and reformers have abandoned integration as a cause," is widening black-white achievement gaps.[8] This report and others have also revealed increasing residential segregation (moving toward pre–civil rights conditions). According to a recent finding from the American Sociological Association, "drastic socioeconomic differences between white and minority families result in a de facto cultural divide."[9] Another report reveals that 28 percent of black children live in high-poverty neighborhoods, compared with 4 percent of white children.[10] One of the most thorough, thoughtful, and chilling studies to confront systemic racism and disenfranchisement in contemporary America is Michelle Alexander's *The New Jim Crow: Mass Incarceration in the Age of Colorblindness*. Alexander cogently indicts America's "justice" system—which incarcerates young men of color (particularly the indigent) at a shockingly disproportionate rate—as a system for racialized social control: "We have not ended racial caste in America; we have merely redesigned it." Reminding readers of the lifelong consequences of felony conviction as a permanent disenfranchisement, she comes to the troubling but logical conclusion that "America is still not an egalitarian democracy."[11]

Despite abundant evidence of the impact of race on socioeconomic status, the national culture still clings to idealized notions of a "post-race," "colorblind" society. So convinced is the Supreme Court of this fiction, apparently, that despite acknowledging that the Voting Rights Act of 1965 (one of America's democratic triumphs) "has proved immensely successful at redressing racial discrimination and integrating the voting process," the justices in 2013 struck down key components of this law as "not justified by current needs."[12] This rationale prompted a retort from Justice Ruth Bader Ginsburg that "throwing out preclearance when it has worked and is continuing to work to stop discriminatory changes is like throwing away your umbrella in a rainstorm because you are not getting wet."[13]

How, one might wonder, is this possible in America—the nation that reinvented democracy two centuries ago, the nation that welcomed the world's "huddled masses yearning to breathe free," the nation that has stood as a beacon for "freedom" and "equality" around the globe and has fought repeatedly (sometimes with minimal provocation) to "save the world for democracy"? It happens, and has happened in varying degrees throughout this nation's history, because (as Alexander reminds us) America has never been an egalitarian democracy. Despite the egalitarian principles undergirding the Constitution, in reality the nation has always operated under specific systems of *exclusion*. Like all nations—and perhaps more so than most—"America" is (to adapt Elizabeth A. Osborne's phrasing vis-à-vis "democracy" in chapter 9) an imagined construct. Or, in the words of the great poet, playwright, and patriot Langston Hughes, it is a "land that never has been yet."[14]

The United States was founded, some eleven score and twenty years ago, on a wave of liberatory enlightenment sentiment and revolutionary rhetoric unparalleled in human history. This new nation did indeed constitute a historic experiment in democracy; its Constitution and Bill of Rights were and would remain for many generations a paradigm of justice, equality, and freedom. Its dream of life, liberty, and happiness would become a clarion call to generations of hopeful immigrants who fled their native lands for America and its promises. It was a utopian dream, in both senses of that term: an ideal community—that did not actually exist. From the beginning, "we the people" was in practice a fairly elite group that excluded a majority of the new nation's adult inhabitants (women, slaves, indigenous Indian tribes, and even white males who owned no property). Among the property American citizens owned were seven hundred thousand human beings, an enslaved population that would increase to four million by the eve of the Civil War in 1860. Nearly half of the Founding Fathers, including the author of the Declaration of Independence (Thomas Jefferson) and the primary author of the Constitution (James Madison), owned slaves.

The men who created America were inarguably men of extraordinary intellectual gifts, and many of them expressed in private correspondence their abhorrence to slavery on principle as an immoral and unjust practice. Few of them possessed the imagination or the grace to transcend the deeply rooted prejudices of their historical moment to envision a multiracial America. As Madison wrote in 1826, "The two races cannot co-exist, both being free & equal. The great *sine qua non* therefore is some external asylum for the colored race."[15] By 1826, it was abundantly clear that indigenous American tribes would never be numbered among "we the people." After five decades of failed governmental efforts to assimilate indigenous peoples coupled with aggressive and usually illegal encroachment on indigenous lands, the U.S. government in 1830 passed the Indian Removal Act, forcing relocation of Native Americans living in the United States to federal territory west of the Mississippi. Eventually, the dictates of manifest destiny led the United States to take the western lands as well, relegating Native Americans to an indescribably perverse existence within a nation reluctant to grant them either citizenship or autonomy. As the modern era dawned, Americans enjoying the rights and privileges of the free and the brave from "sea to shining sea" reacted with alarm to the waves of immigrants who landed on America's shores expecting—sometimes demanding—those same rights and privileges. Americans in power rushed to exclude those deemed unassimilable: Asians, southern and eastern Europeans, Jews. It was the dawning of the American Century, the century in which W. E. B. Du Bois astutely predicted a crisis of race and identity—the "problem of the color line."[16]

This, then, was the state of the American experiment in democracy as the 1900s began. Two centuries of white supremacy, patriarchy, and an unshakable belief in American exceptionalism had forged a nation for whom the very existence of poverty, illness, perceived weakness, want, or need could become grounds to deny full inclusion within an America that was ostensibly strong, free, brave, prosperous, and autonomous. By the turn of the twentieth century, it appeared that the very act of needing America's benefits prevented one from deserving or attaining them. America seemed on its way to becoming a profoundly failed experiment.

This context helps us understand more clearly the historical significance of the many theatrical experiments examined in the preceding chapters of this book. The peoples and cultures represented make up those groups of racial and cultural "Others" that Americans of northern and western European heritage tried to exclude from citizenship: Chinese, eastern and southern Europeans, Jews, Latinos, African Americans, Native Americans. As civil rights activist and politician Julian Bond once stated in an interview with a *New York Times* reporter, "In a still-segregated society . . . people often get their ideas about other groups from what they read, see and hear" through entertainment media.[17] In America's profoundly segregated society of the first half of the twentieth century, people almost certainly formed lasting impressions of other groups (as well as of themselves) through theatrical representations.

Thus it would be difficult to overstate the potential impact on American audiences who saw racially and culturally diverse casts in *Show Boat*, *Othello*, "Fun to Be Free," and Myra Kinch's Federal Theatre Project dance performances; who encountered the representational critiques within *Black Pit*, *Natural Man*, *The Cherokee Night*, the *teatro vernáculo* of La Unión Martí-Maceo, the plays of Josefina Niggli, and FTP's *First Americans* radio series; and who absorbed the deliberate cultural exchanges embedded in *Anna Lucasta*, *The Yellow Jacket*, and *Show Boat*. What a utopian vision of equality and brotherhood, indeed, greeted servicemen at the Stage Door Canteen during a time when the armed forces were (like most schools, hospitals, hotels, restaurants, parks, and public spaces) segregated. With a few notable exceptions (including the Theatre Union and, as referenced in the introduction, the Hedgerow Theatre), auditoriums were segregated, with some theatres barring minority ethnicities entirely. How ironic it is that, although Paul Robeson and Uta Hagen could portray to significant acclaim a married couple on stage in 1943, such a union was illegal in thirty of the forty-eight states. In fact, they would have been hard-pressed to find a restaurant in New York City in which to dine together.

Many of these experiments—originating from members of the dominant culture, or at least from a relatively privileged location on America's complex social continuum—were no doubt ambiguous or even contradictory in effect. Though they held the potential (as Ju Yon Kim suggests in chapter 1) to diminish or exacerbate racial or cultural distinctions, they all represent visions of cultural diversity that intrude on the notion of America as racially or culturally homogeneous. They all, to some extent, promulgate images of racial and cultural heterogeneity in America—harbingers of a more diverse and, perhaps, more egalitarian society.

Psychiatrist and philosopher J. L. Moreno claimed that "spontaneity and creativity are the propelling forces in human progress."[18] Art frequently reflects, but also helps create, reality. In our current cultural climate, we urgently need artist-visionaries to help us imagine and create a better world. More than ever, we need to *perform* democracy if we hope to rescue it from oblivion. We have seen how dehumanization has been deployed to further an agenda of discrimination, disenfranchisement, and exclusion. As our society stands more segregated now than it has been in the past forty years, a new generation of Americans is growing up in cultural isolation—knowing "Others" only through virtual representations. As one of America's most celebrated theatre artists noted in 1949, "You've got to be carefully taught [to hate 'Others']."[19] Theatre, on the other hand, has been proven to contribute positively to personal and social development;[20] to be a powerful tool for changing knowledge, attitudes, and behavior;[21] and to be especially effective in increasing empathy.[22]

There are impressive and important theatrical experiments in democracy continuing today in America, including the work of the Tectonic Theatre Company, whose *Laramie Project* provided an in-depth exploration of the context in which Matthew Shepard was murdered for his sexual orientation; the performances of Anna Deveare Smith, who embodies and performs a cross-section of gendered and racial identities in her project "On the Road: A Search for American Character"; the autoethnographic performances of gay artist/activists like Tim Miller, Holly Hughes, and E. Patrick Johnson; the work of Chicano artist/activist Guillermo Gómez-Peña; the work of Chicana lesbian artist/activist Dora Arreola and the dance ensemble Mujeres en Ritual; the Disability Theatre project; the contributions of many "citizen playwrights" whose works examine urgent social issues through the prism of American heterogeneity (including Tony Kushner, David Henry Hwang, Suzan-Lori Parks, Naomi Wallace, Lynn Nottage, Quiara Alegría Hudes, and Danai Gurira as just a partial list); the collective Fringe Benefits, whose short plays called "Cootie Shots" function as "theatrical inoculations against bigotry" promoting "tolerance and celebrat[ing] diversity by presenting role models of many different races, nationalities, cultures, classes, genders, sexual orientations, abilities, religions, ages and appearances";[23] and the many kindred-spirited ensembles committed to "staging social justice," frequently employing democratic and collective working methods and the interactive theatre techniques of Augusto Boal to promote social awareness and change.[24] New research has confirmed the efficacy of theatre education to raise awareness and change attitudes about gender, race, religion, sexuality, socioeconomics, and a wide range of social issues and, most important, has been shown to inspire action to stop discrimination.

The Constitution of the United States, no matter how imperfectly it may have been executed through the centuries, is a marvel. The principles it espouses are worth struggling for. Despite the injustices that have plagued the nation, despite how long the dream has been deferred, the foundations for its realization have been laid in our Constitution—which democratic activists have wielded as a powerful weapon in the fight to extend the rights and privileges of citizenship. Even if the white, privileged, and propertied men who started the experiment did so largely to the benefit of themselves and their class, the dreams they dreamed, the words they wrote, and the ideal they planted in all our consciousnesses still inspire greatness—of heart, head, hands, spirit. That vision can stir courage within our nation to face up to our past mistakes and to forge a better future. If America and Americans have been capable of unspeakable cruelty, injustice, or greed, they have also been capable of great acts of self-sacrifice and valor in resistance to tyranny and injustice. A love of liberty and a yearning for equality and personal fulfillment have always been part of the American experience, and no injustice, no denial of opportunity to pursue its dream of happiness and freedom, has gone unchallenged. Theatrical performance has been, and will continue to be, an instrument in that ongoing effort.

Denied standard means of access, the disenfranchised and marginalized in America have frequently turned to theatrical performances of dissent, from soapbox speeches to parades and pageants, from street theatre to Broadway stages—rehearsals of power and agency, if you will, that can inspire new realizations of increased power and agency.

It would be easy to let our problems overwhelm us with despair, paralyze us with fear, numb us into apathy. But we would do well to remember that "optimism is a radical weapon," and, as Jill Dolan has eloquently argued, "reanimating humanism and seeing, through performance, more effective models of more radical democracy might reinvigorate a dissipated Left."[25] If disabled playwright John Belluso and Harlem Renaissance writer Langston Hughes didn't give up, how can we?

> O, yes,
> I say it plain,
> America never was America to me,
> And yet I swear this oath—
> America will be![26]

Notes

1. Ralph Nader quoted in *The Radical Reader: A Documentary History of the American Radical Tradition*, ed. Timothy Patrick McCarthy and John McMillan (New York: New Press, 2003), 660. This was Nader's fourth bid for the U.S. presidency.

2. Jake New, "SAE at Sea," Inside Higher Ed, 30 March 2015, https://www.insidehighered.com/news/2015/03/30/u-oklahoma-chapter-learned-racist-song-sae-leadership-cruise, accessed 3 April 2015.

3. "Charleston Church Shooting," NBC News, http://www.nbcnews.com/storyline/charleston-church-shooting, series of news stories, July–October 2015, accessed 20 December 2015.

4. Drew Desilver, "U.S. Income Inequality, on Rise for Decades, Is Now Highest since 1928," Pew Research Center, 5 December 2013, http://www.pewresearch.org/fact-tank/2013/12/05/u-s-income-inequality-on-rise-for-decades-is-now-highest-since-1928/, accessed 11 March 2014.

5. Crystia Freeland, *Plutocrats: The Rise of the New Global Super-Rich and the Fall of Everyone Else* (New York: Penguin, 2011), xii.

6. "2010 Census," U.S. Census Bureau, http://www.census.gov/2010census/, accessed 12 March 2014.

7. "The Unfinished March," Economic Policy Institute, http://www.epi.org/unfinished-march/, accessed 12 March 2014.

8. Richard Rothstein, "For Public Schools, Segregation Then, Segregation Now," Economic Policy Institute, 27 August 2013, http://www.epi.org/publication/unfinished-march-public-school-segregation, accessed 13 March 2014.

9. Ilyce Glink, "U.S. Housing Market Remains Deeply Segregated," CBSNews.com, 20 June 2012, http://www.cbsnews.com/news/us-housing-market-remains-deeply-segregated, accessed 13 March 2014. For a copy of the complete report, contact Daniel Fowler, pubinfo@asa.net.org.

10. "Kids Count Data Book," the Annie E. Casey Foundation, http://datacenter.kidscount.org/, accessed 9 March 2014.

11. Michelle Alexander, *The New Jim Crow: Mass Incarceration in the Age of Colorblindness* (New York: New Press, 2012), 50–55.

12. Quoted in Barbara Arnwine and Marcia Johnson-Bianco, "Voting Rights at a Crossroads," Economic Policy Institute, 25 October 2013, http://www.epi.org/publication/voting-rights-crossroads-supreme-court-decision/, accessed 13 March 2014.

13. Ibid.

14. Langston Hughes, "Let America Be America Again," in *The Poetry of the Negro: 1746–1970*, ed. Langston Hughes and Arna Bontemps (1949; New York: Doubleday, 1970), 193–95.

15. "Madison and Slavery," James Madison's Montpelier, http://www.montpelier.org/research-and-collections/people/african-americans/madison-slavery, accessed 5 March 2014.

16. W. E. B. Du Bois, *The Souls of Black Folk* (Chicago: A. C. McClurg, 1903), 1.

17. Felicia R. Lee, "Protesting Demeaning Images in Media," *New York Times*, 5 November 2007, http://www.nytimes.com/2007/11/05/arts/05enou.html, accessed 11 March 2014.

18. J. L. Moreno, "The Autobiography of J. L. Moreno, M.D." (abridged), Moreno Archives, Harvard University, quoted in "Biographies," Moreno Institute East, http://www.morenoinstituteeast.org/bios.htm, accessed 10 March 2014.

19. The lyric from the song by the same name is by Oscar Hammerstein II and is from the musical *South Pacific*.

20. See, for example, Jenny Hughes and Karen Wilsona, "Research in Drama Education," *Journal of Applied Theatre and Performance* 9.1 (2004): 57–72; and Reed W. Larson and Jane R. Brown, "Emotional Development in Adolescence: What Can Be Learned from a High School Theater Program?," *Child Development* 78.4 (2007): 1083–99.

21. See, for example, Louis Gliksman et al., "The Impact of a High School Alcohol Education Program Utilizing a Live Theatrical Performance: A Comparative Study," *Journal of Drug Education* 13.3 (1983): 229–48; and Barbara

Dennis, "Acting Up: Theatre of the Oppressed as Critical Ethnography," *International Journal of Qualitative Methods* 8.2 (2009): 66–97.

22. See, for example, George Gunkle, "Empathy: Implications for Theatre Research," *Educational Theatre Journal* 15.1 (1963): 15–23; "Developing Empathy through Theatre," changemakers.org, https://www.changemakers.com/project/developing-empathy-through-theater, accessed 10 March 2014; and Laura Gunderson, "How Theater for Young People Could Save the World," *Huffington Post*, 19 March 2012, http://www.huffingtonpost.com/lauren-gunderson/world-theater-for-children-and-young-people-day_b_1343408.html, accessed 27 February 2014.

23. Norma Bowles and Daniel-Raymond Nadon, eds., *Staging Social Justice: Collaborating to Create Activist Theatre* (Carbondale: Southern Illinois University Press, 2013), xiii. See also Norma Bowles, ed., with Mark E. Rosenthal, *Cootie Shots: Theatrical Inoculations against Bigotry for Kids, Parents and Teachers* (New York: Theatre Communications Group, 2000).

24. See Bowles and Nadon, *Staging Social Justice*. I would be remiss not to mention my own institution's Interactive Theatre Troupe, founded by Suzanne Burgoyne and Clyde Ruffin in 2003, and the Center for Applied Theatre and Drama Research. See http://muappliedtheatre.weebly.com/.

25. Jill Dolan, *Utopia in Performance: Finding Hope at the Theater* (Ann Arbor: University of Michigan Press, 2005), 21.

26. Hughes, "Let America Be America Again," 195.

Contributors

Index

Contributors

Cheryl Black is a professor of theatre and Catherine Paine Middlebush Chair in Fine and Performing Arts at the University of Missouri and the president of the American Theatre and Drama Society. She is the author of *The Women of Provincetown, 1915–1922*; chapters in *Staging a Cultural Paradigm: The Political and the Personal in American Drama*, *Feminist Theatrical Revisions of Classic Works*, and *Violence in American Drama: Essays on Its Staging, Meaning, and Effects*; and numerous journal articles.

Garrett Eisler currently teaches theatre studies at New York University's Tisch School of the Arts and the New School's Eugene Lang College. His work has been published in the *Journal of American Drama and Theatre*, the *Eugene O'Neill Review*, *Studies in Musical Theatre*, and the recent *Oxford Companion to Sondheim Studies*. As a critic he has reviewed contemporary theatre for *Time Out New York*, the *Village Voice*, and his blog, *The Playgoer*. He is also a frequent contributor to *American Theatre* magazine.

Harry J. Elam Jr. is the Olive H. Palmer Professor in the Humanities and the Freeman-Thornton Vice Provost for Undergraduate Education at Stanford University. He is the author and editor of seven books, including *Taking It to the Streets: The Social Protest Theater of Luis Valdez and Amiri Baraka* and *The Past as Present in the Drama of August Wilson*. His articles have appeared in numerous journals and critical anthologies worldwide.

Anne Fletcher is a professor of theatre at Southern Illinois University. She is the author of *Rediscovering Mordecai Gorelik: Scene Design and the American Theatre* and a coauthor of *The Process of Dramaturgy: A Handbook* (with Scott R. Irelan and Julie Felise Dubiner) and *Experiencing*

Theatre (with Scott R. Irelan). She is editing the volume on the 1930s in the forthcoming *Decades of Modern American Drama* (series edited by Brenda Murphy and Julia Listengarten).

Stuart J. Hecht is an associate professor of theatre at Boston College, the editor of *New England Theatre Journal*, and an officer of the American Theatre and Drama Society, the Chicago Theatre History Project, and the New England Theatre Conference's College of Fellows. He has authored *Transposing Broadway: Jews, Assimilation, and the American Musical* as well as several chapters and numerous articles.

Lisa Jackson-Schebetta is an assistant professor in the theatre arts department at the University of Pittsburgh. Her research centers on performance, race, and citizenship in the Americas and Spain.

Ju Yon Kim is an associate professor of English at Harvard University and the author of *The Racial Mundane: Asian American Performance and the Embodied Everyday*. She specializes in modern and contemporary American theatre and Asian American performance and literature. Her research has been published in *Theatre Journal*, *Modern Drama*, the *Journal of Transnational American Studies*, and *Modernism/modernity*.

Elizabeth Coonrod Martínez is a professor of Latin American and Latino studies and the director of the Center for Latino Research at DePaul University. Her books include a critical biography of Josefina Niggli and a translation of and introduction to stories by Elena Poniatowska. She is currently preparing a reader on contemporary indigenous literary production in Mexico.

Eric Mayer-García is a PhD candidate in the Louisiana State University's School of Theatre. His research focuses on Cuban avant-garde theatre in Havana, Miami, and New York and its intersection with U.S. Latina/o theatre. He has published and presented original research on nineteenth-century Cuban costumbristas in New Orleans, the popular theatre collective Teatro Escambray, and the theatre of María Irene Fornés, Virgilio Piñera, Reinaldo Arenas, and Caridad Svich. Mayer-García has been a graduate fellow for the Cuban Heritage Collection at the University of Miami and most recently received the American Society for Theatre Research, Targeted Areas Research Grant for archival research in Havana, Cuba.

Andrea Nouryeh is a professor emerita from St. Lawrence University and a dramaturg for the Pascal Theatre Company in London. She has written numerous essays that have appeared in theatre studies anthologies and journals, including *African American Literature Forum*, *New England Theatre Journal*, *On-Stage Studies*, *Research in African Literatures*, *Shakespeare on Film Newsletter*, *Theatre Journal*, *Theatre Symposium*, and *Theatre Topics*.

Elizabeth A. Osborne is an associate professor at Florida State University. Her work appears in *Theatre Symposium*, *Theatre History Studies*, and the *Journal of American Drama and Theatre*. She is the author of *Staging the People: Community and Identity in the Federal Theatre Project* and coeditor of *Working in the Wings: New Perspectives on Theatre History and Labor* (with Christine Woodworth).

W. Douglas Powers is an associate professor of theatre at Susquehanna University. His publications include the monograph *An Eliadean Interpretation of Frank G. Speck's Account of the Cherokee Booger Dance* and a midrashic study of *Cat on a Hot Tin Roof* and *Angels in America* in *South Atlantic Review*. He is a member of Actors' Equity Association.

Margaret F. Savilonis is an assistant professor of English at the University of New Haven. Her publications include chapters in the anthologies *International Dramaturgy: Translation and Transformation in the Theatre of Timberlake Wertenbaker* and *Taking It to the Bridge: Music as Performance*.

Jonathan Shandell is an associate professor of theatre arts at Arcadia University. His scholarship on African American theatre history has been published in *African American Review*, *Theatre Topics*, *The Cambridge Companion to African American Theatre* (edited by Harvey Young), and other publications. He served as the president of the Black Theatre Association for 2014–16.

Index

Italicized page numbers indicate figures.

Theater in the Americas

The goal of the series is to publish a wide range of scholarship on theater and performance, defining theater in its broadest terms and including subjects that encompass all of the Americas.

The series focuses on the performance and production of theater and theater artists and practitioners but welcomes studies of dramatic literature as well. Meant to be inclusive, the series invites studies of traditional, experimental, and ethnic forms of theater; celebrations, festivals, and rituals that perform culture; and acts of civil disobedience that are performative in nature. We publish studies of theater and performance activities of all cultural groups within the Americas, including biographies of individuals, histories of theater companies, studies of cultural traditions, and collections of plays.

Queries and Submissions
Scott Magelssen, Editor
magelss@uw.edu

Founder and Editor, Robert A. Schanke, 2000–2014

Other Books in the Theater in the Americas Series

Shadowed Cocktails: The Plays of Philip Barry from "Paris Bound" to "The Philadelphia Story"
Donald R. Anderson

A Gambler's Instinct: The Story of Broadway Producer Cheryl Crawford
Milly S. Barranger

Unfriendly Witnesses: Gender, Theater, and Film in the McCarthy Era
Milly S. Barranger

The Theatre of Sabina Berman: "The Agony of Ecstasy" and Other Plays
Translated by Adam Versényi
With an Essay by Jacqueline E. Bixler

Staging Social Justice: Collaborating to Create Activist Theatre
Edited by Norma Bowles and Daniel-Raymond Nadon

Messiah of the New Technique: John Howard Lawson, Communism, and American Theatre, 1923–1937
Jonathan L. Chambers

Composing Ourselves: The Little Theatre Movement and the American Audience
Dorothy Chansky

Ghost Light: An Introductory Handbook for Dramaturgy
Michael Mark Chemers

The Hanlon Brothers: From Daredevil Acrobatics to Spectacle Pantomime, 1833–1931
Mark Cosdon

Richard Barr: The Playwright's Producer
David A. Crespy

Women in Turmoil: Six Plays by Mercedes de Acosta
Edited and with an Introduction by Robert A. Schanke

Rediscovering Mordecai Gorelik: Scene Design and the American Theatre
Anne Fletcher

A Spectacle of Suffering: Clara Morris on the American Stage
Barbara Wallace Grossman

American Political Plays after 9/11
Edited by Allan Havis

Performing Loss: Rebuilding Community through Theater and Writing
Jodi Kanter

Unfinished Show Business: Broadway Musicals as Works-in-Process
Bruce Kirle

Staging America: Cornerstone and Community-Based Theater
Sonja Kuftinec

Words at Play: Creative Writing and Dramaturgy
Felicia Hardison Londré

Entertaining the Nation: American Drama in the Eighteenth and Nineteenth Centuries
Tice L. Miller

Documentary Trial Plays in Contemporary American Theater
Jacqueline O'Connor

Working in the Wings: New Perspectives on Theatre History and Labor
Edited by Elizabeth A. Osborne and Christine Woodworth

Cuba Inside Out: Revolution and Contemporary Theatre
Yael Prizant

Stage, Page, Scandals, and Vandals: William E. Burton and Nineteenth-Century American Theatre
David L. Rinear

Contemporary Latina/o Theater: Wrighting Ethnicity
Jon D. Rossini

Angels in the American Theater: Patrons, Patronage, and Philanthropy
Edited and with an Introduction by Robert A. Schanke

"That Furious Lesbian": The Story of Mercedes de Acosta
Robert A. Schanke

Caffe Cino: The Birthplace of Off-Off-Broadway
Wendell C. Stone

Teaching Performance Studies
Edited by Nathan Stucky and Cynthia Wimmer
With a Foreword by Richard Schechner

Broadway's Bravest Woman: Selected Writings of Sophie Treadwell
Edited and with Introductions by Jerry Dickey and Miriam López-Rodríguez

The Humana Festival: The History of New Plays at Actors Theatre of Louisville
Jeffrey Ullom

Childhood and Nineteenth-Century American Theatre: The Work of the Marsh Troupe of Juvenile Actors
Shauna Vey

Our Land Is Made of Courage and Glory: Nationalist Performance of Nicaragua and Guatemala
E. J. Westlake